MY LIFE IN ART

MY LIFE
in
ART

By

CONSTANTIN STANISLAVSKI

ROUTLEDGE / THEATRE ARTS BOOKS

NEW YORK

I DEDICATE THIS BOOK IN GRATITUDE
TO HOSPITABLE AMERICA
AS A TOKEN AND A REMEMBRANCE
FROM THE MOSCOW ART THEATRE
WHICH SHE TOOK SO KINDLY TO HER HEART

Translated by J. J. Robbins

Published since 1948 by
Theatre Arts Books
29 West 35th Street
New York, New York, 10001

Reprinted in 1996 by
Routledge/Theatre Arts Books
29 West 35th Street
New York, NY 10001

CONTENTS

CONTENTS

CONTENTS

CHAPTER I

I WAS born in Moscow in 1863, a time that may well be taken as a dividing point between two great epochs. I remember the landmarks of the age of serfdom, its icons and icon lamps, its lard candles, its pony express, that peculiar Russian conveyance called the tarantas, the flintlock muskets, the cannon that were small enough to be mistaken for playthings.

My eyes have witnessed the coming of electric projectors, railroads, and express trains, automobiles, aeroplanes, steamboats, submarines, the telegraph, the radio, and the 16-inch gun.

In such wise, from the lard candle to the electric projector, from the tarantas to the aeroplane, from the sailboat to the submarine, from the pony express to the radio, from the flintlock to the big Bertha, from serfdom to communism and Bolshevism, I have lived a variegated life, during the course of which I have been forced more than once to change my most fundamental ideas.

I remember the story of my ancestors, who came from the glebe filled with a strength that was the accumulated result of centuries, and lived through their lives in an incomplete way, unable to take advantage of their natural endowments. Their blood flows in me, and I would like to tell what I remember of their life, of the life of the old generation and its strong spirits.

Here is one chip of the past, — a figure astounding in its wholesomeness and strength. One of my aunts became dangerously ill when she was very old. Feeling the approach of death, she ordered the servants to carry her into the parlor.

"Cover the mirrors, the candelabra and the drapery with canvas," she commanded. The servants hastened to obey her. The dying woman lay in the middle of the room and continued to order them about.

"Put the table for the coffin here. Take the plants to the greenhouse. Put this near the table. That is not right. This to the right, and this to the left."

At last the table was ready to receive the coffin, and the plants were arranged to her taste. She looked about the room with darkening eyes.

"A carpet," she commanded, "but not a new one."

They brought the carpet.

"Put it here, for the reader of prayers. He mustn't spit on the floor."

"Let everybody dress in mourning," the dying woman continued in a weak voice that was almost hushed to a whisper. The servants hurriedly left the room and after a while filed, one after the other, before their mistress.

"Fool, why have you tightened that dress?" the old woman whispered angrily. "Have it remodelled at once. Why did you shorten it, blockhead?" she murmured to another. "Fix the thing at once, or you will be late. Fool!" she hissed in anger at a third girl. But her voice refused to obey her will, her eyes could no longer see, and having prepared everything and everybody for her death, she died in the same room that very day.

And here is the story of a paladin with a restless soul, who seems to have stepped out of the pages of "The Brothers Karamazov." The son of a famous merchant, he harbored in himself much good and much evil, and the two sides of his nature continually warred against each other, creating a chaos in his soul that neither he nor his friends could analyze. He was clever, and strong, and able, and courageous, and kind, and lazy, and meandersome, and evil, and attractive and repulsive. All his actions, his entire life, were un-reasonable and illogical. No sooner would he settle down to work and quiet, than he would leave everything for the sake of a tiger hunt. From one of these tiger hunts he brought home a small tiger cub. Soon the cub grew into a well-sized beast, and the man could find no greater pleasure in life than training the tiger in full view of his terrified household. The tiger escaped, clearing a fence between his estate and ours. There was a city-wide scandal, the tiger was caught and immured in a zoological garden, and its owner was fined. But he immediately imported another tiger cub which soon became a ferocious tigress. The shouts of the trainer and the roars of the beast again reëchoed through the house. The servants came demanding that the beast be done away with, to which the trainer quietly replied:

" Take her, if you can."

The only answer to that was a silence interrupted by the roaring of the tigress.

The man was married and jealous. His wife was being courted by a young manufacturer, fat, large, clean, pomaded, dressed in the latest English fashion, with a flower eternally in the lapel of his coat, a scented handkerchief, and a pair of sharp Kaiserlike mustachios.

On a certain holiday, this young spark came to the house of our man, carrying a large bouquet of roses. While waiting for the appearance of the hostess he carefully twisted his mustachios into sharper points before the mirror. Then something rubbed against his leg. It was the tigress. He moved his hand. The tigress growled. He wanted to change his position. The tigress roared. Petrified in a foolish pose, with the ends of his mustachios in his fingers, poor Don Juan remained motionless for half an hour. He was ready to faint from fatigue when the fully revenged and delighted husband came out of hiding, greeted him very pleasantly, as if nothing unusual had happened, and chased the tigress away.

" I must go home," murmured the dandy, recovering from fright.

" Why? " wondered his host.

"I am not in the best of order," whispered the guest, rapidly leaving the room.

Our hero was a friend of the famous generals Skobelev and Chernyaev. When they began their historical advance into Central Asia, he naturally went with them. He soon became a legendary figure, astounding everybody with his disdain for death.

" Life is dull," he cried out once on a quiet night. " I will visit the khan."

" What! "

" I will visit the khan in his camp."

" Where is your common sense? " wondered his comrades.

He rode to the khan's camp, struck up a friendship with the khan, received a jewelled sword as a gift, and was rumored to have spent a night in the khan's harem. The very next morning, before the Russians advanced, he was back with his detachment, in ecstasies from his unusual excursion.

His wife died, leaving him a son whom he worshipped. Soon afterwards his son also died. The father was shaken to the depths of his soul. All day and all night he sat near the coffin of his dead son, dry-eyed and motionless. All night a nun read prayers above the coffin, in a deadly monotonous voice.

On the next day the bereaved father was almost insane. The people about him feared that he was going to commit suicide. He became restless. He drank heavily to drown his grief. With the evening he sat down near the coffin again. The same nun read prayers over the coffin in her deadly monotonous voice. He looked up at her by accident, and found that she was pretty.

" Let us go to Strelna."

And the unhappy father, in order to deaden his inner grief, took the nun in a troika to the gypsies and spent the entire night in wild carousing until the very beginning of the funeral.

When men like this were able to interest themselves in useful work, they showed the full breadth of their generosity and good intentions. The finest institutions of Moscow in all spheres of social life, including art and religion, were founded by private initiative. The first philanthropists were the aristocrats and the nobles, but after their gradual impoverishment their rôle passed into the hands of the merchants.

" Listen, my friend," my cousin, who was the mayor of Moscow, said to one of these rich business men. " You are rather fat of late. Isn't there a bit of extra money in your poke? Come, let me shake you down for a good cause." And he painted the needs of the municipal administration in striking colors.

" Bow low to me three times, and you will see the color of my money," decided the rich man.

" How much? " The mayor was curious.

" A clean million," promised the rich man.

" And if I bow to you when I am dressed in my uniform, my ribbon and all of my decorations, will you add anything to that?" bargained the mayor.

" Another three hundred thousand," cried the rich man.

" A bargain. Call all the clerks into my office," ordered the mayor. " Bring me my uniform, my ribbon and my decorations."

Having delivered a brilliant speech in introduction to the rare bit of foolishness, the mayor bowed three times to the rich man in the presence of the clerks. The rich man wrote him a check for thirteen hundred thousand, and the clerks gave an ovation—to the mayor.

The poor rich man was hurt. He quieted down only when Moscow became richer by a new and useful institution which bore his name, and to which he devoted all of his spare time.

In the realm of art, private initiative also furnished a great deal of generosity. The endowments were large, and the founders of the new artistic institutions gave their money blindly but in good faith, not always understanding the real usefulness of what they created.

The Moscow Conservatory, which created the music of Russia and all of her famous artists and composers, was founded by private means, thanks to the unusual popularity of its founder, Nikolai Rubinstein, a man almost as talented as his brother Anton, the famous pianist and composer. I remember clearly the manner in which the conservatory was shaped. Nikolai Rubinstein made the acquaintance of all of the rich men of Moscow. In the house of one he played cards; in the house of another he dined and amused all who were present with his ready wit and his remarkable powers of conversation; in the house of a third he played the piano to the great admiration of his auditors; in the house of a fourth he gave lessons in music, and when it was necessary paid court to the ladies. Having collected enough capital, he created the conservatory and founded a series of symphonic concerts which paid the expenses of the school. These concerts became fashionable; not to attend them was considered to be rather shameful, so every one who was anybody came to them, listened, was bored, and engaged in flirtation and the display of dress and jewelry.

It often happened that the concerts were given to the accompaniment of a great deal of noise in the auditorium. Poor Rubinstein was forced to educate the crowd not only in regard to music, but in regard to manners. I was the recipient of one of his lessons — when I was eight or nine years old. Dressed in a fine Russian silk shirt and wide knickers, I walked with the rest of our multitudinous family through the central corridor of the tremendous Hall of Columns where the concerts were given. We were not at all awed by the music, and made a great ado with the shuffle of our feet and the rustle of our clothes. Meanwhile the orchestra was weaving a delicate *pianissimo* lacework of sound. When we reached the very centre of the auditorium, Rubinstein stopped the orchestra, which we had drowned with our noise. It was impossible to play in *piano* against the full *forte* of our triumphal procession. The orchestra stopped, the conductor lowered his baton, turned his face to us and devoured us with maddened eyes. And with him, fifteen hundred pairs of eyes belonging to the public present, and the entire orchestra, seemed to watch our slightest motion. They were all silent, frightened by the anger of Rubinstein, and waited for us to pass.

I was struck by panic. I don't remember anything that happened after that. All I know is that during the intermission my parents looked for me in all the neighboring halls and at last found me hidden in the farthest corner of the most remote room.

Compared to the theatre of Europe the Russian theatre is only a young institution, something like two and a half centuries old. In the second half of the seventeenth century Tsar Alexei, influenced by the noble Artamon Matveyev, entrusted an alien pastor by the name of Gregori with the task of organizing a group of young people for the purpose of teaching them dramatic art. The performances of this group were given in the palace, were open only to the nobility, and bore the character of church mysteries. And only with the beginning of the reign of Peter the Great, who flung wide the gates of Russia to the advance of Western Europe, did the wider development of the Russian theatre find its first opportunity. Foreign companies were imported for the first time, the plays of the western theatre were translated into Russian, and Molière appeared on the Russian stage. In the reign of Elisaveta the theatre made its way into the provinces, and dramatic initiative was manifested by that class of society to which my ancestors belonged. The most prominent part in the creation of the Russian dramatic theatre was played by a good merchant's son, Fyodor Volkov. He collected a company of amateurs in the city of Yaroslavl, whose playing became so famous that the empress Elisaveta commanded their presence in Petersburg, the attention of which at that time was occupied by the performances of the dramatic group of the military college, the so-called Noble Corps.

Thanks to the empress Elisaveta, who was a great lover of the theatre, and who even wrote plays herself, it became fashionable for the rich aristocracy to initiate domestic theatres. The actors and actresses in these theatres were mostly serfs, but at times the nobles themselves took part in the performances. Very famous were the companies of Prince Gagarin and Prince Shakhovsky, and that of Count Sheremetev on his estate near Moscow, the gardens of which might well compete in beauty with the gardens of Versailles. Count Sheremetev went so far as to marry one of his serf actresses.

The life of these slaves of the muse was hard indeed. One day the will of their master would raise them to Parnassus; the next it would send them to work in the stables; the third they would be sold like so many cattle. For instance, in the year 1806, Prince Volkonsky sold his domestic theatre group, consisting of seventy-four souls, for the sum of thirty-two thousand roubles.

But the Russian theatre owes a great deal in its development to the existence of these domestic theatre companies. The masters imported foreign teachers for their serfs and encouraged the development of their talents, competing with each other in the luxury and quality of the plays they produced. The serf company of Count Volkenstein was the cradle of the greatest Russian actor of the first half of the nineteenth century, Mikhail Shtchepkin, whose tradition still lived in the Moscow Little Theatre in the days of my youth. Shtchepkin was a friend of our great writer Gogol, and the educator of an entire generation of great and competent artists. He was the first to introduce simplicity and lifelikeness into the Russian theatre, and he taught his pupils to distinguish the manner in which emotions are expressed in real life. I remember that I tried to become acquainted with everything that he wrote of dramatic art in his letters to Gogol and other friends, and always gave willing ear to the stories told of him by his contemporaries, while with a never-abating interest I followed the productions in the Little Theatre, which at that time was in the very bloom of life and crowned with the work of many prominent and talented artists.

The government was also very generous in the support of dramatic art. In order to raise the level of art in a country it is altogether unnecessary to found hundreds of theatres, but it is necessary that there be one consummate theatre in each sphere of scenic art. These model theatres must serve as examples for other theatres. From the times of Tsar Alexei, and during the reigns of Peter and Catherine, there existed in Russia imperially subsidized theatres and schools which gathered the best artists and pupils, giving them means to live, and an opportunity to enter the service of government theatres that were working out the general creative problems and the traditions of Russian art. Tremendous sums were spent on these schools and theatres, and the best French dramatic artists and world-famous singers were brought to help along in their development. For instance, Sarah Bernhardt and Bartet were regular members of the French company in the Mikhailovsky Theatre.

At the beginning of every season the Opera would publish great posters with the names of practically all world-famous stars as regular members of the company. Adelina Patti, Lucca, Nilsson, Volnini, Arteau, Viardot, Tamberlik, Mario, Stanio, and later Mazzini, Gotoni, Podilla, Bagaggilo and Giammetta were all regular members of the cast of the Opera.

CHAPTER II

THE generation to which my parents belonged consisted of people who had already crossed the threshold of culture, and who although they did not receive the benefits of higher education, and in the majority of cases were educated privately, still made much of culture their own, thanks to their innate abilities. They were conscious creators of the new life. Numberless schools, hospitals, asylums, nurseries, learned societies, museums and art institutions were founded by their money, their initiative and even their creative effort. For instance, the famous clinics of Moscow, large enough to constitute a city in themselves, were built mostly by the initiative and the money of these men and their heirs. They made money in order to spend it on social and artistic institutions. And all this was done in a spirit of humility, in the silence of their studies.

In illustration, the manufacturer Pavel Tretyakov, who collected the riches of art galleries and donated them to the city of Moscow. In order to do this, he worked from early morning till late at night in his office and in his factory, and when he came home gave himself up to his gallery and to conversations with young artists in whom he felt the presence of talent. In a year or two the pictures of the young artists would find their way into his gallery, and they themselves would first become well known and then famous. And how humbly he practiced his philanthropy! Who would ever recognize the famous Russian Medici in the bashful, timid, tall and thin figure with the bearded, priestlike face? Instead of taking vacations he would spend his summers in becoming familiar with the pictures and museums of

Europe, and in his later years, in accordance with a long-maturing plan, he traveled systematically on foot through all Germany and France and part of Spain.

Another Mæcenas, Soldatenkov, devoted himself to the publication of books that could not hope for large circulation, but were necessary to science, to social life, to culture and to education. His beautiful house, built in Greek style, became a library. There were never any garish lights in the windows of his house, and only the two windows of his study shone quietly long after midnight was past. And behind the glass of those two windows Soldatenkov was planning with a scientist or an artist some useful but unprofitable publication.

The merchant Shtchukin collected a gallery of modernistic French painters that included the best works of Cézanne and Picasso. All who wished to see his pictures were admitted freely to his house. His brother created a museum of Russian antiquities.

The merchant Bakhrushin founded the only museum of theatrical art in Russia and gathered in it all that was relevant to the Russian theatre.

And here is the figure of another of the creators of Russian life, which is altogether exceptional in its talent, its many-sidedness, its energy, and the strength and breadth of its impetus: I mean the famous philanthropist Savva Mamontov, who was at the same time an operatic artist, a stage director, a dramatist, the creator of Russian private opera, a supporter of art like Tretyakov, and the builder of many Russian railroads.

It is impossible to say how much Russia would have lost if Mamontov had not built the railroad north to Archangel and Murman to find an outlet to the ocean, and one south to the coal mines of the Donetz Basin, so as to bring coal to the north. And when he began this great labor he was laughed at and called a fortune-hunter and an adventurer. And what would have happened to Russian opera if Mamontov had not supported it? It would have still been ruled by

Italian *bel canto,* and we would never have heard Chaliapin, who would be silent in the darkness of the provinces. Without Mamontov and Chaliapin we would never have known Moussorgsky, who had been pronounced anathema by the wiseacres and called a crazy musician; we would not have known the best compositions of Rimsky-Korsakov, for " Snegourochka, " " Sadko, " " The Tsar's Bride, " " Saltan, " and " The Golden Rooster " were written for Mamontov's opera, and were first produced in his theatre. We would never have seen the canvases of modern art from the brushes of Vasnetsov, Polenov, Serov, Korovin, who together with Repin, Antakolsky and all the other great artists of that time may be said to have grown up in the house of Mamontov. And we would never have seen the wonderful operatic productions that were the result of his own talented direction.

We had another generous philanthropist in the realm of the dramatic theatre — Savva Morozov. But I will not say anything about him now, for he is so closely connected with the Moscow Art Theatre that I will have to treat of him in detail in relation to the history of the rise and development of the Moscow Art Theatre itself.

Neighboring on our estate was the estate of our cousins, who had built up a world-famous manufactory of silks, velvets and other materials. They were very enlightened people, and stood at the forefront of the times, being the first to perfect a complete branch of manufacture in Russia, that of weaving. Their home was a meeting place for some very interesting people. But their friends were a little older than we were, and their manner of life and amusement differed from ours. The evenings were mostly taken up with discussions of social subjects, for that was the period of the great awakening of Russian social life: local agricultural councils were just coming into existence, municipal self-government was still a new experiment, as was also trial by jury.

On holidays preceding the hunting season they would be occupied with target shooting for prizes. From noon to sunset all one heard was the sound of rifle fire. Many of the ladies and gentlemen present took part in the target practice; others were present merely as spectators. Picnicking, promenades in the woods, flirtations and betting provided entertainment for those who wished to escape the noise of rifle fire.

With the beginning of the hunting season, and until the coming of frosts, the kennels came into life. With dawn there would come the sound of the hunting horn; pedestrians and mounted kennel men, surrounded by full packs of dogs in leash, would rush hither and thither, and the hunters themselves would arrive in their equipages, singing, and followed by a wagon with provisions for their breakfast in the forest.

The children, of whom I was one, and who took no part in the hunt, would rise with the dawn to see the hunters off. I still remember the feeling of jealousy with which I looked at the excited faces of the hunters. On their return they would show the animals they had killed during the day, usually hares, foxes and wolves; then there would come a general washing-up, and sometimes even bathing, that is when the weather would allow it. At night there would be music, dances, games and charades. The part of entertaining the guests would usually fall to the share of our house.

At times both families would come together and arrange water festivals. The day would be given over to swimming for prizes, and the nights to rowing in gaudily painted boats. A tremendous row-boat, carrying a brass band, would precede the procession.

On St. John's night old and young would take part in making an enchanted forest. Costumed in sheets, or masked for the purpose, some of us would get into the trees and wait for the coming of the fern seekers on whom we would mercilessly descend from our hiding places. If we hid in the bushes, we would rush out, and if in the grass, we would crawl out, but the result attained would be the same. Others, covering themselves and their boats with large white sheets, would come down the river with the current, standing upright on the boat bottoms, frightening and amusing all of us.

Often on some summer night all the neighbors would come together for the purpose of spending the whole night outside and of meeting the dawn. On one such night the watchman mysteriously acquainted us with the fact that some suspicious-looking characters were seen around the estate.

"Tramps! Let's get them!"

We armed ourselves with sticks, umbrellas, rakes and brooms, and chose a leader. Then we divided, some going to the right, some to the left. We crept through the underbrush, sent out patrols, set ambushes, but at last got tired of it all, and sitting down in a meadow, began to sing songs. The other detachment, hidden in a rye field, slept snugly till the dawn. Meanwhile the supposed tramps, who were in reality some of our neighbors, had stopped looking for a lost pocketbook and were on their way home, when suddenly hearing scores of voices and seeing a group of people crawling in their direction through the grass, they ran to the other side and were met by armed bandits, or so it seemed to them at the time.

We sometimes practiced practical jokes that were even cruel. Their victim was a naïve young German musician, who was our first music teacher. He was as innocent as a twelve-year-old girl and believed everything he was told.

He was once informed that there had appeared in the village a fat peasant woman who was madly in love with him, and who was doing everything she could to find him. This lovesick creation of our minds became a nightmare to the young German. One night, he came into his sitting room, undressed, and taking a candle in his hand walked into the neighboring bedroom, where he found what seemed to him to be a tremendous woman lying on his bed. Scared out of his wits, he ran to a window and jumped out. It was his luck that the window was not very high above ground. The watchdogs, seeing his naked legs, attacked him. He began shouting for help and woke up the whole house. Sleepy, frightened faces began to appear in the windows, and everybody shouted, without knowing what had happened. But the practical jokers, who were still stationed at their posts, interfered with the dogs, and saved the poor half-naked German. Meanwhile, the one who had impersonated the German's beloved left the bed, leaving behind him an article of female clothing, and changing quickly into his own clothes, helped the rest to save the German from the dogs. The mystery remained unsolved, and the myth of the fat woman continued to frighten the naïve German, who was later to become famous in the musical world. We would have driven him crazy in the end, had not my father interfered and put an end to our practical jokes at the young man's expense.

All these jests of the elders paint them as practical jokers, idlers, and high livers, but the beauty of the thing lies in the fact that they were good business men, who knew how to work and how to play. They were the men who created the Moscow of those days. Promptly at six each morning they would leave their estates to board the train for the city. But it was not an easy matter to reach the city in those days. Not a single morning train would stop at our flag station. It was necessary to take a train going the other way and ride to the first station where all trains stopped. There one had to wait an hour until the Moscow train pulled in. And it was on this train that business men would reach the city at half after nine, having spent three and a half hours on their journey to work. You can well imagine what the happy practical jokers would do to amuse themselves during the long and tedious journey.

Here is a characteristic conversation between one of the young men and an old priest.

"Where are you going, father?" begins the young man.

"To Troitse, friend," answers the priest. "And where do you happen to be going?" he continues, in order to make talk.

"To Moscow, father," retorts the joker.

"To Moscow? What do you mean to Moscow?" The priest is wonderstruck.

"To Moscow. To Moscow," the young man repeats.

"I think you are joking," the priest replies, still unconscious that he is the butt of a joke, and ready to become angry.

"To Moscow," the joker repeats again.

"To Moscow and to Troitse on the same train!" exclaims the priest in a hurt tone of voice, "That is impossible!"

This is followed by a comic quarrel, and that ends in general laughter.

And here is another jest to make time pass. One of the stations had a foolish and impudent master, who liked to cause passengers all sorts of inconveniences. He would often make them change from one car to another that was full as it was, or examine their tickets twice instead of one time as was the custom.

We paid him for his every impudence. Just as soon as the train would stop at his station, which was called Mitishchi, one of us would leave the car as if he were in a hurry, and approaching the station master, would remove his hat politely and ask him pleasantly, "Tell me, please, what is the name of this station?"

"Mitishchi," the station master would answer gloomily.

"I am very, very much obliged to you," the joker would say, bowing and retreating. But in a moment he would go back to the busy station master with another polite query.

"Tell me, please, how long does the train stay here?"

"Five minutes," the station master would answer gloomily.

"I am very very much obliged to you."

No sooner had the first joker disappeared, than a second one would appear from another side.

"Tell me, please, this is Mitishchi?"

"Yes," from the station master, even more gloomily than before.

"I thank you," the second joker would say, retreating but returning at once. "I forgot. The train stops here ten minutes, I believe."

"Five minutes," the station master would answer, nervously pulling at his beard.

A third joker would run up to the station master. "Tell me, please, what station is this?"

"Mitishchi."

"How long does the train stay here?"

"Five minutes."

"I am very much obliged to you."

In this manner a fourth and a fifth and sometimes even a sixth questioner would appear, until the train began to move. Then the very last of them, sticking his head out of the window of the disappearing train would shout in a very frightened voice, "Is this really Mitishchi?"

But the station master would not answer.

"How long did the train stop here?" the man in the window would yell but the train was already almost out of hearing.

As soon as they arrived in Moscow all these jokers at once became the most serious business men. They rushed along the streets leading from the railroad station to their offices or factories, in the best of equipages, as if competing for a prize at the races. This was the beginning of a working day that no man who is not a Russian could understand. We Russians cannot work systematically, but no one else can work as intensively and productively as we can for short periods.

At seven in the evening the business men would race along the streets again, this time to the train, and having entered the cars, turned again into care free jesters. And from the way-stations they raced to their homes in their *troikas* in order to get as much of carefree happiness into their lives as they could.

We, the children of the great fathers and creators of Russian life, tried to inherit from them the difficult art of being able to be rich. To know how to spend money properly is a very great art.

The majority of our generation of rich people received a good education and were acquainted with world literature. We were taught many languages, we traveled very extensively, and in a word were plunged into the very heart of the maelstrom of culture. Having become equal in education to the nobles and the aristocrats, class distinctions disappeared as if of themselves. Common political and social work brought together all cultured people and made of them the Russian "intelligentsia"; the last revolution destroyed all the remaining class barriers and pitched everybody into one common heap.

In order to acquaint you with our generation and give you an opportunity to judge how art developed in our time, I will try to describe my life in brief.

CHAPTER III

MY father, a rich manufacturer and merchant, the owner of a mercantile firm a hundred years old, Sergey Vladimirovich Alexeiev, was a pure-blooded Russian. My mother, Elisaveta Vassilievna Alexeieva, had a Russian father and a French mother, — the once famous actress Varley who played in Petrograd in her time as a visiting star. This actress married the rich owner of a quarry in Finland, Vassily Abramovich Yakovlev, who erected the famous Column of Alexander on the Palace Square in Petrograd. A family tradition has it that when the pillar was being transported by sea from Finland, the ship was caught in a storm. During that night Yakovlev grew gray, for Tsar Nikolai the First, a man of very short moods, had ordered that the Column be placed in the square on time. Every means known to the art of navigation was used to save the ship, which hardly escaped sinking.

Varley soon separated from Yakovlev, leaving him two children, my mother and an aunt.

Yakovlev married a woman who had a Turkish mother and a Greek father, and this woman practically brought up my mother. Her house was conducted in a very aristocratic fashion. It seems that the court manners acquired by her from her mother, who was stolen from the Turkish Sultan's harem, at last showed themselves. This Turkish woman had been shipped by her Greek husband from Constantinople in a box, and it was only after the ship that carried them was safely out of the reach of the Sublime Porte that the box was opened and the haremite freed.

My mother's sister, who married my father's brother, was very like her Turkish stepmother. They gave famous dinners and balls and the most prominent merchants felt honored to be invited to these, for members of the aristocratic circle often appeared at them. At that time the aristocracy was still shy of the merchant class, and the breaking of class prejudices was considered a signal honor in our circles of society.

I remember those balls. Instead of tablecloths there were roses brought by express trains from Nice and Italy. The guests would arrive in four-in-hands and six-in-hands, with their lackeys sitting stiff in their liveries in the back seats and astride the horses. Bonfires would be lighted in the street opposite the house to keep the horses warm, and the drivers were served food as they gathered around the fires. The lower stories of the house were given over for the entertainment of the servants. The ladies came with necks and bosoms covered with jewels, and those who liked to figure out the riches of others would be busy appraising the value of the gems. Those who seemed to be the poorest in the company considered themselves unhappy and were ashamed of their poverty. The richer women believed themselves the queens of the ball. More than a few tears were shed because of the prevalence of poverty among the millionaires.

Moscow and Petrograd danced for all they were worth in those days. During the season balls took place every day, and young dancers were often forced by circumstances to attend two or three balls in the course of one evening. Cotillions with the most peculiar figures, with rich gifts and prizes for the dancers, would last till five in the morning. The balls usually ended in broad daylight, and the young men, hurriedly changing their clothes, would go directly to their work in offices and mercantile houses.

Unlike the others of their circle, my parents did not enjoy worldly life and visited these gala affairs only when they could not avoid them. They were very home-loving people. My mother spent all her time in the nursery, devoting herself completely to her children — and there were ten of us. My father, until his marriage, slept in the same bed with his father, who was famous for his old-fashioned patriarchal method of life. After his marriage, my father passed to his conjugal couch, where he slept to the end of his days, and where he died. My parents loved each other when they were young, and when they were old. They loved their children and tried to keep them as near themselves as they could.

Of my infancy I remember most clearly only the very best and the very worst. If I am not to reckon my memories of my own christening, which I created after the stories of my nurse so clearly in my mind that even until now I consider myself a conscious witness of that ceremony — my remotest recollection begins with my first stage appearance.

This took place on our estate, about thirty versts[1] from Moscow, in one of the wings of our house. A small children's stage was erected there, with a plaid cloth instead of a curtain. As custom has it, the entertainment was composed of tableaux, in this case the four seasons of the year. I was about two or three years old at that time, and impersonated Winter. The stage was covered with cotton; in the centre there was a small evergreen, also covered with cotton, and on the floor, wrapped in a fur coat, with a fur hat on my head, and a long beard that would insist on crawling up my forehead, sat I, without knowing where to look and what to do. This impression of aimlessness, bashfulness and the absurdity of my presence on the stage, was felt by me subconsciously at that time, and even now it is alive in me and frightens me when I am on the stage. After the applause, which I remember was very much to my liking, I was placed on the stage again, but in a different pose. A candle was lit and placed in a small bundle of branches to make the

[1] A *verst* is not quite two thirds of a mile.

[23]

effect of a fire, and I was given a small piece of wood which I was to make believe I put into the fire.

"Remember, it is only make-believe. It is not in earnest," the others explained to me.

And I was strictly forbidden to bring the piece of wood close to the candlelight. All this seemed nonsensical to me. Why should I only make believe when I could really put the wood in the fire? And perhaps that was what I had to do, just because I was forbidden to do it?

In a word, as soon as the curtain rose, I put out the hand with the piece of wood towards the fire with great interest and curiosity. It was easy and pleasant to do this, for there was meaning in that motion; it was a completely natural and logical action. Even more natural and logical was the fact that the cotton caught fire. There was a great deal of excitement and noise. I was unceremoniously lifted from the stage and carried into the big house, where I was severely scolded. In short I had failed cruelly, and the failure was not to my taste. These four impressions, of the pleasure of success, of the bitterness of failure, of the discomfort of unreasonable presence on the stage, and the inner truth of reasoned presence and action on it, control me on the stage even at the present day.

In order to keep us children nearer to the home hearth, our parents listened willingly to all our demands. Thanks to this, our house often changed its physiognomy in accordance with what was going on there at any given time. For instance, my father, who was well known as a philanthropist, founded a dispensary for the peasants. My oldest sister fell in love with one of the doctors in the dispensary and the entire house began to manifest an extraordinary interest in medicine. Sick people came from all the corners of the earth and all the comrades of my brother-in-law would gather for interminable consultations.

Soon my second sister fell in love with a neighbor, a young German merchant. Everybody in the house began speaking German and the house itself became filled with foreigners. We youngsters tried to dress in European fashion, and all who were able grew side beards and changed the manner of combing their hair.

But then my oldest brother fell in love with the daughter of a simple Russian merchant who wore long Russian boots, and the entire house became a model of simplicity. The samovar never left the table; all of us drank too much tea; we forced ourselves to go regularly to church; we arranged solemn services, invited the best church choirs and sang early mass in chorus ourselves. Then my third sister fell in love with an expert bicylist, and all of us donned woolen stockings, short trousers, bought bicycles and learned to ride.

At last my fourth sister fell in love with an opera singer, and the entire house began to sing. Many of the famous singers of that time were guests in our house and especially on our estate. We sang in the house and in the woods — romances by day and serenades by night. We sang in rowboats and we sang in the bathhouse. Every day at five, just before dinner, the singers would meet there. They would stand in a row on the roof and begin to sing a quartette. Before the final note they would dive from the roof into the river, and as soon as their heads emerged from the water, they would finish the quartette on a high note. He who finished first was always declared winner. Those who were present would make up a purse for him.

What I remember best are the emotions which I lived through in the period of my struggle with obstinacy and not so much the facts that caused them. One such event took place in my early childhood, in the dining room, during breakfast. I was very mischievous, and my father called my attention to it. I answered him foolishly, without any anger, without thinking much. He laughed at me, and I became angry, not so much at him, I remember, as at myself. Not being able to find what to say, I grew confused and even more angry at myself. In order to hide my confusion and show that I was not afraid of my father, I uttered an altogether senseless threat. I don't know myself how it left my tongue.

" I won't let you go to Auntie Vera. "

" Foolish, " said my father, " what do you mean you won't let me go? "

Knowing that I had said something very foolish, and growing even more angry at myself, I became altogether obstinate, and did not notice myself how I repeated:

" I won't let you go to Auntie Vera. "

My father shrugged his shoulders and was silent. This hurt me. He did not want to speak to me. Then the worse I was, the better it would be.

" I *won't let* you go to Auntie Vera! I won't let you go to *Auntie Vera!* I won't *let* you go to Auntie Vera! " I repeated the same sentence insistently and almost impudently, changing the intonation of the words each time.

My father ordered me to be still, and just because of that I said, very distinctly:

" I WON'T LET YOU GO TO AUNTIE VERA! "

Father read his paper in silence. But I could see that he was irritated.

" I won't let *you* go to Auntie Vera! I won't let you go to Auntie *Vera!* I won't *let you go* to Auntie Vera! " I hammered at him in dull and obstinate anger, powerless to combat the evil force which had carried me away. Feeling how weak I was in its grasp, I began to be afraid of it.

" I won't let you go to *Auntie Vera,* " I said again, after a pause and against my own will, feeling that I could no longer control myself.

My father began to threaten me, and I began to repeat the same foolish sentence louder and more insistently, all due to my inertia. My father rapped on the table with his finger, and I imitated his gesture, accompanying it with the same old sentence. My father rose; I did so also, with the same refrain. My father raised his voice in anger (this had never happened to him before); I raised mine also, but it trembled. He controlled himself and spoke softly. I remember that this touched me greatly and that I wanted to surrender. But against my own will I repeated .the impudent sentence again, which made it look that I was making a laughingstock of my father. My father warned me that he would put me in the corner. I repeated my foolish sentence, imitating his tone.

"I will leave you without dinner," my father said more severely.

"I won't let you go to Auntie Vera!" I said in despair, imitating his tone again.

"Think of what you are doing," said my father, throwing his paper on the table.

Within me there shot up an evil emotion that forced me to throw down my napkin. "At least that will put an end to it," I thought, and shouted as loud as I could:

"I won't let you go to Auntie Vera!"

My father flamed up, his lips began to tremble, but he controlled himself, and quickly left the room, uttering a terrible sentence:

"You are not my son."

When I was alone, and the victor in the field, my foolishness left me at once.

"Papa, pardon me, I won't," I cried after him, my voice drowned in tears. But my father was already in another room and did not hear my cries of remorse.

I remember all the spiritual stages of my childish fit as if the thing took place to-day, and when I remember them I experience again an anguished pain in my heart.

During another fit of obstinacy, I was badly put to rout. I had been boasting at dinner and said that I could lead Voronoy, my father's most ill-tempered horse, out of his stall.

"Wonderful!" jested my father. "After dinner we will make you put on your coat and your boots, and you will show us how brave you are."

"I'll put them on, and I'll lead him out." I was obstinate now.

My sisters and brothers disputed with me and assured me that I was a coward. To prove what they said they reminded me of certain compromising facts. The more unpleasant their revelations became, the more obstinately I repeated in my confusion:

"I am not afraid. I will lead him out."

Again my obstinacy went so far that it became necessary to give me a lesson. After dinner they brought my coat, my hat, my boots, my gloves and my winter hood. Then they dressed me, led me out into the courtyard, left me apparently alone, and went in to await my appearance with Voronoy. I remained surrounded by silence and darkness. The darkness seemed all the darker because of the light in the large windows of the parlor — it seems that I was being watched from above. My heart sank within me, and my teeth closed on the hem of my sleeve as I tried to force myself to forget the darkness and the silence about me. Some few steps away I heard the sound of feet in the snow, the creaking of a threshold and the closing of a door. Perhaps it was the coachman who entered the stall of Voronoy, whom I had promised to lead out. I imagined the great black horse beating the ground with an impatient hoof, rearing up on his hind legs, ready to rush forward and to drag me after him as if I were an inanimate piece of wood. Of course, if I had seen this picture at dinner, I would not have boasted of my prowess. But as I had said the thing as if it came of itself, I did not want to stop now. I was ashamed. I had become obstinate.

I philosophized so as to distract my attention from the surrounding darkness.

"I will stay here for a long, long time, until they become frightened in the house and come to look for me," I decided within myself.

Suddenly I heard a piteous cry, and I began to listen to the sounds around me. How many of them there were! And one is more terrible than the other! Who is that stealing after me in the darkness? Nearer, nearer! A dog? A rat? I took a few steps towards a niche in the wall nearest me. At the same time something fell in the darkness. What was it? Again, again, very near now! Perhaps Voronoy was kicking at the door of his stall or a carriage wheel struck the curb on the street. But what was that hissing? And that whistling? It seemed that all the terrible sounds of which I ever knew had suddenly come to life and broken in chaos about me.

"Oh!" I cried and jumped into the very farthest corner of the niche. Something grabbed me by the leg. But it was only the watchdog Roska, my best friend. Now there were two of us! It was not as terrible as before. I took Roska in my arms and she began to lick my face with her warm, wet tongue. My heavy, clumsy winter coat, tightly bound with the ends of my hood, gave me no opportunity to save my face from the dog's caresses. I pushed away her snout, and she went to sleep in my arms, quiet in their embracing warmth. Somebody was rapidly coming towards me from the direction of the gates. Was it for me? My heart began to beat with expectation. But no, the somebody passed into the coachman's outhouse.

I thought that my family would all be ashamed by now. They had thrown me out, me, a little child, in such a frost — almost as in a fairy tale. I would never forgive them.

From the house came the hollow sounds of a piano.

"That must be my brother playing. As if nothing had happened. He is playing! And they've forgotten all about me. How long must I wait here till they remember?" I became more frightened, and I wanted to get back to the parlor, to warmth, to the piano more than anything else in the world.

"I am a fool! A fool! Why did I think of this? Why did I think of Voronoy? I am a blockhead!" I scolded myself, realizing the foolishness of my situation, which, as it seemed to me, was inescapable.

The gates creaked, there was the drumming of hoofs, wheels crunched in the snow. A carriage stopped near the front entrance. The front door slammed, and the carriage began to turn around in the courtyard.

"Those are my cousins," I remembered. "They were invited to come this evening. Now I won't go back into the house at all. They will call me a coward."

The arriving coachman knocked at the window of the outhouse, our coachmen came out, there was loud talk, the barn was opened, the horses were led inside.

"I'll go in with them, and say later that they would not let me lead Voronoy out. I will ask him to give me Voronoy, and of course he won't. So I won't have to lie and I will be able to return."

I came to life; it was a brilliant thought. I dropped Roska from my arms and made ready to go into the barn.

"How I would like to be able to go through the large, dark courtyard." I made a step and stopped, for another carriage had entered the yard, and I was afraid I would get under the hoofs of the horse in the darkness. At that moment some catastrophe took place — I don't remember what it was — because I could not tell in the darkness. The horses that were tied in the barn began to neigh, then to stamp, and then to beat the floors with their hoofs. It seemed to me that the horse of the newly arrived coachman was also restless. It had gotten out of control and was galloping about the courtyard, the carriage thundering behind it. The coachmen leaped out of the outhouse, crying, "Stop! Hold her! Don't let her get away!"

I don't exactly remember what happened after. I stood near the front door and rang the bell. The doorman came out and let me in. Of course, he must have been waiting for me. In the doorway of the lobby flashed the figure of my father; the governess looked down from the staircase. I sat down on a chair in the lobby without removing my coat. My entrance into the house was so unexpected to myself that I could not decide what to do — to continue in my obstinacy and to affirm that I had only come in to warm myself in order to go out to Voronoy again, or to confess my cowardice and surrender. I was so dissatisfied with myself for my smallness of spirit that I was already ashamed of the rôle of hero. Besides, there was nobody to enjoy my performance. All of them seemed to have forgotten about me.

"So much the better. I will also forget. I will remove my coat, wait a little while, and then go into the parlor."

And that is what I did. Nobody asked me anything about Voronoy. It must be that they had agreed not to.

CHAPTER IV

M Y brother and I were taken to the Italian opera in our earliest childhood, when we were six, or at most eight years old. And I am very thankful to my parents, for I have no doubts that it acted beneficially on my musical hearing, on the development of my taste and on my eye, which grew used to the beautiful. We had season tickets which entitled us to be present at forty or fifty performances, and we sat in the orchestra, very near to the stage. But as we often said at the time, the opera was merely a side line for us, and we begged our parents not to count it as part of our regular theatrical fare, especially the circus. Music made us tired. Nevertheless the impressions I received at the opera are still alive in me, and are much clearer, sharper, and greater than the impressions left by the circus. I think that this is so because the strength of the impressions in itself was tremendous, but was not felt consciously, being received organically, and not only spiritually but physically also. I began to understand and value these impressions at their true worth only much later, in my memory. But the circus amused me in childhood, although memories of it were of no interest to me in my maturer years.

I remember many of the operas I saw at that time, and the casts that appeared in them. My impressions of the Italian opera are sealed not alone in my visual or aural memory, — for I still feel them physically with my entire nervous system. When I remember them I experience again that physical state which was created in me by the supernormally high and silvery note of Adelina Patti, by her coloratura and technique which made me hold my breath, by her full chest tones which caused my spirit to swoon and brought a smile of satisfaction to my lips. Together with this there is sealed in my memory her exquisite little figure and her profile that seemed to be cut from ivory and had something porcelain-like about it, something that pleased my childish fancy.

The same organically physical impression is sealed in my memory by the elemental force of the king of baritones, Cotogni, and the basso Giametta. I still tremble when I think of them. At such times I remember a charity concert in the house of one of my acquaintances. In a little parlor the two paladins sang the duet from " The Puritan," drowning the room in a velvety stream of sounds that poured into the soul, making it drunk with the passions of the south. Giametta had the face of a Mephistopheles and a tremendous, handsome figure; Cotogni, with an open and kindly face and an enormous scar on his cheek, was healthy, virile, and also handsome in his own way.

The strength of the impression left on me by Cotogni in my youth is almost indescribable. In 1910, that is almost forty years after his arrival in Moscow, I was in Rome, walking with a friend through some narrow alley or other. Suddenly from the top story of one of the houses there floated out a note — broad, ringing, stormy, warming, and exciting. And I felt again physically the old, familiar impression.

" Cotogni! " I cried.

" Yes, he lives here," affirmed my friend. " How did you recognize him? " he wondered.

" I *felt* him," I answered. " That note could never be forgotten."

I have the same physical impression of the strength of the voices of the baritones Bagaggiolo and Graziani, of the dramatic sopranos Arteau and Nilsson, and later, of Tamagno. Memories of the pleasant timbre of the voice are still felt by me physically in the case of Lucca,

Volpini and Mazzini, heard in my youth, and of Marcella Sembrich in later years.

But there are impressions of yet another character that I still feel, although it may seem that I was too young to have experienced them. These are impressions of more or less æsthetic value. I remember the amazing manner of singing employed by the almost voiceless tenor Naudin, who was perhaps the best vocalist of the old type whom it was my fortune to hear. He was old and ugly, but we children preferred him to the younger singers. I remember the extraordinary perfection of phrasing and pronunciation (in Italian, unknown to me at that time) of the baritone Podilla, even in the serenade from " Don Juan " by Mozart and in " The Barber of Seville." Of course these impressions were forcefully sealed in me in childhood, and understood at their full worth from unforgettable memories at a later time. I shall never forget the clearness, the finish, the subtlety and the rhythm of the play of the tenor Capoul, who was not only the creator of important rôles, but also of a hairdress very fashionable in its time.

Here for instance is the cast of " The Barber of Seville " which I remember more clearly than many others I saw and heard later on. Rosina was Patti and Lucca; Almaviva-Niccolini; Capoul-Mazzini; Figaro-Cotogni, Podilla; Don Basilio-Giametta; Bartolo — the famous comedian and basso-bouffe, Bossi.

And this was not at a gala spectacle, but simply at a seasonal subscription performance, for all these stars were regular artists of the Moscow and Petrograd operas, under contract to the Russian Government for the whole season, and in no case guests. I do not know whether any other cities in Europe allowed themselves such luxury.

To the amazement and shame of our melomaniacs, these performances enjoyed a great lavishness of production, but very little attention. They saw the beginning of a bad habit which was but a poor recommendation of Russian taste, of late arrivals in the theatre, and of noisy entrances while Patti or Podilla sang their silvery notes or forced the soul to swoon with their *piano-pianissimo*. This was a snobbishness that reminded one of a self conscious maid-of-all-work who conceives good manners to consist of talking of everything with high-handed impudence and disrespect.

There was still another custom, of an even worse order. The clubmen who subscribed to the Italian opera played cards almost all the evening while the performance was in progress, and came to the theatre only to hear the high *C* of a famous tenor, which he delivered in the last act. When the last act would begin the front rows were still empty, but a short time before the famous note was due there would begin the arrival, the crowding and the general disorder of the clubmen. The note was taken, and repeated for several encores, and then the noise would begin again. The clubmen were going away to finish their card games. They wanted to express their satiety and the remarkable sensitiveness of their taste, which considered only the highest note of the most famous singer worthy of their attention in the whole performance. They were tasteless, empty-headed, stupid and useless people.

Alas, the vocal art and the voices of the Italian opera fell before my eyes; the secret of the production of *bel canto* and perfect diction was lost. In the beginning of this century Moscow saw a new craze for Italian opera. Part of the cast of Mamontov's opera, of which I have already written, was composed of the best singers of that genre. Many of them proved themselves to be talented men and women and even artists. But in those who recalled phenomena like Patti, Lucca, Sembrich, and Cotogni, the new impressions were wiped out by memories of the older singers. Chaliapin is an exception. He stands alone on the heights. And yet there were other exceptions, in the sense of elemental voice material. One of them was the famous tenor Tamagno. I remember that he was but little advertised before his first appearance in Moscow. We expected a good singer, nothing more. Tamagno entered in the costume of Othello, his tremendous and muscular figure filling the eye and a thundering note deafening his audience at once. Instinctively, the crowd surged backward like one man as if defending itself from contusion. The second note was stronger, the third and fourth even stronger than the second, and when with the word "mussulmani" the last note rose like lava from a crater, the public seemed to lose its self-control for a minute. We leaped from our seats and improvised an intermission so that we might be able to digest an impression that we had never experienced before in life. Friends searched for each other, strangers turned to strangers with one and the same question, " Did you hear it? What is it? " The orchestra stopped, there was confusion on the stage, the artists must have thought that an accident or a scandal had taken place in the auditorium of the theatre. But suddenly, coming to its senses, the crowd rushed towards the stage, roaring in its rapture for an encore.

During the next visit of Tamagno he sang in the Great Theatre. The opening night coincided with the Tsar's birthday, and so the national hymn was sung before the beginning of the performance. While the orchestra played in the strongest forte and the entire chorus and all the principals (with the exception of Tamagno) arranged on the fore-stage, sang at the top of their voices, there was suddenly heard coming from back-stage, flying forward and covering all the singers, the chorus and the orchestra, one sustained note, then a second, then a third. Nothing but these notes was heard, and we wanted to hear nothing else. It was Tamagno.

He was but a mediocre artist. He was often out of pitch, he sang falsely, he was not in time with the music, he made mistakes in rhythm. He was a bad actor, but he was not talentless. That is why it was possible for him to create wonders. His Othello was a wonder. It was ideal, both musically and dramatically. He studied this part for many years (I want to stress the word *years*) with such masters as Verdi himself (musically) and Tommaso Salvini dramatically.

Let all young artists know what results may be attained by work, technique and true art. Tamagno was great in this part not only because of labor of the two masters, but also because of the temperament, the sincerity and the feeling for truth given him by God. The masters of technique, his teachers, were able to uncover his talented spiritual being. He could do nothing by himself. He was taught to play the part, but the means used to make him do so remained mysteries to him. They were art and technique. Like the majority of actors, he worked on his part, but he was not an artist.

I tell of these impressions because it is important for the development of the book that my reader live through with me my impressions from the sphere of sound, music, rhythm and the voice. In my career and in my work they were fated to play a large part. I found this out not long ago, already at the sunset of my artistic career. I understood at last the meaning of my childish impressions, elemental and tremendous. They were the signposts that led me, and not so long ago at that, to the study of the voice, to its placement, to the nobility of sound and diction, to rhythmical, musical intonation, to a true view of the soul of vowels, consonants, words, phrases, sentences and speech. All of this is demanded for a true understanding of dramatic art. But I will treat of it in detail later on. Meanwhile let my reminiscences leave a trail in the memory of my reader.

I mention all these memories also to show young artists how important it is for us to take in as many beautiful and strong impressions as we can. The artist must look at, and not only look at but know how to see, the beautiful in all the spheres of his own art, of all other arts, and of life. He needs impressions of good performances, art, concerts, museums, voyages, and pictures of all tendencies, from the most academic to the most futuristic, for no one knows what will move his soul and open the treasure house of his creative gifts. All tendencies are good which help to create the beauti-ful life of the human spirit in artistic forms, that is, which reach the fundamental goal of art.

Let the artist live, let him be enchanted, disappointed, happy; let him suffer, love, and live through the entire gamut of human emotions, but let him at the same time learn to recreate his life and his emotions into art!

CHAPTER V

F ROM the memories of my childish emotions and experiences those that have remained with me longest have to do with the need of spectacles and satisfaction. Let me but resurrect in memory some of the circumstances of my early life, and I seem to grow younger again and feel the old, familiar emotions surge through me. Here is the eve and the morning of a holiday; before me is a day of freedom. In the morning one must go again to church, rising early (one must make the best of that); then there is a long period of standing, the tasty holy wafer, the winter sun warming us through the cupola and gilding the iconostasis, around us people in their holiday best, loud singing, and before us a day full of joy. That is necessary to uphold our energy during the long procession of dull school days and weary evenings that lie before us. Nature demands satisfaction, joy, and a holiday, and he who stands in the way of it causes anger and evil thoughts to rise in the soul, while he who helps it along earns tender gratefulness and a caress.

But at tea time our parents declare to us that we must visit our aunt (who is as dull as all aunts), or what is even worse, that our cousins, whom we dislike, are to visit us after breakfast. We turn to stone, we lose ourselves, we do not know what to do in order to save the lost day and to wrestle with the approaching disaster. We feel our helplessness, we feel that we are discriminated against. The hungry have stretched hands to take bread and it was torn from their grasp. The tired swimmer has already raised his hand to take hold of the life belt when it is thrown in another direction. And we, who have so laboriously awaited the coming of the holiday, see it torn from our grasp and turned into a dull week day. How will we ever be able to live till the next holiday? But if the day is lost there is however still some hope for the evening. Who knows, perhaps father, who understands our needs better than any one else, has bought seats for the circus, or the ballet, or the opera at worst. Or at the very worst, for a play. Theatre tickets were in the care of the major-domo. We ask where he is. Did he go away? Where? To the right or to the left? Were the coachmen told not to use the big horses till evening? If they were, it is a good sign. It meant that the large carriage with places for four, in which we children were always taken to the theatre, was needed. But if the big horses had been used in the daytime, all hope is lost. There will be no circus, no theatre.

But the major-domo has returned. He has been in father's study and given him something which he took out of a pocketbook. What did he give him? A red ticket or a yellow one? We watch until father leaves the study. Then we hurry to his writing table. We see only dull business papers — nothing else. Our hearts are lost in anguish. The world has grown dull. But if we see a red or yellow pasteboard, our hearts beat so that we can hear them, and there is joy before us. Then the aunt and the cousins are no longer so dull as they have seemed before. Gratefulness to father makes us want to pay him a hundred-fold. We exchange compliments with the aunt, with the cousins, all so that in the evening, during dinner, father might be able to say:

" To-day the boys were so kind to their aunt that it is very possible that I might do them a little favor, or perhaps a big one. What do you think it is?"

Red with excitement, with lumps of food sticking in our throats, we wait for further developments.

Father silently puts his hand in a side pocket, slowly searches for something there, but finds nothing. Powerless to wait any longer, we rise, we go to him, we surround him, we examine his pocketbook, while our governess cries severely:

"*Enfin, ecoutez donc ce, qu'on vous dit. On ne quitte pas ce place pendant le diner.*"

Meanwhile father puts his hand in another pocket, takes out another pocketbook, opens it, and finds nothing in it either. Then he slowly takes out still another but there is nothing there also. He turns out his pockets unhurriedly, one after the other. There is nothing in them.

"I lost it," he exclaims, playing his part quite naturally.

The blood leaves our cheeks and is lost in our toes. They lead us back to our places, and we sit down. We try to make sure in the eyes of our brothers and friends whether they think that father is only jesting. But he has already taken something out of the pocket of his waistcoat, and says, slyly smiling at us:

"Here it is. I found it," and waves the red ticket above his head.

All the governesses in the world cannot restrain us now. We leap up from the table, we dance, we stamp our feet, we wave our napkins in the air, we push away our governesses, we embrace father, we hang on his neck, we kiss him. How tenderly we love him now! But the same instant sees new cares arise within us. We may be late! We eat without chewing our food, we can't wait for the dinner to end, and when it does end, we run to the nursery to tear off our house coats and put on our best with respect. And then we sit, wait, and torture ourselves, hoping that father might not be late. As if to spite us, he likes to take a nap over his after-dinner coffee in the empty dining room. How are we to wake him? We walk past the dining room, stamping with our feet, dropping heavy objects on the floor, or crying aloud and pretending that we do not know that he is inside. But father is a heavy sleeper.

"We are late! We are late!" We are all lost in agitation, running each minute to look at the great clock. How we want to stop its pendulum!

"We won't be in time for the overture!" We are in despair.

To miss the circus overture! Is that not a sacrifice?

"It is already seven o'clock!" we exclaim. "Till father wakes up, dresses himself, and begins shaving it will be at least seven-twenty. It takes at least fifteen minutes to get there. That will make it seven-thirty-five." We understand that we will miss not only the overture, but the first number on the program also. The younger Ciniselli will give his *volto arrete* without us. How we envy him. Ten minutes pass. Now we are forced to be sorry for one of the most important numbers on the program — the comic entrance of the musical clowns, Moreno, Mariani and Inserti. This is a very serious loss. We must save the evening somehow. So we go to sigh near the door of mother's room. At this moment we think that she is much kinder than father. We sigh, we exclaim. She understands our tactics and goes to wake father.

"If you want to spoil the boys, spoil them, but don't disappoint them," she tells father, waking him up from his nap. "*Tu l'a voulu*, Georges Dandin! It is time to go to work."

Father rises, stretches himself, kisses mother, and goes sleepily to do his duty. We fly like bullets downstairs to order the carriage and to beg Alexey the coachman to drive as fast as he can. We sit in the large carriage, swinging our feet; that gives us a slight illusion of motion. The front door opens and closes, opens and closes, people go in and go out, but father does not appear. An evil feeling for him grows in our souls; not a trace of the former gratefulness is left. At last he comes out and sits down. The carriage, creaking with its wheels in the snow, slowly moves, rolling on its springs. Impatiently we try to help it along by surging forward in our seats. Its glass panes are completely decorated by the subtle paintings of the frost, — one can see nothing through them. To find out whether we have far to go yet, we warm a small circle on the pane and peek through it to see where we are. Suddenly and unexpectedly the carriage stops. We have arrived! Not only the second number, but even the third number of the program is over. But it is our luck that our favorites, Marino, Mariani and Inserti, have not yet appeared. Neither has *she*. Our box is near the artists' entrance. That is good! From here we can see what is doing in the wings, in the personal life of these incomprehensible, marvelous people who live side by side with death and risk their lives as if they enjoyed it. Is it possible that they are not nervous before their appearance? This might be the last minute of life granted them on earth. But they are quietly talking about trifles, about money, about supper. They are heroes!

The orchestra plays a familiar polka. It is *her* number. It has been placed forward on the program. Her partner will execute the Danse de Chale, and Elvira will appear on horseback. There she is herself now. My friends know my secret. It is my number, she is my sweetheart, and all the privileges are mine — the best opera glasses, the best place, the congratulations of my friends. And truly, she is very pretty to-night. At the end of the number, Elvira comes out to acknowledge the applause and passes within two steps of me. Her nearness turns my head. I want to do something out of the ordinary, and I jump from the box, kiss the hem of her skirt, and return rapidly to my seat. I sit like a man sentenced to death, afraid to move, and ready to cry. My friends approve my action, and my father laughs where he sits behind me.

"Let me congratulate you," he jests. "I see you are engaged. When does the wedding take place?"

The last, most tiresome number, a quadrille on horseback, will be performed by the entire troupe. After it will come next week, in a long procession of joyless, gloomy days, without the least hope of returning here next Sunday. Mother won't let father take us out often. And the circus — the circus is the best place in the whole world.

In order to prolong the present satisfaction and to live as long as possible in pleasant reminiscences, I make a secret appointment with one of my friends.

" You must come. You must not fail me."

" What will happen? "

" You will see when you come. It is very important."

My friend comes the next day; we retire into a dark room, and I tell him my great secret. I have decided to become the director of a circus as soon as I grow old enough. In order that I may not change my mind it is necessary to make my decision binding with an oath. We take an icon from the wall, and I solemnly swear that I will be nothing but the director of a circus. Then we discuss the program of the future performances at my circus. We compose a list of the future troupe from the names of the best riders, clowns and jockeys we know.

In the expectation of the opening of my circus, we decided to give a private domestic performance for practice. We composed a temporary troupe of my brothers, sisters, and friends, divided the rôles and decided on the numbers of the program.

" A stallion trained in freedom — I am the director and trainer, you are the stallion. Then I will play a red-headed clown while you spread the carpet. Then there will be the musical clowns."

Being the director, I always took the best parts, and the rest yielded them to me, because I was a sworn professional, who could think no more of being anything else than a circus director than a shorn monk of a worldly career. The performance was set for the nearest Sunday, because there was no hope that we would be taken to the real circus or even to the ballet. There was no talk of the Italian opera. That did not count. Without any perspective of amusement on Sunday it was impossible to live through the tiresome school week. During the time free from lessons we became very busy. First we had to print tickets and money. Then we had to build a box office — that is, stretch a blanket across the door, leaving a small opening in it near which we were to keep guard all the day of the performance. This was very important, for a real box office would perhaps do more than anything else to create the illusion of a real circus. It was necessary to devote some time and thought to the costumes and to the hoops covered with thin paper through which we would jump in the *pas de chale,* and to the ropes and sticks that were to serve as barriers for the trained horses. And then there was the music. That was the most important part of the performance. The trouble was that my oldest brother, who alone was capable of taking the place of the orchestra, was very lazy, careless and undisciplined. He did not look at the affair at hand seriously, and God knows what he might do on the day of the performance. He would start to play, and play, and suddenly in the face of the whole audience would lie down on a mattress in the middle of the parlor, lift his legs in the air, and begin to roar:

" I don't want to play any more ! "

In the end of things, if we gave him a bar of chocolate, he would play. But the performance would be spoiled by his foolish act; all its reality would be lost. And that was the most important thing for us. It was necessary to believe that all this was serious, that it was real. Otherwise it was not interesting.

There were but few in the audience. They were always the same, the tutor, the governess, sisters, brothers, maids, their relatives. But the worst theatre and the worst actors in the world have their admirers. These latter are certain that only they understand the hidden talents of their protegés, and that all other people are not big enough to understand, or do not acknowledge talent because of jealously and intrigues. We also had our admirers, who followed our performances, and came to them for their own satisfaction, not so much as for ours. One of the fiercest of these was my father's old bookkeeper, and for this he was given one of the best places, which flattered him greatly.

In order to help along the work of the box office, many of our home-grown audience bought tickets throughout the day, pretended that they lost them, and came to the box office to declare their losses. In each case there was an explanatory conversation and the director, that is, I, was asked for final instructions. I would leave my work, come to the box office and grant or refuse admittance. So far as the free passes were concerned, there existed a special little book of numbered tickets with the words " Constanzo Alexeiev's Circus " written on every ticket.

On the day of the performance we put on make-up and costumes long before the beginning of the circus. Coats and waistcoats were pinned up, forming evening dress. The clown's costume was made from a long nightshirt which was tied between the knees, thus forming something in the shape of wide trousers. Father's old high hat was commandeered for the director and the trainer and the clowns' hats were made of paper. Trousers rolled above the knee represented the tights of the acrobats. Faces were whitened with the help of powder and lard. Cheeks and lips were painted with cranberry juice, and coal served to mark the eyebrows and the triangles on the cheeks of the clowns. The performance would begin in good order and invariably ended with a scandal made by my oldest brother, after which my friend and I would begin beating him, and his roars as he ran away from us could be heard echoing through the whole house. When this unpleasant incident would close and we returned to the parlor, the audience was already leaving and the performance would break up. A sourness would remain in the soul, and the long, long series of dull days, evenings, and nights of the threatening school week would stretch before us. Again we created a bright perspective for the following Sunday, without which we felt we could not live through the week.

PLAY DAYS

We hoped that because one Sunday had passed without entertainment we might count on being taken to the circus or the theatre.

Another Sunday would come around, and again there was anguish and much guessing during the day, and again there was joy during dinner. This time it was the theatre. Going there was altogether different from going to the circus. It was a much more serious matter. Mother herself was in charge of this expedition. We were washed, dressed in silken Russian shirts, velvet trousers and chamois boots. White gloves were pulled on our hands, and a strict command was given that the gloves remain white on our return from the theatre, and not become completely black, as usually happened. All evening we walked about with stretched fingers, holding our palms as far as possible from our bodies, so as not to soil the gloves. But we would forget ourselves now and then, and hold a piece of chocolate or crush a program whose large black print was still wet. Or we would begin to rub the soiled velvet barrier of the box from excitement, and our gloves would immediately become a dark gray with black spots.

Mother herself would put on her visiting dress and grow unusually beautiful. I loved to sit in her room and watch her hair being dressed. This time the children of the servants are also taken along. One carriage is not enough, and several vehicles trail each other, giving our expedition the appearance of a picnicking party. A board made specially for this purpose is taken along. It is put on two chairs placed far from each other, and about eight children are placed on it. They look like sparrows sitting on a fence.

In the back of the box sit the nurse, the governesses, and the maids, and in the entrance mother prepares a luncheon for the intermission and pours tea, which has been brought along for the children in special bottles. She is visited by acquaintances who have come to take a look at us. We are introduced, but we can see nothing amidst the golden stretches of the Great Theatre. The smell of gas, which was used to illuminate theatres at that time, always had a magical influence on me. This smell, connected with my ideas of the theatre and the delight received in it, made me dizzy and called forth strong emotion.

The tremendous auditorium and the enormous crowd that filled it at the bottom, the top, and the sides, the drone of human voices that did not stop until the beginning of the performance and woke again in the intermissions, the tuning up of the musical instruments, which at that time was still allowed in full hearing of the public, the gradually darkening house, and the first sounds of the orchestra, the rising curtain, the great stage on which men looked like dwarfs, the trap-doors, the fire, the stormy sea made of painted canvas, the wrecked property ship, scores of big and little fountains, fish and whales that swam at the bottom of a stage sea, caused me to redden, to whiten, to sweat, to weep, to grow cold when the kidnapped ballet beauty prayed the terrible pirate to let her go free. I loved the ballet, the fairy tale, the fantastic fable. The transformations, the destruction, the stage earthquakes were also good. The music thunders, something crackles and falls. This may even be compared to the circus. The most tiresome and unnecessary thing in the ballet, I thought, was dancing. The ballerinas take a pose at the beginning of their number, and I am no longer interested. Not one of the dancers can be compared to my Elvira from the circus.

But there were exceptions. The prima ballerina at that time was a good friend of ours, the wife of one of my father's friends. The consciousness of the fact that I knew a celebrity who appeared on the stage of the Great Theatre and became the centre of attraction and attention to three thousand spectators made me feel very proud. I could speak to her and see her in the same room with myself, while all the others had to be satisfied with looking at her from a distance. Nobody knew what kind of a voice she had; but I did. Nobody knew how she lived, what kind of a husband she had and what children; but I did. And now she was the Maiden of Hell, the heroine of the ballet and nothing else so far as the audience was concerned, but I knew her. This is why I treated her dancing with respect. During the ensembles I occupied myself with looking for another friend of mine, my dancing master, and I always wondered how it was that he never forgot all the different movements of the dance that were required of him. In the intermissions great pleasure was mine in running along the long corridors, halls, and numerous foyers, the acoustics of which made the sound of our stamping feet reëcho back from the ceilings.

Sometimes on week days we would give an impromptu ballet. But it was considered impossible to waste a Sunday for it. Sunday belonged wholly to the circus. Our governess was the master of the ballet and the orchestra at the same time. We played and danced to her singing. The ballet was called " The Naiad and the Fisherman " and I did not like it. It called for the representation of love, it was necessary to kiss some one, and I was ashamed. What I wanted was to kill, to save, to sentence, to pardon. But the chief trouble was that this ballet included for some unknown reason dances which we studied with our dancing master. This smelled of the schoolroom and disgusted me.

After many hardships my friend and I became convinced that further work with the amateurs, as we called my brother, my sister, and all but ourselves, was impossible, both in the matter of the circus and that of the ballet. Besides, under the existing arrangements, the most important part of the theatre was entirely lost, that part being the scenery, lighting effects, trapdoors, the sea, fire and storm. How was it possible to reproduce them in a simple room with the help of sheets, blankets and the palms and flowers that were always in the parlor? It was decided to exchange the living actors for actors made of pasteboard, and to begin the construction of a marionette theatre with scenery, effects and a full line of theatrical necessities. This would also give us the opportunity to sell tickets.

" I want you to understand that this is not treason to the circus,"

I said to my friend in my quality as his future director. " It is a sad necessity."

But the marionette theatre demanded expenditures. We needed a large table to put in the wide doorway while above and beneath it, that is, above and beneath the marionette stage, the openings were covered with sheets. In this manner, the public sat in one room, the auditorium, while in the other room, which was united to the first by the doorway, was the stage and all its accessories. It was there that we worked, — we, the artists, the designers, the stage managers, and the inventors of all sorts of scenic effects. My oldest brother also joined us; he was an excellent draughtsman and a fine inventor of stage effects. His help was important because he had a little money, and we needed capital for our work. A cabinetmaker, whom I had known almost from the day of my birth, for he was continually employed about the house, pitied us, and agreed to make us a table if we paid him on the installment plan.

" Christmas is coming soon, and Easter right after it," we said, in persuading him. " We will get money then and pay you."

While the table was still in the making, we began to paint scenery. At first we painted it on wrapping paper which tore and crumpled, but we did not lose heart, for we thought that with time, as soon as we became rich (for we were to charge ten kopeks as admission), we would buy pasteboard and glue the painted wrapping paper to it. We did not ask our parents for money because we thought that they would be dissatisfied with our idea which might make them think that it was taking our time from our studies. From the moment that we began to feel ourselves managers and directors of the new theatre that was being built according to our plans, our life became full. There was something to think about every minute. There was a great deal to do. The only thing that was an obstacle in our path was study — study and tutors and governesses. In the drawer of the table there always lay hidden some piece of theatrical work, the figure of a marionette which was to be painted and dressed, a piece of scenery, a bush, a tree, or the plan and sketches for a new production. On the desk lay our books, but in the desk there was always scenery. Let the governess or the tutor go out for a moment, and the scenery was on the table and covered by the book or placed inside of it. The tutor returns — we turn a page and he sees nothing. In the margins of my books and copybooks there were always sketches of scenery. And no one could ever guess whether it was scenery or a geometric drawing.

We staged many plays, or rather acts. We always chose moments of catastrophic character; for instance an act from "The Corsair" which called for a sea quiet in the daylight, but stormy at night, with a wrecked ship, with heroes swimming for their lives, with the appearance of a lighthouse, an escape from a watery grave, the rising of the moon, prayer, and dawn. Or that scene from Pushkin's "The Stone Guest" which showed the appearance of the Commandor, the descent of Don Juan into hell, with fire issuing from a trapdoor, with the destruction of the house turning the stage into a hell of flames, in which fire and smoke were the chief ingredients. More than once the scenic set burned up and was replaced by a new one. We staged a ballet under the name of "Robert and Bertram," about two thieves who left their prison at night and entered the windows of peaceful burgesses. These performances were always sold out, notwithstanding the high price of admission. Many people came to see them, some to encourage us, others to amuse themselves.

Our faithful admirer, the old bookkeeper, did everything he could to advertise our new theatre. He brought his entire family and his friends. This time we did not need to invent work for ourselves in the box office. There was enough work there as it was, and even more work back-stage. The box office opened in the evening, just before the performance. Once, because of the presence of a large audience, we were forced to move to a larger room, but the artistic side of the performance suffered from this, and we were punished for our greed.

We decided that if we were to occupy ourselves with art, no thought of money must enter our minds.

Now we spent our Sundays happily without the circus or the theatre. And when we were asked to choose between the circus and the theatre, we preferred the latter. Not because we had betrayed the circus, but because our marionette theatre demanded that we go to the theatre and see all of its productions, learn and get fresh material for our own creations. We were, it is true, the stage managers and producers of a very little theatre, but even great theatres often learn by imitation.

Our promenades between lessons took on a very deep meaning. Before that we went to the Kuznetsky Bridge to buy the photographs of circus artists, searching for some that we did not have in our collection. But with the appearance of our theatre there appeared a need for all sorts of material for scenery and marionettes. Now we were no longer too lazy to take a walk, as we had been before. We bought all sorts of pictures, books with landscapes and costumes, which served as material for the scenery and the dramatis personæ of our theatre. These were the first volumes of a rapidly increasing library.

Perhaps the necessity to recreate all that took place about us in real life was in our blood. For instance, with the establishment of universal military service, we also organized an army among the boys whom we knew. There were even two armies. My brother led one, I led the other. The commander in chief of both armies was the same person, a friend of my father's. He gave the word, and many ten-year-old boys turned up from the surrounding hamlets and villages. Everything was organized as it should be. In the beginning each one enjoyed equal rights. All were soldiers, and there was one commander who was to educate commissioned and non-commissioned officers.

PLAY DAYS

There was a great deal of competition. Each of us wanted to unravel the wisdom of military affairs and become an officer. Some of the cleverer boys showed themselves strong competitors, and in the very beginning went ahead of us in the matter of military articles. But when the program widened and it was announced that the ability to read and write was required from the soldiers, and my brother and I were commissioned to instruct the rest, we went ahead of our friends, became noncoms, and soon after that, officers.

We were to be made officers on a day devoted to maneuvers, and we were to lead the two corps into which the army was divided. Before the very beginning, when the entire army tremblingly awaited the battle, standing in closely locked ranks, a hunter's horn was heard in the distance, a sound very reminiscent of a fanfare, and a horseman who was a guest of one of our neighbors galloped into the courtyard. He was clad in a very strange costume which evidently was supposed to be Persian, with a white skirt that reached to his knees. He sprang from his horse, bowed in the Eastern manner to the commander in chief and congratulated us in the name of his sovereign, telling us that the Persian Shah and his court were to make us happy with their presence. Soon we saw in the distance a procession in white bathrobes, with towels wound about their heads, and red belts. Among them there was a person clad in a magnificent Bokhara robe (from the museum treasures of the brothers S., the manufacturers of silks and tapestries). The shah himself was in a very rich Eastern robe with a real Eastern turban and wonderful weapons from the same museum. He rode on an old white horse that belonged to us and which had not lost its beauty in all its years of rest. Above the shah was carried a rich umbrella with tassels, fringes and gold-embroidered velvet pinned to it.

On the terrace in front of the courtyard where the parade was to take place, suddenly appeared a throne as if by magic, ornamented with Eastern carpets and materials. The stairs leading from the yard to the terrace and the throne were also covered with carpets. Flags appeared from somewhere and were quickly fastened to the terrace.

The shah, who did not want to walk because he considered it demeaning, was ceremoniously taken off the horse, carried to the terrace and deposited on the throne. We recognized our cousin, who was to be the mayor of Moscow in his time. His courtiers surrounded him.

The parade began. We passed in review. The shah shouted some terrible and incomprehensible words to us, which were supposed to be Persian. The courtiers sang for some reason, bowed very low, and walked around and around the shah. My brother and I and all the other boys were excited with the ceremony.

After the parade there were the maneuvers. We were told the positions of two enemy armies, our strategical problem, and put in our places. Then began a series of surrounding movements, ambushes, counter-attacks, and at last the battle proper. Heated by the solemn circumstances we began to fight. There was already one casualty — a black eye. But ——

At the cruellest moment of the fight, my mother suddenly ran into the very middle of the fighting boys. She waved her parasol energetically, pushing apart the fighting boys, and cried at us in such a severe manner that the engagement suddenly came to an end. Having put both armies to rout she began to scold us and our elders. No one escaped her tongue. The Persian shah also left his throne and began to scold us in his turn.

"Declare war on Persia!" cried one of the boys. Both armies quickly fell into line, united into one and rushed at the shah. He began to roar. We roared also. He began to run away from us. We followed him. At last we overtook him, caught him, surrounded him, and began to pinch him. This time the shah roared, but no longer in jest. He roared seriously, and from pain. But my mother appeared on the horizon with her parasol, and the army of the allies beat a hasty retreat.

In accordance with the patriarchal custom of that time, our education began at home. Our parents spared no money and secured the best tutors in Moscow for us. From early morning to late evening, one teacher would supplant the other, and in the intermissions between lessons we would occupy ourselves with fencing, dancing, skating, and other physical work. My sisters had Russian, French and German teachers, who taught us boys also, and besides, we boys had an old and excellent educator by the name of Vincent, a Swiss who was an accomplished sportsman, gymnast, fencer, and horseman. This man, with his beautiful personality, played a tremendous part in our struggle with the century-old prejudices in the domestic education of children. He begged our parents to let us go to the *gymnasia,* but our mother, who loved us too much, could not even conceive of such a horror. It seemed to her that strange boys, who might be the sons of janitors, and who were certainly strong and cruel, would beat us, boys of whom she always thought as helpless angels. She imagined that the teachers would continually be sending us to the guardroom, and that in the end of things we would become gamins and forget all we knew of decent behavior. The hygienic conditions in the *gymnasia* seemed dangerous to her. We would certainly catch some disease and bring it home where everybody would at once become sick, some with scarlet fever, some with typhus, and some with measles. She prophesied that the entire house would become a hospital.

At about that time, the government instituted universal military service, with exemptions on the ground of education. Soon other reforms appeared, which forced the question of education into a very prominent place. Life itself made my parents surrender, and when I was thirteen years old, I was led to take entrance examinations to the third class in one of the Moscow *gymnasias.* So that the Lord might make me wise enough to pass the impending purgatory, my nurse hung a little bag with mud from Mount Athos around my neck, and my mother and sisters decorated me with holy images. Instead of getting into the third class, thanks to pull and push, I was able at last to get into the first. I tried so hard to write my composition and pulled the button on my chest to such purpose because of my inability to write, that I made a hole in the little bag, and the holy mud ran out.

I was almost as tall then as I am now, and my classmates, to please a cruel fate, were mostly short. The contrast was so piquant that it turned the attention of all those who visited the class to me. Whether it was the director who came, or the superintendent — I knew beforehand that I would be called on to recite. The smaller I tried to make myself, the worse it was. I only formed the habit of holding my shoulders in an unnatural and rounded position.

In the seventies of the last century, the *gymnasias* underwent a fad in classical languages. Many instructors and professors of Greek and Latin, especially from Bohemia, came to Russia and filled all our institutions of learning, trying to force their dried knowledge down our throats. But soon they found out that it was impossible to sew Russian clothes to a foreign cut. We cannot memorize; we are not patient enough. We must understand the contents of what is taught us, and the rest follows as of itself. A Russian child cannot sit quietly and dumbly for a period of five hours. He needs to expend his surplus energy and find an outlet for his temperament. He must be mischievous, and the strict military discipline the alien instructors brought with them served only to make us unmanageable and made us feel that we were persecuted.

Like our parents, we too were infected with the love of practical joking. And often our practical jokes bore a cruel character. Our estate, which lay about twenty miles from Moscow, was in the midst of a summer residential section. The summer residents would pass by our very windows whenever they happened to be rowing up or down the river. It seemed to us that we had suddenly been transported to a highway which ran through our estate and even through our house. We and our comrades decided to frighten away the unbidden guests. And this is what we did: we bought a large bull's bladder, put a wig on it, drew eyes, a nose, a mouth and ears in the proper places until the bladder resembled the yellow face of a drowned man. To the bladder we tied a long rope which we passed through the handles of two dumb-bells; one of the bells we sunk in the middle of the river, the other near the shore. Pulling on the rope, we sank the bladder to the bottom and tied the rope in some bushes, where we also hid. It was only necessary to untie the rope, and the bladder would leap from below the surface of the water like some strange and unheard-of monster. We waited for the summer residents to come rowing down the river. As soon as they approached near enough, a hairy monster would suddenly appear above the water and as suddenly disappear. The effect can hardly be imagined. It is still a marvel to me that not a single one of those boats ever turned over, although their passengers would always rush to one side in panic. It is true that we were careful and experimented only with large boats. After several such seances, the neighborhood was filled with strange rumors. Each of the rumor-mongers exaggerated what had happened for the sake of effect. Some said that a shark, traveling up the Volga and its tributaries from the Caspian Sea, had taken up its residence near our estate. They recommended that no one swim in the river, for sharks ate humans, and that no one row on the river, for sharks often overturned boats with their tails, which were very strong. Others insisted that it was the ghost of a small merchant from a neighboring village, who had been drowned not long before, and whose body was still unrecovered, and that the drowned man, suffering because he was not decently interred beneath a cross, reminded true Christians of his pathetic state. Mass for the soul of the drowned man was held in our house church.

CHAPTER VI

OUR HOME THEATRE

THE small wing of the house on our estate near Moscow, where I made my début on the stage at the age of two or three, rotted away, and it was decided to put up another building in its place. We were sad to see the building go, for it was full of the memories of our childhood. It was the only place where we could dance, sing, and make a noise, without getting into the way of others. Not only we, but the neighbors begged our father not to destroy our club. At last it was decided to put up a new building with a large hall, which, when necessary, could be transformed into an auditorium. I think that our father had in mind our love for the theatre. Perhaps he was also urged to hold us nearer to the paternal hearth. Whatever the case, everything seemed to encourage our secret love for the theatre. Not only the hall with its balcony that served instead of boxes, but even the back part of the building was wonderfully arranged and gave space for dressing rooms, scenery and properties. The result was a little theatre. And near it there was a large lawn that seemed to be just made for illumination and landscape effects. A little farther out, the river was ripe for our water festivals. We even dreamed of making a new Hermitage à la Lentovsky, who was very much in fashion just then.

Perhaps it was an heirloom from our French grandmother actress, but all of us, brothers and sisters, seemed to be possessed with a love for the theatre, which we even came to call theatroline. All our spare time was devoted to the theatre; all our dreams were about the production of this or that play. At first we did the thing without any special preparations and the cost was covered by the modest sums we received from our parents for pocket money. But having seen various European wonders, our tastes became sharper and we began to demand more of our artistic efforts. The direction and acting plans were not within our means, either financial or artistic. What could we do without real technique, without real knowledge of the stage, and even without material for scenery and costumes? Outside of the old clothes of our parents and our sisters and friends, of some few ribbons, buttons and other things like that, we had nothing. And somehow we did not want to ask our parents for money. Willy-nilly we were forced to replace the luxury of costume and scenery by the unexpectedness of artistic imagination, originality and unusualness. A director was necessary, but since there was none, and we wanted badly to play, it was necessary for me to become a stage director myself. Life and necessity taught us and made us pass through the most practical school of all — experience.

To illustrate that crooked line which the work of an amateur takes without the direction of a specialist, I shall describe several performances which were most important to my future activities. I shall not stick closely to chronology in doing so, for their chronology does not interest me. What is important is the succession of steps or stages passed by the actor in attaining his creative maturity and understanding, and the rises and falls in the crooked line of his progress which distinguish it from the true and fundamental highway of his growth.

The building of the new wing to our house was nearing its end. It was necessary to open the theatre with some sort of performance. Our tutor, a student who considered himself somewhat of a specialist in theatrical affairs, as he was the leader of a dramatic circle, took the stage direction on himself.

There began the ordinary amateurish bother, the reading and the choosing of a play. It was necessary to secure a suitable rôle for every one, a rôle that might fit the taste of its interpreter, a rôle that would not be smaller than that of any one else, but at the same time be short rather than long. In order to please everybody it was necessary to compose the performance of several one-act plays. Only this made it possible to give each one a part to his liking.

What rôle was I to choose for myself?

What was my ideal at that time?

It was to resemble my favorite artist N., of the Imperial Little Theatre, a comedian with a sickly, hoarse voice and funny movements of the face. It was these movements and his hoarse voice that I loved. All my work consisted in trying to imitate his movements and to develop a hoarseness in my voice. I wanted to be his exact double. Of course I chose a play in which he had appeared. This would give me the chance to play exactly as he did. It was called "A Cup of Tea" and was in one act. The chief part in it was considered to be N's artistic crown. I knew every bit of business in it, I knew his every intonation, gesture, and his full scale of mimetics. The director had nothing to do with me, for my part had already been directed by another and all that remained for me was to repeat what I had seen,—that is, to copy N. blindly. I felt that I was right in what I did, and I experienced a certain amount of self-confidence. Confidence on the stage is persuasive — to a certain degree.

When the theatre was filled with the public, I felt myself much better. The thought of make-up, of the performance, of my appearance on the stage in the part caused a tremor of satisfaction, excitement and pleasure to appear within me. This feeling grew tenfold when I actually appeared, and I was no longer able to control myself; it seemed to me that somebody was pushing me on, exciting me, encouraging me, and I flew through my whole part, the bit in my teeth. What excited me was not my lines, not the meaning of what transpired, for the one-acter was devoid of all meaning; what thrilled me was artistic action, the playing before spectators. I was excited by the public, by the publicity of my appearance, by the consciousness of the crowd and of myself on show before it. I was excited by the fact that I had an opportunity to act, to represent some one, to repeat what I had learned, with all the stage hokum that I had seen. I was excited by the madness of the tempo and the rhythm within me which made me hold my breath at times. Words and gestures flew out with the rapidity of lightning. I choked, I lost my breath and could not speak, and my nervousness and lack of restraint were mistaken by me for true inspiration. While acting, I was certain that I held my audience in my power. Judge of my surprise when after the end of the one-acter we were met with rather thin applause, and when I walked back-stage I met with no praise and no enthusiasm.

"Well, it was rather nice," the stage director told me.

What did that "rather nice" mean? Later it was explained to me that no one understood me, so swiftly had I moved, so low and hoarsely had I talked. No one had seen anything, for I had moved my hands in the air with unbelievable rapidity.

What a difference there is between your own impressions while on the stage and the impression created in the auditorium by your acting!

This discovery brought me into complete perplexity. I understood nothing then, and later.

It was altogether different with the rôle of an old man in a one-acter called "The Old Mathematician, or the Appearance of a Comet in a Provincial Town." In this rôle I had no examples to follow, and therefore the rôle seemed to me to be empty, transparent, devoid of life. At that time I was still unable to find my examples in life and recreate them on the stage. What I needed was a ready-made stage portrait. I was forced to ask myself:

"How would this actor, the methods of whose acting I know and can copy, play this part?"

There were some sections of the rôle that called for an imitation I could do, and I felt content with those sections. But in other sections I could not see my familiar interpreter; but I struck by accident on the methods of another actor whom I knew, and only then did I find myself at home on the stage. In still another place I recognized still another actor, in a fourth one more, and so on through the whole part. And so, in one part, I gave ten distinct interpretations; in one man I saw ten distinct individuals. Each separate copied section was passable in itself, but all the sections taken together were impossible. The part resembled a blanket sewn together of rags, shreds and remnants. I felt strange on the stage. There was nothing here in common with the impression I had received in my rôle in "A Cup of Tea." That rôle had given me tremendous satisfaction, but the rôle in "The Old Mathematician" had given me only untold torture. And worse than all, I did not know how to get out of my dilemma.

"God, how easy and pleasant it is to occupy one's self with art!" I could say after "A Cup of Tea."

"How hard, how torturing is art!" I would have said sorrowfully after "The Old Mathematician."

There is no greater torture than that experienced when the part played does not enter into the actor; only to play the part is not enough. It is unbearable to represent something cloudy, strange, and alien to you.

It is easy to play, and it is hard to play; it is a ravishing and an unbearable art. These were the paradoxes created by my début.

I was perplexed.

My début performance, so to say, in "A Cup of Tea" and "The Old Mathematician" took place in September, when I was already studying in the *gymnasia*. My brother and I rode to the city together with the commuters on the six o'clock train, and on the day of the performance, tired by the dress rehearsal the night before, we attended school in the city and returned home in time for dinner before the performance. I have retained that day in my memory with astounding clearness and sharpness of impression. Especially that instant when we drove from the station to the house. Rain, twilight, mud. A four-seated carriage, rolling on its springs, wove its slow way forward, filled with people and properties for the performance. On my knees and occupying my arms was a tremendous wood-pulp box. I embraced it lovingly as if it were the waist of a dear woman. I was afraid it would fall out of the carriage. In it were wigs, hair, glue, make-up. The specific odor of the make-up which is so well known to all artists floated into my nose from every crack in the box and made me drunk. I seemed to be in a dream. That which had been always so far off and impossible was actually taking place. In a few hours I would stand behind the footlights, alone on an eminence, in the eyes of all. Many people would come from Moscow and from the far suburbs for my sake, and I would be able to do with them as I willed. If I willed it they would sit quietly, listen and look at me; if I willed it, they would laugh. My body trembled nervously at such thoughts, and my impatience grew sharper. I wanted to appear before the public as quickly as possible and experience the feeling which at that time I called the feeling of publicness.

When we reached home, I did not recognize the old, familiar rooms. Everywhere were covered tables, hurry, the sound of dishes, caterers and hired waiters came in a large vehicle and were carrying in boxes with dishes; the handles of the doors were being cleaned, the rooms swept.

We were hurriedly given something to eat and sat down to some table covered with a multitude of dishes. How I love these dinners in the midst of preparation for an oncoming holiday. They excite one like the prelude to something great and important.

The artists are eating! The artists are getting ready for the performance! This seemed to me as important as a mystery.

In the theatrical wing, as we called it at that time, there was no less chaos. My sisters and their friends were placing the costumes in the proper dressing rooms. The make-up men were preparing beards, paint and wigs. A young man whom everybody called Yasha flashed from one dressing room into another. I met him that day never to part from him. Yakov Ivanovich Gremislavsky was fated to play a great rôle in the art of make-up in the Russian theatre, and to place that art on the height required of it by the growing and complex problems of contemporary art in general.

The actors sat down in order before the mirror of the make-up man, — my father, my brothers, my tutor, and the other actors, and left it changed into other people. Some became older, some younger and more beautiful; others became bald, still others were altogether unrecognizable.

" Can that be *you*? Ha-ha-ha! — You won't know me! Marvelous! See how he looks! I can't believe it! Bravo! "

Exclamations so common at amateur performances were heard from all the corners of the dressing room where people pushed each other, one searching for a lost necktie, another for a collar button, a third for a waistcoat. Curious onlookers were in our way, filling the air with cigarette smoke and making a great deal of noise, and it was impossible to drive them out of the small dressing room which was hardly large enough to seat ten actors.

In the distance there was the thunder of a military march. The guests, with burning candles in their hands, were marching up the alleyways of the garden before entering triumphantly into the theatrical wing. The sounds of music came nearer and nearer, and at last deafened us so that we could not hear each other talk, but little by little they began to weaken in the distance, and then died out somewhere in the courtyard. Then we heard the tramping of feet, the unceasing sound of voices, and the noise of moving chairs. Talk quieted down back-stage and in the dressing rooms; the actors grew quieter also, forced smiles appeared on their faces, confusion. But in my heart there was joy; something boiled up in me and urged me forward to conquer the whole world. The curtain rose, the performance was on. Instead of joy my début brought me perplexity. It was strange that when I felt myself to be good the public criticized me, and when I felt myself to be bad some praised me.

Soon after that I played in a private house, and all I thought about was this insoluble problem. I played the part of a drunken lackey who declared that another bottle burst in the wine cellar each time he appeared on the stage. The more appearances he made the more drunk he became, and his words grew more and more indistinct. At the end the lackey was completely drunk and spoke no more, but only moved his lips. In this part I did not suffer for lack of living examples to copy. In the good old days there were plenty of drunkards to be seen on every street corner and I could have freely taken examples from life, as Shtchepkin, the great artist and lawgiver of the Russian stage, taught us to do. I learned, as it seemed to me, to copy drunkards to perfection, and I felt myself to be so good in the part on the stage that I could not restrain the inner joy and palpitation which I mistook for inspiration at that time. With each of my entrances I tried to give stronger and stronger expression to what boiled within me. But the audience criticized me.

In another house I played one of the best rôles of my favorite actor, N. I imitated him perfectly. Again I felt at home on the stage, again there was inspiration, and the more it excited me, the more the audience criticized my rapid patter, my incoherent diction, my hoarse voice, my murmuring speech, my rapid gestures, my strained and exaggerated efforts.

At a third performance I was reproached for shouting, for grimacing instead of mimicking, for exaggeration and the absence of a *feeling of true measure,* without which everything I did seemed inartistic and unnatural. These words — *a feeling of true measure* — now entered my soul for the first time. They helped me to a dim understanding of something about the stage.

CHAPTER VII

OUR productions were few and far between and in the interim we suffered from having no artistic work to do. In order to assuage our artistic thirst we would engage in the following things. As soon as evening would arrive we would make ourselves up as beggars or drunkards and go to the station. There we would frighten everybody, and more than once the watchmen would chase us from the platform. The worse they treated us, the more we were satisfied. For in life one must be more subtle and truth-like than on the stage, where illusion is almost ready-made for you. If we were not good actors we would get into trouble. But since we were chased away, we must have played our parts well.

Our greatest success came to us in the rôles of gypsies. A passing gypsy camp that had stopped between our estate and the station gave us the proper clue for making costumes. Gypsy women and children could be seen on every road near the summer residences. One evening we expected a cousin, a beautiful young woman who was in love with a neighbor of ours and with whom all of us were in love. We know that she liked to be told her fortune. Not long before her arrival a new governess appeared in our house, with whom our cousin was still unacquainted. The new governess told fortunes brilliantly. Having told her all the secrets of my cousin, I, she, and the small son of one of the maids secretly assumed the guise of gypsies. We walked on the road to the station, and meeting my cousin in her carriage, we started running after her, shouting something in a broken gypsy jargon. The young woman was frightened, and ordered the coachman to get her home as quickly as possible. Having reached the house, and told one of my brothers the secret, we waited near the gates. Soon the excited young woman and her family came to visit us. Putting her hand through a break in the fence she asked for her fortune to be told. She was told everything. The effect was indescribable, — then somebody suddenly cried that he had lost a ring.

"The gypsies stole it. Search them."

We began to run to the wood, followed by the entire crowd. But my cousin, pleased by what we had told her, had managed to put a small diamond pin in the hand of the governess. Next day, this pin suddenly appeared on my cousin's dress. Mystification, conversations, guesses, and then new mischief.

There was a time when we could not arrange any performances, but we wanted to play very much. And so we, that is, my two sisters, my friend and I, decided to rehearse by ourselves for the sake of practice two vaudeville skits translated from the French, "The Weak String" and "A Woman's Secret." Much later I learned that our precursers, the famous actors of the Russian stage, were not brought up in tragedies which force youth to tear passion to tatters and overstrain the abilities of the young novice, but in the simplest vaudeville skits. The French vaudeville act enjoyed special honor. But it demanded good technique, inner and outer agility, faultless diction, elegance, and a verve that gave the skit the necessary piquancy, just as sparkling gas gives champagne its taste. Without tearing passion to tatters, without straining the soul of youth, the old school first worked out its technique by means of the vaudeville skit. And only after that technique was present did it pass on to the more difficult problems of the spirit.

The vaudeville plots were simple indeed.

Two students love two grisettes, and seek for the weak strings in their souls in order to play on them and so win their love. But what is the weak string of a woman? A male canary beats a female, and the latter, after a good beating, kisses the former. Is not this the weak string of a woman? One must beat them. The students try it and receive strong slaps in return. But in the end they fall in love with each other and marry. Truly, is it not clear, pure, and naive?

And here is another simple subject. An artist and a student by the name of Megrio (I played Megrio) court a grisette. The artist loves the grisette, and the student helps him. But they have discovered a terrible secret — the grisette drinks — rum has been found in her room. Perplexity and sorrow! In the end it is proven that the grisette used the rum for her hair only. The rum is consumed by the student and the janitor, and the grisette falls in love with the artist. The latter two kiss in the finale, while the first two roll under a table and sing a very funny duet.

An artist, a grisette, an attic, a student, Montmartre — in this there is style, enchantment, grace, and even romance.

Taking advantage of the fact that we lived all that summer in the village, we could rehearse as much as we pleased and then be able to play in a perfected manner. We would rise in the morning, bathe, and then rehearse one skit. Then we would breakfast and rehearse the other. After a walk we would repeat the first. In the evening if a guest came out to visit us, we would propose at once:

" Don't you want us to play for you? "

" Go right ahead, " he would answer.

We would light a kerosene lamp, for the scenery was always set and ready, lower the curtain, and dress — one would get into a blouse, another into an apron, a bonnet, a kepi — and the performance would begin before our solitary listener. We considered such performances in the light of rehearsals at which we put before ourselves continually new problems in order to become perfect. Here the phrase that I had heard at random once, " the feeling of true measure," was studied from every angle. At last I inculcated the actors with such a feeling of true measure that our lonely spectator would fall asleep from boredom. "It is good, but rather — quiet," he would say in a confused manner.

This gave us a new problem — to speak louder. Another spectator would come and say that we were shouting. That meant that there was still no feeling of true measure and it was necessary to speak neither loudly nor softly, but find a middle road. This problem, so simple at first sight, we could not solve. The hardest thing on the stage is to speak neither louder nor softer than is necessary, and at the same time be simple and natural. But to speak softly means to wipe out the entire rôle, and so we were forced to speak louder than was necessary. Loudness for the sake of loudness is not a creative goal.

"The vaudeville skit must be played in full tempo, in full tone," said still another spectator.

"The act takes forty minutes to play," I said to myself. "When it takes only thirty minutes it will mean that we are playing at full tempo."

At last we reached thirty minutes.

"When it will take us twenty minutes, we will be doing well," I thought.

There was created a sort of a sport, to play for the sake of swiftness, and we reached twenty minutes.

It seemed to us that the skit was being played in the proper tempo at last, and in full tone, that is, loudly. But when our critic came again he refused to grant us any degree of success.

"I don't understand a single word you are saying, or anything that you are doing. This is a madhouse."

"This means that the business is to remain the same," I decided. "I won't allow another minute to be added to the time the skit takes on the stage, but it must be done so that every word, every gesture, and the entire plot of the skit is completely understood. "

If we had been successful in solving this hardest of all problems, we might have become great vaudeville artists and comedians. But of course, we were not successful. Nevertheless we came to some results, and our work brought us a great deal of outer technical craftsmanship. We began to speak more clearly and to act more definitely. This in itself is a result not to be sneered at. Yet the swiftness was merely for the sake of swiftness, the loudness for the sake of loudness, the full tone for the sake of the full tone, the rapid tempo for the sake of the rapid tempo. All these four things existed, but they did not live *in* us. And the creativeness of an actor must come from within, while his voice and his body remain obedient instruments in the sure hands of a virtuoso. There is trouble when a violin has a false tone. No matter how well the violinist feels, he cannot interpret what he feels. A false instrument will mutilate and distort all the interpretative creativeness of the artist. Our instrument — the mutual assumption of voice and body — was distorted, and it was for this reason that we exaggerated and ex-perienced a nervousness very much like that of a jockey who races for a prize.

At another time, wishing again to give a performance which would use only those who lived all summer together, after a long search for a suitable play, we decided that we were going to write the text and music of an operetta. As a basis for our new work we laid down a naive principle: each of the actors would invent a rôle to suit himself and explain what he wanted to play. Putting all these orders together, we would invent a plot that could be com-posed of the ordered rôles, write the text and the music, which last labor was undertaken by one of our friends. We, the newly baked writers and the composer, learned by experience all of the tortures of creation. We found out what it meant to create a musico-dramatic work for the stage and in what the difficulty of such a work lay. There is no doubt that some parts of the work were successful. They were suitable for the stage, joyous, and gave good material to the stage director and the actor. But when we tried to unite the separate parts and to tie them together into a plot, we found that the plot was bad, that it would not hold. There was no single basic idea which might lead the author to a definite goal. Just the opposite; there were many altogether differing ideas, a few from each of the actors, which tore the plot into many separate pieces. The parts in themselves were all right, but the play would not stick together. We did not really understand the reason for our literary failure, but the very fact that we had had to think of it ourselves was very useful.

It was necessary to decide whom I wanted to play. Of course I must be handsome, in order to sing tender love arias, be successful with the ladies, and resemble some famous singer whom I could copy in voice, singing, and in stage manner, — that I might imitate his qualities, and most of all his individual faults. I was in that stage of artistic development when the youth does not understand and does not want to recognize his special gifts. A short man wants to be tall, an ugly woman to be beautiful, an awkward lout agile, a man devoid of lyricism to act a sweet lover, a man devoid of passion to play Don Juan, a fool to play a philosopher, a coward to play a hero, an atheist to play Sophocles or Dostoyevsky, whose whole meaning lies in the search for God. Ask an amateur what part he wants to play most. You will be amazed by his choice. People are always attracted by what they have not, and actors often use the stage to receive there what they cannot get in real life. If a woman cannot be a beauty in life she wants to be beautiful at least on the stage. This is the logic of those who are completely ignorant of pure art. What can a performance that has no basic life element give to the artist? To be beautiful and successful is not a creative goal that can make a work of art. And the imitation of a favorite actor can only create an outer method, but not the soul, without which there can be no art. Such a performance only makes for bad craftsmanship and works out a ready-made manner of acting which at times becomes a mechanical habit. But the misunderstanding of one's true ability and calling in the art is the strongest obstacle in the further development of an actor. It is a blind alley which he enters for tens of years, and from which he cannot get out until he realizes his mistake and returns to the avenue that leads to the gates of pure art.

But even this performance proved to be interesting because of one very educative incident. My cousin, who was to play the leading part, and who came to live with us for the sake of playing the part, was forced to leave in the middle because she was needed at home. There was no one to take her place. It became necessary to give the part to my oldest sister. Until that time she had been a Cinderella who did only the rougher work around the stage, like preparing costumes, renewing scenery, and calling the actors when it was their turn to appear; she appeared on the stage only on the most extraordinary occasions in the rôle of a super or at most in a small part. And suddenly, the leading part was hers. She agreed to help us in a spirit of self-sacrifice that was worthy of admiration.

Not believing in the successful result of this change, I rehearsed her only because I had to, and often could not hide my bad feelings for her, although she was innocent and did not at all deserve any bad wishes. I tortured her, and at one of the rehearsals reached the last limit of her breaking patience. She could not make her own the strongest and most important moment of the rôle, without which all that followed would be incomprehensible. I decided not to go any further until she had reached success in the part. With tears of despair in her eyes, my sister played the most important scene so that we all became seriously affected. The ice had cracked and the water was at last free; the bars had dropped and the prisoner was at liberty. The timidity that had chained her was broken by her in her despair and the strong temperament of an artist found its way to the surface. With the same passion with which I had persecuted her, I now glorified her. Without letting her stop to dry her tears I begged her to continue. Encouraged and inspirited by me, experiencing the feeling of a soul opening, she continued to amaze us with her suddenly discovered talent. From that time on my sister began to believe in herself and tore out the thing that had corked up her soul. We had a great new artist, and I dreamed of only one thing — to show her to the public in a part that fitted her.

The performance of our operetta, which was called "Let Every Cricket Know his Hearth," was not very successful, and brought us more harm than good, but then it had given us a new actress for whose sake we began to look for a play.

My sister did not have a good singing voice, so we decided to choose a drama for her. Our choice fell on a rather weak play, "The Practical Man" by Potekhin, because it had good parts for me and for the rest of the amateurs who were living in the village that summer. Again rehearsals took place several times a day, and sometimes all day without a stop. Here is how we managed to do it.

In order to become better acquainted with a part and to enter into it, habit and continual practice are necessary, — so we decided. It was therefore agreed that on a given day we would live no longer as ourselves but as the people whom we were to play, and under the circumstances of the play in question. Whatever might happen on that day in the real life around us, whether we went for a walk, or gathered mushrooms or went boating, or strolled out of the house, or sat indoors, we were to be controlled by the circumstances of the play and to be dependent on the spiritual make-up of each of the rôles played. It was necessary to turn our real life into use for the sake of our rôles. For instance, in the play, the father and mother of my future bride forbade me strictly to see their daughter because I was poor, ugly, and a student. It was necessary to plot in order to meet my sweetheart without the knowledge of her parents. But here there comes my friend, who is to play her father. It was necessary to use all possible speed to part from my sister so that he might not notice us, or to explain our meeting and give some valid and logical reason for it. My friend in his turn was forced to act on these occasions not as if he were meeting us in real life, but as he would have acted if he were the practical man whose part he was playing, and whose double he was to be all of the day. The hardship lay in the fact that it was necessary to be not only an actor, but also the author of all sorts of impromptus. Often there were not enough words or subjects for conversation, and then we would leave our parts for a minute, consult as to what was supposed to happen to the *dramatis personæ* under the given circumstances, and decide what thoughts, words, actions and movements were to appear as the result of the living conditions we met on our way. After our consultations we returned to our rôles and continued our experiment.

As we practiced and gathered material, we found our work easier,, and at last after long and obstinate trials, we reached the stage where it was very easy for us to go through all the circumstances into which we might place the characters. Apparently we were entering into our rôles.

Even here, according to my old habit, I began by imitating the well-known actor Sadovsky of the Imperial theatres, in the rôle of the student in the play " Talents and Admirers " by Ostrovsky. I worked out the same awkward, web-footed walk that was his, his short-sightedness, his clumsy hands, the habit of patting the almost growing hairs of my beard, and of righting the spectacles and the long hair that gathered in waves about my forehead. As I advanced towards an understanding of real life that surrounded us, this copying, unknown to me, began to pass into a habit, and later into a true experience. In the atmosphere of the stage, among properties and made-up people it was possible to conventionalize, but in the atmosphere of life where all was truth, it is impossible to lie. Perhaps this forced me to play no longer for the sake of showing off myself, but so as to persuade my audience of the truthfulness and faithfulness of my interpretations to life and reality. Apparently in this production I learned what was the feeling of true measure. But alas, I could not force that feeling into my consciousness at that time. It appeared in this role just as unexpectedly as it disappeared in others. But I do not doubt that the work we then accomplished, although it was temporary and soon forgotten, nevertheless planted certain seeds of the future in our souls. What I had taken from Sadovsky had at last become mine. This was the first part in which I was praised by the spectators, especially those among them who understood the stage. But the young ladies said, " Isn't it a pity that you are so ugly! "

It was pleasanter for me to believe the young ladies, and not those who really knew, and I began to dream of being handsome on the stage at my next appearance.

It was a pity. I had left a blind alley, and the broad highway was already before me. And now I went back to the blind alley to try all possible sorts of rôles except those which nature intended for me. Poor, poor actors that have mistaken their calling on the stage! And as for you, young men and women, try first of all to understand what your calling really is.

CHAPTER VIII

I N order to create a position for oneself," my uncle and cousin told me, " it is necessary for you to occupy yourself with some sort of social work. You must become the honorary president of some school or of a poorhouse, or a member of the Duma." And from that time my sufferings began.

I went to some sort of meetings and tried to look imposing and important. I feigned interest in the question of what kind of waists or bonnets were made for the old women in the poorhouse and in the progress made by my school. I thought out some strange methods for the betterment of child education in Russia without knowing a single thing about what I was doing; with great artfulness, like an actor, I learned how to keep silent in a wise manner when I did not understand what was said to me, and to pronounce the following with an air of great meaningfulness, " Hm, yes. I will think of it." I learned to listen to other's opinions and then cleverly make them my own. It seems that I played the part very well for every charitable institution in the city began to ask for my services. I never had time to attend to everything, I became tired, and my soul was filled with coldness and sourness and a feeling that I was engaged in evil work. I was not doing my own work, and I could find no satisfaction in what I was doing. I was making a career of which I stood in no need whatsoever. Nevertheless, my new activities took greater and greater hold of me, and I could not refuse to continue fulfilling the tasks I had undertaken. Happily for me, a solution was found. My cousin, who was a very active director in the Russian Musical Society and Conservatory founded by Nikolai Rubinstein, was forced to leave his post for a higher one. No one could be found to take his place except myself. I took the position so as to be able to get rid of all the others on the ground of lack of time. It was better to occupy myself with a strange affair in artistic circles among interesting people than in poorhouses and schools which were not only alien to me, but unbearable.

At that time the Conservatory was filled with really interesting people. It is enough to say that among my co-directors were the composer Petr Tchaikovsky, the composer and pianist Taneiev, one of the founders of the Tretyakovskaya Gallery, Sergey Tretyakov, and among the professors preparing future artists, men like Vassily Safonov, well known even in America.

At about this time there visited Moscow the famous tragedian Ernesto Rossi. He played throughout Lent in the Great Theatre, surrounded by a second-rate troupe.

In those days performances in Russian were forbidden during Lent, but performances in foreign languages were allowed. This explains Rossi's presence in the Great Theatre at that time.

I subscribed to all the performances mostly because there was nowhere else to go. But apparently my educator, Fate, did not send me there in vain. Every actor who was a contemporary of Rossi's was in duty bound not only to see him, but to study him. He was astounding in his unusual plasticity and rhythm, notwithstanding the fact that he was far from handsome. He was not an actor of elemental temperament like Salvini or Mochalov, who were gods to-day and dwarfs to-morrow. Rossi was always finished in his work; he was a genius as a craftsman. Craftsmanship demands a talent of its own and often rises to genius. Rossi was such a genius.

This does not mean that Rossi gave the impression that he had no temperament, expressiveness and inner force of effect. Just the opposite; he had all of them to a large degree, and more than once we rejoiced and wept together with him in the theatre. But they were not the tears that pour from the springs of the soul as the result of an overwhelming organic shock. Rossi was not elemental enough to do that. Rossi was irresistible, but he owed it more to the logic of his emotions, to the consequentialness of his plan of the part he was playing, to the repose of his interpretation, the sureness of his craftsmanship and his effects. When Rossi played, we were certain that he would persuade us with his acting, for his art was truthful. And truth is always persuasive. In his speech and in his movements he was exceptionally simple. I saw him first in the rôle of King Lear. I confess that my first impression of him on his appearance was not favorable. The picturesque side of his rôles was almost always very weak. He paid almost no attention to it — a banal operatic costume, a badly glued beard, an uninteresting make-up.

It seemed that the first act showed nothing extraordinary in him. The spectator simply grew used to listening to a foreign actor playing a part in an incomprehensible language. But the more the great master unrolled before us the plan of the rôle and drew its spiritual and physical contours, the more it grew, broadened and deepened before our eyes. Unnoticeably, quietly, consequentially, step by step, Rossi led us up the spiritual ladder to the very strongest point of the rôle, but there he did not give us the last elemental burst of a mighty temperament which creates a miracle in the hearts and souls of men, but, as if he were being merciful to himself as an actor, often passed into simple pathos or used a bit of hokum, knowing that we would not notice it, for we would finish ourselves what he began and the impetus would carry us to the heights alone, and without him. This method is used by the majority of great actors, but not all of them are so successful as Rossi was in using it. In lyric passages, in love scenes, in poetic descriptions, Rossi was inimitable. He had the right to talk simply, and knew how to do it. This is very rare among actors. He had a fine voice, a wonderful ability to handle it, an unusually clear diction, a correctness of intonation, a plasticity that had reached such perfection that it became second nature with him. And his own nature was created mostly for lyric emotions and experiences.

And all this despite the fact that his physical gifts were not of the first class. He was short, his mustaches were dyed, his hands were stumpy, his face wrinkled, but he had remarkable eyes, — eyes that were mirrors of the soul. And with these qualities, already an old man, Rossi interpreted Romeo. He could not play the part any longer, but he drew its inner image to perfection. It was a courageous drawing, almost an impudent one. For instance, in the scene with the monk, Rossi rolled on the floor from despair. And this was done by an old man with a round little abdomen. But it was not funny, because it was required by the inner image of the rôle, by the correct and interesting psychological thread of the creation. We understood the wonderful idea, we admired Rossi, we sympathized with him.

I am trying to remember how actors were taught in dramatic schools at that time. There were different methods. The majority of the so-called professors of dramatic art were charlatans, as they have remained till the present day; and prominent individual actors were in the possession of some fundamentals which they either worked out themselves, or received as a heritage from the great actors of the past generations. But not a single artist will ever betray his secrets. How he works and creates is a mystery which he carries into the grave with him. Some do it simply because they don't know themselves, because they create intuitively and have no conscious relation to their creations. Others know very well what, why, and how things are done. But it is their patented secret, which it does not pay to pass on to some one else. They teach correctly, but they never open the eyes of their pupils, although they could do it if they wished.

Long ago, dramatic teaching was a simple matter indeed, as I have been told. And who knows, it may be that it was a more proper one than the one practiced now.

"Do you want to get into the theatre, to become an actor? Go to the ballet school. First of all it is necessary to teach you how to walk. And extras are always needed, if not for dancing, then for crowd effects, for court pages. If we make a dancer of you, good. And if we see that you have no abilities for the dance, but that you have some for the opera or the drama, we'll send you for lessons to a singer or an actor. If you are not successful, return, play pages, become a stage hand, or an administrative official."

This order of things made it possible for only those who had talent to reach the stage. That was as it should be. Without talent or ability one must not go on the stage. In our organized schools of dramatic art to-day it is not so. What they need is a certain quantity of paying pupils. And not every one who can pay has talent or can hope to become an artist. Actuality has it rather the other way; talented people do not pay even if they are materially able to do so. Why should they? Those who pay are the less talented, or the talentless. They support the school materially, they pay the salaries of the professors, they pay for the heat and the light and the rent. In order to graduate one man of talent one must deceive at least a hundred who are not gifted. Without such a compromise no school can exist at the present time.

How did they teach in the past? They taught only those who were really fit, and who were chosen from among the pupils of the ballet school of the theatre.

They were sent for their education to the best artists. The pride of our national art, the man who re-created in himself all that the West could give and created the foundations of true Russian dramatic art and its traditions, our great lawgiver and artist, Mikhail Semyono-vich Shtchepkin, took his pupils into the heart of his family. They lived with him, they ate with him, they grew up and married under his guidance. But let one of his pupils, a famous artist of the Imperial Little Theatre, Fedotova, speak instead of me.

"Here is how our never-to-be-forgotten Mikhail Semyonovich Shtchepkin taught me. I lived in his house when summer would free me from school. Often I would play croquet with the other children when suddenly I would hear a tremendous shout reëchoing throughout the whole garden. 'Loushenka — a — a!' The old man had awakened and come out into the garden in his bathrobe and with a little pipe, and was calling me to take my lesson. Well, I would be angry, and weep, and throw down my croquet hammer from vexation, but I would go, little father, I would go, because it was impossible not to obey Mikhail Semyonovich. Why it was impossible I don't know myself, but it was impossible, impossible, impossible, my friend. So I would go, with a pouting face, sit down with a book, and turn my face away from it.

"'Gather your lips up, forget that you are angry, and read me that little page,' the old man would say. 'If you read it well, I will let you go at once, but if you don't, please don't be angry at me if I keep you at it till evening or till you do.'

"'But Mikhail Semyonovich, my dear, I can't. Let me do it later. I will read ten pages if you will.'

"'Come, come now, we've heard enough talking. You had better read now and stop wasting time for me and yourself.'

"Well, I would begin to read, and nothing, absolutely nothing, would come of it.

"'Did you come here to learn the alphabet, or to read in syllables? Read it as it has to be read. You know very well how to read it.'

"I would struggle and struggle, and concentrate all my attention, but I could not drive the thought of the croquet game from my mind. And when at last I did and thought as hard as I could of the part and what was in it, something would really come of it.

"'Well, you can go now, my clever one.' And I would run away as fast as I could. We would begin playing again, there was noise, laughter, and then suddenly, the voice of the old man: 'Loushenka

—a—a!' And I would begin all over again. This is how the old man trained me and developed my power of will. An actor must have a strong power of will. The first duty of an actor is to learn to control his will."

And here is another story she told me.

"At last I made my début, I passed through my baptism of fire. There was noise, applause, curtain calls. I stood like a fool and did not know what to do. Then I made a curtsey, and ran into the wings, again on the stage, again a curtsey, again into the wings. And I was so tired, my friend, so tired. But there was a joyous warmth in my soul. Could it be that it was I who did all of that? And in the wings stood Mikhail Semyonovich himself, leaning on a cane and smiling. And his smile was so kind, so kind. You can never know what it meant to us to see Mikhail Semyonovich smiling. Only we and God will ever know. I would run into the wings, and he would wipe my face with his kerchief, kiss me and pat my cheek. 'Well, my clever one,' he would say, 'it was not in vain that I tortured you and you tortured me so long. Go, go and take your bow while they are applauding you. Take what you have earned.'

And I would go out on the stage again, and curtsey to all sides of me, and back into the wings. At last they were silent.

" 'Well, and now you come here, clever one,' Mikhail Semyonovich called me. 'Why did they applaud you, clever one? Do you know? Well, I am going to tell you. Because your face is young and pretty. But if I, with my old face, played as you played to-day? What would they have done to me?'

" 'What would they have done to you?'

" 'Why, they would have driven me from the stage at the wrong end of a stick. Remember that. Well, and now you can go and listen to their compliments. We'll talk later about this, you and I. We have our score to settle yet.'"

After her first success, when she was already considered to be an artist of the Little Theatre and played in its repertoire, Fedotova, and others like her, still continued to dance in the ballet.

Another famous artist of the same period, Samarin, passed through almost the same experiences. His début was successful, and he was accepted by the Little Theatre as a leading juvenile and played many parts in the repertoire, but at the same time continued to represent a lion pierced with an arrow in the ballet " Tsar Candale." The famous artist could die so well that no one could be found to take his place. So he continued to appear in the ballet.

" Let him dance, let him play a bit. Why should they idle their time away? They're young, they need work, or they will get into trouble," said the old teachers and the administration of the theatre.

But there were still other methods of teaching in the same theatre. Here is how one of the most talented actors of the Russian stage treated a young, but self-important actor who had just graduated from the school to the stage. They played together in a vaudeville skit, whose entire point lay in having the young man drop a letter which caused the development of the whole plot. The young actor did not drop the letter accidentally, but as if he premeditated doing so.

" I don't believe you! Once more! I don't believe you! Remember how you drop your own love letters; I'll wager you do it differently. Now it is better. Once more! I don't believe you again! "

He tried to make the young man do what he wished him to do for hours. And the management of the theatre patiently waited until the young man might drop his letter properly.

The vaudeville skit was produced, and the juvenile became even more self-important than before.

" I've got to give him a lesson," said the older artist. " Stepan, my dear, give me my coat," he said in the presence of others, in a kind voice. " And my rubbers right over there. Get them. Don't be lazy, get them for the old man; bend down and put them on for me. That's it. Now you may go."

The first thing taught in the school was a full round of general culture, but not too much of it at that. Lectures on the history of art were read by professors famous at that time, and discussions were held with the pupils for the sake of their development.

As far as special study was concerned, and that of dramatic art in particular, it was taught in the following manner.

Let us say that the pupil could not pronounce the sounds S, KH, and SHTCH. Then the teacher would sit down in front of him, open the mouth as wide as possible, and say to the pupil:

"Look in my mouth. You see what my tongue is doing; it lies on the roots of my upper teeth. Do the same. Say it. Repeat it ten times. Open your mouth wider, and let me look into it to see if you are doing it correctly."

I have become convinced, from my own experience, that after a week or two of concentration and practice, it is possible to correct the wrongly placed consonants, and to know what to do in order to pronounce them rightly. I passed through the same course and I affirm that the results were wonderful.

Voice teachers among the opera artists placed the voices of chosen pupils from the dramatic department, and besides, teachers of declamation forced them to read hexameters and chant them in about this way: let us say that the first syllable struck on the note *do*. Then the pupil read the whole line in the same tone. The second line was to be read in the next tone of the scale, the third in the next, and so forth. It cannot be denied that this method develops the voice. But it also does tremendous harm. The habit of saying words without any meaning for the sake of the exercise of sound, and not in order to express inner feelings and thoughts, breaks the direct connection between soul and word, voice and emotion. Words must be guarded, for they are precious!

In the classes of diction they studied verse and learned to declaim it. Here a great deal depended on the instructor himself. Those who loved false pathos, which they claimed was necessary for tragedy, taught the chanting of words, but others, who preferred inner pathos, tried to reach simplicity and power by entering into the soul of what was read. Of course, this was incomparably harder, but it was also incomparably more true.

Parallel with this, some rôle was studied, either for a public performance or for the sake of practice and for the gala evenings given by the school.

According to oral stories, Mikhail Shtchepkin could approach his pupils, look into their souls and possess himself of their emotions so that they understood him at once. How he did it is a mystery about which no evidence is left except some few of his letters to Shumsky, to Alexander Schubert and Gogol, one of which, that to Shumsky, I quote in full, because of its tremendous practical importance.

Take advantage of every opportunity, labor and develop the abilities given you by God to their fullest extent. Never cease to listen to criticism, and enter as deeply as you can into its core in order to set yourself right, and for the sake of good advice. Always have nature before your eyes; enter, so to say, into the skin of the rôle you are playing, study well its social locale, its education, its peculiar ideas if they are present, and do not forget to study its past life. When all this is learned, then no matter what situations are taken from life and transplanted to the stage, you will always play correctly. At times your acting may weaken, at times it might be somewhat satisfactory (this depends on your spiritual state) but you will always play correctly. Remember that perfection is not given to man. But if you study diligently, you will approach it insofar as Nature has given you abilities. For God's sake, never think of amusing your audience, for both the ridiculous and the serious flow from a true conception of life; and believe me, in two or three years you will see a difference in the way you act your rôles; with each year they will become rounder and more natural. Watch yourself sleeplessly, for although the public may be satisfied with you, you yourself must be your own severest critic. You must believe that inner reward is better than all applause. Try to appear in society as much as your time permits, study man in the mass, do not let a single anecdote pass without giving it attention, and you will always discover the reasons why the thing happened as it did and not otherwise. This living book will serve you instead of theories, which unhappily are still non-existent in our art. Therefore study all classes of society without prejudices on this side or that and you will see that everywhere there is both good and evil. This will give you an opportunity when acting to give each class its due — that is, if you are playing a peasant you will not be able to observe the social amenities in a case of extreme joy, and when playing an aristocrat you will not shout and wave your hands when angry, as a peasant would do. Do not consider yourself above hard work over situations and details noticed in life, but remember that they are only to aid you, and not to become your goal, that they are good only when you have learned to understand your goal in acting.

Only in extreme cases, when the pupil could not understand of what feeling, image, or inner action the teacher spoke, did Shtchepkin come on the stage and act himself.

When the rôle was played, each new performance was treated in the light of a rehearsal, after which the pupil was praised or criticised and the necessary explanations given to him. If the pupil failed, he was told why he failed, what it was he lacked, what demanded most work on his part, what was good. Praise of course encouraged him. And the other remarks led him in the proper direction. But if he were conceited, his teachers did not use any ceremonies with him. They *taught* in the old days.

The heirs and successors of these great artists brought to us the remnants of these simple, wise, unwritten traditions and pedagogical methods. They tried to go in the way planned by their teachers — some, like Fedotova, her husband Fedotov, Nadejda Medvedeva, V. N. Davidov, and other talented persons were able to interpret the spiritual reality of the traditions. Others, less talented, understood them more on the surface and talked more of their outer form than of their inner contents. Still others talked only of the methods of acting, and not of the art itself. These little fry copied the outer style of Shtchepkin, they taught *à la* Shtchepkin. They simply showed a long procession of samples and taught how any given part was *acted*, explaining what the *result* of playing the part in the given manner would be. Little by little the tradition of Shtchepkin grew paler and disappeared, in tragedy, in comedy, in the theatre and in the school.

In my time they required a rather complete course of general culture, and many subjects of a general nature were introduced, which raised to a great degree the general intellectual level of the actors. But exceptional talents appeared less often, perhaps because they could not stand the dry school régime.

Pupils were taught to read and play with the aid of instructions, so that each of the pupils first learned to imitate his teachers. The pupils read very correctly, putting in all the commas and periods, obeying every law of grammar, and resembled each other in their outer form which, like a uniform, hid the inner reality of the man. It was not for that the poet wrote his poems; it was not of that he talked in them; it was not important for him to know what readers tell us from the concert stage. I knew teachers who taught their pupils in the following way:

"Make your voice sharp and read. Strain yourself, thicken your voice. Read as you wish."

In another school a well-known teacher, after he had looked at a part of a gala performance, came back-stage in my presence and was indignant.

"You did not move your head. When a man speaks he always moves his head."

It is necessary to explain the origin of this moving of the head. At that time there lived a good actor who was very successful and who had many imitators. He had one bad fault. He had a habit of moving his head. And all his followers, forgetting that he was a talented man with wonderful gifts and a marvelous technique, took from him neither of these qualities, which they could not take, for they were in him and his own, but only his fault, the movement of the head. Whole graduating classes left the theatrical school with moving heads.

In a word, it was required of the pupils that they copy their teachers. And they imitated their teachers, but did it badly because of the lack of talent and technique. But they would have done well what was required of them if they had been allowed to do it in their own way. Perhaps it would have been incorrect, but anyway it would have been sincere, truthful and natural, and one could believe them. One can do much in art, one can even walk on his hands, but it must be done artistically and persuasively. Remember what Shtchepkin writes in his letter: " It is not important that you play well or ill; it is important that you play truthfully."

But nevertheless, let me repeat, that notwithstanding all these minuses, which accompanied the mass production of dramatic art in Russia, the spirit of Shtchepkin still managed to hold its own in the schools and the theatres, and reached us, although in a dying form, through the work of talented individual teachers.

At this time there appeared on the horizon of school life Vladimir Nemirovich-Danchenko, who taught in the dramatic school under the supervision of the Moscow Philharmonic Society. But I will talk of this in due time.

The dramatic school where I was accepted was a little better than the others, because it was founded by " the house of Shtchepkin himself " as the Imperial Little Theatre was nicknamed.

Around a table covered with green cloth sat several artists and many non-artists, pedagogues and officials who had no relation to art whatsoever. They decided by a majority of votes after one cursory reading of some verses the fate of the talented ones and dunces who were taking their examinations. Compare it to the system which existed in the old days and in the old theatre, and you will understand the tremendous difference. I know by dint of many years of experience that those who passed the examinations with flying colors very seldom justified the hopes placed in them. A man with a good appearance, with a little experience in amateur dramatic circles and at concerts, will find it easy to deceive the most experienced teacher during an examination, especially as the teacher wants to find in every new face the traces of a real find, of real talent. He does everything he can in order to make things easier. It is very pleasant to discover new talent. It is even pleasanter to vaunt a talented pupil. True talent is deeply hidden in the soul. It is not easy to lure it from its hiding place. This is why many artists who are famous now were far from being the first at the entrance examinations. And many of them, like Orlenev and Knipper were refused admittance at one of the best of our theatrical schools.

I, who had already acted much as an amateur, passed on the strength of my experience. Each of the examiners must have felt about me : " Of course, that's not what we want. He doesn't fit in at all. But he has height, a voice, a figure, and you meet those very seldom on the stage."

Besides, I was acquainted with an actress of the Imperial Theatres, Glikeria Fedotova, who was one of the examiners. I had often been at her home and was a friend of her son's, who was a student and a lover of the theatre and especially of the drama. Despite my bad reading I was accepted, and found myself in a group of pupils who were much younger than I. There were schoolboys and schoolgirls among them, fifteen years or thereabout, while I was a manufacturer, one of the directors of the Musical Society and the chairman of many charitable institutions. The difference between us and our attitude towards life was too great for me to feel at home in the school and among the pupils.

Subjects of general culture were not needed by me, for I had passed them long before. I could not attend the lectures on the history of the theatre, art, and costume and customs, because I did not have the time for it. But I would leave my office on any pretext and at times was able to attend special classes in drama and the rehearsals of school exercises.

Learned professors filled our heads with all sorts of information about the play we were rehearsing. This aroused thought, but our emotions remained quiescent. We were told very picturesquely and with much skill what the play and the parts were supposed to be, that is, of the final results of creative work, but how we were to do it, what road or method to use in order to arrive at the wished-for result — nothing was said about that. We were taught collectively or individually to play a given rôle, but we were not taught our craft. We felt the absence of fundamentals and of system. We were taught practical methods without these methods being systematized scientifically. It was not this that I wanted, it was not for this that I had entered the school. I felt that I was a piece of dough out of which they were baking a bread of definite taste and appearance. I was frightened by the thought that like 'the rest of the pupils, I would be deprived of my own individuality, bad as it was. And I dreamed of one thing only — to be myself, to be that which I can and must be naturally, something that neither the professors nor I myself could teach me, but nature and time alone. To all this was added the hardship and the impossibility of accuracy in my school attendance, due to my work in the factory and the office. Remarks about my tardiness, the jests of my fellow pupils at my expense because of the allowances I received and which they did not, in the sense of my failures to attend, all this became unbearable to me, and I left the school, after I had been there no more than three weeks. Glikeria Fedotova, for whose sake I had entered the school, also left at about that time.

CHAPTER IX

UNDERSTANDING the superlative qualities of dramatic art in the sense of the breadth and depth of its problems, and conscious of the difficulties of studying this art, I gave all my thoughts, my time and my material wealth to it. At that time the temple of dramatic art was our beloved Imperial Little Theatre which was nicknamed " The House of Shtchepkin," just as the Paris Comédie Française was dubbed " The House of Molière." The teachings of Shtchepkin still lived within the walls of that theatre; they were striking in their simplicity and amazing in their artistic truth. There was the real atmosphere of art, which formed a broad, free, artistic soul better than any prisonlike academy could. I can bravely affirm that I received my education not in the *gymnasia* but in the Little Theatre. I prepared myself for every performance there. For this purpose there was organized a small group of young people who read in common each play produced in the theatre, who studied all that was written about the play, and formed their own opinions, and then went as a group to the theatre, and after the performance, in a series of discussions exchanged their impressions and their thoughts and established their own evaluations of the play. Then they would go to see the play again and discuss it anew. These discussions very often proved our ignorance of the varied problems of art and knowledge. We tried to correct our ignorance by making researches and conducting lectures. The Little Theatre became the lever which controlled the spiritual and intellectual side of our life. To this admiration of the Little Theatre there was added the idolization of its individual actors and actresses. The common idol was the great pride of the Russian stage, Maria Nikolaevna Yermolova, whom God still spares to us. But of her later. In view of the fact that we consider ourselves the heirs of Shtchepkin let me say a few words about his " House."

The brightest pages in the book of the Little Theatre had been written before my time. But I still managed to see the last glorious chapters chronicled.

I saw the wonderful, extraordinary artists of the Little Theatre in their full glory. Spoiled in my childhood by an Italian Opera that consisted only of stars, I was spoiled in my youth by the copious wealth of talents in the Little Theatre. How could these shining pages of art remain a secret from Europe that looked down upon us at that time, and from America which was not interested in us? That period in the life of our theatre could be well compared with the theatre of Molière, Shakespeare, Goldoni, Gozzi, Schroeder, Goethe, Schiller, and the Weimar Theatre. We were creating our own school, our own actors, and dramatists and poets like Pushkin, Lermontov, Gogol, Griboyedov, Ostrovsky, Turgenev, Pissemsky, Chernishevsky and countless others.

Have you ever noticed that in theatrical life there come long, torturing periods of inactivity during which there appear no new and talented writers on the horizon, no actors, no stage directors? And then suddenly, unexpectedly, nature spews forth a whole theatrical troupe and adds to it out of its bounty a writer and a stage director, who, all together, create that wonder, an epoch in the theatre. And at once, to balance the scales, there appear their opponents, who try to destroy the new enterprise with their own even newer one. But fashion changes. The eternal remains.

This was the case with Shakespeare and Ben Jonson, with Molière and ——. I forget the name of the fat actor who was Molière's rival and who died on the stage from apoplexy.

Then there appear the continuators of the great men who have created the epoch. They accept the tradition and bear it to the next generation. But tradition is capricious, it takes on strange forms, just like the blue birds of Maeterlinck, and becomes a trade, and only one seed of it, the most important one, retains life till the new rejuvenation of the theatre, which takes the inherited seed of the great eternal and creates its own and new eternal. In turn this eternal is carried to the next generation and most of it is lost on the way, with the exception of a small seed which finds its way into the common treasure cave of the world which houses the material for the great future human Art Religion.

In the Russian theatre there were such talented groups also: that of Volkov at the time of Catherine the Great, and that of Shtchepkin during the last century. Nature created a complete group of Russian geniuses and talents, beginning with Shtchepkin himself. There was the famous tragedian Mochalov, his rival Karatygin, the Sadovskys, Shumsky, Samarin, Lensky, Yermolova, Fedotova, Nikulina, Nikulina-Kositzkaya, Ryazantzeva, Jivokini, Akimova, the Vassilievs, the great Martinov, Samoilov, Varlamov, Davidov, Savina, Strepetova, and others. All these artists created themselves by intuition. Some of them, like Shtchepkin and Samarin, were in the beginning illiterate serfs and educated themselves until they counted Gogol, Belinsky, Aksakov, Turgenev, and Dostoyevsky among their nearest friends.

I still remember the famous old Sadovsky, whom I saw once in my early childhood. He played in some vaudeville act in which he had almost nothing to say. The entire rôle consisted in the fact that he was getting ready to say something important, but suddenly stopped, and sedulously felt for a hair that had gotten into his mouth from his fur collar, which hair did not allow him to finish the sentence. For a long time he moved his tongue about and tried to take the hair out with his fingers while the sentence he had begun remained unfinished. This theatrical piece of hokum, invented to fill the emptiness of the rôle, was performed eternally, once and for ever, otherwise it would not have remained alive in my memory during the decades that have passed since the time I saw him.

In my early childhood I also saw, but once only, the tremendous scenic figure of Vassily Jivokini. I remember that I was taken to see him partly because my mother had been enchanted by the acting of Jivokini at the time she expected my birth, and wanted me very much to see him before he died. It was even said that in the first days of my life my face reminded her of the face of Jivokini. I remember that Jivokini came out on the stage before the performance and walked right into the audience. Standing before the footlights he greeted the audience in his own name. He was given an ovation and only after this did he begin to play. This action, which seems impossible for a serious theatre, he could not be denied, for it fitted his individuality and his eccentrically artistic personality to a tremendous degree. After his meeting with the public the soul of each spectator was filled with gladness. Jivokini was given still another ovation because he was Jivokini, because he lived at the same time with us, because he gave us wonderful moments of happiness that lived with us for the rest of our lives, because he was always wide-awake and happy, because everybody loved him.

But the same Jivokini could be tragically serious in the most comic and even farcical parts of his rôles. He knew the secret of making seriousness ridiculous. The face and the mimetics of the comedian cannot be described. He was an enchanting ugly man whom one wanted to kiss, to caress, to love. His kindness and restfulness on the stage were not only simple, they were universal. When he began to suffer in earnest, to run about the stage, to call for help with all the sincerity of his talent, he was unbearably funny in the seriousness of his reactions to noise and trifles. He was also one of those who could create in the realm of farce " eternally, once and forever."

The third genius, Shumsky, I remember very well indeed. With what world-famous artist can he be compared? I think best of all with Coquelin, in the sense of his artistry, the interesting drawing of the rôle, and its finishing touches. But Shumsky had the advantage of always being sincere. He could have taken the palm from any French Sganarelle. Shumsky played not only in comedy, he played in tragedy also, and here too his finesse, his artistry, his aristocratism did not leave him.

Samarin, in his youth a dandified young interpreter of French parts, in his maturity an ideal aristocrat and enchanting actor with his aged, somewhat plump handsomeness, his unusual voice, diction, rare manners, and great temperament.

I remember Medvedeva well not only as an actress but as an interesting human being, self taught. To a certain degree she was my teacher and exercised a great influence over me. In her youth she was considered to be a fair-to-middling interpreter of young rôles, but later on she reached her real forte on the stage, intended for her by nature — that of a character actress — and she found in herself that bright color which enabled her also to play " eternally, once and forever." She was a character actress by the grace of God. Even in private life she could not live a single hour without impersonating a gallery of characters she saw about her. She spoke in images. When she told you that she had had a visitor who expressed such and such a thought, you at once saw who had been there and how he said what he said.

Once I was present at a characteristic scene in her house. She was ill and could not appear in a new play which was running at the Little Theatre. Knowing that she was torturing herself with the thought that another actress was taking her place in the new rôle, I went to visit the old woman in order to make her ordeal lighter for her. Her apartment was empty, for everyone had gone to the theatre. The only one who was home with her was an ancient woman who lived on Medvedeva's charity. I knocked at the door and quietly entered the parlor. In the center of the room, confused and disheveled, sat Medvedeva. I was frightened at first, thinking that something had happened to her, but she reassured me and said:

"You see, I'm acting. It is time for me to die, old fool that I am, but I am still acting. I suppose I'll be acting in my coffin also."

"But what are you acting?" I was interested.

"A fool," she answered and began to explain: "A fool, either a cook or a simple village peasant woman, came to a doctor, came and sat down, and laid a package of vegetables down at her side. She sits and looks about her. A picture hangs on the wall. She looks into a mirror, is glad and begins to laugh. She pushes her hair under her shawl — see — that one in the mirror is doing the same thing. She can't restrain herself, she smiles."

And really, it was hard to imagine a smile more foolish.

"The doctor comes in, calls her. She goes into another room, but carries the vegetables with her. 'What's the trouble with you?' he asks. 'Where does it hurt you?' 'I swallowed it.' 'What did you swallow?' 'I swallowed a nail.' 'A big one?' 'Like that.' And she shows a nail a few inches long. 'You would have died, old woman,' says the doctor, 'if you had swallowed such a nail.' 'Why die, when I'm living?' 'Well, and how do you feel?' 'Well, it's coming out here, and here and over there,' and the old woman points to various parts of her body. 'Well, undress.' The doctor goes out, and the woman begins to undress. She takes off her coat, her shawl, her waist, her skirt, her shift; she tries to take off her shoes, but cannot, her abdomen is in the way. She sits down on the floor, takes one shoe off, then the other; pulls off a stocking, helping herself with the free foot. She is naked now, and begins to rise, but can't. At last she rises, sits down on a chair, folds her hands, and sits, like this."

Medvedeva's acting almost persuaded me that a naked woman sat before me.

My educator, Fate, pushed me into the kingdom of Terpsichore, to see and learn what was on foot in the sphere of plastic art. This is necessary for our ilk, for dramatic actors. I began attending the ballet without any preconceived notions. I first went quite accidentally, being bored with nothing to do. I wasted my energies in all directions at that time, and so I had gone to the ballet in order to see what my comrades the lovers of the dance had found in the ballet. I came to laugh, and I remained to be one of them.

Ballet lovers perform a great service in a way. They never miss a performance, but they always come late, in order to find their seats to the sound of music. It is an altogether different thing if *she,* that is, the object of their admiration, happens to appear in the first number. Then the ballet lover goes to his seat accompanied by the sounds of the overture. God help him if he is late. *She* will be insulted. After *she* finishes her number, and there is no generally recognized diva on the rest of the program, a diva who is a true priestess of Terpsichore, it was considered unworthy of a true lover and connoisseur of the art to remain in the theatre to see mediocrities. Between dances it was the custom to go to a special little den in the smoking room and to sit there till an usher came to each one with the words, " They are beginning." This meant that the object of the admiration of this or that ballet maniac would soon appear on the stage, and that it was his turn to be present in the auditorium. It was not necessary for the object of his admiration to be very talented. In affairs of the heart art retires to the background, and knighthood holds the fore-stage. Of course, one must look at *her* without taking the opera glasses from the eyes, and not only when she dances, but when she is still. Here the mimetic telegraph would put in its siege of work.

For instance: She stands aside while some one else dances. Now she looks over the footlights at her admirer. She smiles. This is a good sign. She is not angry. But if she does not smile and thoughtfully looks in the distance or aside, or down and quietly retires into the wings, she is angry and does not want you to see her. Matters are at a bad stage. The heart of the poor admirer grows small and his head is in a whirl. He throws himself headlong at a friend, feeling himself publicly insulted and begins to whisper.

"Did you see?"

"I did," his friend answers gloomily.

"What does it mean?"

"I don't understand. Were you present at the Passage?"

"I was."

"She smiled?"

"Yes."

"She sent a kiss through the casement?"

"She did."

"The duenna was not there?"

"I could not see."

"Then I cannot understand it at all."

"What am I to do? Send her flowers?"

"Are you crazy? Flowers to a pupil, and back-stage? Shame. Have you become a lover of the ballet only yesterday?"

"Then what am I to do?"

"Let me think. Wait. Mine is looking at me. She is smiling."

"Yes, she is smiling. Ah, happy man!"

"Bravo! Bravo! Applaud her!"

"Bravo! Bravo! *Bis! bis!*"

"No, she is not going to give an encore. This is what we are going to do. You buy the flowers, and I will write a note to her and send it with the flowers, but I will send it to mine, and not to yours, understand? She will pass the flowers on and explain everything."

"Marvelous! My friend, let me embrace you. You always help me out. You alone understand me! I am going."

In the next number *she* appears with a flower in her corsage. She looks at the guilty ballet maniac and smiles. He leaps up in joy and runs to his friend again.

"She smiled! She smiled! Thank God! But the question is why she was angry."

"Come to my home after the performance, and you will learn everything from mine."

After the performance the ballet maniac must take his admired one home. And those who are in love with the pupils of the school wait for them near the artists' entrance. The following scenes take place here. A great carriage stops before the door. The front door of the carriage is opened. *She* leaps into it and stands at the other door of the carriage, covering it entirely. The glass is lowered. He approaches, kisses her hand or gives her a note, or says something brief but full of meaning, that will occupy her thoughts all night. Meanwhile the other pupils pile into the carriage through the front door.

The more courageous ballet maniacs would bravely abduct the objects of their admiration, put them in a special carriage waiting some distance away, and rush at top speed through several streets. When the theatre carriage arrived at the school, the runaways were already there. *He* would put his lady in through the back door while the other pupils would go out through the front door and cover the appearance of the runaway from the sharp eyes of the duenna. But this was a difficult maneuver and demanded the help of the coachman, the doorkeeper and all of the pupils.

Having taken the pupil home, the ballet maniac goes to his friend, or rather to his friend's friend. Here everything is explained quickly and simply. The sad event was caused because to-day all were in the Passage which is opposite the windows of the Theatre School at the appointed hour, sending kisses through the casements, and making all sorts of cabalistic signs whose meaning was being discussed by us, but the duenna appeared in a window below (the duenna being the class monitor) and the ballet maniacs hurried to hide themselves. After some time they returned. But the guilty ballet maniac did not come, and the lady of his heart was teased cruelly by her comrades.

In the furnished rooms where the unmarried dancers lived there was much to remind one of a student's life in an attic. The other lodgers would come in for a visit, some one would go out to buy food, others shared what they had brought, admirers brought candy and treated each other to it, a supper was improvised, tea, a samovar.

During this feast the last performance was criticized thoroughly. Sometimes both actresses and administration came in for a thorough drubbing. Or the last gossip of the theatre and the back-stage was aired. In these moments, which were the most interesting for me, I listened and tried to enter into the mysteries of the art of the ballet. For him who does not intend to become a specialist in a given art, but who simply wants to learn its general outline, and tries to understand things that he may have to learn in detail later on, it is interesting and instructive to be present at the discussions of specialists who talk of something one has just seen, and to the truth of which one can bear witness. These discussions of living examples with demonstrations of the principles in question opened a way for me to the mystery of ballet technique. When a ballerina could not prove her case with words, she proved it with her legs, dancing her proof on the spot. Many times I had to serve in the rôle of a dancing partner in such discussions. I would drop the ballerina and my awkwardness would disclose to me the technical secret of some method or piece of hokum. If one is to add to this the eternal discussions in the smoking room of the theatre, where I would often go and meet clever, well-read and discriminating æsthetes, who discussed dancing and plastics not from the point of view of their outward technique, but from the side of the æsthetic impression created by them and the creative, artistic problems which they entailed, then one can see that the material I gathered for my conception and study of the ballet was more than elementary. I repeat that I did all this without any thought of study at the beginning but only because I liked the mysterious, colorful and poetic life behind the scenes.

How beautiful, how haunting are the regions back of the scenery, with unexpected glimmer of light on reflectors, projectors, magic lanterns. Here it is red, there it is blue, here again it is violet. Over there there is a chromotrope of moving water. Endless heights and gloom above. Mysterious depths below, in the pit. Picturesque groups of artists in their gaudy costumes waiting for their entrances. And in the intermission bright light, mad movement, chaos, work. Falling and rising canvas drops, with mountains, cliffs, rivers, seas, cloudless heavens and thunderclouds, the flora of paradise and the pit of hell. Tremendous, painted walls of pavilions sliding along the floor; columns in relief, arches, architectural parts. Tired workers, sweaty, greasy, excited. And side by side with them an ethereal ballerina who stretches her butterfly legs and arms, ready to fly out on the stage. The dress coats of the musicians, the liveries of the ushers, the uniforms of officers, the dandified costumes of the ballet maniacs. Noise, cries, an atmosphere of nervousness — all is in chaos. The whole stage has become naked so that after the earthquake all might again gradually reach order and create a new, graceful, and harmonious picture. If there is anything wonderful on our earth, it can surely be found on the stage.

Can one keep from falling in love in the midst of such an atmosphere? And I did fall in love, and for six months I looked at only one of the pupils of the ballet school, who, as my friends assured me, was madly in love with me, and it seemed to me that she smiled at me and made mysterious signs intended for my understanding alone. We were introduced to each other only before the Christmas vacation. I found out that during six months I had looked at an altogether different girl. But I liked this one also, and fell in love with her on the spot. All this was childishly naïve, mysterious and poetic, and best of all, pure. People think in vain· that a spirit of debauch reigns in the ballet. I never saw it, and I remember the time I spent in the kingdom of Terpsichore with gratefulness in my heart. The ballet is a beautiful art, but not for us, not for dramatic artists. We need something else. We need other plastics, another grace, another rhythm, another set of gestures, another manner of walking, another method of movement. We must only borrow the amazing capacity for work and the knowledge of how to train the body from the artists of the ballet.

CHAPTER X

MOSCOW received news from the novelist Turgenev that the talented Nikolai Rubinstein had died in his arms beyond the border. His body was brought to Moscow for interment some time in March or April, 1881, just at the time when mud made it almost impossible to walk the streets of Moscow. My cousin, who at that time was the chairman of the Russian Musical Society and Conservatory, which was the fruit of the labor of Rubinstein, asked me to help him in meeting the body and in arranging the funeral. I was only twenty years old then, and was very much flattered by the offer, as I found it rather pleasant to figure publicly in the rôle of a manager at the funeral of a man as famous as Rubinstein. My work was to manage and place the deputations at the head of the procession. This meant that I was to lead the procession and necessitated that I seek my cousin, who was the manager of the entire funeral, on many occasions to solve some of my problems, such for instance, as the route of the procession, which had not been explained to me clearly enough. The distance from the head of the procession, where I was stationed, to the coffin, where my cousin was, was at least a good mile, and the streets were covered with ankle-deep mud. Like most of the assistant managers, I was tired to death at the end of the first day when we met the coffin and carried it to the University Church. The following day was to see a longer route of march to the graveyard of a monastery beyond the city limits. It was decided that the managers would come on horseback. I was very fond of riding at that time, and the decision made me enthusiastic. I owned an unusually handsome mount, and thought that if I could get funereal accoutrement for the horse and mourning clothes for myself, I could cause a sensation at the funeral. Evidently the actor's desire to flaunt himself before the public had already managed to poison me.

On the following day, mounted on my horse in its black harness, dressed in black boots, a long black coat and a black high hat, I took my place at the head of the procession, which was soon on its way. My mount walked in dance step and I felt very fine indeed. Just as the procession moved, two mounted gendarmes suddenly appeared at my sides and the effect on which I had reckoned was somewhat spoiled.

" And who's that? " I heard among the spectators who lined the streets. " That fellow in black, between the gendarmes? "

" That's the dead man's coachman. And that's his horse. That's why he's leading it."

" Oh, no, that's the chief undertaker."

Unconscious of the impression I was making, unsuspecting that all the other managers had deceived me and appeared on foot, I played my foolish part to the end, and for a long time was the butt of jokes, pleasantry and caricature. Whenever any one met me the first words would be, " Ah, that's the fellow in black, on horseback."

This was not the first time that I experienced a fiasco publicly, and soon my mistakes made me famous.

There was a long search for a successor to Nikolai Rubinstein for the work of conducting symphonic concerts in Moscow. At last, after having tried many men, the choice fell on the famous conductor and fine musician Max Ermansdoerfer. He was at the zenith of his Moscow career at the time when I was a director of the Musical Society.

The wife of the cousin, whose place I had now taken in the Conservatory was very friendly with the wife of Ermansdoerfer. I was young then; I occupied a position of sorts; I was rich. In a word, I had everything needed by a bridegroom. Some women cannot see a bachelor on whose forehead the word "good match" seems to be engraved. They cannot sleep in peace unless they bind the happy, free bachelor who still wants to live for himself, to see the world, and not to rest near a home hearth, in the holy bonds of matrimony. In a word, they wanted to marry me off, and a proper object for their art appeared in the person of a rising young German violinist, Miss Z., who was playing as a visiting star with the symphony orchestra. She was young, blonde, sentimental, talented. She was guarded by a strict mother who valued the good points of her daughter. That willing matchmaker, my sister-in-law, began to arrange dinners and suppers mostly for the sake of the young girl and myself. She praised me to the mother of the girl, telling her that although I was so young I was already a director of the Musical Society. At the same time she said to me, "How wonderful she is! How can you be so blind and cold at your age? Get up and hand her a chair. Take her arm and lead her in to dinner."

I would take her arm and lead her in to dinner, sit at her side all through the meal, but I could not guess what my sister-in-law wanted. Apparently there entered into the plot against my single bliss even Petr Tchaikovsky, the composer, whose brother was married to a sister of my sister-in-law. He was almost a member of the family and was a constant visitor at her house. I was invited to intimate musical evenings and suppers arranged by the composers and musicians at the Hotel Billot, where most visiting musicians stopped, including Miss Z. The best musicians and composers of the city came to these evenings, played their new compositions, and the young violinist would acquaint them with those numbers of her repertoire which she did not play at public concerts. Tchaikovsky liked the young woman, and he would put me side by side with her, although, due to his timidity and eternal confusion, he was never able to *"faire les honneurs de la maison."* The kindness of Tchaikovsky would confuse me. He loved to repeat to me that in his opinion I could play the part of Peter the Great in youth, and that when I would become a great singer, he would write an opera on that theme for me.

At these musicales Ermansdoerfer and his wife showed me very particular attention and I heard on the side that they liked me very much and were happy that I had become a director of the Musical Society.

At the end of the musicales, the mother of Miss Z. would invite me and some of the musicians, for the sake of propriety, to drink tea in their suite. Tchaikovsky would come in, for a minute, as was his wont, his soft fur hat under his arm, where he liked to carry it, and would leave as suddenly as he had come. He was always nervous and afraid of society. Ermansdoerfer, his wife, and my sister-in-law would remain longer than the others. But they also disappeared mysteriously, and Miss Z., her mother and I would remain alone. But I was far from eloquent in my German, and for this reason, if for no other, the young diva began to give me violin lessons. Her Stradivarius would come out of its precious case, I would take it awkwardly, afraid to crush it, into one hand, while my other hand held the bow even more awkwardly, and in the silence of the orderly German hotel already plunged into sleep, there would echo the terrible shriek of a tortured violin string. But the diva soon left, I presented her with roses, the petals of which she sadly tore from the flowers and threw in my direction one by one as her train pulled out from the station. Our romance remained incompleted.

I received my share of scoldings from my matchmaker for my dullness.

During this time we came into very close touch with Ermansdoerfer's family. He was a very talented, nervous and temperamental man, whom one had to know how to approach. Apparently I guessed that secret, although I cannot say the same of the other members of the direction, who could never get used to him. This had strange results. When it was necessary to ask the great artist for something, he was not approached by his comrades, artists as great as he was, but the business in hand was entrusted to me, a young and inexperienced man. In the majority of cases I did not influence him directly, but through his clever and attractive wife, who knew how to handle him. Little by little he got used to dealing with his wife and with me only, and did not want to talk to any one else. It may sound funny to say it — I don't know how it happened myself, but I arranged the programs of a whole year with him at one time, and I knew positively nothing about music. It must be that he allowed me to be with him, so that there might be some living object in the room with him with whom he could speak. Or perhaps I was needed by him to write down his notes. Before my meetings with him, really great musicians made use of me to put through the programs they wanted. I, who knew nothing about music, was forced to give advice to a famous musician. Happily I had one good quality, very important in the practice of life. I was able to be quiet when that was necessary and to make a serious face and utter a much-meaning " So! " Or to mutter thoughtfully, " Also, *sie meinen* " or to hiss through closed teeth, " So, so, *jetzt verstehe ich.*" Or to shake my head negatively over some proposed number in his program. *" Nein? "* he would wonder. *" Nein,"* I would answer confidently. *" Dann was denn? "* *" Ein* Mozart, *dann ein* Bach," I would say, calling in order all the numbers that had been suggested to me beforehand. Evidently my prompters were not fools, for my talented friend was always amazed by my good taste.

If he did not surrender at once, I would be forced to make the affair more complex than it was. " What is this? " and I would hum a melody that seemingly appeared to me fit for the program. *" Aber spielen sie,"* the great conductor would say. And I sang whatever came into my head. Of course, he never understood me, and would sit down to play the tune himself. " No, no, not that! " and I would again sing something impossible, and again he would run to the piano and play something, but I would not be satisfied. In this way I took his mind off the track, and he would forget what he wanted or grow cold to it, and then leap up as if he had struck on a brilliant thought, walk like the Pythian priestess about the room, and dictate the new, prompted program, which apparently also amazed him by the taste and understanding it evinced on my part.

In this manner I was able to do a great deal of what my comrades in the direction asked me. One may judge the liking this dear and kind man had for me if he did not suspect my almost transparent slyness. In this new rôle there was a large opportunity for an actor. It was necessary to play very subtly so as not to be caught. I confess that my success gave me a certain sort of artistic satisfaction. If it were impossible to play on the stage, I could at least act in life.

CHAPTER XI

L ET me say a few words about the famous composer and pianist Anton Rubinstein, because my meeting with him, although it does not present great interest in the facts that caused it or the words that accompanied it, nevertheless left an impression on my inner artistic conscience. Even a surface acquaintance with great men, the mere proximity to them, the unseen exchange of spiritual currents, their often unconscious reaction to the phenomena about them, their exclamations, their words, their eloquent pauses leave a mark on your soul. Later, when the artist develops and meets analogous facts in life, he remembers the words, the opinions, the exclamations, and the pauses of the great man, deciphers them and reaches their real meaning. More than once I have remembered the eyes, the exclamations, and the meaningful silences of Anton Rubinstein during the two or three meetings with him that fate granted me.

This was at the time when I was a director of the Russian Musical Society. I was very young — I could not have been more than twenty-two or three. All the other directors of the society were absent from Moscow, and Rubinstein was expected to come from St. Petersburg to conduct a symphonic concert. The entire administrative responsibility for the concert was left to me. I was very much confused, for I knew that Rubinstein was very severe, truthful to a point of sharpness, and suffered no compromises or remissnesses in art. Of course, I went to meet him at the station. But unexpectedly, he had come on an earlier train, and I met him and introduced myself at his hotel. Our talk was very short and of the most official character. I asked him whether he had any orders to give me about the concert.

"What orders? The affair is arranged," he answered in a high voice, his intonation lazily stretched, his sharp glance piercing me. Unlike us earthly beings, he was not ashamed to look at people as if they were things. I noticed the same habit in other great men whom I met, for instance in Lev Tolstoy.

His answer and his gaze confused me. It seemed to me that he was amazed and disappointed.

"Just see what a stage affairs have reached! What directors are in order now! He is a raw boy. What does he understand? And here he is, offering his services!"

His lionlike repose, the mane of his hair, the complete absence of effort, his lazy, graceful, kingly movements, like those of a beast of prey, oppressed me. Alone with him in the little room, I felt my nonentity and his greatness. I seemed to be the guest of a lion in his cage. I suddenly remembered how this quiet giant could become fiery at the piano or behind the conductor's stand, how his long hair rose like the mane of a lion, what fire gleamed in his eyes, what headlong and unexpected movements he made, in the grip of his lavalike temperament. Lion and Anton Rubinstein became one in my imagination.

An hour later I met him at the rehearsal of the orchestra, and again I felt and saw all that I had felt and seen when I met him first. In the moment of his highest creative effort, his unbridled temperament swept through him like a whirlwind, lifting his hair — which covered half his face — and his arms, his head, his body so that a beast of prey seemed to embrace the whole of the storming orchestra. He tried to outshout it in his high voice; he shrieked to the trombone players:

"Lift your snouts higher!"

There was not enough sound and strength to interpret the emotions loose within him, and he demanded that the trombone players lift the openings of their instruments higher so that their roar might fly out at the public without any obstacles in its path.

The rehearsal ended. Rubinstein, like a lion after battle, lay on his couch, a feline softness in all of his tired body, streaming with perspiration. With a beating heart I stood near the door of his dressing room, guarding him and praying to him, looking into the crack between the door and the jamb. The musicians were all in ecstasy, and they accompanied him with trembling respect when after resting, he went to his small room in the hotel.

Imagine my surprise when several excited trombone players approached me and declared that they would not appear at the concert unless Rubinstein would apologize to them.

" Why ? " I wondered, remembering the beauty of what I had just seen and heard.

" He said —— He said —— " they cried in broken Russian, for they were Germans, " He called our heads snouts ! "

" This is not a snout, it is a head ! " exclaimed one of them, pointing to his head. " I will not let him —— "

They began talking all at the same time, mixing Russian and German. No matter how hard I tried to explain to them that the word " snouts " did not apply to them, but to their instruments, they would not be at peace. But at last I persuaded them to appear at the concert. If Rubinstein would promise me that he would ask their apology they would play. If he would not, they would not play.

I went to Rubinstein at once, excused myself for coming, stuttered and mumbled of what had happened, and asked him what I was to do. The lion lay in the same restful pose in which I had seen him at our first meeting. What I told him did not make the slightest impression on him, although I was sweating with excitement and fear of the coming scandal, and the helplessness of my responsible position.

"Goo-oo-ood! I will te-e-ell them!" he squeaked. If the intonation he used could be quoted as well as his words, they would have meant, "Good, I will show them how to raise scandals! I will give them something to think about!"

"Then I may inform them that you will apologize?" I tried to stress the word "you."

"Good, good, you may tell them so. Let them sit down in their places," he said even more restfully, lazily stretching his hand for a letter which he began opening.

Of course, I should have waited for a more definite answer, but I did not dare to disturb him any more and could not insist on my demands, and I went away dissatisfied, anxious, and not at all assured that the concert would take place.

Before it began, I told the musicians that I had seen Rubinstein and had told him of all that had happened, and that he had told me, "Good, I will tell them!" Of course I kept secret what I had heard in his intonation, and what was the real meaning of his words. The musicians were satisfied, and their anger almost died out.

The concert passed with tremendous success. But how cold the great man was toward it, and how disdainful, or rather not to it but to the public that glorified him. He would go out and bow mechanically, and as it seemed to me, forgot those who glorified him; and in their very sight he conversed with some acquaintance, as if the applause were not intended for him. When the impatience of the public and of the musicians, who were beating their music stands from excitement, reached a point where it seemed that they would make a scandal if he did not give an encore, and I as the administrator was sent to remind the great man that the evening was not yet over and that he was expected to appear again, I fulfilled my duty timidly and received a completely quiet answer:

"I hear them myself."

In other words, " It is not for you to teach me how to handle them."

I was still innerly ecstatic and envied the right of genius to such majestic indifference to glory, to such repose in success, and the consciousness of his superiority to the mob.

Out of the corner of my eye I saw the trombone players, who were outshouting all the others present.

I met Anton Rubinstein again, and although I played a very foolish part at the meeting, I will tell of it, for the stronger traits of the genius showed in it again.

This was also at the time when I was a director of the Musical Society. The two hundredth performance of the opera " The Demon " was being celebrated in the Imperial Great Opera Theatre. The flower of Moscow society filled the theatre. The gala lights, the high-named guests in the imperial boxes, the best of singers even in the smallest parts, the grandiose welcome of the great favorite himself, the singing of " Glory " by the whole chorus and the soloists and then the rising of the curtain — and the overture. The first act was over. There was tremendous applause. Curtain calls. The second act began. The composer conducted, but he was nervous. His lion-like gaze did not burn a single soloist or musician. One could see impatient, vexatious movements. One could hear a whisper throughout the theatre, " Rubinstein is in bad spirits! He is dissatisfied! "

At the very moment when the Demon appeared from a trapdoor and rose above Tamara, who was lying on a couch, Rubinstein stopped the orchestra and the performance, and nervously beating the conductor's stand with his baton, impatiently addressed some one on the stage:

" I told you a hundred ti-i-imes, that —— "

It was impossible to hear the rest of what he said.

As it was explained later, the whole trouble was caused by a reflector that should have illuminated the Demon from the back and not from the front.

There was a tomblike silence. People ran across the stage and in the wings one could see hands waving, heads moving. The poor artists, deprived of the music and of customary action on the stage, stood as if lost, as if they were suddenly undressed and ashamed and trying to cover their nakedness. It seemed that a whole hour passed. The crowd, which had been silent in confusion, began to come to its senses little by little, then to criticize, to be indignant. Chaotic noise rose in the auditorium. Rubinstein sat in a restful pose, almost like the one in which I had seen him at our first meeting. When the noise of the crowd reached its highest, he rose quietly, lazily and severely turned his back to the auditorium, and struck his stand with his baton. But this did not at all mean that he had surrendered and wanted to continue the performance. It was a severe reminder to the crowd and an order that they keep quiet. A silence ensued. Quite some time passed, until a strong light struck the back of the Demon, making his figure look almost like a transparent silhouette. The performance was renewed.

" How wonderful! " one could hear in the auditorium.

The ovation in the next intermission was rather smaller than before. Perhaps the public was insulted. But this did not seem to bother Rubinstein. I saw him in the wings talking quietly to some one.

The next act was opened by us, that is by one of my codirectors and myself. We were to present the composer with a tremendous wreath with long ribbons. As soon as Rubinstein had approached his stand, we were pushed through the opening between the red portal and the curtain. It was not to be wondered at that it was funny to see us crawling through that crack. Unused to the bright footlights of the Great Theatre, we were at once blinded. We could see nothing in front of us. It seemed that a mist rose from the footlights and

hid everything on the other side. We walked, walked, walked ——
It seemed to me that we had walked a whole mile. There was talk
in the auditorium that little by little turned into noise. Three thousand people were shouting with laughter, and we continued walking,
walking, not knowing what had happened, until the box of the director of the theatre, which bordered on the stage, suddenly rose before
us from the mist. We had lost ourselves on the stage. We had
passed the prompter's box, in front of which, with his back to the
orchestra, stood the composer. Shading our eyes with our hands
from the footlights, and looking over them into the auditorium, forgetting the tremendous wreath whose ribbons dragged on the stage
behind us, we were a comic pair indeed. Rubinstein, forgetting his
mood, was rolling with laughter. He was beating his stand with his
baton despairingly to let us know where he was. At last we found
him, handed him the wreath, and left the stage in confusion at a
quickstep that resembled the pace of an expert runner. The laughter
became louder, and the intermission was continued until it subsided.

Apparently I was in bad luck in honoring both dead and living
Rubinsteins.

CHAPTER XII

ATTEMPTS IN OPERETTAS

THE new theatre in our Moscow home was ready. It was a large room connected by an arch with another one in which we were able to place the platform of a stage or to take it away, forming a smoking room. On week days the large room was a dining room. On days of the performance it was the auditorium of our theatre. We ate dinner in it and then used it for a rehearsal hall. To turn it into a theatre it was only necessary to light the gas footlights and lift the fine red curtain with gold designs behind which was the stage. Behind the scenes we had taken care of all our necessities. Two doors led from the stage to a wide corridor and through a small hall to an addition to the house where we were able to construct many dressing rooms. The wide corridor served as a storeroom for scenery and properties. Here were also the stopcocks for the control of the lights. All we had to do was to open the theatre.

At that time I brought from Vienna a new operetta by the name of " Javotta." Its only good point was that it had never been played in Moscow, and that it had suitable rôles for all of our actors. But we did not have any one for the duke, a part that demanded a trained singer and was much too hard for any of us. We were forced to invite a professional who was just finishing the Conservatory, and had a well-trained and beautiful baritone voice, but a bad appearance, for he was small, ugly, had all the banal manners of a poor operatic artist and did not possess an iota of dramatic talent. His partner was my cousin, who was always preparing to appear on the operatic stage and never found courage to make her debut. From the very first rehearsal two groups formed, one consisting of us poor amateurs, and the other of the two learned singers. One could not say anything to the baritone, to such an extent was he sure of his superiority to us. So much the worse for him, I decided, giving free rein to my badly insulted actor's self-admiration. Jealousy gave us amateurs redoubled energy in our work. A great obstacle was the fact that the learned baritone quickly learned his part and did not desire to rehearse it with our ignorant chorus. I was forced to study his part in order to help the chorus in its rehearsals.

When everything was ready, the baritone appeared and kindly gave his approval to the work of the amateurs. We had rehearsed according to a system which we had worked out ourselves — first of all to memorize the text so that the words repeated themselves mechanically, as we had done in " The Weak String " and in " A Woman's Secret " and to live not in our own selves but in our rôles, as we did in " The Practical Man." Of course this did not lead us anywhere, for the methods of experience in life continually created a need for impromptu work, and the methods of memorizing words completely excluded the possibility of impromptus. Like every coarse and mechanical method, the memorizing of words conquered. No sooner did my partner finish saying a speech and I heard the well-known final words than my tongue would take up my own words. This mechanical confidence was accepted by us at that time for the sake of its swift tempo on one hand and for the feeling of security it gave us on the other.

It is not good for amateurs to use special professional hokum without understanding its inner meaning.

Nevertheless a sort of ensemble, if I can call it that, resulted from our many rehearsals. We became used one to the other, and mechanical memorizing gave the illusion of well-rehearsed perfection. The plan of the production and the distribution of parts was perfect in our own opinion and in good taste, worked out by us in imitation of the good example set by the great foreign artists who visited Moscow. Without any doubt there was a great deal in our favor when we compared ourselves to the trained singers. But the baritone would take one high note — and he knew well how to take it — and our audience would forget us and make an ovation for the man in whom it felt the presence of a specialist.

"But he is a blockhead!" we cried with open envy.

"Of course," some would answer us, "but you know yourselves that he has a voice. What strength! What an ability to sing!"

"What's the use of working?" we would say, exchanging glances with our other actors.

The trained baritone was the hero of the performance. We only helped him along. Anger and indignation at this injustice forced us to think deeply. What were we to do? How were we to work? We were willing to learn. We only waited for some one to tell us where and how. But when time passed and the sound of the high note was obliterated, the public began to remember the few artistic things that we had done. We were reassured. I did not forget that besides art and talent there was such a thing as ability.

The Russian operetta reigned in Moscow at that time. The well-known manager Lentovsky gathered a fine company among whom there were really talented ones, singers and actors of all descriptions. The energy of this exceptional man created something unusual in theatrical enterprise, if we are to judge what he created by its richness and many-sidedness. A whole city block was turned into a park with mounds, meadows, ponds and walks. This garden was called the Hermitage. There is nothing left of it now, as the entire block has long been built up. Everything one can think of could be found in this garden. There were boats in the ponds, and remarkable displays of fireworks that represented naval battles and the sinking of ships; there were ropewalks above the ponds; there were water festivals with gondolas and illuminated boats; there were bathing nymphs in the water, a shore ballet and a water ballet, and two theatres. One had a seating capacity of several thousand and was used for the operetta and the other was in the open air and housed a faery melodrama called " Anteus." This theatre was in the shape of a Greek amphitheatre. There were wonderful productions and fine orchestras, ballets, choruses and artists, if we were to judge them by the standards of that time. Right alongside of the theatre there were two large clear spaces with a stage for acrobatics and a tremendous auditorium for the public under the open sky.

All that was famous in Europe in the kingdom of the open-air stage, beginning with cabaret divas and ending with hypnotists and eccentrics, found a welcome in the Hermitage. Those who were invited to Moscow saw their stock rise in the universal theatrical market. The second open space, the larger of the two, was given over to a circus, to animal trainers, and so forth. There were many shaded walks and intimate summer houses and poetic benches in the garden and on the shores of the pond. The garden was illuminated by countless lights, reflectors, shields and lamps. Processions, foot races, wrestling matches, military bands, gypsy choruses, Russian folk singers, — all were here. All Moscow and all visitors to Moscow came to the garden. The buffet did a wonderful business.

Family people, the common people, aristocrats, cocottes, the gilded youth, business men, all came to the Hermitage in the evenings, especially in the summer days when it was hard to breathe in the city, because of the tropical heat.

Lentovsky took good care to see to it that family people came to his garden, and was very severe in maintaining a fine moral tone in his enterprise. In order to uphold this tone he terrorized the public by issuing the most unbelievable rumors about himself. He was supposed to have thrown a famous scandalist by main force over a fence. In order to bring a drunkard to his senses he was supposed to have held him by the collar in the pond. The cocottes feared him like fire and were on good behavior in the garden, no worse than young ladies at the most aristocratic boarding schools. If any one did anything to spoil the good name of the garden he or she was never admitted again.

It could all be believed, for the manager was really very strong, his figure was impressive, his shoulders wide, his beard black and abundant, his hair cut long in the fashion of an ancient Russian boyar. A Russian coat of thin black cloth, and high lacquered boots, gave his figure knightly grace. He wore a thick gold chain bedecked with all sorts of knickknacks and gifts from famous persons and even royalty, — a Russian cap with a large visor and a tremendous stick that looked like a club and was the terror of all mischief-makers. He had a loud voice, an energetic, convincing manner of walking. Lentovsky would appear unexpectedly in some corner or other of his garden, and watch all that was going on with a falcon eye.

The Hermitage, loved by all the young people of that time, became a model for our imitation, and the dream of our theatrical desires. Not only the actors of the operetta, but even the outdoor attractions drew us like magnets. We also wanted to build a stage for music, we also wanted lamps and tables for those that wished to drink tea, and an aerial program and water fireworks. All this was to be continuous, exactly as it was in the Hermitage. No sooner was the performance in the theatre over than the music was to play outside, calling the guests to new delights. No sooner were these over than a new performance was to begin in the theatre. One can easily imagine how much work was necessary to arrange such an affair for one evening, and in the absence of a large public. The larger part of the work in illuminating and decorating of the garden we did with our own hands, because we did not have enough money to hire any one. And parallel with this work there were the rehearsals of the operetta with a large chorus and cast. We played "Mascotta," in which I of course took the part of the shepherd Pipo. I am ashamed to look at my portrait in that rôle. All that is bad in confectionery barber-shop beauty was taken for my make-up — curled mustaches, curled hair, tightly clad legs. And all this for a simple shepherd who always lived near to nature. How can I place my comparatively decent taste in other things alongside of the absence of all taste in my own make-up?

It is tiresome to repeat the same details again — there were the same operatic gestures, but all that was good and that we had recently made our own was absent. Art always revenges itself. All I had to do was to enter the magic circle of an operatic lover's part, and I could see nothing living around me, but only a dead and empty space as if I were surrounded by a stone wall. Of course I sang like an amateur, imagining that I had an operatic voice.

The other actors were rather nice in their parts. The choruses were composed of all the servants who had the slightest pretensions to voice and of friends who were forced to come daily to the village to rehearse. They came at seven in the morning and would leave at two or three next morning — sometimes. And on the next day some would rise at six to go to Moscow, and return to the evening rehearsal. I must confess that the training was good. In the majority of cases we often did not sleep at all, because after rehearsal we would go into a large room reserved for ourselves and the choristers (our rooms were given to the ladies). The entire area of the large room was covered with beds. There was only one small free path in the center. You can imagine what would take place here. Witticisms, anecdotes, gossip, laughter, the imitation of animals, of monkeys that leapt from the closets in the costume worn by Adam, night bathing in the river, circus and gymnastics. Affairs reached such a stage that the floor of the room gave way, and the plaster began to fall in the parlor down-stairs. It became necessary to unload our room and place the choristers in other rooms. But we would not stop even here and would visit each other in groups. Perhaps not a single one of our choristers could read notes. They had to be taught with music, until their parts could be sung by them mechanically. I wondered at the patience of my older brother, who accomplished wonders with them.

The same hardships faced the stage director. I had to train every chorister individually.

Both indoors and outdoors the affair was crowned with success. It is clear that I received not a jot of use from the performance. Just the opposite; there was only harm, because I became more rooted in my mistakes.

In those days the popularity of the operetta reached its highest point. The well-known Anna Judic, an operetta artist and *diseu.e,* was queening it in Paris then, and she often came to perform in Petersburg and Moscow. We followed the fashion, and it became our dream to produce an operetta.

And it seems that here Life again took our education in its hands. The operetta and vaudeville make the best school for actors. It was not for nothing that our old actors always began their careers in the operetta or in vaudeville. Without overburdening the soul, with deep emotions, without attempting the solution of problems too difficult for young actors, the light genre demands a tremendous amount of outward technique. Voice, diction, gesture, movement, light rhythm, unforced and sincere joyfulness which easily infects the spectator are the first necessity in the light genre. The genre of Judic, besides all this, demanded a truly French sharpness of out-line, humor and subtlety that cannot be reached without the technique of a virtuoso. We could not satisfy ourselves with anything less, for our highly developed tastes demanded subtle and artistic operetta. And I was tall, awkward, ungraceful and had a faulty diction. It was necessary to work over my voice, my diction, my gestures, and to torture myself in order to get anywhere. This work often ap-proached the stages of mania.

I was awkward to an extraordinary degree. Whenever I walked

into a small room its owners hurried to remove any breakables in it, for I was certain to break something. Once at a ball I overturned a palm tree in a barrel. At another time, while dancing, I tripped, caught hold of a piano which as it later turned out had a defective leg, and went to the floor together with the piano. I broke still another piano, but of that later.

All this made my awkwardness famous. I did not even dare to suggest that I wanted to be an actor, for that would only cause laughter among my friends. I remember that I decided not to go to the country, although it was a hot summer, and that I refused the bless-, ings of outdoor and family life. And I made those sacrifices only for the sake of continuing my studies in the empty city house. There, in a large hall before a tremendous mirror, I found it pleasant to work over my gestures and my plastics, and the marble walls and staircase gave my voice unwonted resonance. During all summer and autumn, every day after I finished my work in the office, I worked according to a self-made program till three or four in the morning. It is impossible to recount all that I did during that time. All that came to hand, whatever it might be, was used for the creation of the outward image, which I created myself. Looking at myself as my own audience in the mirror I became acquainted with plastics, and listening to myself I worked out my diction and intonation. What else could I do? I was inexperienced, and I did not suspect the evil that lay in working before a mirror. Nevertheless I gained something from that work. I came to know all my faults of gesture and plastics, and the outward manner of combating them. But the chief use I drew out of my work during that summer and fall was in the matter of diction.

My sisters returned from Paris transported by the work of the famous Anna Judic. They had seen her in " Lili," a musical comedy in four acts. In this operetta there were but few parts, and it had many musical and dramatic qualities. My sisters did more than tell us the contents of the piece in an orderly, almost stenographic fashion; they sang us all the musical numbers. Only the sharp memory of youth is able to remember so correctly a performance seen once or twice on the stage.

We began immediately to write the text and find words for the music. Usually, French when translated into Russian falls into very long sentences. We decided to write the text in sentences much shorter than the French originals. For instance, one of the persons in the plays cries " *Suis je on?* " " *Dame.* " Answers another.

One of our Russian translators had it this way, " Was I created a man in your opinion, or not? " " A woman," answered the other.

But we translated it in a much shorter fashion. " Am I a man? " " Ba-ba " (Woman).

Each of the translated sentences was examined by the one who was to say it. Each of them was to give the actor an opportunity to intone and accent it in the French manner. Happily, almost all of the actors knew French well and understood its music and its peculiar character. It was not in vain that French stage blood flowed in our veins. Some of us, especially my oldest sister, reached perfection, but because of the incoherency of our diction at that time and for a long period later, it was impossible to tell whether she spoke in French or Russian. It is true that she, like the rest of us, made little of the meaning and the meat of the sentence and used it more for the sake of sound and the French accentuation of the intonation. The spectators saw a performance in Russian and thought that it was being given in French, for often it was impossible to get the meaning of the words. Even in movement and action we found a rhythm that was more typical of the French than the Russian. We knew and felt the methods and manners of French speech.

The stage business and the production were of course slavishly copied from the Paris production as our sisters reported it.

I rapidly made my own the methods of speech and movement in

my French rôle, and this at once gave me a sort of independence on the stage. Perhaps I did not play the type created by the author, but there is no doubt that I succeeded in creating a true image of a Frenchman translated into the terms of the Russian language. And this was real success in a way, for if I did imitate, it was not the stage I imitated, but life. Feeling the national characteristics of the part, I found it easy to justify the tempo and the rhythm of my movements and my speech. This was no longer tempo for the sake of tempo, rhythm for the sake of rhythm, but this was an inner rhythm, although one of general character, typical of all Frenchmen and not of the individual type I played.

The performance was crowned with noisy success and was repeated many times before packed houses. The possibility of repeating our performances filled us with pride. It meant that we were becoming successful. The heroine of the evening was my sister and I played well in the rôle of Planchard, which I loved. This Planchard is a bugler by the name of Piu Piu in the first act, an officer in the second, and an ancient general in retirement and with gout in the last. In these three gradually ageing images I felt myself at home on the stage.

In this play I returned again by accident to a more or less true path in the sense that I approached my rôle through its character, although only through its outer and general character. But even this method, far from the ideal as it was, did not enter into my consciousness and therefore did not bring any quick results.

In a year my sisters went to Paris again and saw Judic in the operetta " Mlle. Nitouche." Once more they memorized the text and we wrote it down and fitted it to the parts of the play. The songs were translated to fit the orchestration which they also brought with them. Again my oldest sister played the leading part, and I played the rôle of a comic organist in a convent who secretly composed and produced an operetta whose chief rôle, due to altogether unbelievable circumstances, was sung by one of the girls educated in the convent. My new rôle demanded first of all colorful characterization on my part. The clumsiness necessary in it was already mine through my playing of the student in " The Practical Man." I changed it a little and this helped me find a characterization, thanks to which I felt myself at home on the stage again, and which was another step in the right direction.

But again there were young ladies who pitied the fact that I was not handsome and who inflamed in me a bad actor's passion for admiration and the desire to be liked by the spectators.

The next winter season saw our home circle preparing the production of the Gilbert-Sullivan operetta " The Mikado." During all that winter our home resembled a nook of Japan. A troupe of Japanese acrobats, who were appearing in the circus, stayed with us day and night. They proved themselves to be very decent people and they helped us very much. They taught us all the Japanese customs, the manner of walking, deportment, bowing, dancing, the handling of a fan. In accordance with their instructions we had Japanese muslin rehearsal costumes with belts made for all the actors, and we practiced putting these on. The women walked all day with legs tied together as far as the knee, the fan became a necessary object of everyday life. We already felt the necessity to explain ourselves during conversations with the help of the fan, a Japanese habit.

Returning from the office or the factory, we donned our Japanese costumes and wore them all evening, and during holidays, all day as well. At the great dinner table and at tea there sat Japanese men with fans which seemed to crackle and talk when they were opened and closed.

We had Japanese dancing classes and the women learned all the enchanting habits of the geishas. We knew how to turn rhythmically on our heels, showing now the right, now the left profile; how to fall to the floor, doubling up like gymnasts; how to run with mincing steps; how to jump, coquettishly lifting our heels. Some of the women learned to throw the fan in the dance so that it might describe a semicircle in its flight and reach the hands of another dancer or singer. We learned to juggle with the fan, to throw it under a shoulder or a leg, and what is most important, made our own all the Japanese poses with the fan, without exception, of which a tremendous amount was distributed in the songs and in the text exactly like notes in music. In this manner, every passage, bar of music, and strong note had its definite gesture, movement and action with the fan. In the mass scenes, that is in the chorus, each of the singers was given his own series of gestures and movements with the fan for each accented musical note, bar, and passage. The poses with the fan depended on the arrangement of the groups, or rather on a kaleidoscope of continually changing and moving groups. While some swept their fans upward, others lowered and opened theirs near their very feet; others did the same to the right, still others to the left, and so on.

When this kaleidoscope came into action in the crowd scenes, and fans of every size, color and description swept through the air, the soul was in ecstasy from the theatrical effect. Many platforms were prepared so that from the fore-stage where the actors lay on the floor to the background where they stood some feet above ground, the entire arc of the stage could be filled with the fans. They covered it like a curtain. The platforms are an old but comfortable method of the stage director for theatrical groupings and picturesqueness. With their help one can show the actors standing in the rear; all that is necessary is to lower the front and lift the back platforms. At that time I was still not experienced enough, and did not take advantage of other more subtle methods for filling the stage with mass groups. I could not show all my actors without having too many people on the stage and without letting them get into each other's way.

All the movements with the fans were made in time with the music. At that time this was a novelty. But it was only an outward rhythm with the accentuation on all the loud notes. And only some of us intuitively created to the rhythm of the music our own original rhythm that corresponded to our individual reactions to the music, the text, and what we lived through on the stage.

Add to the description of the performance the picturesque costumes, many of which were really Japanese, the ancient armor of samurais, the banners, the pretty faces of the women, our youthful heat and temperament, and it will be clear that for a domestic performance there was enough to make it highly successful. I am not trying to make little of it. In the performance there was something never shown on the stage before, — real Japanese life, original plastics, an agility of acting, juggling, acrobatics, rhythm, and dances. The performance had its style, its original physiognomy. There was only one blot in it, — an unexplainable and strange double division. As the stage director of the performance I worked to find a new tone and style of production, but as an actor I did not want to part from the most banal, theatrically operatic, postcard beauty. Having worked out my movements in that foyer of which I have already talked I could not leave them, and tried to be a handsome Italian singer in the Japanese operetta. How could I disfigure my tall, thin figure in a Japanese manner, when I had always dreamed of making it straight. In this manner, in my rôle of actor I again rooted myself in my old mistakes and in banality, but as a stage director I reached rather decent results with the aid of my older brother. But all these attempts were entirely accidental, never understood or connected with what had been done before. They were found by accident, and they were lost by accident.

We became disgusted with operettas. Besides, our greatly developing demands in the sphere of production made the performances costly out of proportion with our means, and my lessons with Kommisarjevsky drew me to the opera. The dream of being a singer took more and more hold of me. The days of the operetta were counted. It was decided to make our next performance a production of a drama.

At that time the Russian stage was mainly occupied with adaptations of foreign comedies. One such play, called " Mischief " made its way into our theatre. It is not worth while stopping on it, for its production was amateurish in every way conceivable, and I imitated to a point of disgust the most talented and attractive actor I had ever seen, A. G. Lensky. But it is impossible to imitate talent and personality. For this reason my imitation had none of his good qualities and all of his faults.

If I am not mistaken, the same evening saw the production of a one-acter called " A Peculiar Disaster." The subject was most banal — in order to give his wife a lesson the husband stages a tragedy. He pretends to have taken poison which has an immediate deadly result. The one-acter finishes with an explanation and kisses.

This vaudeville skit was needed by me not for the sake of playing the comic part and making my public laugh, but in order to try out my tragic powers and to shock my audience. But what is power from the viewpoint of the audience? Power is loudness, power is strain from which the face becomes purple, the eyes red, the voice hoarse, and so on. Was it possible to reach a tragic shock in a vaudeville skit? But I foolishly persisted. This caused many farcical scenes during the rehearsals and the performance.

" Does it make an impression? " I asked after a rehearsal.

" I don't know, but somehow it makes none — on me," a spectator would tell me.

" Well, and now? "

And I would run to the stage and strain myself more than before, making it worse.

But my make-up was not bad; add my youth, a loud voice, a theatrical effectiveness, good examples which I copied, and in the end some one liked it. And as there exists no actor who has no admirers of his own, I had some in this rôle, and I recognized only their competency to judge me, and explained all the uncomplimentary remarks I heard as jealousy, foolishness and the inability to understand. There exists such a great number of reasons for the justification of your own mistakes and false enthusiasms that one is never at a loss for an explanation.

In this manner this performance, foolish though it may seem, was the first attempt at a dramatic rôle and a passing to a new sort of acting for me. The hues of tragedy are more noticeable, brighter, and more striking than those of comedy, and all my mistakes seemed greater this time. It is unpleasant to be untrue in half voice, but it is much more unpleasant to be untrue in full voice. This time I was untrue in full voice. Fate must have trembled for an actor who was just beginning and was already lost.

Our dining-room theatre was closed. But the stage platform was still in its place and accidental rehearsals, performances and impromptus still took place there. For instance, the danseuse Zucchi visited us very often. After dinner she would often dance on our stage. We were clever enough to persuade her that she had to dance for us. This happened in the following way.

My brothers had a hunchbacked tutor. An Italian superstition has it that in order to be lucky it is necessary to embrace and kiss a hunchback so and so many times.

And so we intrigued Zucchi into rehearsing a performance of a ballet on our stage, the ballet to be Esmeralda, — to apportion all the rôles, and to ask the hunchback to play Quasimodo. Then, excused by the rehearsals and the repetition of certain parts of the ballet, she would be able to embrace and kiss him the necessary number of times.

The rehearsals began and Zucchi was the stage directress and played the part of Esmeralda. We knew her both as a dancer and as a stage director, and as one who played together with us. This was all that we needed. It was good that Zucchi, thanks to superstition, took the work very seriously. She found it necessary to create the proper sort of stage business to make the hunchback believe her. She had to make him believe her. This demanded reality and creativeness. And we admired and watched closely the work of a great talent, and learned much that was interesting and educative. She was first of all a dramatic actress, and only after that a dancer, although she was a great dancer also. I saw at these foolish rehearsals her limitless imagination, her fertility of combination, her originality, her taste in the choice of new stage problems and stage business, her unusual experience and most of all a naïve, childish faith in what she was doing at the moment and what was taking place around her. She gave this all of her attention whole-heartedly and completely. She seemed to pour her own desires into the souls of her actors, like a hypnotist who enters into the soul of his subject.

I was struck by the softness of her muscles in moments of great spiritual stress in the drama that took place during the ballet, when I touched her in order to support her as her dancing partner. I myself was always strained on the stage and my imagination was always drowsy, for I took advantage of the creations of others. My scenic inventiveness, adaptiveness, and taste were occupied only with making myself resemble the actors whom I was imitating. I did not have an opportunity to use my own taste and originality, because I used those of others, those which were always ready to hand. Naïveté and childish faith could not be born under these circumstances. I gave my attention not to what was happening on my stage, but to what had once happened on other stages whence I took my examples. This is why I was helpless on the stage, and my helplessness caused physical and spiritual strain. The only thing which was developing in me was the ability to handle stage business to a certain degree.

Zucchi forced me to take thought of all this.

CHAPTER XIII

BUT soon we got tired of the operetta. It had brought its small share of use, but now we wanted to do something else, something serious. At that time Moscow saw a reawakening in opera. The brilliant work of the Italian opera was over. But national opera began to come to life. Tchaikovsky and other lights of Russian opera appeared on the scene. I believed in my vocal gifts on the ground of what I knew of them through our domestic operetta, and secretly made up my mind to prepare for a career in the opera. From that time on, while still continuing to appear in the operettas whenever they were given, I took lessons from the famous tenor Fyodor Kommisarjevsky, the father of the present stage director of the same name whose work New York has had an opportunity to judge. Each day, as soon as I got through with my work in the office, I would go to the other end of the city for a lesson in singing. I don't know what brought me more use, the lessons or our conversations after them.

It seemed that my opera studies had moved forward to such an extent that I was ready to appear in a part. Apparently my teacher, F. P. Kommisarjevsky, was aching to return to the stage. He also wanted to play. Our dining-room theatre was empty in the sense of artistic life. And so we decided to give a performance of chosen scenes — for the pupils of Kommisarjevsky. I was to sing in two scenes, Mephistopheles in the first scene of " Faust," with Kommisarjevsky as Faust, and the Miller in the first act of " The Mermaid " by Dargomijsky. Other scenes were prepared for the other pupils of Kommisarjevsky, in which real opera stars whose voices were much superior to mine were to take part. At the second rehearsal I became hoarse, and the more I sang the hoarser I became.

But how pleasant and unusually easy it is to be an operatic artist in the dramatically imaginary meaning of the word. All is ready-made by the composer; all you have to do is to sing what has been written. And it is so easy to understand what is necessary. The music is orchestrated, the character of the individual instruments, the musical leitmotif are so clear and eloquent, that it seems even a dead man could play. One must only not get into his own way; one must yield entirely to the magic power of sound. Besides, I found it easy to play because the operatic images of Mephistopheles and the Miller are so definite, clear, and established forever that no doubts can be raised about them. Imitate — that is all you have to do. My ideals were confined to those words at that time. I wanted to resemble certain actors. In Mephistopheles I wanted to resemble Giametta, in the miller the famous Russian singer Melnikov.

The production did not go any further than a dress rehearsal. We came to understand that it would add no glory to my name. Besides, due to the daily work, my voice became worse and worse, until it was only a whisper in my throat.

Standing on the same stage with good singers I understood that my voice was not fit for the opera and that I did not have sufficient musical preparation. It became clear to me that I would never be a singer and that it was necessary for me to part forever with the idea of an operatic career.

My dream was broken and there was nothing else left for me than to occupy myself with the drama. But I knew that the latter was the hardest and the most exacting of all forms of scenic art.

The singing lessons stopped but I still went almost every day to my ex-teacher, Kommisarjevsky, to speak with him about art and to meet at his house people who were connected with music and singing, and the professors of the Conservatory where Kommisarjevsky taught voice culture. I may disclose the secret that I entertained the thought of becoming his assistant, but that I did not dare to speak of it. I could not forget the enchanting impressions that remained in me of rhythmic acting to music, and I could not understand how singers were able to unite several completely different rhythms in the same breath. The orchestra and the composer have their own rhythm and time. The singing is in complete accord with them, the choruses move, that is they lift and lower their hands automatically, in another rhythm. Each of the singers, ruled only by his mood or his digestion, acts, or rather does not act, in his own rhythm, or rather without any rhythm.

I was attracted to mimodrama and I tried to show Kommisarjevsky the necessity of creating a class in mimodrama for singers. He was in accord with me. We had already found an accompanist-improvisator, and in the evenings we lived, moved and sat in rhythm. In the beginning I began with the most primitive outward rhythm to mark with movement and action each strong note, but later I came to understand all the coarseness and unmusicalness of this method and began to find another more subtle and more true and fundamental inner rhythm.

The Conservatory refused to let Kommisarjevsky start the proposed class. I became sour, and our attempts were discontinued. But even now, as soon as I hear music, rhythmic movement and mimetics in the same form I felt them at that time break out in me.

Involuntarily those unclear fundamentals broke out in me on the stage also, but I could not understand what it was that controlled me when I swam on the crest of this or that rhythmic wave. I know that there were performances and even parts in which I seemed to swing in one tiresome monotonous rhythm as if on top of dead water. First I called this " dead water," then " camel rhythm " and " oxlike rhythm " (because of the likeness of their uniform motion). But I was not understood and I could not explain and formulate my disturbances.

Some other thing attracted me and for the time being I unconsciously laid aside but did not forget the things which my growth had not yet reached. This is not the first hint of something important which discovered itself to me and was laid aside — as the future showed me — only for the time being.

In the period of the inactivity of our domestic theatre there was still another performance given, for a charitable end. The attraction was that several artists of the Imperial Little Theatre played with us, the amateurs of the Alexciev Dramatic Circle. We produced " The Lucky Man " by Vladimir Nemirovich-Danchenko who was at that time the most popular and talented playwright in Russia. Among those who acted were the famous Glikeria Fedotova, Olga Sadovskaya, and other artists of our glorious Little Theatre, to which I owed so much. I felt my nonentity in front of these great artists who touched me by their fine relations to us.

My amateur friends seemed to me to be cold and indifferent to this. This seriously disturbed me.

The play was in the repertoire of the Little Theatre, where it was played many scores of times each season. But for us amateurs it was altogether new. The rehearsals were held for our sake and not for the sake of the artists of the Little Theatre.

Nevertheless the famous artists who had played the drama so many times came an hour before rehearsal, appeared on the stage at the appointed time, and waited for the amateurs (of course not for me). The famous artists rehearsed in full tone and the amateurs (myself excepted) whispered their lines and read the text from manuscript. True, they were all very busy people who had no free time at all. But what affair is that of art's, or artists' or the theatre's?

For the first time in my life I stood on the stage with highly talented artists. It was an important moment in my life. But I was timid, I was confused, I was angry at myself; I could not hear my cues and did not understand what I was saying. My chief care was not to be angered, not to hold back, to remember, to copy what was told me. This was exactly the opposite of what is needed for true creativeness. But I could not do otherwise. They could not make the rehearsals lessons in dramatic art, all the more so because I had just left the Imperial Dramatic School and with it Glikeria Fedotova, at whose side I was now playing as a real artist.

Thanks to my amateurish inexperience the piles of my part, in actors' parlance, did not hold. I would flame up and then suddenly die down. This made my speech and action become energetic and then my voice could be heard, the words sounded clearly and reached the audience — or all would grow dull and I wilted, my voice would begin to murmur, my words could not be heard, and the spectators would cry " Louder! Louder! "

In actors' parlance this is called " dropping tone." Of course I could force myself to speak loudly, to act energetically, but when you force yourself to be loud for the sake of loudness, courageous for the sake of courage, without any inner meaning and inspiration, you feel ashamed on the stage. This cannot put you into a creative mood. And side by side with me were real true-to-goodness artists, who seemed to be always full of something. Something seemed to hold them at the same temperature of heightened energy and prevented them from sinking. They could not help but speak loudly on the stage; they could not be anything but courageous. They may have heartaches or headaches or pains in the throat, they will nevertheless act energetically and speak loud. It was altogether different with us amateurs. We needed somebody outside to warm us, to encourage us, to make us joyous. We did not hold our public in our hands. Just the opposite, we expected it to take us into its hands, to say something complimentary and then perhaps we would begin to want to play.

" Why is it so? " I asked Fedotova.

"You don't know, my friend, from which end to begin. And you don't want to learn," Fedotova pricked me with her singsong voice and caressing intonation. "There is no training, no restraint, no discipline. And an artist cannot live without that."

"And how can I work out discipline for myself?" I asked again.

"Play a little oftener with us, and we will teach you, my friend. We are not always like to-day. We can be severe when the need for it comes. Oh, my friend, we can scold. Oh, how we can scold! And the artists of to-day sit with folded hands and wait for inspiration from Apollo. In vain, my friend, he has enough of his own affairs to attend."

And true, when the curtain rose on the performance, the trained actors began speaking in the proper tone and dragged me after them as if by a bridle. You couldn't drowse with them, you couldn't let the tone down. It even seemed to me that I played in tone and with inspiration. Alas, it only seemed so to me. My rôle was far from being completely made.

The training and discipline of real artists showed still clearer when "The Lucky Man" was repeated with almost the same cast, that is with the artists of the Little Theatre and myself, in another city — Ryazan.

I had been abroad and just returned home. On the platform of the station I saw Fedotov, the son of Glikeria Fedotova, who played a part in the performance. He came in the name of all those in the cast of the play to ask me to help them in their trouble. It was necessary to go at once to Ryazan to play my part in the place of an artist of the Little Theatre who had fallen ill. It was impossible to refuse and I went in spite of my exhaustion after my long journey from abroad, and without seeing my parents who were waiting for me at home. We were taken to Ryazan in the second class. I was given a book to look through my part, which I had half forgotten, for I had never known it well, and I had played it only once. The noise in the car made my head feel heavier than it was and I could hardly make out what I was reading. I could not remember the text and I was almost in despair because the thing I feared most on the stage was a poorly memorized text.

"Well," I thought, "we will arrive and God will grant me a free room in the theatre where I can be alone long enough to go through the part at least once with real attention."

But it was fated to be otherwise. The performance was to be given not in a theatre but in some regimental club, — on a small amateur stage, and near it a room divided into sections by screens. This room contained everything, dressing rooms for both men and women, and a dining room where a samovar was going full blast. Here they also squeezed in the military band in order to free as many seats as possible in the auditorium. When the band began to blow and the drums began to beat while we were dressing and making up, I almost fainted. I threw down my text and decided to rely on the prompter, who happily was a very good one.

When I came on the stage, it seemed to me that some one whistled — again — once more — stronger. I could not understand what had happened. I stopped, looked into the audience and saw that a few of the spectators were whistling me down.

"Why? What had I done?"

Later it turned out that they whistled at me because I had come instead of the slated artist Yuzhin. I became so confused that I went back into the wings.

"I deserved it!"

I cannot say that it was pleasant. But I did not find anything bad in it. Just the opposite, I was rather glad, for this gave me the right to play badly. It could be interpreted as an insult, or as a direct invitation to play badly. This encouraged me, and I went out on the stage again. This time I was met with applause, but because of self-love I treated it disdainfully, that is, I paid no attention to it, stood as if petrified, as if the applause was not for me. It is self-evident that I could not play an unprepared rôle well. This was my first experience with a prompter. What horror it is to be on the stage without a memorized text. A nightmare!

At last the performance ended. Thank God! Still in our make-up we were taken to the station that we might go back to Moscow. But we were late for the train, and we were forced to spend the night in Ryazan. While we looked for rooms, the admirers of Fedotova and Sadovskaya arranged an impromptu supper. Oh, if you could see the sorry figure I cut, pale from a headache, with weakened legs, with a bent back, with muscles that altogether refused to serve me. In the middle of the supper I fell asleep, while Fedotova, who was old enough to be my mother, was fresh, young, joyful, coquettish, talkative. She could be mistaken for my sister. Sadovskaya, who was also far from young, was running a close second to Fedotova. " But I am just from abroad," I justified myself.

"You are from abroad, but my mother has a temperature of a hundred and one. She has a cold and she is sick," Fedotov told me.

" This is training and discipline! " I thought.

If things were to go wrong they would go wrong to the very end. I reached my bed and was already on the point of falling asleep when my companion Fedotov began to snore. And I cannot bear snoring. What was I to do? I rose, afraid to move my head, which seemed to be cracking from pain. Carefully turning the sleeping man from his back to his side, I lay down again. The snoring stopped. I was falling asleep. One moment more and I would have slept. But Fedotov turned on his back again and choked with snoring. I rose once more, restraining myself from irritation, again turned the sleeper on his side, but could not fall asleep as I was waiting for the snoring to begin again. This soon happened. Fedotov began to snore more loudly than before. Restraining myself with difficulty, I repeated my maneuvers again and again, losing more and more patience each time.

"Throw him out! Strangle him! Kill him!" whispered the inner voice of revenge in me.

And this is what I invented, because I was ill, I suppose. I rose, angrily, with irritation, with a course of action planned out beforehand, poured water in a glass, bent above the sleeping man and waited for him to sigh deeply before he snored again. I caught him right in the middle of a sigh and poured the water into his mouth. I was mad. The water got into his nose and his windpipe. He began to strangle, leapt up in a fit of coughing, ran to the middle of the room and fell to the floor in a spasm. It seemed that he was coughing his lungs out. I was certain that he was dying.

I was scolded till six in the morning when we had to make our train.

CHAPTER XIV

THE MAMONTOV CIRCLE

NOT far from our house in Moscow there lived the well-known philanthropist Savva Ivanovich Mamontov of whom I have already written at the beginning of my book when I described and characterized those men who in their time created Russian life and the new intelligentsia. As I have already stated, the house of Mamontov was a sanctuary for all young and talented painters, sculptors, actors, musicians, singers and dancers. Mamontov was interested and well versed in all arts. Once or twice each year performances for children were given in his house, and sometimes performances for adults also. Oftener than not the plays were of his own making or his sons'. Now and then composers of his acquaintance produced an opera or an operetta. The plays of established writers were also produced, for instance, Ostrovsky's "Snow Maiden" for which Victor Vasnetzov painted all the scenery and designed all the costumes, which were later reproduced in many illustrated artistic publications. These famous productions, unlike the productions of our Alexeiev Circle, were always produced in a hurry, during Christmas or Easter, when children did not go to school. The play was rehearsed, costumed, and the scenery designed and painted in two weeks' time. During this time work did not cease day or night, and the house would become a tremendous workshop.

In one of the rooms Vasnetzov designed the first act of the play, in another Polenov the second, in another Korovin the third, in another Serov and Vrubel the fourth, in another Repin himself the fifth. Young men and women, children, relatives, came to the house from all the ends of the city and helped in the work. Some mixed paint, others prepared the ground on the canvases, others worked on the furniture and the props.

In the ladies' quarters they prepared and sewed costumes under the supervision of the artists themselves, who would now and then be called upon to explain or to help. Heaps of all sorts of material lay in the corners of the room, tables would be placed for cutting, the costumes were fitted on the actors who would be called from the rehearsal for that purpose, and volunteer tailors as well as professionals worked day and night in full shifts.

In still another corner of the room the musicians would go through an aria or a song with one of the young songbirds who was evidently destitute of great musical ability. All this work was done to the accompaniment of the hammers of the carpenters that reëchoed through the entire house from the large room that was the study and work-room of Mamontov, where they were building a stage. Without taking any notice of the noise one of the stage directors would go over the play in rehearsal with his actors. Another rehearsal would be taking place near the main stairway of the house. All questions of acting and stage direction were taken down on the run to the chief stage director, Mamontov himself.

He sat in the large dining room at the tea table which was never bare of food. Here were always crowded the volunteers who wished to help in the productions. In the midst of all this noise Mamontov was writing the play while its first acts were being rehearsed upstairs. The hardly finished sheet of paper was copied on the spot and given at once to an actor who ran upstairs and began to rehearse what had just been written. Mamontov had a remarkable ability of working in public and doing several things at one and the same time. He conducted all of the work on the production while he was writing the play, jesting with the young people, dictating business letters and telegrams in his complex railroad-building affairs of which he was the manager and the initiator.

The result of the two weeks' work was a performance peculiar to itself, that amazed one and made one angry at the same time. On one side there were the wonderful decorations of the best artists, and a stage director's idea which created a new era in the decorative art of the theatre and forced the best theatres in Moscow to pay attention. Against this wonderful background played completely untaught amateurs, who had not only been unable to rehearse their parts well, but who could not even remember them. The unholy amount of labor on the part of the prompter, the helpless stops and pauses of the timid actors, whose faint voices could not be heard, convulsions instead of gestures, which were due to stage fright, the complete absence of technique, made the performance inartistic and the play itself, the fine idea of the stage director and the wonderful production, unnecessary. True, now and then this or that rôle would gleam with talent for a moment, for among the people on the stage there were several real actors. Then the whole stage would come to life for a time, while the actor was on it.

These performances seemed to be created for the purpose of showing the primary importance on the stage of the actor himself and the entire lack of necessity of the whole production and all beautiful scenery in the absence of the most important person in the theatre — the actor. It was at these performances that I learned this truth, and saw with my own eyes the meaning of completeness and long rehearsals in theatre affairs. I became convinced that in chaos there can be no art. Art is order, grace. What do I care how long they worked on the production, a day or a year? What is important to me is that the collective creation of all the artists of the stage be whole and complete and that all those who helped to make the performance might serve for the sake of the same creative goal and bring their creations to one common denominator. It is strange that

Mamontov himself, who was such a sensitive artist, found a peculiar joy in the very carelessness and hurry of the work. On this ground we always debated and quarreled with him, and on this ground there was created the well-known competition and antagonism between his productions and the productions of the Alexeiev Circle. Nevertheless I tried to take part in Mamontov's productions; once or twice I played parts in them and was sincere in my admiration for the work of the artists and stage directors, but as an actor, I never received anything but pain from these productions.

The productions of Mamontov played a great part in the decorative art of the Russian theatre; they interested talented artists, and from that time on, true painters appeared on the horizon of the theatre who gradually began to supplant the horrible house painters who were the only decorators the theatre had known in the past.

I began to understand that singing was not for me. I stood at the crossroads. I could no longer return to the domestic operetta because I had learned too much from Kommisarjevsky about the higher aims and problems of art. Besides this, our domestic group was falling apart. My sisters were married.

The only thing left was the drama. I had not forgotten it even before and always paid a great deal of attention to the work of the Imperial Little Theatre, so famous in its time, and also the work of one of the best private theatres in Russia, that of Korsh, where the best provincial actors of the time appeared.

Thanks to frequent appearances at amateur performances, I became quite well known among the amateurs. I was often invited to take part in single performances and also in dramatic circles, where I came to know all the amateurs of the time, and worked under many stage directors. I had an opportunity to choose the rôles and the plays I appeared in, which gave me the chance to try myself out in many parts, especially in those that were dramatic, and of which young men always dream. When it is strong and imaginative, youth always tends to " tear passion to tatters."

I will not say anything of the great evil that this experience caused me. It is dangerous to sing Wagnerian parts with an unplaced voice. It is just as dangerous for a young man without the necessary technique to undertake dramatic parts too difficult for him. When you are called on to perform the impossible, you naturally have recourse to tricks, and that leads you away from the fundamental roadway of development.

My eyes gradually opened and I began to understand that in the realm of the stage it was possible to say the most and the best in the drama. Fyodor Kommisarjevsky, whose friendship I retained after our singing lessons were discontinued, upheld me in my new efforts.

Besides, our operetta circle had been split and broken. Nothing was left but to follow the usual road of all amateurs, that is, play at all chance performances, in rapidly rising and rapidly disappearing dramatic circles, in dirty, cold, and small amateur halls, with terrible scenery, and very often in unpleasant society. The continual change of rehearsals, flirting instead of work, gossip, and performances rapidly thrown together which the public attended only because of the dances that followed them, could not cool my ardor. Sometimes we played in unheated theatres where our costumes would freeze to the walls before we put them on our warm bodies. In the worst frosts I managed to have a dressing room in the house of my sister and in the intermissions I would go there in a cab to change costumes or make-up. Behind the wings we sat in fur coats and arctic boots.

Both rehearsals and performances had only one end, — flirting, tea drinking and strong liquor that caused more than one scandal.

I remember that at a certain vaudeville performance in which fifteen persons were to take part only two came, and we, who were playing in another playlet on the same program, were forced to play in the vaudeville act without knowing a single line in it.

"But what are we to play?" we asked in wonderment.

"It doesn't matter. Walk out and say whatever you wish. The performance must be finished. The public has paid for its seats."

And we walked out on the stage and said whatever we could think of at the moment, and when we could say no more, walked off. Others walked on and did exactly as we had done. And whenever the stage was empty we would be dragged on again. Both we and the public roared with laughter at the senselessness of the whole thing. At the end of the performance we were called before the curtain by applause and the manager was in very high spirits.

"You see," he cried, "and you did not want to go on!"

Often I was forced to play in the company of suspicious-looking people. What could I do? There were no other places to act, and I so wanted to act. Among these amateurs there were gamblers and demimondaines. And I, a man of position, a director of the Russian Musical Society, found that it was dangerous for my reputation if I appeared. It was necessary to hide behind some pseudonym. I sought a strange name, thinking that it would hide my real identity. I had known an amateur by the name of Doctor Stanislavski. He had stopped playing, and I decided to adopt his name, thinking that behind a name as Polish as Stanislavski no one could ever recognize me.

At last I secured the rôle of a comedy lover in a three-act French farce whose action took place in the dressing room of an actress. With hair curled, in the costume of a dandy of the period, I flew out on the stage, carrying a tremendous bouquet. I flew out — and stopped. In the central box sat my father, my mother, my tutor and the governesses of my sisters. And I remembered that in the following acts I would have to go through love scenes and even a little beyond love scenes, a thing that had always been forbidden by our domestic censorship. Instead of a worldly, gallant young man I played a modest, well-reared boy and caused the failure of the whole play. After the performance I returned home ashamed of myself and did not dare to appear before the family. On the next day, my father settled the matter in one sentence.

" If you want to play on the side, found a decent dramatic circle and a decent repertoire, but for God's sake, don't appear in such trash as the play last night."

My old governess, who had known me since my days in the cradle, could not understand that I had grown up. She said, " I never, never thought, that our Constantin, who was such a clean boy, could ever do a thing like that. It is terrible, terrible. Why did my eyes behold it? "

The German governess said, " *Abscheulich*."

The French governess said, *"C'est rigolo."*

And so, another failure.

There was still another practical result of my wanderings in amateur circles. I came to know the most talented amateurs of Moscow, men and women who later became leading figures in our amateur circle — The Society of Art and Literature, and still later passed into the ranks of the Moscow Art Theatre: Artem, Samarova, Vonsiatsky and Sanin, now famous as a stage director in Paris, London, and Madrid, who has worked with Diaghilev, and who has independently produced opera.

CHAPTER XV

A T that time there appeared in Moscow the famous stage director and actor, Alexandr Fillipovich Fedotov, the husband of
the famous actress Fedotova and the father of my friend Alexandr Fedotov, who often appeared with me at amateur performances.
He arranged a performance in Moscow to remind the city of his existence. His son, of course, took part in the performance, and through
him I was also invited. The play was " Les Plaideurs " of Racine in
Fedotov's translation. The chief part was played by the artist, amateur,
and æsthete, Count Fyodor Salogub. As for me, I played the chief
part in Gogol's one-act comedy " The Gamblers." At this performance I met for the first time the talented stage director of the old
French school. He had just returned from Paris, bringing with him
the newest methods of acting. Rehearsals under his direction were
the best possible school for me. It seems that I interested him, for he
tried to bring me together with his family.

The performance arranged by Fedotov was crowned with success.
After it I could no longer return to my former amateurish wanderings.

" Everything, but not that," I said to myself, whenever I remembered those performances. All those who had taken part in Fedotov's
affair did not want to separate, and Fedotov himself, who was a great
dreamer, began talking of the creation of a large society that might
unite all amateurs into one dramatic circle and bring all other artists
in Moscow under the roof of one club where there was no card play.
I had already talked on that subject with Fyodor Kommisarjevsky, and
it only remained to bring Fedotov and Kommisarjevsky together in
order to reach a final decision about the projected society.

When you want something very badly, it seems to you that your desire is both simple and realizable. And it seemed to us that it would be easy to get the necessary money from club dues and donations. Like lava that rolls down a hillside, our new idea, as it developed in our minds, embraced more and more branches which it seemed to us would bring in money and help us to realize our aims. Fedotov was the representative of " The Society of Writers and Actors " ; Kommisarjevsky the representative of music and opera, Count Salogub the representative of the artists. And behind them there was a large group of people who dreamed of joining our ranks. For instance, the publisher of a large literary and artistic magazine took advantage of the society in order to begin and to popularize his venture. Besides, as talk of the new society progressed it was decided to open schools of the drama and the opera. Could we have gotten along without them once we had two such marvelous teachers as Fedotov and Kommisarjevsky?

Everybody thought a great deal of our venture and prophesied success for it. Only Count Salogub, who was much older than I, but who was so young in spirit that we became friends and comrades, tried to cool off my imagination and save me from many impractical steps.

Mme. Fedotova also called me to visit her on several occasions in order to use her motherly influence and save me from some impending disaster. But because of my headstrong nature which forced me to use every effort to get that which interested me, their voices of reason did not enter much into my calculations. I explained the pessimism of Fedotova as due to her private dissensions with her husband, and I did not at all believe in the practical experience of Salogub as he was too much of an artist to be practical. And then luck would have it that my father's business had a very good year, and I received a bonus of about thirty thousand roubles. Not being used to so much money I considered myself a rich man, and gave a large part of the money in order to get hold of certain premises which seemed to us to be more than necessary for the success of the society. The premises demanded a great deal of reconstruction, and since there was no one else to furnish the money for that, I again contributed, blindly believing in the future of the society. In the middle of the winter of 1888 our Society of Art and Literature gave its first gala affair in its well-furnished headquarters in the centre of which there was a large auditorium that on occasion could serve as a ballroom also. Around the auditorium there was a foyer, and a large room done in ancient Russian style for the artists. They painted the walls themselves and designed the furniture. In this strange room they met and drew their sketches, which were sold on the spot at auction, the proceeds of which they used for buying food.

Actors from every theatre of Moscow appeared at our concert, as readers or impromptu players; others danced, still others sang, and what amused all was that dramatic artists would appear in the rôle of operatic artists and dancers, and the artists of the ballet would appear in the rôle of dramatic artists. The entire intelligentsia of the city was there that evening and thanked the initiators of the society and me for the fact that we had gathered them together under one roof, and assured us that they had long waited for the appearance of a society like ours. The press met our opening enthusiastically. A few days after the gala opening we produced Pushkin's " Miser Knight " before a full house, together with Molière's " Georges Dandin." In the first I played the part of the Knight, and in the second the part of Sotanville. The scenery of the " Miser Knight " was designed by Count Salogub, and the scenery of " Georges Dandin " by a young artist then just at the beginning of his career, and now famous, — Korovin. Both plays were directed by Fedotov.

In early spring it had been decided to open the theatre of the Society of Art and Literature with these two plays, " The Miser Knight " by Pushkin in three scenes, and " Georges Dandin " by

Molière, in three acts. I think that no amateurs could have made a more difficult choice. Pushkin is one of the curtest, sharpest, most poetical, most perfect in form and deepest in inner content of artistic writers. Each of his sentences is a theme for a work of art, or at least, for a whole act. To play the few pages that house his creation is the same as to play several long dramas. This tragedy of miserliness, which occupies only a few pages, covers all that was said or will ever be said of that human fault.

In studying my part, I tried to add something of my own to what had been said by Pushkin. Thirty years have passed since that time, and I have still found nothing to add. The genius of Pushkin is all-embracing. The hardest thing in all art is to be brief and full of content. Metternich once wrote, " Excuse me for the length of my letter, as I have not had the time to be brief."

Molière also embraces human passions and faults broadly. He describes what he has seen and what he knows. Being a genius, he knows all. His Tartuffe is not merely the individual Tartuffe, but all human Tartuffes taken together. He writes of life, of plots, of individuals, but the result is a general human passion or fault. In this he is near to Pushkin and to all great writers generally, for in this respect all great writers are the same. They are great because they have wide horizons and broad vision.

I played in both dramas. In the first I played the Knight, a tragic rôle; in the second, the comic rôle of Sotanville. Nothing is harder for us actors than to act in such plays. Our parts in such plays must be cast like bronze monuments. This is too hard for an amateur who is just beginning to play, for what he needs is an interesting plot and outward action, which hold the attention of the spectator by their own power. But in Pushkin the outward plot is simple, and there is almost no outward action. All the action in the play is of an inner character.

A mediaeval baron descends of nights into the cellar of a tower where his riches are hidden, and takes toll of the pleasure of being with them. Each night he adds a handful of gold pieces, exulting over the price of each, now murder, now hungry death, now debauch, now corruption — all human virtues and faults, everything — lies in the gold pieces. The baron has money, and all human kind is in his hands. He is all-powerful, he is above all desires, he despises everybody. But everybody thinks that he is poor. And this power which is at his command is even dearer to him because it is secret. His tenderness for gold reaches the heights of passion, and his consciousness of power the ecstasies of madness. Among his open trunks, his gleaming candles and the blinding flash of gold, he is drunk with the consciousness of his power. He chokes with bliss, but remembers at once that his bliss is not eternal, that death takes everything away and gives his treasures, bought at the cost of sleepless nights, of pangs of conscience, of privations, of hunger, to his worthless son, a spendthrift who will drink all this wealth away with his comrades of the tavern. Oh, if he could sit on his trunks after death as he sits now, and protect his treasures from the hands of the living. These despairing shrieks of the crazed miser are the end of the play.

"Whom shall I take for an example? Whom will I imitate? I never saw any one in this part on the stage, and I can't imagine how a given actor would play the part," I said to myself with despair. "The only man who can save me is Fedotov. I will place myself in his hands."

"To-night I will sleep, or rather, I will not sleep with you," Fedotov told me. "Arrange it so that we can pass the night in the same room, and that we may lie opposite each other."

I made the necessary arrangements.

Fedotov was already an old man, with a head of thick gray hair, with bristly, cropped mustaches, which had grown used to the razor, with lively mimetics and a nervous movement of facial muscles. His eyes were forever moving and winking. Asthma had bent his figure, but it could not restrain his inhuman energy. He always smoked thin, perfumed cigarettes, lighting new ones from the butts of the old ones.

In his nightshirt, his thin aged legs naked, he began to describe the decorations, plans and *mise-en-scène* which he had worked out for the tragedy. He spoke with enthusiasm and a talent which he possessed to no small degree. Fedotov called the *mise-en-scène* worked out, but I saw that he did not know himself how the thing would look in the end. He dreamed before me an impromptu in order to enthuse me as well as himself towards creativeness. I have done the same thing myself many times, and I know this old method of the *régisseur* very well indeed. It does not matter that everything on the stage will be diametrically different than you imagine in the beginning. Often one does not believe that one can do on the stage what one pictures in imagination. But even such imagining fires one for the work at hand. While Fedotov talked, I put some of my own thoughts and remarks into his project. Then we threw everything to the winds, and began from the very beginning, in an altogether new way. But we would meet with obstacles, and were forced to create still another plan. In the end, of all the fantasies there remained something in the shape of a crystal, or an elixir, which was rich in content, and brief, like the Pushkin play itself. Enthused by his imagination, Fedotov would leap from his bed and demonstrate outwardly what he beheld in his inner vision. His bent, aged figure, his thin, emaciated legs, his nervous face, and his talent were already creating a hint of the barely discernible future image, which I also seemed to see. It was the image of a weak, nervous old man, interesting in its inner and outer characteristics. But I dreamt of another, an image more grandiosely quiet in its faults, without any little nervousnesses, but just the opposite, with a monumental self-control and an unbreakable belief in his rights. It seems that Fedotov was also searching for the same image, and his nervousness was only due to his exhaustion after a day's work.

But there was a difference. It lay in the fact that his image was that of a man older and more characteristic than mine. It seemed to be taken from the paintings of the old masters. Do you remember those typical faces of old men lit by reddish candlelight, bent above swords that they are cleaning of bloodstains, or bowed above a book? My image was another one; simply speaking, it was a noble opera father or an old man, like St. Brie in "Les Huguenots." I had already begun to imitate one of the famous Italian baritones, who had good legs in black tights, wonderful slippers, wide breeches, and a well-cut doublet around the waist, with a sword. The sword was the most important thing of all. It had been the sword that had attracted me to the rôle. From that night on a torturing division began in me. Two entirely different images lived and fought in my soul like two bears in the same den.

I could not decide which of the two images it was better to imitate, that of Fedotov or that of the baritone. In some places I liked Fedotov's; I could not deny the talent and originality of his creation. But in the greater part of the rôle, the baritone won the victory. Could I have denied myself the good leg in tights, the sword, the high Spanish collar, — denied myself in a moment when I had at last won a beautiful operatic rôle, which I had just missed singing when I was a singer? It seemed to me at that time that to sing and to recite verses was the same thing. My inartistic taste seemed to frighten Fedotov. Feeling it in me, he lost his fire, grew silent, and quickly put out his candle.

Our second meeting and discussion took place at the demonstration of the sketches of the scenery and costumes made by Count Salogub.

"How awful!" I said to myself when I saw them.

Imagine an ancient old man with noble, aristocratic features, in a dirty and torn leather headpiece that looked like a woman's bonnet, with a long, uncut imperial that looked like a full-grown beard, with thin, careless mustaches, in wide, worn-out tights that lay along the leg in awkward folds. Long slippers that made the feet look thin and narrow, a severe, well-worn, half-buttoned shirt stuck into old breeches, a waistcoat with wide sleeves like those of a monk. A well-defined, aged stoop. The whole figure — tall, thin — bent like a question mark. He stooped above a chest and through his thin, bony fingers gold pieces flowed into the receptacle below.

"What! A pitiful beggar instead of my handsome baritone! Never!"

I was so hurt that I could not hide my feelings and began to beg through tears that the part, which had become hateful to me, should be taken away from me.

"I can't play it anyway, any longer."

"But what do you want?" asked the confused artist and stage director.

I told them sincerely of what I had dreamed, and what attracted me in the rôle. I tried to draw what I had imagined. I even showed the portrait of the baritone, which I always carried in my pocket secretly.

Then they began performing an operation that was an amputation, a search and a shaking out of all the theatrical artificiality that I had gathered through my amateur years. Fedotov and Salogub taught me a lesson that I will never forget. They laughed me down and showed me as clearly as two and two is four all the backwardness, insolvency, and vulgarity of my taste at that time. At the beginning I was quiet, then I became ashamed, and at last I felt all my nonentity. Something seemed to give way in me. All that was old was no good, and there was nothing new. They had not convinced me of the new, but they had certainly made me distrust the old. In a whole series of conversations, the demonstrations of the pictures of old and new masters, and very talented instructions and lessons, they began to put into me single seeds of the new. I began to feel like a capon that was being stuffed with nutritious nuts. I put the portrait of the baritone into a drawer and was ashamed of my erstwhile dreams about him. Was that not success?

But I was still far from what my new teachers wanted.

The next step of my work in the rôle was to learn to interpret an old man outwardly, physically.

" It is easier for you to play a very old man than a middle-aged one," Fedotov explained to me. " In a very old man the contours are much clearer."

I was a bit prepared for the playing of old men. While I had practiced before the mirror in our city house during the summer, I had played everything, an old man included. Besides, I watched and imitated one of the old men I knew. Then I began to feel physically in myself that the normal state of an old man resembles the state of a young man after long exhaustion. The feet, the hands, the spine become wooden. Before rising one must get ready to bend the body forward in order to move the centre of weight, to find a fulcrum, and to rise with the aid of the hands, for the legs half-refuse to serve. On rising, you do not straighten out the back at once, but you unbend it gradually. Until the legs stretch, you walk with small steps, and only after a time begin to move swiftly, but then it is hard to stop yourself. All this I understood not only theoretically, but I felt it in practice. I could live with these experiences of age adapted to a condition of youthful exhaustion. It seemed to me that this was good. And the better it seemed to me the more I tried to put it into the part.

" No, this won't do. It is too exaggerated. This is how children imitate old men," Fedotov criticized me. " You mustn't try so hard. Go a little easier."

I tried to control myself, but nevertheless there was still too much.

" Again, again!" he commanded.

And I tried to let down the tone of my performance more and more, until I no longer strained myself and retained the rhythm of age only through inertia.

" This is the real thing," Fedotov commended.

" I don't understand a thing. I stopped to imitate an old man and you tell me that I did well. And when I used the methods that I had discovered for the playing of an old man, you told me that they are not worth anything. This can only mean that no methods are necessary." I threw away the methods that I had found out, and stopped playing, but they would cry, " Louder. We can't hear you!"

No matter how hard I tried, I could not understand the secret.

My further work over the same part gave no results. In the simple, more quiet places, I felt something, but these were my personal feelings, which had no relation to the image itself. I lived through something outwardly and physically also, but this bore a relation only to the aged characteristics of the rôle. I was also able to say the words of the text simply, but not because of the inner causes by which Pushkin's baron lived. I spoke simply just for the sake of speaking simply. One can imagine an exercise of the following order — to make oneself limp on one foot, and while limping put a room in order, singing a song at the same time. In the same way one may walk in the manner of an old man, perform the necessary stage business and action and declaim mechanically the lines of Pushkin. It seems that I could reach no greater result at that time, so hateful had the part into which I could not wholly enter become to me. I had put on the rôle as if it were a coat, in a hurry, using only one sleeve. That was not enough. I was hardly able to use half of what I had reached in the quiet places. And in the strong places I could not handle even the little that I had found in the part. At such moments I was visited by what I had once called inspiration, and I began squeezing my voice, hissing, and straining my whole body and read the lines and read them badly, provincially, with bad actor's pathos and an empty soul.

The rehearsals ended, and I went to Vichy and tortured myself all summer over the part, continuing more and more to make it my own. I could think of nothing else. It had entered my soul and become a sickening, fixed idea. The worst of all human tortures are the pangs of creation. They are the true tortures of Tantalus. You feel the *something* that is lacking in the part; it is very near, here in yourself, and all you have to do is to take hold of it, but as soon as you stretch your hand it is gone. After this, with an empty soul, without any spiritual contents, you approach a strong part in the rôle — it is only necessary to open the gates of your soul — and now some sort of buffers seem to crawl out of the soul and do not let it approach strong emotion. This condition is reminiscent of the case of a bather who cannot make up his mind to dive into the icy water.

In my quest for a solution I decided on one means which at that time seemed to me to be the idea of a genius. Several miles from Vichy there is a mediaeval castle and under it a tremendous cellar. "Let them lock me in there for several hours, and there, in that true ancient keep, in the midst of solitude, I might find that feeling, that condition or that emotion." I didn't know what it was I needed and for what I was looking then.

I went to the castle and got them to lock me in the cellar for two hours. I felt creepy and lonely; it was dark, damp; there were rats, and all these inconveniences only interfered with my concentrating on the rôle. And when I began to repeat in the darkness the text that had become cold in me, the whole thing grew foolish. Then I grew chilled and began to fear that I might finish with pneumonia. This fear did away with any thought of the rôle that I might have entertained. I began to knock but no one unlocked the door. I became really frightened, but my fear had nothing to do with my rôle. The only result of the experiment was a bad cold and despair. Apparently, to become a tragedian it was not enough to lock myself in a cellar with rats. Something else was necessary. But what? It seemed that one had to take oneself high and higher, to the top floor, to the clouds. But how was one to get there? No one would tell me. The stage directors explained only the results that they wanted. They were interested only in the result. They criticized, telling you what was bad, but they would not tell you how to get at what was desired.

" Live the thing through, feel it stronger, deeper, live it," they would say. Or, " You are not living it through. You must live it through. Try to feel it."

And I would try, and strain all my strength, and tie myself into knots, and squeeze my voice till I grew hoarse and the blood would rush to my head and my eyes would pop out of their sockets, while I tried to do what was required of me until I grew exhausted. One rehearsal would tire me so that I would not have the strength to repeat the scene again at the demand of the stage director.

If this happened at ordinary rehearsals, what would take place at the performance when nervousness would make me lose all control of myself? And to say the truth, my acting on the first night was all a matter of stage fright, as actors say.

But the performance was successful. Wonderful scenery, costumes designed by that talented artist Count Salogub, remarkable stage business, the whole tone and atmosphere of the performance, its fine balance — due to Fedotov — all was new and original for that time. There was applause. Who was to take it but I? And I walked out and bowed, and the public accepted me, because it cannot differentiate the work of the artist from the work of the stage director, and the work of the stage director from the work of the actor. There was praise also for me. I believed it and I sincerely thought that if there were praise, then the work I did must have reached the public, must have made an impression, must have been good, and that this hissing and spasm was inspiration. It follows that I had felt my rôle truly and everything was crowned with success.

But the stage director scolded. From jealousy! If he is jealous, there must be something for him to envy.

There is no escaping this magic circle of self-deceit. The actor is caught in the quicksands of flattery and praise. That which is pleasant is always victorious, because one wants to believe it. One listens to the compliments of charming admirers and not to the bitter truth of the expert.

Young actors, fear your admirers! You may pay them attentions, but do not talk with them of art. Learn in time, from your very first steps, to hear, understand and love the cruel truth about yourselves. Find out who can tell you that truth. And talk of your art only with those who can tell you the truth.

CHAPTER XVI

W ORK on the other rôle for the same performance, that of Sotanville in "Georges Dandin," was also far from easy. The hardest thing was to begin. And the larger the work of art the more amazed you stand before it, like a pedestrian before Mont Blanc.

Pushkin, Gogol, Molière, and other great poets are dressed once and forever in the old uniforms of all kinds of traditions, which make it almost impossible to get down to the living soul of their works. The works of Shakespeare, Schiller and Pushkin are called by actors and theatrical workers *Gothic* pieces; the works of Molière are known under the name of *Molière*. In the very existence of the nickname and in the grouping of these several names under it there is already hidden the hint that they are all of the same cut. If in a drama there are verses, costumes, the Middle Ages, pathos, that is, romanticism, that is Gothic scenery and costumes; in one word, it is a *Gothic* play. Not only actors and theatres are to blame for the creation of such prejudices and the defacing of great masterpieces by false traditions; those more to blame are the pedagogues who spoil the glow of the youth's first acquaintance with a work of art while his impressions are fresh and strong, his intuition powerful, and his memory impressible. They speak of the Great in one general, dry, old and uninteresting tone of pedantry. Homer, Herodotus, Ovid — are beautiful. But when children in the secondary schools are forced to commit them to memory for the sake of grammatical exercises so that they might best remember the much hated *nu efelkiustikon,* the soul of the child is filled with a sourness towards masterpieces which it takes long years to conquer.

And how are classical Gothic dramas played? Is there anybody who does not know it? Any high-school boy will show you how high feelings are interpreted in the theatre, how verses are declaimed and chanted with pathos, how costumes are worn, how the actors stride triumphantly over the stage and assume various poses. The gist of the matter seems to lie not in the author and his style, but in Spanish boots, in tights, in swords, in the verses, in the voice badly and falsely placed, in the bearing of the actor, in his animal temperament, in beautiful limbs, in curled hair, in penciled eyebrows.

The same thing happens with Molière. Who does not know the uniform of Molière? It is the same for all his plays and for all plays like his. Try to remember a production of any of his plays on the stage. And you will .at once remember the productions of all of his plays in all theatres. In your eyes there will leap all the theatrical Orgons, Cleanders, Clotildas and Sganarelles that you have seen who are as like each other as two drops of water. And this is the holy tradition sedulously guarded by all theatres!

And where is Molière? He is hidden in a pocket of the uniform. He cannot be seen for his tradition. But if you read his " L'Impromptu de Versailles " you will become convinced that Molière himself condemns bitterly all that goes into the making of the so-called Molière traditions. God, what can be more boresome than the Molière traditions on the stage, this Molière *As Always,* Molière *As He Is Supposed To Be,* Molière *In General!*

This phrase "In General" is the bane of the theatre. It stood between me and Molière's Sotanville like a stone wall. Not seeing the real Molière because of that wall, I told myself that I knew everything even at the very first rehearsal. It was not in vain that I had seen Molière on the French stage. Of course, I had never seen " Dandin " on the stage, but that did not trouble me. I had Molière

" In General " before me, and this was more than enough for me, for a born imitator.

At the first rehearsals I was already copying all of the Molière hokum that I had seen, and feeling myself thoroughly at home.

" You must have seen a lot in Paris," said Fedotov, smiling, to me. " You have brought the whole orchestration with you."

Fedotov knew how to surmount the wall that lay between an actor and his rôle, and how to rip off the uniform of false tradition, giving instead of it the true traditions of real art. As was his habit, he would mount the stage himself and play, creating what was true and full of life, and so destroying all that was false and dead. He played the plot of the play, but the plot was thoroughly connected with the psychology, and the psychology with the image and the poet. The comism of the work, its satire, discover themselves if one treats all that happens seriously and with great faith. This seriousness was very strong in Fedotov; besides, like a truly Russian comic actor, he was bright and rich in characterization. In other words, he had all that was necessary for Molière. It was not in vain that during the flowering of the Russian theatre it was thought that the best Molière actors in the world were the Russians Shtchepkin, Shumsky, Sadovsky and Jivokini. Besides, Fedotov had studied every subtlety of the French theatre, and this gave his acting a finish, a delicacy and a lightness all its own. Fedotov would play a part, and his playing would make the part clear. The organic nature of the part would show itself in its full beauty.

How wonderful and how simple! All that one had to do was to get on the stage and do the same. But as soon as I felt the boards under me all that I had thought seemed to be reversed. There is a far cry between seeing a thing done and doing it yourself. Once on the boards and all that seemed to be so easy while you were in the auditorium becomes devilishly hard. The hardest thing of all is to stand on the boards and to believe and take seriously all that takes place on the stage. But without faith and seriousness it is impossible to play satire or comedy, especially if it is French, especially if it is classical, especially if it is Molière. Here the entire gist is in seriousness, in sincerely believing in one's foolish, or impossible, or helpless position, in becoming sincerely excited and in suffering sincerely. One can play at that seriousness, but then the comedy revenges itself. To live over or to play at living over — there is a difference between these two as large as the difference between natural, organic comism, and the outer antics of a talentless court fool.

I played artlessly at living where Fedotov lived organically. I tried to look as if I were serious and believed in what was happening to me on the stage. Fedotov had real, living life; I had only a report of that life. But what Fedotov showed was so beautiful that it was impossible to deny to myself what he had shown. I was a captive in his hands — the usual result of what he did and showed on the stage. True, the wall was breaking, but instead of it there rose between me and the rôle Fedotov's alien image. I had to surmount this obstacle now in order to reach my Sotanville and become one with it. But nevertheless, a living image is much better than a dead tradition. Fedotov himself discussed what he showed much more simply and practically.

" What can I do with amateurs? " he justified himself. " How can I avoid showing the thing to them, when there is so little time before the performance? I can't open classes for them. They will copy a bit, and then will enter into their parts somehow."

But when Fedotov noticed the slightest glimmer of independence in creativeness, he was as glad as a child and did everything he could to help the actor find himself.

And so I began to imitate Fedotov. Of course I copied him only outwardly, for it is impossible to copy the living spark of genius. The trouble was that I, a sworn imitator, was at the same time a very bad imitator. Imitation is a special gift that I did not possess. When my imitation was unsuccessful, I left it and caught hold of my old methods of play, seeking life in the tempo of patter and waving my arms, then in acting without a pause so that the spectator might not have time to be bored, or in the straining of all my muscles and the squeezing out of temperament, or in the loss of text. In a word, I was fatally returning to my former amateur and musical comedy mistakes, which can be covered in one sentence:

"Play as hard as you can while your audience is not asleep."

"They praised me for it before. I was joyful and light and funny on the stage."

But my attempts to commit my former errors were not accepted by Fedotov. He would cry from his place:

"Don't mumble! Clearer! Do you think that this will make me, the spectator, laugh? Just the opposite; you bore me, because I don't understand anything. Your stamping, and waving your arms, and walking, and all your numberless gestures interfere with my vision. There are spots in my eyes and a noise in my ears. Whatever made you think it was funny?"

We were rapidly approaching the dress rehearsal and I was still, so to say, sitting between two chairs. But luckily for me, I accidentally received a gift from the lap of the gods. One feature in my make-up gave a living and comic expression to my face, and something suddenly turned within me. All that was dim became clear, all that was groundless suddenly had ground under its feet, all that I did not believe suddenly found my trust. Who can explain this unexplainable, sudden, and magical creative motion! Something had ripened within me, slowly filling with life while it was in the bud, and now at last it bloomed. One accidental touch, the bud opened and from it burst fresh young petals, seeking the warmth of the sun. And with me, an accidental touch of the make-up brush on my face served to open the flower of the rôle in the shining glow of the footlights. This was a moment of great joy, that paid for all my former pangs of creation. What can I compare it to? With a return to life after dangerous illness, or with the successful end of birth pangs. How good it is to be an artist in such moments, and how rare these moments are among artists. They always remain bright stars that burn like watch fires and point a way to further quests and the achievements of new goals for the artist.

Looking back and evaluating the results of that performance, I understand the importance of the moment that I lived through at that time. Thanks to Fedotov and Salogub, there had taken place in me a movement away from a point of inertia. I seemed to have crept out of the quicksands where I had struggled for such a long time. I did not find a new road, but I came to understand my former mistakes, and that is very much. For instance, I had mistaken stage emotion, which is only one kind of hysteria, for true inspiration. After this performance my mistake was clear to me.

Imagine that I had been taught from childhood to call peas meat. I would eat them, thinking that I was eating meat. But peas only blow you up, without nourishing you. And I would walk around with an enlarged stomach, but hungry.

That empty stage emotion which I had mistaken for inspiration — that is the food that blows up the soul of the actor, but does not nourish it.

But at last I had understood my mistake, and had I substituted true inspiration for false stage emotion I might have gained a great deal of creative strength from the change.

We have retained random thoughts uttered by Shakespeare, Molière, Ekholm, Schroeder, Goethe, Lessing, Riccoboni, the De Briennes, Coquelin, Salvini, and other individual lawgivers in the realm of our art. But all these valuable opinions and advices are not systematized, and are not reduced to one common denominator, and therefore the fact remains that fundamentals which might guide the teachers of our art are missing. In Russia, which has reworked in itself all that the West has given her, and created her own national art, the absence of fundamentals which might have fixed that art, is even more striking. Notwithstanding the mountains of written articles, books, lectures and theses on the art, notwithstanding the researches of the innovators, with the exception of a few lines from Shtchepkin's letter, we had written nothing that might be of practical aid to the actor in the moment of the realization of his creativeness, or that might be of aid to the teacher at the moment he meets his pupil. All that has been written about the theatre is only philosophizing, very interesting, very deep, it is true, that speaks beautifully of the results desirable to reach in art, or criticism of the success or failure of results already reached. All these works are valuable and necessary, but not for the actual practical work in the theatre, for they are silent on how to reach certain results, on what is necessary to do firstly, secondly, thirdly, and so forth, with a beginner, or what is to be done with an experienced and spoiled actor.

What exercises resembling solfeggi are needed by him? What scales, what appreggi for the development of creative feeling and experience are required by the actor? They must be given numbers, just like the problems in a mathematical textbook, for systematic exercise in the school and at home. All books and works of the theatre are silent on this score. There is no practical textbook. There are only attempts, but as far as they are concerned, it is either too early, or altogether unnecessary to speak of them.

In the region of practical teaching there exist a few unwritten traditions left by Shtchepkin and his heirs, who learned their art intuitively, but who did not make sure of it by scientific methods, and who did not fix all that they discovered in a definite and concrete system. Is it necessary to say that there can be no system for the creation of inspiration or system for creation itself? There can be no system for the making of a great virtuoso violinist or a singer like Chaliapin. They have been given the most important thing by Apollo himself.

But there is a certain thing, small and insignificant though it may be, that is necessary even for a Chaliapin, a Paganini, a chorister, and a fiddler in the orchestra in the same degree. For both Chaliapin and the chorister have lungs and a system of breathing, a nervous system and a physical organism, one more and the other less perfect, which live and act for the production of sound according to a law common to all mankind. In the realm of psychic life there is a great deal that is necessary for all men, and the approach to which is the same for all men. These organic laws of creation, common to all mankind, and perceptible to our consciousness, are not many in number. The part they play is not very honorable and is confined to small fields, but nevertheless these laws that are perceptible to consciousness are necessary for every artist, as it is only through them that he can release his superconscious creative apparatus, the substance of which will always remain a secret to man. And the more talented the artist is, the greater and more mysterious this secret, and the more necessary the technical methods of creativeness perceptible to consciousness for direct reaction on the hidden springs of superconsciousness that are the source of inspiration.

These very elementary psychic laws, information, researches, practical exercises, problems, solfeggi, appreggi, scales, counterpoint, composition, perspective are lacking in relation to the art of the actor, and make of that art an accidental impromptu, often inspired, but oftener sunk to the level of a simple trade of a definite mold and method, fixed now and forever. Do actors study their art and its nature? No, they study how to play this or that part and not how it is created organically. Craftsmanship teaches the actor how to walk on the stage and play. But true art must teach him how to awaken consciously his subconscious creative self for its superconscious organic creativeness.

CHAPTER XVII

MARRIAGE

SOON after the "Miser Knight," we produced "Bitter Fate" by Pissemsky, a play of peasant and land-gentry life. I played the part of the peasant Ananiy Yakovlev, who goes on business to Petersburg. Meanwhile his wife Lizaveta falls in love with a neighboring squire, a good but weak-willed man, and bears him a child whom the squire wants to adopt. He also wants to take Lizaveta to himself. Ananiy returns unexpectedly to the village and learns everything. With great nobility he explains himself to the squire and refuses to grant the latter's desire. And when the village council nevertheless decides to take the child forcibly from him and the councilmen come for it, Ananiy, in a fit of anger and excitement kills the child with a blow of an axe, for which act he is sentenced to prison in Siberia, where he goes in humility to expiate his sin.

The play is written masterfully by one of the most famous Russian authors; after Tolstoy's "Power of Darkness" it is the best drama of the life of our peasants.

The rôle of Ananiy, which I played, demands at times not only dramatic, but also tragic strength. The parts of the play were well taken care of by the amateurs who played in it, and some parts, especially that of Lizaveta, the wife of Ananiy, found exceptionally fine interpreters.

Just as I did before, I gave myself a new problem to solve this time also. This consisted in working out in myself scenic restraint. I understood that in a moment of strong upheaval which I mistook for inspiration, it was not I who controlled my body, but it was my body that controlled me. But what can the body do where the work of creative emotion is desired? In such moments the body is strained with impotence, and knots seem to be tied in various points of it, or spasms appear that petrify the legs and arms, shorten the breath, and tie all the organs. Or just the opposite, due to impotence, the entire body becomes subject to anarchy, the muscles move against one's will and call out a numberless amount of nervous movements, little, unconscious reflex actions, meaningless gestures and poses, nervous movements of the face, and so on. This often makes emotion seek a hiding place in its secret sources. Is it possible to create, live over, think under such circumstances? It is apparent that the first thing to do is to overcome these circumstances in one's self, that is, to destroy the anarchy and free the body from the power of the muscles, at the same time putting it into the power of the emotions.

At that time I understood the word *restraint* only in its outward meaning, and therefore I tried to destroy every unnecessary gesture and movement, that is, I taught myself to stand on the stage without moving. It is far from easy to stand motionless on the stage in the full sight of more than a thousand pair of eyes. I was successful, but only at the cost of a tremendous bodily strain. I ordered my body not to move and stood like a wooden Indian at my own command.

But habit is second nature. Little by little, from one rehearsal to another, from one performance to another, I untied the knots of the muscular spasms which were strewed in all the centers of my body. I changed general straining into particular and local straining, that is, I seemed to gather the strain of my whole body and centralize it in one given spot, in the fingers, the toes, the diaphragm, or rather what I took at that time to be the diaphragm. Closing my fists with all my strength, I pressed the nails of my fingers into the palms of the hands, often leaving bloody marks in their wake. I drew together the toes of my feet and pressed them with all the weight of my body into the floor, often leaving blood in my shoes as a result.

Creating local and particular strain, I removed the general strain from the rest of my body, giving it a chance to stand free without any unnecessary movements. In my further work, I learned to wrestle with the local strains in the hands, the feet, the diaphragm, and so on. But for a long time I was not successful. As soon as I freed the strain in my fists it would travel over all the rest of my body. In order to get rid of these spasms it was necessary to gather them once more into my fists. This was another magic circle that seemed to have no break in it. But at last I found that break.

Even outward and artificial restraint which freed the body from strain, created a sense of physical well-being on the stage that approached real restraint. This truth carried with it a spiritual atmosphere that warmed me on the stage, and at times it was easy and pleasant to stand motionless. I believed in my large figure that seemed to have grown into the earth, and felt in it a source of strength, confidence and stability. Faith has great meaning for the actor. Physical truth, and faith in that truth, call out inner spiritual truth and faith, and these free emotion, which comes from its secret hiding places and begins to enter into all that takes place on the stage. At such moments emotion takes the initiative into its hands, directing all energy towards a definite creative goal, and then muscular strains, general or local, disappear as of themselves, perhaps because there is no longer energy enough to support the spasms, which, at the command of emotion, are given another and a more reasonable direction.

These are moments of great artistic joy. They did not remain without notice on the part of the stage director, who would cry, " Good! fine! simple! There is no exaggeration!"

It is a pity, but these moments were rare, accidental, and they did not last.

And another discovery. The quieter and more restrained my body felt on the stage, the more there arose in me the necessity to supplant gesture with mimetics, intonation of the voice, and look of the eye.

Then I felt in my new method something akin to the methods of the great actors whom I had studied in my time. How happy I was in those moments! It seemed to me that I understood everything at last! That I could use my discovery to its fullest! And I would give full freedom to mimetics, to the eyes, to the voice.

Unexpectedly, the voice of the stage director would sound in my ears, " Don't shout! " or " Don't grimace! "

And again I was in the quicksands.

" Again something is the trouble. Why do I feel that I am right, and they feel that I am wrong? " I asked myself. Once more, due to the doubt that attacked me because of the warring of my emotions within me, all that I had discovered would leave me, and my gestures would fall back into anarchy, and again I would be forced to chain them down with the help of strained hands or feet.

" What is the trouble? " I tried to find out.

" What is the trouble? The trouble is that you are grimacing."

" That means that I am not to use any mimetics."

And I tried not only to cut out mimetics, but even to hide it. No remark was made by the stage director but I noticed something myself. In the scene of explanation with the squire I only had to try to appear quiet and indifferent and emotion would at once boil within me. I had to hide this by main force, but the more I hid it, the more it raged. And again I felt warm and at home on the stage. The hiding of emotion enrages it all the more. But why was there no remark from the stage director at this moment?

It was not enough for me that after the act was finished I received general praise from all for all of my work. How important it would have been to receive the stage director's praise during the very moment of my inner satisfaction. But stage directors did not, it seemed, recognize the importance of that yet.

This is what happened in the quiet parts of the rôle. But during the mob scene, which was finely written by the author, finely produced by Fedotov, and finely played by the actors, a scene which I could not play indifferently, I gave myself up against my own will to the general atmosphere of excitement prevalent, and could do nothing with myself. No matter how much I strained in order to control my gestures, in the end my temperament mastered me and my consciousness, and I lost all control of myself to such a degree that after the performance was over I could not remember what I had done on the stage. Covered with sweat from excitement, I walked across the hall to the table of the stage director in order to share my troubles with him.

"I know, I know," I waved my hands, "what you will tell me. That I let go of my gestures. But it was more than I could do to restrain them. Look, I have scarred my palms with my finger nails."

What was my surprise when all present attacked me with exclamations of praise.

"Fine! you made a wonderful impression! What restraint! Play like this on the first night, and nothing more is necessary."

"But at the end I let go my gestures, and no longer controlled myself. I dropped all restraint."

"That is what was necessary."

"It was necessary that I let go of my gestures?"

"Yes. What does controlled gesture mean when a man is carried out of himself?" I was told. "What was good was that we saw how you controlled yourself more and more, until at last something tore in you, and you could control yourself no longer. This is what is called growth, crescendo, a musical passing from *piano* to *forte*. Emotion rose from the lowest to the highest notes, from calmness to insanity. This is what you must remember. Control yourself while you have strength to control yourself, — the longer, the better. Let the gradual rise to the top be long, and the last moment of striking short, otherwise your blow will lose its effect. Mediocre actors usually do the very opposite. They leave out the most interesting gradual growth of emotion and leap directly from the *piano* to the *fortissimo* where they remain for a long time."

"Ah, so that is the secret? That is something from the region of practical advice which is so necessary to the actor. This is my first, my necessary stage baggage, which I will guard faithfully."

Around me there was triumphal joy, the best witness of my own impressions. And I asked everybody I could, not to satisfy my, actor's vanity, but in order to make sure that there was a relation between what I had felt on the stage, and what they had felt in the auditorium. Now I know something about this striking difference. It is very much like the opera. From the background of the stage sound reaches the public later than sound from the orchestra, for the orchestra is in the auditorium itself. Therefore in the background of the stage one must sing one quarter note before the orchestra, and only when this is done is perfect sound heard in the auditorium.

On the dramatic stage it is also necessary to know how to act differently from life on every portion of the stage, so that truth may pass over the footlights. Without this there will be no agreement in what is done, and things will look false. The same thing applies to the voice. In order to make the effect true, one must do things to it that in real life are not true. The same applies to make-up. One must paint, and pencil the brows to make an effect in the auditorium. But when you take a close look at a man in make-up, especially in the daylight, the effect is one of a mask.

Happily, this time also, the make-up reminded me of a familiar peasant's face; it was not forcefully painted on me, but it coincided with what I felt within myself. Even the mirror passed on my outward appearance. And this time I did not see a strange image, but my own. Having found it, I rode my hobby again, as I did in the rôle of Sotanville, and began to imitate. But it is much better to imitate an image created by yourself than another's methods of play or another's mannerisms.

MARRIAGE

The performance was crowned with success. The play, the production and the actors were praised by the press and by the public. The play remained in repertoire and the more I played in it the more I felt myself at home on the stage. Much that I felt on the stage coincided with what was told me by the spectators, and I was happy with my success, and with the fact that I had discovered the secret which might guide me, and on which I might depend in my further work on the stage.

Physical bodily restraint, the taming of the anarchy of muscles, to reveal emotion in the strong places and think of nothing, to work out my own image which I was to copy and imitate.

These are the whales whose backs I mounted in order to adventure further.

I took advantage of my new methods of play for but a short time. I only had to hear Pushkin's verses in " The Stone Guest," in which I first played Don Carlos and then Don Juan, I only had to don Spanish boots and a sword with a jewelled hilt that was brought from Paris, and all that I had reached with such hardships disappeared, and instead of it there appeared the powerful falseness of what I had learned in my many years of amateur acting. To yield to old habits is the same thing as beginning to smoke again after a year's abstention from nicotine. The organism embraces the old experiences with added strength. It got along without them temporarily, but in secret it never stopped dreaming of tobacco.

In this manner I advanced in art two steps at a time and retreated three. Why did I assume to play parts for which I was not yet ripe? The greatest obstacle in the artistic development of an actor is hurry, the forcing of his immature powers, the eternal desire to play leading parts and tragic heroes. To give heavy work to weak emotions is the same thing as to sing Wagnerian rôles with an immature voice. No, it is even worse. For the actor's nervous and subconscious apparatus is much tenderer and more complex and more easily spoiled and harder to correct than the vocal apparatus of a singer. But apparently man is so created that he dreams of what he has not and what he must not have; the child is all agog to smoke and curl a wicked mustache; the little girl wants to flirt instead of playing with dolls and studying; the youth wants to make himself look older in order to arouse interest in himself. From jealousy, from conceit, from foolishness, and from inexperience, each desires to be what he cannot or must not be. An actor just beginning wants to play Hamlet, a rôle which is the crown of a long stage career. He does not understand that his hurry forces and destroys his tender spiritual apparatus. But no matter how many times you say this to the pupil or the young actor, it is in vain. Let a good looking high-school girl applaud the young actor, let another praise him, let a third send him a letter with his portrait and beg for an autograph, let a fourth one ask for an appointment, and all the advice wise men can give him retreats before his conceit.

I played Spaniards, ordered my boots in Paris, and violated my immature acting abilities for the sake of the praise of high-school girls. The worst thing of all was that I was forced to take the rôle of Don Juan itself, as its interpreter was forced to give it up after the first performance. Here again, conceit rose in me.

"When I asked for the rôle, they did not give it to me, but now when there is no one to play it, they come to me themselves. Well, they understand and value me at last!" my actor's conceit told me. I accepted the rôle in a spirit of charity. I was flattered by the fact that I was necessary in the repertoire.

The performance was given. I was applauded because high-school girls do not understand anything, and cannot discern the actor from the part, and I rushed forward like a fool, mounted on all my old mistakes. They became even more noticeable because now I could play with restraint, which I learned in the rôle of Ananiy. All that is bad, as well as all that is good, simply increases its quality when it is shown on the stage with restraint. Even the fact that I had learned to reveal emotion in strong places was bad in my new rôle; the more I opened up, the more false theatrical pathos there was in my acting, for in my soul I had nothing else for the part. Again I imitated the baritone in Parisian boots and a jewelled sword at his belt. But no one could dissuade me of the fact that I had learned the secret of how to play not only simple peasant parts but also the parts of lovers in tragedies.

My work in Don Carlos and Don Juan pushed me back at least ten strides in my development.

It is a pity that the next rôle I attempted that season was, if not Spanish in verses, still so in long boots, sword, love speeches, and high style. I played the part of Ferdinand in the tragedy by Schiller, " Villainy and Love." But there was a *but* which to a certain degree saved me from new mistakes and without which we could never have gotten along with the tragedy.

Louisa was played by M. P. Perevozchikova, whose stage name was Lilina, the same amateur actress who, in spite of society's opinion, came to act with us. It seems that we were in love with each other, but did not know it, but we were told of it by the public. We kissed each other too naturally, and our secret was an open one to the public. In this performance I played less with technique than with intuition, but it is not hard to guess who inspired us, Apollo or Hymen. Right after the performance, there appeared willing matchmakers. In the spring at the end of the first season of the Society of Art and Literature, I was proclaimed a bridegroom, and on July 5 was married. Then we went on a honeymoon and returned in the autumn to the theatre with the news that my wife could not fulfil her duties in the theatre during all of next year. Everybody will understand why.

In this manner " Villainy and Love " proved itself to be a villainous drama. It was played only two or three times, and was later entirely removed from the repertoire. Could we, after the marriage, as man and wife, still possess that same artistic technique and inspiration that we possessed until our engagement? Or would the rôle of Ferdinand, if repeated, fall to the same level as that of Don Juan and Don Carlos, and be a reprimand to my obstinacy?

Just as in the former performances, the experienced hand of the stage director Fedotov was able to take advantage of rather passable artistic material. We listened to the guiding remarks of our experienced director gladly. They helped us, but we did not understand them consciously, and these performances hardly moved us forward as actors. The performances were successful and I was triumphant, for it proved all my theories about romantic rôles which, after Don Juan, became even more liked by me.

"So I can play tragic rôles," I said to myself. "So I can play lovers, and my technical principles found in 'Bitter Fate' are effective in tragedy also!"

The first year of the existence of the Society brought me a large deficit, but did not shake my faith in its future success.

Towards the beginning of the second season great changes took place in our Society. Because of the jealous competition between the two schools, that of the drama and that of the opera, and their directors, that is, Fedotov and Kommisarjevsky, there arose quarrels whose whole weight fell on my shoulders. For instance, as soon as Fedotov produced a new successful play, the operatic department would arrange a new concert which caused new expenses but did not add any gains. This loss was always borne by me, for I was the only one able to bear it. And I, awed by my directors, and attracted by the art of both, did not have the strength to cut out either of the two losing departments. At the end of the year the family evenings for artists and actors became boring. The actors said, "We are tired of playing in the theatre. We would rather play cards in the evenings, and there are no cards here. What kind of an artists' club is this, anyway?"

The artists did not want to paint, without cards, the dancers to dance, the singers to sing. And here there was a conflict after which the artists left the society. They were followed by many of the actors and the club under the auspices of the Society died out of itself. There remained the dramatic department and with it an operatic dramatic school.

CHAPTER XVIII

CHARACTER PARTS

THE second season of the Society of Art and Literature, 1889-1890, began with the production of " The Usurpers of the Law " by Pissemsky, the same man who wrote " Bitter Fate." I played the part of a general-en-chef of the times of the Emperor Paul I. Both the play and the part are skilfully but cruelly written in the difficult language of the epoch. General-en-chef Imshin goes to the war at the command of the Emperor, and leaves in the care of his brother, the dandy and Lovelace Prince Sergey, his young wife, who was taken by him from a family of a ruined nobleman. She is secretly in love with the handsome officer of the guards Rykov, a fact which Prince Sergey accidentally finds out. " Either she is to give herself to him, or he will send a courier with the news to his brother ! "

But the general seems to have sensed the danger. He secretly returns home, walks into the library through the garden, unseen, and hears everything, both the treachery of his brother and the faithlessness of his wife. The young officer appears in the house to see the wife and meets the old husband. Here there is a fine, strong scene in which the general plays with the lovers like a cat with a pair of mice. He locks both in a cellar and there, under the presidentship of his beloved fool, the general conducts court, at which he sentences the lovers to life imprisonment. For days at a time the general sits near the window of the lovers' prison and is tortured by pity and jealousy.

But the father of the woman, a drunken warrior, with the face of the great Russian general Suvorov, comes with a band of robbers to the house. He attacks the estate in order to free his daughter. There is a real battle on the stage. The robbers climb over the fence, cut down the trees, break in the windows of the cellar and free the prisoners. A swiftly organized domestic troop under the command of the general himself attack the robbers. The robbers retreat, but Imshin is wounded and dies, and before dying he gives his wife to Rykov. The play, which begins like a real tragedy, at its end sinks into a melodrama.

Much of what had been discovered before was useful to me in this new part: restraint, the hiding of my inner jealousy under the mask of outer calm, mimetics and the play of the eyes (a thing that comes of itself when the anarchy of the muscles is done away with), the full spiritual revelation of the soul in moments of high stress, and my " old-man " methods from the " Miser Knight." The hardest thing for me, as in the " Miser Knight," was the speech of old age. I did not guess it intuitively and was forced to seek it by artificial means, technical means, and the methods of creating the pronunciation of age.

First of all I turned to the old man that served me as a model and looked in his mouth to see what happened there when he removed his upper plate of artificial teeth. Between the lower teeth and the upper gum there is formed a crack. I tried to make exactly such a crack between my upper and lower teeth. In order to do this I had to move my lower jaw forward. This made me lisp and interfered with my speech. Nevertheless, having created this obstacle, I did not try to make it greater, but tried to speak as clearly as possible and to pronounce every letter. In order to do this I was forced to pay more attention to my speech and to speak more slowly than was my wont. There appeared a slow rhythm of speech and this reminded me of a very old man whose state I guessed emotionally.

I remembered that almost the same principle was used in my

search for the walk and the outer action of the Miser Knight. In this way I tried first of all to understand and study the physiological cause of the physical process, that is, why the rhythm of action and speech is so slow with old men, why they rise so carefully, why they straighten so slowly, walk so slowly, etc. Becoming aware of these principles and their results, I began to apply them on the stage. Before I would rise I looked for something to rest my hands on, and rose with the help of my hands, slowly straightened myself in order to ease my back, for I knew that without this carefulness old men may be attacked by lumbago. Conscious relation to action that was typical to old age guided me and as a result I tuned my own feelings to the physiological phenomena of senility. This created a kind of method from the outer to the inner, from the body to the soul, based upon an unbreakable bond between physical and psychical nature.

All these technical means, although they did not create the image, prepared the soil for it, and to a certain degree filled the inner emptiness on the stage that was so terrible to the actor. There was something from which one could advance. True, in the rôle there were dangerous reefs; for instance, high boots, costumes of the eighteenth century, a sword, words and feelings of love, and if not verses, still the high language of the court, but Imshin is too much Russian to be afraid of the Spaniard in me. And his love was not young, but old and more characteristic than romantic in outline.

It was said that an image appeared even in spite of me, but I did not notice from where. The technical methods of play pushed me on to the truth, and the feeling of truth is the best awakener of emotion and the sense of living over a thing, imagination and creativeness. At first I did not have to imitate any one, and I felt well on the stage. There was only one unpleasantness — the public complained about the play. "It is very unbearable!" they said. It seems that there was a reason for that.

Together with the "Usurpers of the Law" another play was in

rehearsal in which I did not take part, but simply came to watch. When my opinion was asked I made my remarks. Good and true words come not when you want to say them, but only when you do not think of them, when they become necessary themselves. For instance I cannot philosophize and think and create aphorisms in solitude. But when I have to explain my thoughts to another then logic is necessary to me for proof, and aphorisms come of themselves. This happened this time also. What is done on the stage is seen better from the auditorium than from the stage itself. Looking from the auditorium I comprehended the mistakes on the stage at once, and began to explain them to my comrades.

"Understand," I said to one of them, "you are playing a hypochondriac. You are nagging yourself all the time, and seemingly take care only that your part might, God forbid, not be that of a hypochondriac. But why worry about it, when the author himself has taken care of it already? The result is that you are painting the picture in only one color, and black only becomes black when some white is introduced for the sake of contrast. So let in just a bit of white color as well as some other colors of the rainbow into your rôle. There will be contrast, variety, and truth. Life is never like bad plays on the stage where some people are all black and others are all white. So, when you play a hypochondriac, seek where he is happy, virile and full of hope. If after this you return to your nagging, it will not bother you any longer. Just the opposite, its strength will be redoubled. Continuously complete nagging like yours is just as unbearable as a toothache. When you play a good man look for the places where he is evil, and in an evil man look for the places where he is good."

Having uttered this aphorism accidentally, the rôle of General Imshin became suddenly clear to me. I had made the same mistake as my comrade. I played a beast, but there was no necessity to take care of that, the author himself had taken care of it; what was left to me was to look and see where he was good, suffering, remorseful, loving, tender and sacrificing. And this was new baggage in my actor's train.

When you act an evil man look to see where he is good.

When you play an old man, look to see where he is young. When you play a young man, look to see where he is old, etc.

In relation to how much I took advantage of this new discovery, the general tone of " The Usurpers of the Law " became softened, and complaints about its heaviness became rarer.

All the second season of the Society of Art and Literature passed along the line of almost the same artistic quest and technical problems as the first.

It was a pity that Fedotov did not put the same old fire into his work, but he was dissatisfied with something; he did not agree with Kommisarjevsky and grew cold to the business.

During the second year I played several character parts and one dramatic part. I played the rôle of Paratov in " The Dowerless Bride," then in Fedotov's play " The Rouble " the part of a stock-broker. I repeated the brightly characteristic rôle of the German Frese in an empty three-act vaudeville sketch, " The Favorite," which we had played before. I also repeated the old one-acters " The Secret of Woman " and the " The Weak String," which were played in our old Alexeiev Circle, and at last I played one big new part, that of Peter in Ostrovsky's play, " Don't Live to Please Yourself but to Please the Lord."

Had I learned to approach my rôles? And if I had, then by what method? There is no doubt that Fedotov had created a complete perturbation in me. I understood now that to approach a rôle by imitating another actor does not yet create the necessary image. I understood that I had to create my own image. I understood that it was necessary to create something within myself, for without that there could be no excitement and no quickening of the creative spirit.

While one is cold one cannot create. But I did not know how to look for an approach to the image unless the stage director like Fedotov showed me how, or chance itself would, as was the case in the rôle of Sotanville. I believed then that emotion, pose, costume, make-up, manner and gesture could lead me to the image. I learned further that by a whole series of technical approaches one could create within himself the feeling of truth, which awoke creativeness.

For " The Dowerless Bride " I had many such technical approaches which led me to a feeling of the truth and so to creativeness. Judge yourself.

Here are the contents of " The Dowerless Bride ": Volga, freedom, breadth, and care-free Russia. In a small trading town on the Volga there live modernized merchants who go to foreign countries, dress in fashion, but keep in their hearts the impulses of the beast. In the same town lives the beautiful Larissa, a half gypsy that has grown up in Bohemia. Guitars, gypsy songs, gypsies in a famous inn that teach her to sing the gypsy songs — that is her sphere. She has a tender soul that seeks great passion. Her mother, an ex-courtesan, dreams of selling her daughter as dearly as possible, to find a good setting for her jewel, but the daughter is hopelessly in love. But the man she loves is far away. In despair Larissa decides to marry an official, narrow-minded and reserved, called Karandishev. The mother is in terror.

Meanwhile, down the Volga in his own steamer comes an ex-guardsman who is now a shipowner, Paratov. He is brave, powerful, strong, broad-natured, and handsome. He wears a white guardsman's cap with a bright red band, a tight fitting coat of that period, an artistic bow tie, his stately legs are in riding breeches and high lacquered boots, a carelessly worn military overcoat lies on his shoulders like a Spanish cloak. In his hand is a horse-whip which he knows how to use on men also. His arrival is an event. The town is in turmoil. The gypsies go in costume to meet him at the pier head. The local rich men also go there to welcome him. The restaurant kitchen is preparing for a holiday.

Paratov visits Larissa and finds out about her slated wedding. His masculine conceit is wounded. He decides to revenge himself on his rival and for this reason visits him at the engagement dinner, makes the bridegroom drunk, laughs at him in the eyes of the bride, and takes her with him for a ride on the Volga in a rowboat accompanied by the gypsy chorus. During this boat ride Larissa gives herself to Paratov, thinking that she will always belong to him, but, Paratov, at the end of the boat ride, shows her a wedding ring, the gold of which prevents his marrying her. Larissa is shamed. She tries to leap from a cliff into the Volga, but cannot make up her mind to do so. She is saved by her sobered bridegroom who wants to revenge himself on Paratov. With a pistol in his hand, seeking his rival, in his excitement, he shoots and kills his bride. She dies to the singing of the gypsies that comes from the restaurant where Paratov is feasting.

I played Paratov. In the rôle there were words of love, high boots and a coat like a Spanish cloak, all dangerous reefs for me. There was preparing in me a duel between my former " opera baritone " methods and my newly acquired technical methods of approach. Again I called on their help, that is on the help of restraint, on the hiding of my emotions, on facial play, on the use of a variety of colors, in a word, on all that I had discovered. This created a fine state of mind and a feeling of well being in which I began to believe. Imagination had free play, details began to appear as of themselves; for instance, the habits and characteristic traits of Paratov himself, like his military bearing. With all this baggage I was no longer empty on the stage; I had something to do on it, I did not feel myself naked. With the advance of the rehearsals I became used to the technical approaches, and the breadth that is so characteristic of the Russian in Paratov opened my soul. Happily I had a rather typical make-up. I saw Paratov's outer image, and everything became orderly. In this way, I first created artificially and then intuitively my image, grounded on something, and to a certain degree justified, and all that remained was to copy it according to the habit that still was in me.

But in this rôle there appeared one unpleasant feature. I could not handle the text. Notwithstanding the marvelous language of Ostrovsky, in which one cannot change the placing of a single word, the text, as actors say, " did not take to my tongue." I felt that at any moment of my presence on the stage I could make a mistake. This made me nervous, frightened me, and caused stoppages and unnecessary pauses, creating scenic misunderstandings which denied to the play and to the part the comedy lightness that belonged to them rightly. The fear of the text was so great that every pause threw me into a sweat. Once I mixed up my text so that I lost all control of myself and did not even know how to find my way out of the labyrinth of words. I left the stage, breaking up one of the best places in the rôle of another actor, and I was roundly scolded and called an amateur, which word had already become a term of disapprobation with us.

This actor's stagefright which began in me at that time showed itself in other rôles also and took away from me that confidence in myself which I had already begun to possess. When I did not think of my new fault, it would disappear. This was proof that it was of purely nervous origin. And here is another example of the truth of such a hypothesis. I became seriously ill on the day of one of the performances of " The Dowerless Bride." I was almost semiconscious. But in order to show an example of discipline to my comrades, I came to the theatre in the great frost. They put my make-up on me while I lay on a couch, and thanks to the fact that I did not have to change my costume during the play, I was able to lie down in the intermissions and whenever I was not needed on the stage. The other actors were afraid that I would leave the theatre during the progress of the play, but I, occupied with thoughts of my sickness, played more confidently and freely than ever. Only in the last act — due to my weakness — I had to give up.

Work over the rôle of Paratov and the results of that work were of great educational value to me in the sense that they pointed clearly to my peculiar and real *emploi* and talents in the theatre. I am a character actor. Because of that I had been able to conquer all the hidden reefs of the rôle of Paratov, its coat like a Spanish cloak, its high boots, its love speeches and all the other temptations in it that were so dangerous to me. Through being a character actor I could have with time reached tragedy. But to approach it by the direct road and in my own original way — I still could not do that.

Why?

There are artists, mostly leading men and heroes who are in love with themselves, who always and everywhere show not images or creations, but themselves, their persons, and who never change themselves. An actor of that kind does not see the stage or the rôle in so far as he himself is not concerned. Hamlet and Romeo are needed by them only as a new dress is needed by a light-minded girl.

On the other hand there are actors who are ashamed to show themselves. In playing a good or a kind man it seems immodest to them to claim those good qualities as their own. Playing evil, debauched or dishonest men, they are ashamed to make their own the qualities their portrayal calls for. But, having masked themselves, they are no longer afraid to show their faults and their virtues and can speak and say what they could never afford to do in their own person and without a mask.

I belong to the actors of this second type. I am a character actor. Not only that, I claim that all actors must be character actors, of course not in the sense of outer, but of inner characteristics. But even outwardly it is best for the actor to leave himself at times. This does not mean of course that he must lose his individuality and his personality; it means that in each rôle he must find his individuality and his personality, but nevertheless be different in every rôle. Why are all lovers handsome and curly-haired? Can it be that young men who are not handsome have no right to love? Yet in the whole course of my life I saw only one such lover, who was not afraid to make himself ugly in order that he might the better show his pure, loving heart, just as the ill-smelling coat of the drainman Akim in " The Power of Darkness " stresses his crystal-pure soul.

It is a pity that all beginning actors, and I was a beginner myself at that time, dream only about playing lovers and heroes. It is the accepted fashion to reckon lovers and heroes the rarest, most valuable and first in all our art. The lover is liked most by the ladies, he is the most tempting, handsome and effective figure on the stage. The question here is not at all in the success of the actor but in the success of the man. The stage is transformed into platform for exhibition and the actor becomes a prostitute who appears so many hours each evening for the purpose of exhibiting his beauty, his legs, his breast, his muscles, his animal temperament and passion, his loud voice and all that might enchant a woman. This is a hateful and shameful trade that lowers the dignity of the actor.

My next work was the rôle of the stockbroker Obnovlensky in " The Rouble," by Fedotov, the contents of which play I no longer remember. Like the rôle of Sotanville, after long tortures this rôle became successful because of an accidental touch in my make-up. The wigmaker, in his hurry, glued the left half of my mustache lower than the right half. This gave my face an expression of slyness. To help the mustaches along, I drew the right brow higher than the left. The result was a face that enabled me simply to repeat the text of my speeches and everybody understood at once that Obnovlensky was a scoundrel, not a single one of whose words was trustworthy. If I were to describe the zigzag line of the development of the rôle until I received that "gift" of Apollo, I would simply repeat what I have written before.

This rôle was also a success and passed under the ægis of character acting.

That same season I played the part of Peter in Ostrovsky's "Don't Live to Please Yourself but to Please the Lord." These are its contents in short:

Peter, a rich merchant's son, is debauching as only a true Russian can. He is in love with Grusha, the daughter of the mistress of an inn, who is also loved by the young and foolish merchant Vassya, who wants to marry her. Peter is afraid that he is not successful in his love-making, and Grusha tortures him and leads him on. One of the habitués of the inn, the blacksmith Yeremka, limping, terrible, red-headed, like Satan himself offers his services to Peter. Tradition has it that blacksmiths, who pass their lives in the red light of their forges, have dealings with the evil one, that they know how to make love philtres and how to poison a rival. Yeremka agrees to make a love philtre for Grusha and to rid Peter of his rival. The crime takes place. Later Peter confesses.

Both play and rôle have breadth, swing, strong passions, interesting psychological development. It seemed that I had the necessary temperament also, and the figure and the voice. Besides, there were also tried methods for the technical creation of the image, and restraint, which is necessary always and everywhere, and a certain ability to variegate and design the spiritual colors of the part interestingly. I was also beginning to understand the necessity of inner psychological consequency that led by degrees to the climax of the rôle and the necessity of leashing my temperament in so far as I could. In separate moments I was sometimes successful in removing the spiritual buffers that tried to protect my soul from those parts of the rôle that were difficult for my feelings. I could give myself to the moment until I forgot myself, until I almost lost consciousness.

But all these new technical approaches suddenly disappeared as soon as I undertook the rôle of Peter. From the very first step I traveled along the upper folds of the rôle, along its periphery, aided by purely outward methods that I had memorized. I glided along the surface of the part, without touching any of its inner characteristics. I made as much noise as an unconnected belting in a factory while the machine which it is supposed to run is stationary. The belting works, but there are no results. The actor can also work like the belting, along the outer nerves and the periphery of the body, without touching the soul, which remains cold and inactive. The actor tries more than is necessary, he runs, he moves his hands, he loses the whole text of the rôle because of his hurry; he blushes, he pales, he is sincerely moved by some emotion altogether useless for the part, he shouts, and becomes hoarse. All this is done in an insane rhythm and tempo so that the spectator might not have time to grow bored and might pay more attention to him.

But all this work is barren. It is no more productive than the whirling of the unconnected belting. Words, gestures, movements, fly past real emotion like an express train past local stops. Nothing takes hold of any of the inner being of the rôle, for mechanical outward play is a long way ahead of true inner experiences. In order to stop this meaningless movement along the surface of the rôle, it is necessary to give the initiative of creativeness to intuition and emotion, which become the helmsmen of the ship of acting. But how can one stop the ship that has broken its anchor chain, or cast the moving belting over its proper cog, or cease the meaningless surface movement of the actor along the periphery of nerves and body? How can one force the emotions to leave their secret hiding places and take the initiative of creation into their hands?

To do this it was necessary to attract emotion by means of the interesting inner image of the mighty Peter, by means of his broad Russian spirit, his elemental character, his great love passion that passed into jealousy, despair and madness. But emotion was silent, and I could not attract it to appear artificially. At that time I did not know the conscious methods of inner technique for the creation of subconscious creative intution and emotion.

Only for a moment, with the aid of strained movements of the legs and arms, could I awake emotion, and at such times it was so unreasonably excited and mechanical, that it died out almost at once. It reminded me of a spoiled watch. If the hands are turned for a long time from the outside, they begin to hiss and show life inside, and to strike in irregular rhythm, but their blows suddenly cease. In the same way, inner emotions called out by outer physical excitement woke momentarily in me in a chaotic condition and then died out. But did they have some relation to the spiritual substance of the rôle or were they simply mechanical excitations that were momentary and lifeless? But I had no other means. I only had to take the part of Peter in my hands, and my emotions and imagination fell asleep, my intuition was silent, and I was helpless before the part whose emotions were alien to me.

Together with my inner helplessness I was strong in my outer, stagy manner of playing. Without any inner guidance I knew how to imitate tragedy. Like the frog in the fable I tried to look bigger and stronger than I was in order to resemble a paladin. But I only imitated a paladin, and I could not become a paladin. I violated myself and my drowsy emotions. The results are obvious. There appeared spasms and petrifications of the body, strain and the anarchy of muscles, bad craftsmanship, acting of the old cut, and so forth.

Of all existing stencils, the worst is that of the Russian paladin, of the Russian knight, the son of a boyarin, or the village strong man with their width and breadth of soul and character. For these there exists a specific manner of walking, wide gestures that are established once for all, traditional posing with hands on the hips, a mighty heaving of the head to free it from the falling waves of their hair, a special manner of holding the hat, which is mercilessly crumpled for the mechanical strengthening of passion, brave vocal attempts at the high notes of the register, and a chanting diction in the lyric places of the part. These bad faults have entered so much into the ears, eyes, body and muscles of Russian actors that there is no possibility of getting rid of them.

At that time the opera "The Enemy's Host," by Serov, was very much in fashion. This opera was written on the theme of Ostrovsky's play which we were rehearsing. If the stencil of the Russian paladin is bad in drama, then in the opera it is altogether unbearable. The opera stencil of Peter is the worst of all possible stencils of that character. And it was exactly that stencil that took possession of me, for a secret admiration of the opera was still extant in me. I only had to feel the old familiar stage methods and their companion feelings and like a smoker after a long period of denial of the weed, I would give myself up into the power of all the bad habits of stagecraft that I knew.

Must I say anything about the artistic side of the performance? The result is self-evident. It was negatory. It is more important to say something about the degree of harm which a rôle that is too difficult can bring to a young actor. One must have a practice and an experience of more than thirty years of the stage to value that harm at its true worth. In what does it express itself?

That bad craftsmanship and old stencils cripple the emotions and the body — that is, the true living over of the rôle and its natural personification — that they force creative emotion is so true that it is unnecessary to speak of it after all that has been said already. In the calm minutes of the part the harm is great. But it is even greater in those places where a tragic climax is forcibly created against the desires of the emotion itself, for in such places the forcing becomes tenfold in strength. But in what does the harm lie? Imagine that you are being pushed into the cage of a lion. It is natural that you will resist. If you are made to leap across a wide chasm in the hills or to climb a perpendicular cliff or to lift five hundred pounds, it is natural that you will resist and perhaps lift your hands to defend yourself against the person that tries to make you do those things. You will do all this because you feel your helplessness and the impossibility of doing what is required of you.

The same thing happens with emotion: the more it is violated, the more it resists and throws out its invisible buffers before it, and these, like hands, do not allow emotion to approach that part of the rôle which is too difficult for it. The more times emotion is forced to attack problems too difficult for it, the more timid it becomes and the more used to its buffers. And the more the buffers are developed, the harder it is for emotion to appear when needed and the more necessity there is for old stencils and stagy craftsmanship. The more stamps and staginess, the farther emotion runs from them. All that creates the necessity of using protective buffers works out a stencil and is harmful to the greatest degree.

Tragedy, which demands strong strain, may violate emotion more than anything else, if that emotion does not awaken of itself, intuitively, or with the help of a correctly acquired inner technique. This is the reason why the harm done by tragic rôles can be so great, and I must warn young actors, who have not yet acquired technique and who already wish to play Hamlet, Othello and other tragic rôles which should come not at the beginning but at the end of the actor's career. Rather than undertake such difficult work let the young actor acquire more of the methods of inner technique, that is, let him first learn to awaken by conscious means the superconscious creativeness within him.

Neither Ostrovsky's play nor my part were successful. The result was despair and the loss of faith in myself. But as not a single untalented creation on the stage does not find its admirers, I also found them. My failure did not make me give up hopes of tragedy, and

I continued obstinately to dream of it, holding back the natural growth of my art.

Strong moments of great climacteric force and the strain of temperament are even worse, even more dangerous and harmful for the artistic nature. In order to reach such moments naturally, one needs a great deal of preparation for them. If the first steps are logical, and lead you higher and higher, as if you were traveling up the steps of a ladder, then in the end of things you can, with the help of consciousness, reach a certain final height which is the beginning of the higher spheres of superconsciousness. Impetus may make you rise into this region and surrender yourself to the power of emotion only. The whole gist is in the first steps which create the impetus. But if there are no steps that lead higher and the part moves on a flat plane, now backwards, now forwards, mounting at times and falling again, there is no possibility of developing enough impetus to rise. Nothing is left but to squeeze emotion out of yourself by main force. There is no greater harm than the harm in the mechanical forcing of the emotions from outside, without the creation of an inner spiritual stimulation. Under this method emotion remains in a drowsy state and the actor begins to strain himself physically. The muscles of the actor are willing tools that are worse than the worst enemies. Every young actor who forces his will to undertake parts too difficult for him only develops his stage muscles, and nothing else.

CHAPTER XIX

I DON'T know how to explain my remarkable and extraordinary success in the vaudeville act " The Secret of Woman," where I repeated the part of the student Megrio, played by me once before. I changed nothing in my interpretation, and the former principle of my acting, on which I had created the rôle before, was doubtless false. This principle was to play as swiftly as one could, so that the spectator had no time to be bored. The patter of words, action without any stop, the raising of tone just for the sake of tone, the swiftness of tempo for the sake of swiftness, all the mistakes that I had committed before I now committed again. But to my amazement it was all liked by the severe evaluators of my play, by Fedotov, Kommisarjevsky and Salogub. The only explanation of this was in my youth and the fire with which I played. This is an important quality which is lost in later years.

Having accidentally mentioned this, I must confess that all the rôles towards which I behave so seriously, criticising them now with the weight of my experience behind me, were filled with the same fire, which gave them life on the stage of itself. This is why I often hear my old admirers tell me that in those days, when we were not learned in our art, we played much better than we do now, when we know a little about it. How can one learn to keep that young fire in one's self? What a pity it is that it disappears, — but there is not a shadow of doubt that one cannot build the foundations of art on that fire alone. We have lost that fire because our technique is not yet perfected.

It must be that I lived by the virtue of that fire in the rôle of Megrio, and this was good and useful to me. That is why I remember that vaudeville sketch so kindly, a sketch that we repeated during many years. Listening to the sound of applause after the fall of the curtain I would say to myself, " So, after all, I can play a lover; so after all, I can play myself, and all the false operetta tempo and patter are allowable."

And again I would begin to believe in them and their roots would come to life within me.

To meet our deficits a gala ball and concert were given in one of the best halls of Moscow, with the help of all the best artists and actors of the city. For the first time in the history of the city, real artists decorated a hall. The large gypsy chorus, composed of the pupils and members of the Society, was especially successful. The soloists of the chorus were the two daughters of Kommisarjevsky, who had fine voices and a good manner of singing. They had come from Petersburg just to appear at the ball. This was the first public appearance of one of the greatest of all Russian actresses, Vera Kommisarjevskaya.

The concert more than paid for itself, and materially aided the Society and partly myself.

During Lent, Moscow was visited by the famous ducal players of Meiningen, headed by the stage director Kronek. Their performances showed Moscow for the first time productions that were historically true, with well-directed mob scenes, fine outer form and amazing discipline. I did not miss a single one of their performances, I came not only to look but to study as well.

It was said that the company did not include a single talented actor. This was untrue. There were Barnay, Teller, Link, and others. One may generally disagree with German pathos and the German manner of playing tragedies. I must confess that the Meiningen Players brought but little that was new into the old stagy methods of acting. But it is not right to maintain that all they did was only outward. When Kronek was told so, he exclaimed:

" I brought them Shakespeare, Schiller and Molière, and they are interested in the furniture. What kind of a taste have they, anyway? "

Kronek was right, for the spirit of Schiller, Shakespeare, and Molière lived in his players.

The Meiningen Players were able, by using purely stage-direction methods, without the help of extraordinary stage talents, to show much in the creative works of the great poets. I can never forget a scene from " The Maid of Orleans." A skinny, piteous, forlorn king sits on a tremendous throne; his thin legs hang in the air and do not reach the floor. Around the throne is the confused court, which tries with all its strength to uphold the semblance of kingly ritual. But in the moment of the loss of power the deep bows of etiquette seem out of place. Into this picture of the destruction of a king enter the English ambassadors, tall, stately, decisive, courageous and impudent. It is impossible to bear the scorn and the despising tone of the conquerors cold-bloodedly. When the unhappy king gives his demeaning order, which insults his own dignity, the courtier who receives the order tries to bow before he leaves the king's presence. But hardly having begun the bow, he stops in indecision, straightens up, and stands with lowered eyes. Then the tears burst from them and he runs in order not to lose control of himself before the entire court.

With him wept the spectators, and I wept also, for the ingenuity of the stage director created a tremendous mood by itself and went down to the soul of the play.

The same fine stage direction was seen in the other moments of the demeaning of the French king. The heavy atmosphere of the court artfully creates the moment of the appearance of Jeanne in it. The stage director thickened the atmosphere of the defeated court so that the spectator waits impatiently for the coming of the Maid, and he is so glad when she does come that he does not notice the cheap acting of the woman who uses the worst stage methods in her play, rolling her eyes and giving vent to vocal fireworks. The talent of the stage director hid the faults of the actress, but ——

The stage director can do a great deal, but he cannot do everything. The most important thing is in the hands of the actor, whom one must help, who must be guided in the proper direction. The Meiningen directors seemingly paid but little attention to helping their actors. The director was obliged to create without the help of the actor, and the actor without the help of the director. And therefore most attention was paid not to the acting but to the production. Yet the plans of the director were spiritually deep and wide. How could they be made to live without the great help of the actor? It was necessary to take much from the actors' balance cup and put it into the director's. The necessity to create for everybody created the despotism of the stage director.

It seemed to me that we amateurs together with our director were in the same predicament as Kronek and the Meiningen Players. We also wanted to give luxurious performances, to uncover great thoughts and emotions, and because we did not have ready actors, we were to put the whole power into the hands of the stage director. He had to create by himself, with the aid of the production, scenery, properties, interesting *mise en scène* and the stage imagination. This is why the despotism of the Meiningen stage directors seemed to me to be grounded in necessity. I sympathized with Kronek and tried to learn his methods of work. Here is what I found out from persons, who dealt with him and who were present at his rehearsals.

Outside of the theatre Kronek's relations even with the third-rate actors of his company were simple and friendly. He even seemed to flaunt this simplicity of conduct. But as soon as a rehearsal began and Kronek mounted his usual place, he would be reborn. He sat in complete silence and waited for the hands of the clock to reach the time allotted for the beginning of the rehearsal. Then he would ring a large bell and declare in a quiet voice, *"Anfangen."* Every-thing quieted down. The rehearsal would begin at once and continue until he rang the bell again. Then he would make his remarks in a dispassionate voice, ring the bell again, repeat the fatal *"Anfangen"* and the rehearsal would continue.

And now there was an unexpected stop and confusion on the stage. The actors whispered, the stage managers ran about. Something seemed to have happened. One of the leading actors was late, and it was necessary to leave his scene out. One of the stage managers tells this to Kronek and waits for his orders near the prompter's box. Everybody is quiet. Kronek tires them out with a long pause. This pause seems to be endless, threatening. Kronek pauses, decides, while everybody stands as if awaiting sentence. At last he pronounces:

"While we are in Moscow, the rôles of the actor who is late will be played by actor Y, and as far as X is concerned, I will let him lead the mob actors in the rear. *Anfangen!"*

And with the fateful sound of the bell, the rehearsal continued, with an understudy in the part of the actor who was late.

No matter how much I am ashamed to acknowledge it now, at that time, when I was not yet in full agreement with my actors, I liked Kronek's despotism, for I did not know to what a terrible end it might bring an actor.

At another time, Kronek, after a performance of Schiller's "Robbers," conducted a court martial. One of his assistants, who seemed to be a light-minded young man, was late in letting a group of extras out on the stage. After the performance Kronek called him over and began to reproach him in a soft, aged voice. But the assistant tried to justify himself laughingly.

"Herr Schulz," Kronek said to a stage hand who was passing at that time, "tell me, please, at what words in such and such a scene does a group of robbers come on the stage from the left?"

The stage hand declaimed a whole monologue with pathos, trying to show his acting abilities. Kronek patted him on the shoulder, and turning to his assistant, said to him almost severely:

"He is a simple stage hand. And you are a stage manager and my assistant. Shame on you. Pfui!"

The restraint and the cold-bloodedness of Kronek were to my taste and I wanted to imitate him. With time I also became a despotic stage director. Very soon the majority of Russian stage directors began to imitate me in my despotism as I imitated Kronek. There was a whole generation of despotic stage directors, who, alas, did not have the talents of Kronek or of the Duke of Meiningen. These directors of the new type became mere producers who made of the actor a stage property on the same level with stage furniture, a pawn that was moved about in their *mises en scène.*

Only with time, as I began to understand the wrongness of the principle of the director's despotism, I valued that good which the Meiningen Players brought us, that is, their director's methods for showing the spiritual contents of the drama. For this they deserve great thanks. My gratitude to them is unbounded and will always live in my soul.

In the life of our Society and especially in me the Meiningen Players created a new and important period.

Our losses were so great that we decided to close the Society. We appointed a liquidation meeting at which a report of the closing of the Society was written. While I was in the act of signing it, some one's hand stopped me. This was Pavel Ivanovich Blaraembergh, one of the members of our Society, who was respected by everybody, a famous composer, and also the editor of one of our best newspapers.

"What!" he exclaimed, "You are going to liquidate such a beautiful beginning which has already been able to show such a spirit of life. I won't allow it. Shorten your expenses, cut away all the dead-wood, but guard all that is in flower. This circle of amateurs must continue its existence in spite of all obstacles. You only need a few cents to do so, and I don't believe that it will ruin any of you rich men. Right after this liquidation meeting you will eat supper in a restaurant and you will leave there enough money to provide a month's support for the Society. Sacrifice four or five suppers and save this good beginning that might do so much to advance art. Give me a sheet of paper. I am not rich, but I will sign my name first. And tear up your report."

The list passed from hand to hand. It gave little, but that little was enough to begin a simple amateur circle on the very humblest of bases. Nevertheless, we went to supper right after and spent enough to support our Society for a month.

At the beginning of the season our Society of Art and Literature found a small apartment and furnished it in some way. Administrative duties were divided among the members and were fulfilled by them to the dot. There was not enough to pay the director, and therefore, willy-nilly, I was forced to take upon myself the work of Fedotov.

The further support of the big headquarters of the Society was beyond our means. We were forced to rent it to the Hunting Club which asked us to give one performance a week for their family evenings. We took on ourselves the tremendous task of producing a new play each week, as was the custom in all the other theatres of Moscow. But the professionals had practice and the technique of the trade for such work. We did not possess these, and therefore what we undertook was beyond our strength. Yet there was nothing else to do but accept the great hardship in order to maintain the material welfare of our Society.

First of all, we repeated the old plays.

During one of the rehearsals of Pissemsky's "Usurpers of the Law," Glikeria Fedotova, the ex-wife of Alexandr Fedotov, who had just left us, entered the room. Two years before she had warned me of the danger in founding the Society; now she sat down near the director's table, and said to me:

"Two years ago I warned you, but you did not listen to me. And I did not come to you. But now, when everybody has left you, I have come to work with you. Begin, little father. And may the Lord bless us." She crossed herself, and the rehearsal began.

We came to life. Fedotova had an altogether different method of work from her husband. The latter saw a picture, images, and drew them. She felt emotion and tried to recreate it. Fedotov and Fedotova seemed to complete each other.

Fedotova became the leader of the dramatic department of our circle. She looked over and perfected the productions that we prepared. As soon as we saved a little money, we invited old practiced actors of the Imperial Little Theatre to help Fedotova. With them we produced many plays for our scheduled performances in the Hunting Club.

What did these new directors give us? While Fedotov was an artist of *mise-en-scène* and of the whole production in general, and Fedotova recreated emotion, the new directors drew the image, and not so much from its inner as its outer side. Besides, because of the arrangements with the Hunting Club, which forced us to give a new performance each week, the new directors showed us the trade side of hurried work, and stage methods of acting in a stencil worked out once and forever. With the help of these methods, we worked out a great deal of specific stage experience, the habit of the stage, resourcefulness, and confidence in our action, and thanks to practice, our voices became stronger, and the habit of talking loudly and being confident on the stage appeared in us. We received the right to go out and remain on the stage; the spectator believed that we were rightfully on the boards, and not there by accident; that we had the right to speak and that the spectators must listen to us. This distinguished us from amateurs who come out on the stage and seem to doubt if they have business on it. And the spectator, looking at such amateurs, is not sure that he must listen to them. Of course in places, despite the will of the amateur, he is suddenly fired, and the spectator with him. But the artistic fire dies out at once, and the helpless actor stands on the stage like an accidental guest, while the spectator ceases to believe in him. In a word, our practice made us scenic on the boards of the stage.

At that time we considered this success, not knowing that there is an altogether different scenic quality, founded not on the outward practice of a craftsman but on the inner working out of the creative spirit of the actor. I don't know whether we could, with the help of Fedotov and Fedotova, produce the enormous quantity of plays for the weekly performances of the Hunting Club. I doubt if either of these talented directors would have agreed to do such work, and besides, their demands were too hard for us. We were not enough prepared to understand and evaluate the substance and subtlety of the art of Alexandr Fedotov. The problems given by Glikeria Fedotova, who endeavored to guide our creative emotions, were even more complex. Her art was to be learned systematically and in easy stages.

The new directors fitted us exactly. They simply taught us to act the play, and we liked it, for it gave us the illusion of great and productive work.

I will keep quiet about our sad trade, that is, about the weekly club performances. They did not create taste in me nor did they move me forward as an actor. Just the opposite; they seriously interfered with my artistic development. All that was bad in the commercial theatre was repeated by us perhaps in a larger degree. Now I call all of our exercises of that time the factory of stencils. These performances brought lots of unnecessary rubbish that was irrelevant in the actor's development. There are decent stencils, — for instance, a properly created part, with time and careless treatment of its inner soul, becomes an outward and empty stencil, but in it there is fixed what was once well lived.   Although I cannot welcome such a stencil, still I must distinguish it from bad stencils.   A bad stencil is the same thing not only in actors but in all men.

What does a man do when he is faced with the necessity of performing an impossibility?   He strains with impotence.   Now he flexes the muscles of his legs and his whole body, now he presses his teeth together, now hunches his shoulders upward, or clenches his fists, now without any need contracts his throat and stops breathing; in a word, by any means open to him, he tries to leave his uncomfortable position and to create for himself the illusion that he is doing the impossible thing that is required of him.

Exactly the same thing happens to the actor.   He is forced to weep when he does not want to weep, to laugh when he is sad, to suffer when he is happy, to feel and to recreate the feelings that he has not in his own soul.   Hence all kinds of compromises to lead him out of the quicksands.   But the actor does not leave the quicksands and everything ends only with forced strain and false conventionalities of play with which the actor wants to deceive himself and the public, imagining that he is doing what he is told to do by the creative laws of artistic nature.   This bad stencil was being worked out in me at that time in a tremendous quantity.   The harm done by these commercial performances is self-evident and does not need explanation.

Here I want to stress one fact which had a significance for us and for Russian art.   At that time there came to Moscow the daughter of Kommisarjevsky, Vera Kommisarjevskaya, who in time became a famous actress whom America knows from her appearance in New York.   After a family catastrophe Vera returned to her father, who at that time still conducted his opera class in our Society, limited to a minimum quantity of pupils.   He lived in an apartment in the Society, and his daughter lived with him.   She was given a corner furnished with stage properties and furniture.   Hiding from all, she, to the accompaniment of her guitar, hummed sad gypsy songs of lost love, treason and the sufferings of a woman's heart.

We asked her for help in one of the critical moments of our theatrical life. We asked her to take the place of an actress who had fallen ill. I played with her a rather elegant one-acter called " Burning Letters." This was the first and very successful début of the future celebrity.

In the very midst of this season there was a disaster. The headquarters of the Hunting Club burned down. Our performances stopped, while we waited for the completion of the new and even more luxurious apartments of the Club. In this manner we remained without lucrative work and were forced to support ourselves by our own performances.

CHAPTER XX

WE were lucky in getting Lev Tolstoy's play, " The Fruits of Knowledge." It was written in jest for a domestic performance and was produced in Yasnaya Polyana. Everybody was certain that permission to produce the play publicly could never be secured. But we received a permission from the censor to give a private performance unadvertised. The name of Tolstoy was so popular that his new play easily bore up under this hardship.

The direction of " The Fruits of Knowledge " was put into my hands and was my first directing experience in the realm of the drama. The play has great hardships for the stage director because of the many *dramatis personæ* in it and the complexity of its *mise en scène*. One needs great experience to make each of the quickly changing groupings interesting and typical. I approached my work simply. It was necessary to produce a performance, and I produced it as best I could. I showed what my imagination saw to the actors and they imitated me. Where I was able to feel things rightly the play came to life. Where there was only outward ingenuity the play remained a dead thing. The only good quality of my work at that time was the fact that I tried to be sincere. I sought the truth, and falsehood, especially theatrical and commercial falsehood, became for me, after all I had lived through, unbearable. I began to hate the theatre in the theatre. More than all I wanted living, truthful, real life, not commonplace life, but artistic life. Perhaps at that time I could not make out the difference between artistic and commonplace life on the stage. From the director's table in the auditorium one sees falsehood clearly and sharply, and I saw it at once. This helped me to give a true, real and scenically interesting outward *mise-en-scène* which pushed me on to the truth. The truth awoke emotion, and emotion excited the living over of the rôle. Maybe this road from the outward to the inward is not the most correct but it is possible and allowable. Besides in this performance chance also helped me, for the fact was that the rôles were very well distributed among the interpreters. The very actors seemed to be created for the parts they played and were one with them. In the play one sees aristocrats, servants and peasants. The aristocrats were played by real society men, which was very rare in the theatre at that time. Others were vulgar enough to play the servants, and among the peasants there was Vladimir Lopatin, the brother of the famous Russian philosopher, Lev Lopatin, that very amateur who had captured Tolstoy by his performance of the part of a peasant at the domestic spectacle in Tolstoy's house. Feeling a good actor who understood the soul of a Russian peasant, Tolstoy wrote him a large part instead of his old little one.

In this performance there were very successful interpretations by many of the present actors of the Moscow Art Theatre and other persons, who later became well known in theatrical life; Samarova, Lilina, Luzhsky, Artem, and Sanin, who is at present a well-known stage director of the opera in Paris, London, and Madrid.

This performance taught me the administrative side of the director's work. It is not easy to rule a group of actors at the moment when they are under strain and excitement. The organism of an actor is capricious and whimsical. One must know how to handle an actor during a rehearsal. One must have a director's authority, which at that time I still did not possess. I conquered all with my fanatical love of my work, my ability to work, and the strictness of the demands I made on myself first. The first person I fined was myself, and this was done with such belief that it did not seem to be a pose. Lateness at rehearsals, a badly learned part, discussions during work, absence from the rehearsal hall without permission were punished by me with special cruelty. Garishness of attire, especially as far as the women were concerned, was banned from the rehearsals. It was not needed for work. The tremendous hats of the actresses were not allowed at all. All the women were to come without hats. Flirting was forbidden.

"As much as you can of serious love. It uplifts you. Shoot yourself for the sake of women, drown yourselves, die, but one does not need the atmosphere of flirtation which drags you downward." This was my Puritan thought at that time.

Our poverty did not allow us even to dream of luxurious scenery. And yet good scenery is the salvation of amateurs. How many actors' sins are covered by the artist, his line and color. How easily he gives an artistic shading to the whole performance. It is not in vain that so many talentless actors and directors forcibly hide themselves behind the scenery, costumes, color spots on the stage, impressionism, cubism, futurism, and all the *isms* that frighten the inexperienced spectator and the naïve bourgeois. Just the opposite, with bad scenery that does not deserve a second look, the actor and the director can be seen at their best or their worst. A play must be well played and directed to show what is valuable and makes the substance of the play and to interpret this inner substance by means of typical images, actions and situations. And this was useful for the beginning actors as well as for me, a director who was also just beginning. We tried honestly to interpret what was so beautifully written by the author. Of course we could not enter very deeply into the play. Perhaps we mostly glided along the surface of the plot and local color but we justified that direction of the play. And this was all that could be demanded of us at that time.

Of course even here there were many sins, for it is hardest of all to be simple and sincere on the stage and it is easiest to exaggerate. Now and then we fell back to the ordinary road of conventionalities and stencils, but it was good that we acknowledged it, and said sincerely that we could not do any better, without trying to justify ourselves with loud words and theories. At that time we lived over without choosing all that we could find and feel in the play, in the rôle, the *mise en scène,* in the costume and the scenery, in ourselves, in our partners, in properties, in accidents that came of themselves. We did not have an exact internal plan of creation. Our guide was young, hot, sympathetic intuition. Where there was not enough intuition the play was empty and dead. We were powerless to do anything with our emotion. We did not have even the common technique of commercial actors for it, which copies experience coarsely and primitively and ends in spasms and physical strain which force the actor to redden, strain and become hoarse. Those places which we could not feel of themselves, we simply said in tempo, as if wishing to pass them by as quickly as we could. I had torn many passions to tatters at amateur rehearsals and now I was willing to do anything but that. These were the foundation and the road of my first stage directing work.

The performance was extraordinarily successful. The play ran till late spring, and helped us out of our financial difficulties.

I consider the success of this production purely accidental. Its usefulness lay in the fact that I had found not the highway but a side-path to the soul of the artist, the road from the outer to the inner, from the body to the soul, from the embodiment to the inner creation, from the form to the substance. I learned by Fedotov's example to simply make the *mise en scène* in which the inner seed of the play was hidden. I showed the actors what to do, because it was necessary to show them in order to make the production, because it was impossible not to show them, because I did not know how to do the director's work otherwise. There was success, because I had felt the *mise en scène.* What was new in this production was that nothing that was bad in the old was admitted.

FIRST EXPERIENCE AS A DIRECTOR

One could say about the Hunting Club that the fire did a great deal to make it look better. And the Society of Art and Literature found a decenter headquarters. Performances were still given once each week after several rehearsals, and so far as our souls were concerned, we prepared one play a year under my directorship and without any hurry. These productions that displayed our artistic work and not our mere craftsmanship we housed in another place and the money we made through them we used for new productions and artistic researches.

At the beginning of the season the Hunting Club rented and remodeled the house where the Moscow City Council had met. With the opening of this house we renewed our scheduled performances for the Club.

For our next yearly artistic production we chose my dramatization of Dostoyevsky's story " The Village of Stepanchikovo and its Inhabitants," the types of which seemed to be especially created for the stage. And as Dostoyevsky's widow told me, Dostoyevsky had begun writing the thing as a play, but because its production on the stage would have been accompanied with a great deal of trouble on account of the censorship, especially for him who was always persecuted by the police, and because he was in terrible need of funds, he was forced to reshape his play into a story and sell it. My dramatization of the story was forbidden by the censorship. Then, acting on the advice of experienced men, I changed the names of the *dramatis personæ,* as well as the name of the author himself. That is, I called Foma Opiskin — Foma Oplevkin, Obnoskov — Otrepiev, Mizinchikov — Palchikov; and myself — the author of the play. In this shape I sent the play to the censor. Its production was permitted almost without any changes in the text, except that the words *God, Holy Mother,* and *Christ* were stricken out wherever they appeared. Of course the name of the author was absent from the posters we printed, but everybody knew who he was.

" The Village of Stepanchikovo " is radically different from anything else that Dostoyevsky has written. There is no seeking for God in it, but nevertheless the cruel genius of the author is evident in every stroke of his pen. It is a poisonous pamphlet directed at the literary passers-by of the time. On the stage it is a torturing tragedy with a comedy denouement which is not exactly satisfactory. Let me sum up its contents.

Colonel Rostanov, the uncle of the story-teller, and young Nastya, the governess of his children, are in love with each other. In order to retain Nastya near him, the colonel wants to marry her to his nephew, whom he calls for this purpose to the village. In the household of Rostanov, like a spider in his web, there sits this Foma Opiskin, a man pretending to be a writer, but in reality an ignoramus who is full of learned words and verbose expressions. The half-crazy mother of Rostanov and her group of companions consider Foma almost a saint. With the help of this saintlihood, his false pretensions to learning, and the synod of crazy women, Foma exploits Rostanov, terrorizes him and holds him in the hollow of his hand. But the extraordinary kindness of Rostanov, his trustfulness, his childish goodness of heart, his saintly naïveté, his sacrificing spirit and his delicacy force the spectator to lovable laughter, to amazement and indignation, to love and admiration and at last to a loss of patience and of hope. For material purposes Foma tries to arrange a marriage between Rostanov and a crazy old woman who is rich. Happily this woman is abducted by Obnoskin, whom Rostanov has supported in his house. And here Foma surprises Rostanov and Nastya kissing in the garden. The climax is at hand. Foma declares that it is his name-day, and the whole family comes together, carrying flowers and presents to the litterateur. Foma delivers a foolish speech in which he denounces the debauchery of Rostanov, whom he is forced to leave, and the dust of whose hospitality he shakes from his heels. He denounces and dishonors Nastya, taking pleasure in crossing every *t* and dotting every *i* in his speech. Rostanov can bear all but the insult to the woman he loves. He changes from lamb to lion and throws Foma out of the house while a storm rages outside. But Rostanov's anger does not last long. He himself rushes to save Foma, who, in order to regain the love of his uncle and his former influence in the house, blesses the marriage of Rostanov and Nastya. The end of the play sees a general bowing and scraping to Foma.

In the repertoire of an actor, among the large number of parts played by him, there are some that seem to have been creating themselves in his inner consciousness for a long time. One only has to touch the rôle and it comes to life without any of the tortures of creation, without any quest or technical work. Life itself has created that rôle in its own good time, life and nature. Organically living the rôle that has been created within you, you even cease to understand the usual question put to the actor, " How do you interpret Dostoyevsky, his play and the part? "

" In no way," I could have answered conscientiously. "The part, the play, and Dostoyevsky are what they are. They cannot be otherwise. Is it possible to analyze and divide such a part into the elements that compose it? No, this would be just as hard as analyzing your own soul."

I believed everything in this rôle, and in this I had the same point of view as Rostanov himself. I was told that he is naïve, that he is not very clever, that he makes a great ado about nothing, but I did not agree. In my mind all that excites him is very important from the viewpoint of human nobility. I was told that he is as innocent as the soul of a virgin. I did not see that. Just the opposite; when I played the part, I was ashamed of myself that I, an old man, had fallen in love with a young girl. Were we equally matched? It was said that Foma is a scoundrel. But if he really cares so much for me that he spends nights in prayers for my soul, that he teaches me for my own good, then he seems to me to be self-sacrificing. And can I get along without Foma? Will I be able to handle all these old women that have made an asylum of my home? No, they would have finished me. They say that when Nastya is insulted the lion awakes in Rostanov. But I look at it much more simply. He did what any man in love would have done. Entering into the life of the play, I see no other way for Rostanov than the way he chose himself. Within the limits of the play I live the life of Rostanov, I think his thoughts, I cease to be myself. I become another, a man like Rostanov. Do you understand this phrase that is magic for the actor, *to become another?*

Gogol has said the following, " Anybody can imitate an image, but only a true talent can become an image." If that was true, then I had talent, for in this rôle (although it was almost the only one) I had become Rostanov, while in my other rôles I merely copied and imitated the necessary images and sometimes my own image.

What a happiness it is to feel even once in a lifetime what a true actor must feel and do on the stage! Imagine that you have been granted a glance at paradise, that you have come to know that it really exists, that you have felt the bliss that fills the souls of those who live there. Can it be that after that you will not want to try to get there by means of faith and hope? To know the paradise of art! To glance into it and to feel its bliss! Can one make peace with anything else on the stage after an experience like that?

I lived through a happy moment in my artistic life. I had received a true gift from Apollo. Were there no technical means for a conscious entry into the paradise of art? When technique reaches the possibility of realizing this hope, our stage craftsmanship will become a true art. But where and how is one to seek those roads into the secret sources of inspiration? This is the question that must serve as the fundamental life problem of every true actor.

I don't know how I played the part, and I will not undertake to praise or criticize myself. I was happy with true artistic joy, and I was not at all hurt by the fact that the performance was not successful financially. Only a few individuals valued Dostoyevsky on the stage and our work in putting him there.

I am happy that among those who appreciated our work was the famous writer and critic Grigorovich, a comrade of Dostoyevsky's and Turgenev's, who was very much like the latter in figure and face. After the performance Grigorovich almost ran in on us in his ecstasy.

"After 'The Inspector General,'" he cried, "the stage has not seen such bright, colorful images."

It was seen that the genius of Dostoyevsky had again captured him and had carried him back into his memories, which he shared with us on the spot. He spoke of the enmity between Dostoyevsky and Turgenev, of how Dostoyevsky hated Turgenev, of the terrible moments of ecstasy in Dostoyevsky's life that opened the boiling hell that raged in his soul. But these are memories of such an intimate nature, and they were told us in such full confidence, that I do not consider that I have the right to make them public if Grigorovich himself did not think it necessary to do so.

Grigorovich, like Turgenev, was a nobleman in the full sense of the word, in his outer appearance, in his manners, in his tastes, in his habits. Like Turgenev, he loved to paint peasants and he knew them well. It is not in vain that Tolstoy said that Grigorovich was the first literary man to give a true picture of the Russian peasant.

We appeared in "The Tutor," a comedy by Dyachenko. How shall I explain the choice of such a worthless play? Let me confess that at the time I was very much attracted by the French theatre, and especially by the Comedie Française, and I always dreamed of playing a part in French. But how was I to do it, and where? The rôle of the tutor was written half in Russian and half in French. Even before the choice of this play I had to a certain degree made my own a French accent in Russian, and my French pronunciation was more or less correct. Both these things somehow gave a certain character to the image. This warmed me even at the first rehearsal. Besides,

I had an heirloom for this rôle from the time when I had been playing in the operettas *à la* Judic and in a complete cycle of rôles of the same character. French gestures, the manner of bearing myself, the methods typical of Frenchmen in general were still alive in my muscular, aural, and optical memory and only waited for application. In the old days, playing in Russian, we had reached the illusion of French speech and French manner. It was so much easier to reach the same illusion in French, which itself pushed you on to the proper rhythm, the proper accentuation and all the manners and tricks which are usually connected with them. Because I had gone often to the French theatres in Paris, I still retained all the intonations of the speech of the best actors in the Comedie Française. Besides, I could always take advantage of the wonderful living model of the French correspondent in our factory office, with whom I at once established the friendliest of relations. In this manner there was no lack of material for the rôle.

I had never felt so free, joyful and easy in any other rôle; without thinking of the image I was playing the image itself, for it had come to me instinctively from correct self-consciousness on the stage. Perhaps the outward image was at first created instinctively and innerly. Who knows, but that the French blood of my actress grandmother showed in me this time? It is possible that in this part I had found its characteristics and proceeded forward from them; it is probable that I enjoyed a great success in the part and that the play was very successful too. I loved the part, the performances gave me pleasure; I had again, for the time being, left the quicksands and was on the true road.

CHAPTER XXI

LEV TOLSTOY

IN 18— our amateur circle, which was later recreated into the Moscow Art Theatre, gave several performances in Tula. The rehearsals and all the other preparations for the performances were held in the hospitable home of N. V. Davidov, who was a close friend of Tolstoy. The life of the entire household was forced to run in the channels made necessary by the needs of our company. Between rehearsals there were noisy dinners, accompanied by practical joking. Even the host himself, who was far from young, became a veritable schoolboy.

During one of these dinners, at the very height of our merry-making, the figure of a man in a peasant's coat appeared in the vestibule. Soon there entered an old man with a long beard, dressed in a gray blouse, with a belt around his waist, in felt boots. He was met with happy acclamation. At first I did not guess that it was Lev Tolstoy. Not a single photograph and not even any of his portraits can give the impression made by his living face and figure. Can a photograph show the eyes of Tolstoy, which pierced the soul and seemed to judge it on the spot? They were the eyes of a man wise in the wisdom of the heart, now sharp and pricking, now soft, sunny, warming the soul. When Tolstoy looked at a man he grew motionless and concentrated. Then he entered into the soul and seemed to suck all its substance out of it, good and evil. At such moments his eyes hid behind his heavy eyelids like the sun behind clouds. At other moments he would jest like a child, burst out in sympathetic laughter, and his piercing eyes would become joyful and humorous, coming out from behind his heavy eyelids and shining like the sun after storm. Let any one express an interesting thought, and Tolstoy would be the first to appreciate it. He would become youthfully expansive and movable, and in his eyes there would burn the fire of the artist's genius.

At the moment when I first met him, he was tender, soft, calm, kind, and filled with aged courtesy. The children leaped from their places and surrounded him in a tight ring. He knew each by name and nickname, and asked each questions about their intimate domestic life that I could not understand.

We, the guests, were led up to him, in turn, and he held the hand of each one, trying us with the sharp glance of his eyes. I felt that I had been pierced by a bullet.

While Tolstoy lived we Russians would say, "How happy we are to live while he lives!" And when life or spiritual experiences became unbearable, and all men seemed to be beasts, we consoled ourselves with the thought, "There, in Yasnaya Polyana, lives Lev Tolstoy," and the love of life would come back to us.

The unexpected meeting with the great old man brought me into an almost petrified state. I was only half aware of what was taking place in myself and around me.

Lev Nikolaevich was placed at the table in a chair exactly opposite mine.

I must have appeared very funny and very strange, for he looked at me many times with curiosity in his eyes.

But now he bent toward me and asked me something. I could not concentrate enough to understand him. There was laughter around me. I became even more confused.

Tolstoy wanted to know what play we were to give in Tula, and I could not for the world remember its name. Somebody helped me out.

Although it was the most popular play by Ostrovsky, which any educated Russian knows, Lev Nikolaevich forgot the contents of the classic, and made no ado about saying so, simply, publicly and without any shame. Only he could have acknowledged so simply and publicly something that most of us would have hidden so as not to seem ignorant. He had a right to forget what any simple mortal is obliged to know.

"Remind me of its contents," he said. All grew still in the expectation of my story, and I, like a schoolboy that had failed at an examination, could not find a single word to begin my story. All my efforts were in vain and only aroused the laughter of the others at the table. My neighbor was not any braver than myself. His story also aroused laughter. Davidov saved us by telling Tolstoy in brief of the contents of the play.

Confused by my failure, I was quiet, looking guiltily at Lev Nikolaevich.

The servant brought in a roast.

"Lev Nikolaevich, don't you want a little piece of meat?" The adults and the children began to pester the vegetarian.

"Why not?" Lev Nikolaevich jested.

And large pieces of meat began to fly from all parts of the table into his plate. To the laughter of all, the famous vegetarian cut himself a small piece of meat, began to chew it, swallowed it with hardship, and put down his fork and knife.

"I can't! I can't eat a corpse! It is poison! Leave meat alone. and only then will you understand what is health, good spiritual condition and a clear head!" Having mounted his hobby, Lev Nikolaevich began to develop his well-known theory of vegetarianism.

Tolstoy was able to speak on the most boring of themes so that it became interesting. This ability was clearly shown when after dinner, in the semi-gloom of the study, over a cup of coffee, he retailed to us for more than an hour his conversation with some Arian. The Arians are an ancient Christian sect that base everything on symbols.

An apple tree against a red sky means a certain event in their lives and augurs something good or evil. A dark pine against a moonlit sky means something altogether different; the flight of a bird across a cloudless sky or the appearance of a storm cloud — all have their special meanings. One must wonder at the memory of Tolstoy, who for more than an hour recounted all the symbols of the sect and forced us by some innate power to listen to him with tremendous interest.

Then we began talking about the theatre, having decided to boast before Lev Nikolaevich of the fact that we were the first in Moscow to play "The Fruits of Knowledge," which he had written for a domestic performance, and the public performance of which was forbidden by the censorship.

"Make an old man happy; free 'The Power of Darkness' from censorship and play it."

"And you will let us play it?" we cried in chorus.

"I never forbid any one to play my plays," he answered.

Without having killed our bear, we began to divide his skin, that is, without having removed the censorship, we began to divide the rôles of the play among us. We were already deciding who would direct the play and how, — we had asked Lev Nikolaevich to come to the rehearsals, — we hurried to take advantage of his presence to decide which of the variants of the fourth act we were to play, and how to unite the variants so as not to interfere with the culminating growth of action and mood in the act. We attacked Lev Nikolaevich with all our young energy. One would think that we were considering an affair that could not wait and that the rehearsals of the play were beginning to-morrow.

Soon we found it easy to talk to Tolstoy, for he easily surrendered himself to our young enthusiasm. His eyes, with that deep inward gaze or search into the soul of the man he was looking at, that had been hiding behind his heavy lids, were shining now like the sun in the cloudless sky; they were like the eyes of a young man.

[220]

"Yes," Lev Nikolaevich suddenly became alive with a newly born thought, "write out a plan of how to connect the parts and give it to me, and then I will work over the play according to your instructions."

The young man to whom these words were addressed became so confused that he could not answer and hid behind another man. Lev Nikolaevich understood our confusion and began to encourage us, saying that in his offer there was nothing that could not be fulfilled by us. Just the opposite; we would be doing him a favor, because he was not a man of the theatre, and we were specialists. But even Tolstoy could not persuade us of that.

Some years passed and I had not seen Tolstoy again.

I was passing the autumn in Biarritz, where at that time lived the well-known publisher of " Novoye Vremya," and the creator of the theatre of the Literary Art Society, the publicist and critic, Alexey Suvorin. Once he came to me on business that could not wait. He had decided to produce in his theatre " The Power of Darkness " and he wanted to use all his influence in order to have the censorship ban removed from it. He had corresponded with Tolstoy, who wrote him among other things that he should see me and take the synopsis of the fourth act in which the two variants of the act were united, from me. No matter how much I told Suvorin that I had no synopsis, he insisted on having it. It was hard to argue with him, for I was a young man and he was many years older than I. I sat a few days and nights over the work, and at last carried it to Suvorin. The censorship was lifted from " The Power of Darkness," and it was produced by Suvorin and in all of Russia. Of course it was played as Tolstoy had written it, and my scenario was not used. It was said that Tolstoy had seen many performances of the play, that he liked some things in it and disliked others.

Some more time passed. Suddenly I received a note from one of Tolstoy's friends, which informed me that Tolstoy wanted to see me.

I went at once and Tolstoy received me in one of the rooms of his Moscow house. He was not satisfied with the performances and the very play itself.

"Remind me how you wanted to change the fourth act. I will change it, and you will play it," Tolstoy said this so simply that I found it just as simple to remember and explain my plan, which had long slipped from my memory.

We spoke a very long time, without knowing that his wife, Sofia Andreievna and the family were in the next room.

Put yourself in the place of Sofia Andreievna for a minute. She was always very jealous of her husband. And now there came a young man that took the masterpiece of her husband and began teaching its talented creator how it was to be written. This was the height of impudence if one did not know what had taken place before.

Sofia Andreievna could not bear it. She ran into the room and attacked me. I confess that I got a fine dressing down. I would have gotten even a finer one if Maria Lvovna, the daughter, had not come in and quieted her mother. During the whole scene Lev Nikolaevich sat without moving, calmly playing with his beard. He did not utter a single word to defend me.

And when his wife left us, and I remained completely nonplussed, he smiled courteously and said:

"Don't pay any attention to it. She is very nervous and in a bad mood."

Then, turning back to our broken conversation, he continued:

"And so, where did we stop?"

I remember another accidental meeting with Tolstoy in one of the alleys near his house. This was at the time when he was writing his famous diatribe against war and against the military class. I was walking with a friend who knew Tolstoy well. We met him. I was timid because his face was very severe, and his eyes were hidden behind his lids. His voice was also different. It had become hard. He was nervous and irascible. I walked behind him courteously, afraid to excite him. But I was listening very carefully to his talk. He was talking of what he later wrote in his essay. With unusual temperment and heat he expressed his accusation of all legalized murder. He attacked military men and their customs, and all the more persuasively because in his time he had gone through more than one campaign. He did not base his words on theory but on his own experience. His hanging eyebrows, his burning eyes in which the tears were ready to appear at any moment, the severe and at the same time excited and suffering voice I will always remember.

Suddenly from behind a corner there grew before us two tremendous guardsmen in stately, long military coats, with shining helmets and swords loudly ringing against the stones under their feet. Handsome, young, stately, tall, with courageous faces, with a manly, correct and schooled manner of walk — they were wonderful.

Tolstoy seemed to become stone, stopped in the middle of a word, his mouth half-opened, his hands caught in the midst of the gesture, and his eyes drinking in the two soldiers. I stood where I could clearly see the expression of his face and his eyes. Like the dawn that gradually pierces the darkness after deep night and before the rising of the sun, so the face and the eyes of Tolstoy gradually began to shine with the inner light of an artist, and, as if they were lit by the rising sun, began to gleam with enthusiasm and youth.

" A-ha! " he whispered so that he could be heard in the whole alley. " Good! What fine fellows! " and with great enthusiasm he began to explain the meaning of military bearing. In that moment one could easily recognize in him an old and experienced military man.

Much time passed. Once in going through the contents of my desk I found an unopened letter from Tolstoy. I was frightened. He wrote me several pages in his own hand about the epic of the Dukhobors, and asked me to help in collecting money for their emigration from Russia.

How the letter could have been lost for years in my desk I do not understand even now.

I wanted to explain this in person to Tolstoy and to justify my silence. My friend Sulerjitsky, who was very close to Tolstoy's family, offered me to take advantage of the fact that Tolstoy had an appointment with a dramatist which Sulerjitsky had arranged. He hoped that before or after this appointment he could lead me in to see Tolstoy. My appointment did not materialize, for the dramatist used up all of Tolstoy's free time. I was not present at their appointment, but I was told what had happened in the room at the time I waited outside.

" First of all," said Sulerjitsky, " imagine his figure, the thin, tired, shaven writer with long hair combed in the style of the eighteen thirties, with a large soft collar, without a tie, sitting as if on needles and speaking a whole hour in a strange language with newly invented words of how he seeks and creates a new art. A fountain of foreign words, quotations from all kinds of new authors, philosophy, excerpts from poems in the new style, which illustrated the newly invented bases of poetry and art. All this was said for the sake of showing the plans of a new monthly magazine which he was preparing to issue and where he invited Tolstoy to publish some of his work.

" For more than an hour Lev Nikolaevich listened attentively and patiently to the creator of the new art, walking up and down the room. At times he stopped and pierced the man with his sharp gaze. Then he would turn away as if he was disappointed, and putting his hands in his belt paced up and down the room, listening attentively.

" At last the writer grew quiet.

" ' I have said everything,' he completed his hour-long speech.

" Tolstoy still continued to pace up and down the room and think, while the writer dried his perspiration and fanned himself with his handkerchief. There was a long silence. At last Tolstoy stopped before him, sent his piercing gaze into the soul of the man, and looked for a long time, his face serious and severe.

" ' Indefinite!' he said, stressing the letter *e,* as if trying to say ' Are you trying to fool me?'

" Having said this, Tolstoy went to the door, opened it, made a step over the threshold, and turned to the writer again.

" ' I always thought that a writer writes when he has something to say, when something is ripe in his mind and he is ready to transfer it to paper. But why I must write for a magazine only in March or October — that I could never understand.' After these words Tolstoy went out."

CHAPTER XXII

THE special production for this season was " Uriel Acosta." Let me summarize the contents of the play. Acosta, a Jewish philosopher, has written a book which is blasphemous from the viewpoint of the fanatical rabbis. During a festival in the garden of the rich Manasseh, whose daughter is in love with Acosta, the rabbis appear and curse the heretic. From this moment Acosta becomes outlawed and accursed. In order to cleanse himself he must publicly deny his ideas and beliefs. His teacher, his bride, his mother and his brother beg him to repent. After a superhuman inner struggle between the philosopher and the lover, the lover is victorious in Acosta. The philosopher goes to deny his own ideas of religion in the synagogue for the sake of his love. But during the denial the ideas conquer love again. Acosta publicly repeats his heresy and a mob of fanatical Jews tries to kill him. Acosta sees his beloved for the last time at her wedding to a rich man. But true to her love she has already taken poison and dies in the arms of the heretic. Acosta also deprives himself of life. Love celebrates its victory with two deaths.

In my interpretation of Acosta, it was the philosopher who conquered the lover. All those places in the rôle that demanded persuasion, hardness, courage found in me the spiritual material for their recreation. But in the love scenes I fell as usual into flabbiness, effeminateness and sentimentality, that is, into all the surrogates of real feeling. Think of it; I was large, I had a strong figure, I had a big deep voice — and all of a sudden I used the methods of a weak opera tenor of decided effeminateness. Could one with such gifts as mine look with languishing eyes into the distance, sentimentally and tenderly admire his beloved, weep (what can be worse than a weeping man on the stage) and wipe my tears with a sour face, or with artificial passion squeeze and break the hands of my beloved, displaying animal passion? It is not in such methods that true lyricism, tenderness, love and passion lie hidden. All these are masculine feelings that are to be interpreted in a masculine manner. The effeminate methods of the tenor were not for me, as they are for no one.

The difference between all my physical qualities and the effeminate method of scenic play created an unpleasant dissonance. Ladies and girls, why did you applaud me at that time? Why do you still applaud saccharine tenors? What would you say if an effeminate, sweet and sentimental lover came to you in life, put his hand on the place where his heart is supposed to be, rolled his eyes languishingly, placed his left foot behind him, resting it against the heel of his right shoe, and said with a sugary smile:

"I am yours. Be mine all your life."

Tell me truthfully, would you decide to marry such a creature? Don't do such a foolish thing. You will perish with a husband like that. He cannot support you. You will torture yourself all your life with him. Then why do you give ovations to men like him on the stage? Cry to them, "Be a man. Don't make love to us in that way!"

If you had cried so to me at that time, I would have understood that there is a masculine lyricism, a masculine tenderness and dreaminess, masculine love, and that sentimentalism is only a weak surrogate of real feeling. I would have felt that the most tenor-like tenor, the tenderest ingenue lyricist must first of all take care that his love emotion be strong and masculine. The more lyrical and tender love is, the clearer and stronger must be the color that characterizes that love. Sentimentality that is as yielding as a custard pie in a healthy, strong and beautiful girl, because of its contrast with her nature, creates a dissonance. And the younger the actor or actress is, and the older and more yielding their sentimentalism, the more horrible is it to behold it.

And I, fool that I was, imagined that only these over-sweet methods that had become legitimate in the theatre could interpret lyricism on the stage.

Therefore it is not surprising that the love scenes of the rôle were lost in my interpretation. But luckily for me, there were very few of them in the play. The strong places of the rôle, in which the strong beliefs of the philosopher showed themselves, were successful, and if it had not been for the traces of opera technique which remained in me to a considerable degree from the old days, the part would have been played to my complete satisfaction.

There was still another great fault, which I did not want to acknowledge to myself. I was out of tune with the text. Part of this fault must be blamed on my naturally defective memory. This even forces me to watch myself in the moments of complete spiritual revelation and when I am completely in the grasp of my intuition and emotion. In those moments my memory seems to throw out its buffers, without giving me the opportunity to touch that high point where the region of the superconscious begins. My memory, which distrusts itself, is almost completely devoid of mechanical action, and forces me to watch myself continually so that I may not break the continuity of the text. Otherwise there would be trouble. There would be a pause, a white blot on the sheet where the words of the part are written, complete helplessness and panic. This great fault takes away from me at least twenty-five per cent of my temperament in climacteric moments. My faulty oral memory is stressed by the fact that in calm scenes and pauses, or during rehearsals, when I speak my own words without having learned the text, I can freely reveal myself at full and show all that is in my soul. Besides this bad fault a prejudice also lived in me at that time. I said to myself:

" The gist of the matter is not in the text. The text will come of itself, when I feel the rôle."

True, this sometimes happens. But at times it is altogether different. While the text is weak, the rôle is not felt. The dropping of words from the text, the unclear interpretation of thought, the crumpling of sentences and words, the quietness of voice and unclear pronunciation interfered not only with my acting, but with the public hearing and understanding me.

Under the influence of the Meiningen Players we put more hope than necessary on the outward side of the production, especially on the costumes, the historical truthfulness to the epoch of the play, and most of all on the mob scenes, which at that time were a great novelty in the theatre and brought success and created a sensation for the production and the Society. With the despotism that was part of me at that time, I took nothing into account, and took all into my directing hands, ordering the actors about as if they were mannequins, with the exception, however, of the more talented among them, like V. V. Luzhsky and G. S. Burdzhalov, who later became famous in the Moscow Art Theatre, A. A. Sanin and N. A. Popov, who later grew to be well-known stage directors, and several others.

The other amateurs demanded despotic treatment. Talentless people must be subjected to simple training, dressed to the taste of the director and made to act according to his will. If one is forced to give talentless actors big parts one is also forced, for the sake of the performance, to hide their faults. For this there are many excellent ways which I learned to perfection at that time. These cover the lapses of the bad actors like screens. Without mentioning colorful scenery and garish costumes which distract the eyes of the spectator, and exaggerated props which also occupy the attention of the audience, there exist unexpected hokum and clever *mises en scène* which, at the will of the stage director, distract the attention of the spectator from a bad actor at any given moment.

Let us say that in the second act of " Uriel Acosta " at the festival in Manasseh's garden, the actors on the stage are talentless. Choose the most beautiful woman and the handsomest man among them, dress them in the most garish costumes you may find, and let them have the most prominent spot on the stage. Let the man energetically make love to the woman, let her flirt piquantly, or, if it becomes necessary, invent a scene for them containing interest in itself and drawing the spectators' attention away from the faulty actors. Only in the places necessary for the exposition of the play, stop the action of the extras temporarily to give the spectators an opportunity to hear the important words. Is it not all very simple? Of course, the stage director will assume the blame for all of this. But it is better to be blamed for too much trying than to be conscious of the lack of substance in one's theatre. Besides, for the success of the play and its interpreters there are necessary climaxes, the culminating moments of the play. When real means for producing these climaxes with the help of actors only are lacking, it is necessary to accept the stage director's help. For this the stage director has many methods for the " fooling of the public." Let me explain by quoting an example.

In Uriel Acosta there are two places that must leave a large impression on the spectator. I say " large," making peace beforehand with the quality of the word. This yielding is a compromise on my part. The first of these places is the cursing of Acosta in the second act during the festival in Manasseh's garden. The second of these places is the renunciation by Acosta in the synagogue in the fourth act. One scene, is, so to say, of a society character, the other of a proletarian nature. For the first scene I needed beautiful society women and young men (I hid the awkward and the ugly among them by means of characteristic make-up and costumes). For the second climacteric scene of the proletarian crowd I needed young hot-headed students whom I had to hold back from fighting and from hurting Acosta, that is myself.

When in the second act the curtain rose on the scenery of a garden with many differently placed platforms which gave all sorts of chances for picturesque groupings in a very primitive manner, and the spectator saw a bouquet of real society buds and society men in marvelous costumes and gleaming jewels, the public rose from its seats from surprise. The impression was made. The lackeys carried about wine and sweetmeats, the gentlemen courted the ladies, the ladies flirted sentimentally, rolling their eyes and covering their faces with their fans, the music played, some danced, others made picturesque groups. The host would pass with old men and honored guests who were welcomed and seated. Acosta appeared also, but the guests left him one by one until he was alone. There entered Judith the daughter of Manasseh and joyfully approached the heretic. The noise of happy holiday voices became one with the music, until all these sounds were pierced by the threatening sound of a horn accompanied by many wheezing little pipes and bass voices singing a Jewish melody. The merrymaking stopped for a moment, people remained petrified in their places, listening, and were then taken up in disorder, becoming more and more panic-stricken. They moved like a wave backwards to look into the distance. And Acosta himself and the family of Manasseh already felt what awaited them.

Meanwhile, in the back, from under the floor, like inescapable fate, enter the black and terrible rabbis, with candles, with the servants of the synagogue who carry the holy books and the scrolls of the Law. Praying cloths are thrown over ball costumes and the foreheads of the ladies are bound with boxes with the commandments instead of tiaras. The black servants carefully lead every one away from Acosta, and the terrible rite of excommunication begins, accompanied by singing and religious ceremony.

But Acosta protests and justifies himself, and the young Judith, in a fit of indignation, throws herself, ecstatic with love, on the neck of the accursed and demonstratively proclaims her love for him. This is sin, blasphemy. All remain in one position and then silently, confusedly disperse, while the rabbis, with revenge hidden in their souls, go down back to the synagogue to tell of what has happened. All this director's work gave the necessary mood by itself and created a strong impression, thanks to which my theatrical pathos passed for the real climax of inspiration.

The Russian stage saw such a mob scene for the first time, and all this pointed to large theatrical success. One can imagine what took place after this scene. Husbands, wives, brothers, sisters, fathers and mothers, admirers and friends of the amateur extras, who filled the auditorium of the club, stormed the footlights with cries that reached a roar, waved handkerchiefs and broke chairs until the curtain was lifted again and again and all the actors and extras in the scene came out on the stage.

The second mob scene was made altogether differently, and strove to create an impression of another character. After a religious ceremony in the synagogue, after singing and a public examination, Acosta mounted an elevation amidst the crowd to read his denial. First he stuttered, then stopped, and at last, being no longer able to bear up, fainted. He was lifted, revived and forced to complete the reading of the act of denial in a semiconscious state. The servants supported him, giving him no chance to fall. But suddenly his brother, who pitied him, cried to him that his mother had died and that his bride was plighted to another. Feeling that the ropes of love had fallen from the soul of the philosopher, Acosta comes back to life, leaps to his full height and like Galileo cries with his full voice, " But it turns around anyway!"

No matter how the crowd was held back from touching the accursed man, a thing that according to religious belief was dangerous, all those who were present at Acosta's new blasphemy began to tear him to pieces. Shreds of clothing began to fly in the air, Acosta fell, disappearing in the crowd, and rose again, dominating the mob and crying out his new blasphemy with all his strength.

My own experience was that it was dangerous to stand among the excited young students at that time. This was the climax of the play, its highest culminating point. The crowd helped me, the Acosta. It carried me on its waves without giving time for my spiritual buffers to push me away from the highest point of my artistic desire, without letting me put obstacles in the way of the impetus of my instinctive scenic movement forward.

It was altogether different in the fourth act where there was also a great tragic climax. But I had to create it alone, without outside help. Again, as I approached it, my spiritual buffers reached out, pushing back my creative goal and giving me no chance to approach it. Again inner doubts obstructed the course of impetus. Something seemed to be locked in my soul, and I could not move forward without looking back into the superconscious sphere of the tragic. I experienced the feelings of a bather who is about to dive into icy water. I felt myself to be a tenor without a high C. I remembered and I envied great actors like Salvini, Duse, and Yermolova, and I asked them in my thought what they did in order to rise freely to the highest point of their passion. It must be that they have some secret technical method to do so. Without knowing that method I stood impotently as if surrounded by a Chinese wall which I had to surmount. Other places of the rôle that did not demand self-forgetfulness and complete self-revelation, but only a certain depth of feeling, were more successful. And those places that were colored by the philosophic thoughts of Acosta, which demanded only simple saying, reporting to the spectator, were crumpled by me, due to my imperfect speech. Again some words fell out of the text; others did not reach the public because I spoke too quietly; still others were crumpled, and the philosophic thought itself became incomprehensible. It could not be made one's own, just as one cannot understand a melody which is played on a piano with broken hammers.

At this performance I made the acquaintance of one of the future workers of the Moscow Art Theatre, Alexey Alexandrovich Stakhovich, an acquaintance that later bore fruit for our art. But I will let him tell about it himself.

This is how he told it to me.

"Stakhovich," said Grand Duke Sergey Alexandrovich, to me at breakfast, "you will go to the amateur theatre with us to-day."

"I am at your orders, your highness," I answered.

"Are you glad to go?" jested the grand duke.

"I am always glad to be where your highness is."

"Take more cigarettes with you," jested the grand duke, who knew my habit of running out of the auditorium and spending the whole act with friends in the smoking room.

"Oh, no, Grandmother Strekalova won't let you. She is in love with these amateurs and has ordered everybody to see them," declared the grand duchess Elizaveta Fyodorovna.

"Grandmother Strekalova is the kindest being on earth and a marvellously philanthropic lady, but I never knew that she was very strong on matters of art, and so, with the permission of your highness, I will bring more cigaretttes," I answered.

"Stakhovich is incorrigible," the grand duke decided.

"In the evening we were at your performance in the Hunting Club, and I really received an order from Grandmother Strekalova to watch the performance from beginning to end.

"I am at your orders," I answered, and went out to smoke.

"But towards the end of the act, in order not to hurt the grandmother, I stole into the auditorium, sat down in my seat in the darkness, and unwillingly looked up at the stage, and, well — the scenery, the lighting, the costumes, the make-ups seemed interesting to me.

"The devil take it! These are not amateurs!" I said after a minute. "What a pity that I lost the whole of the first act in the smoking room."

" Soon the curtain descended, and of course I did not tell Grandmother Strekalova that I had disobeyed her orders. I praised all that I had seen and praised it sincerely. The grand duke and all our companions were very much interested in the performance. The auditorium was alive. In the intermission we visited each other and compared notes. You know how I love to hear theatrical discussions in the audience.

" The curtain rose again and I saw on the stage a bouquet of beauties. What costumes! What jewels! *Ce tenue! Ce ton!* I thought that I was in Paris, in the Comedie Française, and that Bartet, Richambert, Worms, Le Bargy, Févre, were before me. We all looked at each other with enthusiasm, shrugged our shoulders with surprise, moved our heads in approval. I worked more than everybody. But when Judith entered! I can't tell you what happened to me! Never in my life had I seen such a beautiful woman! I was already in love with everybody and did not know where to begin to pay court. Well, after that there was the scene with those black men and then the mob scene! Just as soon as the final scene was over, I ran headlong back-stage. I found out that Stanislavsky was the leader of the circle. I made my way to him. I met him, I met all the actors. Now all of them are my best friends. I love all of them. I have kissed the hands of every lady in the company! And in the next intermission I brought the grand duke and the duchess back-stage and was in enthusiasm because all the actors bore themselves proudly, restrainedly, with dignity. Both the men and the women, especially the women.

" During the whole next week at the Court, at dinners and balls, ' Acosta ' was the only topic of conversation. I advertised you left and right. Stanislavsky, his wife Lilina, the beautiful Andreieva, never left my tongue.

" This is how I first became an admirer and a friend of the Circle, and later a friend of the Art Theatre, one of its directors, and at last an actor."

How clearly I remember my friendship with this brilliant adjutant of the grand duke, this tall, handsome colonel with a Roman profile, elegant mustaches and a coquettishly cropped beard, who spoke French like a Parisian, this clever jester and punster Alexey Stakhovich. He was very popular among the actors of our theatre. "Handsome like Stakhovich! Elegant like Stakhovich! An aristocrat like Stakhovich!" These exclamations became commonplace in our theatre. And Stakhovich himself became a model for imitation. Some tried to imitate his elegant gestures, others the plastics of his hands, fingers, his manner of talking. And when one needed an authority about the customs of the highest circles of society, of what, where and how was to be worn an evening coat, a tuxedo, a visiting coat, a black or white vest or tie, all would say in one voice, " Ask Stakhovich."

The production of " Uriel Acosta " with large mob scenes *à la* the Meinigen Players made much noise and attracted the attention of all. Moscow. People began talking about us. For a time we seemed to have received a patent for mob scenes. What theatres of that time except ours could have given much time for the rehearsal of mob scenes? What other theatre could have supplied the costumes that we had learned to make? This side of scenic art was at a very low level in the other theatres of Moscow. The costumers' shops knew only of two styles, those of " Faust," and those of " Les Huguenots." And we, besides knowing costumes, were already collecting a museum of arms, materials, and other things that supplied fine color on the stage. What theatre could have collected a mob of extras from among society ladies and young men who so willingly came to us? When these society ladies covered their bosoms with jewels, the ball at Manasseh's house received such rich tone that the breaking up of the society festival by the rite of excommunication received a tremendous scenic importance.

And when the grand duke and the grand duchess came to one of the benefit performances of " Acosta," the effect created in Moscow was beyond description. At that time Moscow was proud that at its head was a member of the royal family. Noblemen and merchants tried to attract the duke and duchess to visit them. After the duke and duchess came to our performance, the following question was asked everywhere, " Whom did the royal guests visit? Was it the nobleman, that is the Hunting Club, or us, that is the Society of Art and Literature?

Those who had until that time avoided us now called us their own. Basing themselves on the fact that I was the leader of the Society and that I came from a merchant's family, it was decided that the grand duke and the grand duchess had honored the merchants. This helped us, as the wide public which seemed to be blind and deaf to our existence, suddenly noticed us. We became the talk of the day, and the production of " Acosta " became fashionable and attracted full houses.

Our financial affairs began to look brighter. The members of the Society, the actors who were already despairing of the success of our enterprise, began to believe in it again and decided to remain in the Circle. Under the same fashionable flag of the luxurious costumes of the Meiningen production and mob scenes, we staged " Othello," " Much Ado About Nothing," " The Polish Jew," " The Sunken Bell," and other plays.

CHAPTER XXIII

"THE POLISH JEW"

THE next production of the Society of Art and Literature was "The Polish Jew," a play by Erckmann and Chatrian.

There are plays which are interesting in themselves. But there are others which may be made interesting if the stage director approaches them in an original way. For instance, if I tell you the dry plot of "The Polish Jew," it will bore you. But if I take the outline of the play and embroider it with all the possible designs of a stage manager's imagination, the play will come to life and grow interesting. I have chosen this play especially not because I liked it in the original, but because I came to love it in that production which I imagined. And now I will tell of it not as it is written, but as it was produced by the Society of Art and Literature.

Imagine a cosy interior in the home of a burgomaster in a border village of Alsace, in the hills. The stove is burning, the lamp is bright, a Christmas supper is in progress. The daughter of the burgomaster is there, her fiancé who is an officer in the frontier guard, a forester and another hillsman. Outside there is a snowstorm, the wind howls. The window panes rattle, the wind enters through the cracks in the frames and oppresses the soul. But the people in the room are happy; they sing hill songs, they smoke, eat, drink, talk. But the gusts of wind are so strong at times that the people in the room stop in their merriment now and then, and are forced to listen to what is going on outside. One wind gust even frightens them. They remember another snowstorm like the present one, some years ago; at that time they seemed to have heard the thin sound of sleighbells amidst the gusts of wind. Somebody was driving in the storm. But the voice of the wind drowned the silver bells until the wind died down and the ringing pierced the air again, becoming more and more audible. Some minutes more, and it became even clearer. Then it rang very near, and stopped. There was the sound of footsteps in the snow, the door banged, some one stamped his feet outside, opened another door, and the tremendous figure of a man wrapped in a fur coat and covered with snow, stood on the threshold.

"Peace be with you," said the new arrival and began to remove his coat, shake the snow from his hat, his clothing and his long beard. He was one of those rich Polish Jews who often passed through that neighborhood. Having removed his coat, he took off his belt and laid it on the table in such a manner that the money hidden in it rang. A few coins dropped to the floor. After warming himself and waiting for the storm to stop, the Jew put his money belt on again, wrapped himself in his coat and went away. Next day his horse and sleigh were found in the hills, and he and his money belt had vanished without leaving a sign behind them. But now the officer of the frontier guard says that some evidence has been discovered and that the murderer of the Jew will soon be captured by the police. Then the burgomaster arrives. He is a man respected by all. The merriment is renewed to the accompaniment of the gusty wind.

Suddenly there is the hardly audible sound of bells. Now it is not heard, now it is heard again. Somebody approaches outside. There is the sound of footsteps in the snow, the banging of a door, the stamping of feet, the opening of another door, and on the threshold appears a large figure wrapped in a coat and covered with snow.

"Peace be with you," the newcomer says. He removes his coat and lays a heavy money belt on the table. The belt rings and several coins roll to the floor. All those present seem to be turned to stone. It seems to them that they see a ghost. The burgomaster cannot stand

it and falls to the floor.   There is chaos.   They begin to bring him to
— but the curtain falls.

The second act takes place in a large room in the house of the burgomaster.   It is the day of the wedding of the burgomaster's daughter
to the young officer of the guard.   The domestics are all at church, and
one can hear the sound of church bells.   Only the burgomaster is home;
he is still ill from his fright.   The bridegroom comes to see him.   While
they are talking, the burgomaster suddenly begins to listen to something.
In the ringing of the church bells he seems to hear the thin, piercing,
silver sound of the sleigh bells.   And truly, one seems to hear it.   Perhaps it only seemed so.   No, no, it was really the sound of sleigh bells.
And yet, it was impossible.   In order to quiet the sick man, the officer
assures him that the murderer will soon be found, and justice will revenge the death of the Jew.   But this does not at all quiet the burgomaster.   Meanwhile the domestics come back from the church, the
guests come to the wedding, there is the notary, the friends of the bride
with tremendous black Alsatian bows on their necks, the well-to-do
peasants who are the friends of the burgomaster, and behind them all
are the musicians, who are standing in a window niche ready to strike
up at the first sign.   The ceremony takes place.   The bridegroom, the
bride and the witnesses sign their names in the book of the notary.   The
bridegroom, the bride and the burgomaster are congratulated, but the
burgomaster has grown strange again; he seems to be preoccupied with
something; he is listening to something again.   And the audience seems
to hear the far sound of sleigh bells.   But the musicians begin to play
and that sound is drowned.   There is merriment and dancing.   But
clearer and clearer the sleigh bells are heard in harmony with the instrument.   They are heard by the audience; they pierce the sound of the
orchestra; they float wider and wider as if they embrace all other
sounds, and at last they are heard, sharp and painfully piercing.

The maddened burgomaster, wishing to drown the bells, shouts that
the musicians should play louder.   He throws himself at the first woman

he sees and begins to whirl with her in an insane dance. He sings together with the music, he shouts, but the bells are stronger and stronger and more piercing, and nothing that he can do drowns their sound. Everybody has noticed the insane conduct of the burgomaster, they have stopped dancing, they press themselves to the walls, while he still whirls in his mad dance with his unhappy partner who cannot escape from his embrace.

The third act takes place in the attic. There is a slanting ceiling, a stairway from below with a small partition instead of a banister. In the back wall there is a low window with shutters almost on the level of the floor. Through the bars of the shutters one can see that it is night. There is a large bed in the center of the background. On the fore-stage there is a table, benches, a wardrobe, a stove, all with the back to the audience. It is dark. From below comes the happy sound of wedding songs, music, young, ringing voices, drunken cries. Many people mount the stairway, talking. They are taking up the burgomaster who is tired and wants to sleep. They say good-by. They go away, and the pale, tortured burgomaster hurries to the door in order to lock it. Then he sits down to rest and from below there comes the sound of dishes through which one, if he listen attentively, may perhaps discern the sound of the fateful sleigh bells. Listening to that sound with grief and excitement, the burgomaster undresses in order to lie down and seek relief in sleep. He puts out the candle, but in the darkness there again begins a musical symphony of terrible sounds.

It is an hallucination of the ear, in which happy singing subtly passes into funereal harmony, and the glad voices and exclamations of the young guests change into the gloomy, deathlike voices of the drunkards, and the sound of dishes and winecups at times are reminiscent of church bells. And through all these sounds, like the chief leit-motif of a symphony, there pierce, now torturingly and insistently, now triumphantly and threateningly, the fateful sleigh bells which have not left the burgomaster since the appearance of the Jew in the first act. When he hears them, the burgomaster groans in the darkness and pronounces some ununderstandable words. It seems that he is moving, for the bed groans and something falls, perhaps a chair that he has pushed.

And now in the middle of the room, where the bed was, it seems to grow lighter; bluish-gray rays of light appear no one can tell from where. Imperceptibly this light grows stronger, then weaker. Gradually, to the accompaniment of the hallucinatory symphony, there is limned a figure sitting high above the place where the back of the bed was, which back has now become a balustrade. The head of this figure is lowered and crowned with hanging white hair. Its hands are tied and when it moves them one hears the ringing of chains. Behind the ghostly figure there is a pillar with an inscription which cannot be read. One may think that it is a pillar of shame with a criminal chained to it.

The light grows and becomes grayer, greener, and more threatening. It spreads along the back wall and becomes a gloomy back-ground for black beings, for ghostly silhouettes who have placed themselves before the footlights, with their backs to the public. In the middle, where the table was, a large, plump man in a black cloak and a judge's hat sits on a raised platform. To each side of him there are several other such figures with hats that are not quite so tall. To the right, where the cupboard was, a long serpentlike figure in a black cloak is stretching towards the criminal, and to the left, where the stove was, with elbows on the *cathedra,* eyes covered by a hand, stands a motionless weeping figure, the figure of the defender, also in a black cloak and a legal cap.

The examination of the criminal takes place as if in a nightmare, in whispers, with always changing rhythm. The criminal lowers his head more and more, his hanging hair covering his face. He refuses to answer, and now from the corner where hung the burgomaster's clothes, there grows a long, thin figure which seems to grow larger as it crawls along the wall and reaches the ceiling, then lowers itself above the criminal and looks directly at him. This is a hypnotist. Now the criminal is forced to raise his head, and the audience recognizes in the tired, old, thin face the face of the burgomaster. Under the influence of the hypnosis, weeping, pausing, quieting down, the burgomaster begins to give evidence in broken words. To the question of the procurator as to what he did with the murdered and robbed Polish Jew, the criminal refuses to answer.

Then there rises a storm of nightmare sounds; the hallucinatory symphony of sounds is renewed; the stage gradually darkens and a crimson glow appears behind the glass of the door which leads to the stairway. The burgomaster in his nightmare thinks it is a forge and runs to it in order to squeeze the tremendous body of the murdered Jew into the narrow opening of the fiery stove and destroy all the evidence by burning it. For he has burned all that already, and with it his soul. All is embraced in darkness.

The red rays of the rising sun are seen through the openings in the shutters and the glad and drunken cries of the wedding guests are heard from below. The guests mount the stairway to wake the burgomaster, for it is already broad daylight. There is a knocking at the door. This is answered by silence. At first there is laughter at this silence, and there is knocking again, but still there is no answer. The guests outside are amazed, then excited, frightened, they break the glass, open the door, enter, and find the burgomaster dead.

The change of the room into a chamber of justice took place almost unnoticeably and created the impression of such a nightmare that at almost all of the performances nervous women left the theatre and sometimes even fainted. But while the audience was frightened by the nightmare, I, in the rôle of the burgomaster, saw an altogether different picture. The amateur actors who impersonated the judges, among whom were very many respectable citizens, and even an important civil general who played the part of the procurator, and had a large, well-fed figure, crawled in the darkness on all fours, hurrying to their places so as not to be caught by the light in their progress. Many of them would be a little late, and they would push each other from the rear. This was so funny that it would insist on occupying my mind before the last and culminating scene of the play. I closed my eyes and thought, " So this is the stage! Here it is funny, and from the audience it is terrifying."

I like to create deviltry in the theatre. I am happy when I find a piece of hokum which deceives the spectator and which the spectator cannot explain. In the realm of the fantastic the stage can still do a great deal. Not even a half of what can be done has been done.

I confess that one of the reasons for the production was the hokum in the last act, which seemed to me to be interesting on the stage. I had not made a mistake. It was successful. There were curtain calls. For whom? For me. Why? For my stage direction or my acting? It pleased me to think that it was for the latter, and I thought that I must have played well indeed, and that I was a true tragedian, for this rôle was in the repertoire of such great tragedians as Irving, Barnay, Paul Mounet and others.

At present, looking backwards, I think that I did not play the part badly. There were the characteristics of an old man, an important, solid citizen, and there was restraint. The interest in the play and the rôle grew, but this interest was not created by the psychology and inner life of the human spirit of the rôle, but by the plot of the play itself. Who was the murderer? This was the puzzle which interested the spectator and demanded solution. There were the climacteric moments necessary to tragedy also; for instance in the finale of the first act when the burgo-master faints; in the finale of the second act where the burgomaster dances madly; and in the third act, in the strongest moment of the hokum scene. But who had created these strong moments, the stage director with his production or the actor with his playing? Of course it was the stage director, and the laurels were his rather than the actor's. And the preponderance of usefulness was also in the balance cup of the stage director.

This experiment as a stage director helped me once more to learn how to help the actor from the outside. And at present I see still another use in it for the stage director — it is to learn how to show clearly the plot of the play and its outward action. Often we see a play in the theatre without clearly understanding the logic of events, the time of them and their dependence on each other, that quality which the poet Pushkin calls the " given circumstances." And that is the very first thing which must be made clear in any play, because without it, it is hard to speak of the play's inner nature. But even here there was a great fault which emanated from the actors. Our amateurs were not masters of speech, nor was I, and wherever the action of the play was explained in a monologue or a story, much was lost to the spectator because of our poor diction and wrong phrasing. We were greatly blamed by critics and spectators for this, and were told to learn how to speak from the better actors of other theatres, but we were instinctively afraid of something and reasoned in the following way:

" We will better talk without clearness rather than talk as the other actors do. They either flirt with their words or take pleasure in running the whole gamut of their vocal register, or they prophesy. Let some one teach us to speak simply, musically, nobly, beautifully, but without vocal acrobatics, actors' pathos and all the odds and ends of scenic diction. We want the same thing in movement and action. Let them be humble and not completely expressive and scenic in the theatrical sense of the word, but then they are not false, and they are humanly simple. We hate the theatrical in the theatre, we love the scenic on the stage. That is a tremendous difference."

This production persuaded me to a certain degree that I was able to play not tragedy itself, but an approach to tragedy. Like a tenor without a high C, I was a tragedian without the highest note of tragedy. In moments of the highest tragedy I needed the help of the stage director, which I received in this production even more than in that of " Uriel Acosta." The usefulness of this production lay in the fact that I grounded myself in what was good in the new.

CHAPTER XXIV

THE PROFESSIONAL THEATRE

IN my quest for a helper in the theatre of which I was dreaming, with whom I might share the reins of rule in the complex theatrical affair and who might become the administrator and one of the founding directors of the theatre, and also in my quest for actors who might fill out the skeleton of our troupe, I turned to professional actors and managers, and tried to make several productions with them. For instance, I took upon myself the production of Gogol's " Inspector General " at one of the summer theatres near Moscow. I came to the rehearsal and was met with honor, although at that time I was only a beginning amateur. Who does not know the properties and the *mise-en-scène* of " The Inspector-General " ? Everything was in its place, the divan, the chair and every smallest trifle. The rehearsal progressed smoothly so that it seemed that the actors had played together hundreds of times. There was not a single intonation, not a single trait that was created by themselves, but all the stencils fixed once and forever, against which Gogol has himself protested so vigorously in his well-known letter on the production of " The Inspector General." Purposely I did not stop the actors, and after the end of the first act paid them many compliments, and said that there was nothing left for me but to come to the performance and applaud, for the production was ready and only waiting for posters, a full house, and the rise of the curtain. But if they wanted to play the real Gogol as I understood him, then nothing that they had done from the very beginning to the very end was of any use. The actors insisted that they wanted my manner of production and were ready to change everything as I told them to do.

"Then let us begin," I said, mounting the stage. "This divan is at the left. Put it on the right. The exit is on the right. Put it in the center. You began acting here, on the divan. Go to the other side." It was in such manner that I talked to professional actors with all the despotism that was part of me then. "Now we will begin," I said, having purposely converted the whole stage.

The confused actors, with long and surprised faces, walked to the other side of the stage and were lost in amazement as to where they were to sit down. I helped them, for they were completely helpless in the creation of a new *mise en scène*.

"And what further?"—one was lost.

"And where do I go now?" asked another.

"How am I to say this sentence?" a third asked me, having lost all his aplomb and seemingly turned into a simple amateur.

I began to order the actors about exactly as I ordered about amateurs. Of course they did not like it, but they obeyed, for they lost all ground beneath their feet. What I said and what I wanted was right. I saw the truth of that in the following years in many productions of "The Inspector General." But the means I used for attaining my new ideas and influencing the actors were not the right ones. Simple despotism does not persuade an actor in his inner self; it only violates his inner self. A black cat seemed to have run between us already. I found out personally the meaning of actors' intrigues, gossip, undermining, and what the Americans call "kidding." I also came to know that it is much easier to destroy the old than to create the new.

The performance was not successful, for the actors had no time to unlearn the old and to make the new their own. I had taught them nothing. I only disturbed them. But they had taught me a great deal.

My first experience with professional actors was far from successful.

My second attempt was much more successful. One very well-known manager, a man of much talent, intuition and experience, but of course, like all professional theatrical men, eaten through by theatrical rust, invited me to produce Hauptmann's " Hannele " in the tremendous theatre of Solodovnikov. This production was in preparation at the very time of the coronation of Nikolai II. The work was responsible, as not only Russians would come to see it, but foreigners also. Besides the opportunity that this offered to me to become known to a wide public, I also wanted to learn the methods of work of the famous manager.

Perhaps he was that director whom I was seeking!

This took place during Lent, when actors from every corner of the provinces had come to Moscow to get engagements for the following season. I was invited to take part in the making up of the company, and to examine the actors who were to be hired for the coming performance. At the appointed hour I came to the address given to me and found myself in a store that had just been left by its ruined owner. Dirt, rubbish, paper, broken boxes and shelves, an old divan with broken arms and back, several armchairs in the same condition, old advertisements of manufactured goods, a circular stairway that led to a low attic with a dirty window and a ceiling which I continually struck with my head, and a mass of old boxes. Here on some boxes sat the manager with his assistant. People came to them, poor, ragged, dirty people, to whom he spoke very familiarly.

" Come, show me your leg," the assistant said to a young girl. " Higher. You need a good leg for tights. It is not so bad. Show me your bust."

The confused girl took off her coat in the unheated kennel and tried to look as stately as she could.

" Show me your voice. Sing."

" I am a dramatic actress. I don't sing."

" Write her down as a beggar," the manager decided.

The young actress moved her head in assent and walked out. They began calling in others, but I stopped them, closed the door and asked for an explanation.

" Pardon me," I began as tenderly and caressingly as I could, " I can't continue this work. Do you think that one can occupy himself with art and aesthetics in a pigsty? Aesthetics has its demands which must be fulfilled even if they are very badly fulfilled. Without this aesthetics ceases to be aesthetics. Here is the minimum demand not only of aesthetics but of the simplest cultured society. Tell them to sweep out this rubbish, wash the floors and the windows, heat the place, put a few chairs and a simple table in the room and place an inkwell and a pen on the table, so that one might write on the table and not on the wall as you are doing now. When all this is done, I will begin my work with great enthusiasm, for it interests me, but now I cannot, because I am nauseated.

" And another condition. You are the director of an establishment which must enlighten society. And actors are your closest cultured assistants. Let us remember this and speak to them not as if they were prostitutes and burglars but people who deserve to be called actors. If what I have said has not insulted you, but has inspired you to the creation of a clean and a good piece of work, give me your hand and let us say good-by until the next time. If what I have said sounds like an insult to you, let us say good-by for the last time."

I had not made a mistake in the manager. He was a sensitive and a decent man. My words confused him, and he could only say, striking his forehead:

" Why did I, old fool that I am, not understand this before? "

He embraced me, and we said good-by.

When I came again the place was heated and shone with cleanliness. Both top and bottom were furnished like palace halls in an operetta. Luxurious curtains covered with theatrical designs, with very golden fringes, gilded and silvered chairs, velvet and silken tablecloths, property vases made of pasteboard, a pasteboard clock on the table, carpets, water, glasses, ash trays, and tea for the actors. The upper room was turned into a real office for the director. The actors, amazed by the change, hurried to remove their coats, bring themselves into order and to conduct themselves in the manner they had grown to use in the Spanish plays of their repertoire. The bonton of this parlor was of a peculiar sort. But nevertheless, my goal had been reached, and it was possible to talk to people in a human manner.

The work began to boil; all were in good spirits, everything promised something new to the poor provincial actors who had become tired and worn by the theatrical indecencies of the provinces. Apparently I had become popular. It seemed that every one wanted to show this in his relations with me. The theatre, which was hired only for a period beginning with the week ahead, forced us to rehearse in our temporary quarters. First of all I committed to memory the names, patronymics, and families of all the actors. Imagine the surprise of an extra or a third-rate actor who in the decades that he had acted had heard only the words " Listen here," when he was first called at a rehearsal by his name, patronymic and family. This was such bribery on my part that not a single one of them could hold out against it.

The rehearsal began according to a program and methods that were new to all of them. This time, after the lesson I had learned with " The Inspector General," I was more careful. The actors understood me better, and everything progressed well to the joy of the manager and myself. He showered me with compliments for my so-called ability in handling the actors. That entire ability lay in the fact that I treated them as I would any other people. But for the theatre this was a new discovery.

A week passed, the theatre was free; we moved there in excitement and were shocked by the dirt and coldness of the ill-kept stage, auditorium and dressing rooms. Unwillingly we were obliged to put on our coats, hats and rubbers again. The actors were forced to push past each other in the corridors, waiting for their entrances, and gossip because they had nothing else to do. The discipline fell at once, and we were sorry that we had left the old store.

In order to save the situation a *coup d'état* was necessary. I called off one of the rehearsals, left the theatre and left word for the manager that I repeated all that I said at an analagous occasion in the dirty store which was later turned into a palace. A few days passed, and I received an invitation to a rehearsal. The theatre was heated, cleaned, and washed. A good room furnished with opera properties had been prepared for me, and two foyers for the actors, one for the men, one for the women. But according to immemorial theatrical habit, far from all of the actors guessed that they were to remove their hats, and the atmosphere of the back stage seemingly poisoned them with terrible stage habits and carelessness with which I struggled and which did not allow us to attack the work with clean hands and open hearts.

Then I was forced to another *coup d'état*. One of the small parts was played by an old and deserving actor who was famous in the provinces. He began the play. I asked him secretly to appear at the rehearsal in a hat, in rubbers, a coat on his shoulders, and a stick in his hands, and to mumble his part, as is the habit in some theatres. Then I asked him to help and to bring a sacrifice to the altar of the theatre: namely, to let me, a young amateur, give him, an old actor, a severe scolding and order him to take off his coat, hat and rubbers, to rehearse in full tone, and to repeat his text without the aid of written words.

The actor was intelligent and wise and agreed to do what I asked. All was done as it had been planned. I made my remarks to him very politely, but loudly, and with the consciousness of my right to do so.

If a young amateur allows himself to speak in such a manner to an old and honored member of the profession, what can he not do with unknown actors if they do not obey him? What confused them most of all was that at the fifth rehearsal I demanded that they know the text of their rôles completely and did not allow them to look at their written parts. At the next rehearsal they knew their parts.

After my second *coup d'état* it was possible to conduct the rehearsals in the theatre. Then the manager began to drink from joy, and to conduct himself with more freedom than was necessary. Another drunkard also appeared. I suspected a third man of drinking. And again the work began to give backwards and downwards. I felt that a third *coup d'état* was necessary. I was forced to stop rehearsals again, excuse myself before the actors for a lost evening, and without saying anything to anybody, go home. A silent insult is always mysterious and terrible. That same evening I sent the manager a decisive refusal to continue my work, and stated categorically that under the existing conditions, that is, while he was drunk, I could not and would not do anything. I was told later that the manager used drugs and all the means known to medicine in order to stop his fit of drinking and bring himself into a state of respectability. I knew that he had nowhere to go. He had spent almost all his money on the new production, he had debts and he could ask no one but me to help him. Clean, shaven, perfumed, he came to visit me and swore by all the saints that the drinking fit would not be repeated. I agreed to come to a rehearsal in the evening. It is a pity that the manager's oath was broken shortly. This is what happened.

In " Hannele " is depicted the life of beggars in an asylum. At first the author paints a sharp and truthful picture of naturalism. But with the second act the tone of the play is completely changed. Naturalism passes into mysticism. Hannele, who was in the process of dying a naturalistic death in the first act, says farewell to the body and to realistic life in the second act, passing into eternity, which is depicted on the stage. Her comrades of the asylum, coarse and realistic beggars, become the shades of themselves, tender, caressing, and kind. Their treatment of her becomes loving, and she turns from a beggar girl to a fairy princess and rests in a glass coffin.

At last we reached this scene, and I was breaking my heart as to how I was to turn real people into shades. The stage was not yet lighted, and from behind a piece of scenery fell a bright ray of bluish light, giving a mysterious air and only hinting at the presence of walls in the room. All the rest of the stage was drowned in darkness. The actors were coming for the rehearsal, meeting on the stage, talking, walking at times into the way of the ray of light, and their elongated shades crept over the floor and across the walls and ceiling. When they moved their bodies looked like silhouettes and their shadows ran, met, parted, united, broke away from each other; all became confused, and they were lost amidst their shadows and looked like shadows themselves.

Eureka! I had it. All that remained to find out was where and how the light was situated, for often accidental lighting is impossible to repeat on the stage. Calling the electrician, I wrote everything down with him, — the strength of the light, the strength of the lamp, and marked the lamp which lay on the floor with a special mark, and also the place where it lay. In addition to this I had to find complementary play for the actors. But this was easy, for the light-effect prompted all the rest. I taught the actors to speak and move like the figures in our sick-dreams or nightmares, when some one seems to whisper mysterious words in your ear, — then a pause on a broken word, a long pause, and all shiver and breathe, then again a slow, broken, often-accented speech in a rising and falling chromatic scale. Again a pause, a silence — an unexpected whisper — the slow, monotonous, movement of the shades of the crowd that stand on the floor, across the walls and ceiling. Then suddenly, the sharp sound of an opening door, the strong creaking of a hinge, the sharp unpleasant voice that one hears when one is in fever.

" Some frost on the street! " the unpleasant voice whines, sounding like a pain of the heart that pierces a man through and through. All comes to life and the shades fly to all sides along the walls; all is in chaos as when your head whirls around. Then again a gradual silencing, all stop, moving from side to side — a long, long pause. Then some one's soft half-whisper in a tearful moan, "Hannele! Ha-a-a-nne-e-le!" The stronger chromatic lift of a sigh, and then the sharp chromatic fall of intonation, a helpless whisper, "Hannele is dead!" The crowd of shades move; one can hear tender, girlish and aged sobs and moans. At this moment, from the distance, from the very farthest dressing room a tenor cries in a mad voice in his highest note while a man shakes his shoulders, giving his voice a trembling sound, "The-e-e-e-e-ey bri-i-i-i-i-ing the gla-a-a-a-ass co-o-o-o-offii-i-i-i-in!" After several minutes of this far-away, hardly audible cry, that seems to come from some mysterious messenger, the shades become restless and repeat the same sentence, but stressing all the hissing and sonorous consonants, "They brrrring the gggggglassss coffffffinnnn." This whistling and hissing which began calmly, strengthened and thickened with the rising disorder of the crowd. Then it came nearer and nearer, while extras placed in the wings began to repeat the phrase again and again with the hissing and whistling of consonants. When they had carried this hissing to a *forte,* everybody would join, including stage hands and some of the musicians who offered their help. The result was a grandiose hiss accompanied by the whirling of the shades on the walls. Meanwhile in the center of the stage appeared a glass coffin brightly illuminated, in which lay Hannele in the costume of a fairy princess. The other Hannele remained on the forestage in the costume of a beggar and lay as motionless as a corpse. With the appearance of the coffin everything gradually calmed down into blissful contemplation and returned to the slow moving of the shades. There was a tremendous pause.

At this very moment, I don't know myself from where, some one's drunken bass voice said quietly, clearly and distinctly, as if awaking from sleep, without any pathos, like a reflex in a dream, "They carry the glass coffin." This unexpectedness frightened us, it seemed that electricity had passed along our nerves. The manager, I, and several other sensitive people who sat in the theatre leapt up with fear and confusion. The manager was already running towards me.

"What was it? What was it? It was the work of a genius. One must notice it. One must leave it in. One must repeat it!" And the manager and I mounted the stage to embrace the new genius who had created such a superhuman effect.

This genius was the completely drunk assistant of the director. The poor fellow, who had heard that one could not drink while one worked with us, and understood that he had betrayed himself, ran out of the theatre in fear. And no matter how we tried to recreate the effect, no matter how much the manager gave him to drink, he was afraid to come on the stage drunk, and from that time on came to the theatre sober, which deprived him of the possibility of repeating his moment of inspiration.

Despairing of him, the manager found a contra bass from a church choir. First we tried him sober. We were unsuccessful. We made him drunk. The sound was good, but he could not say the words in the proper time, either being late or saying something that no one could understand. Besides, the manager himself began to drink with him. Having noticed this, I protested against the genial touch entirely. The manager consented, but did not stop drinking, and said that he was sick. I pretended to believe that he was ill but I warned his family not to let him come to the theatre while he was ill. It is said that the sick man roared that he was drinking for the sake of art and that no one but he could make the genial touch. Time passed, his illness was over, and he returned to the theatre, talented and attractive as ever, and one could not help loving him. I did not say a single word to him about his illness and we continued to be the best of friends.

CHAPTER XXV

NEW STAGE EFFECTS

HAUPTMANN had appeared earnestly on the theatrical horizon. In other countries he was already an idol, but in Russia not a single one of his plays had yet found its way to the boards. Our Society of Art and Literature was the first in Moscow to produce his " Sunken Bell," a lyrico-tragical fairy tale in which, with a great deal of philosophy, there is also much of the fantastic. The old woman Wittichen is something of a witch. Her daughter Rautendelein of the golden hair, the beautiful child of the hills, is the dream of the poet, the muse of the artist and sculptor, who dances under the rays of the sun and weeps above a brook. Her counselor and friend is the philosophic Nickelmann, who comes from the water, blows like a walrus, wiping his face with webbed paws that look like fish fins, and in important cases always pronounces his deep-meaning " Bre-ke-ke-kex." The Wood Sprite with the beast's face, in a furry skin with a tail, leaps from stone to stone along the sides of precipices, climbs the trees and knows all the news and the gossip which he communicates to his friend the Nickelmann. A crowd of beautiful young elves appear in circling dances under the moon, like our Russian mermaids. Little animals that resemble moles crawl from everywhere at Wittichen's call to feed on the remnants of her food.

There is also a cliff with a cavern in which Wittichen lives, and a small platform covered with fallen stones where Rautendelein dances and warms herself in the sun, and a mountain lake with murmuring waters out of which the Nickelmann appears, and a tree that has fallen across the brook, on which the Wood Sprite nimbly balances himself, and an endless amount of platforms that extend in all directions, up and down to the trapdoors, giving a chaotic appearance to the floor.

Into this fantastic Devil's Dell falls Master Heinrich, whose part I played. My appearance, rather cleverly planned, made a big impression. I rolled head downwards along a smoothly polished board that was placed at an angle to a high platform in the wings. This board was masked as a side of the cliff. Together with me there descended a flood of stones, small trees, branches, whose pasteboard noise was drowned in the terrible crash of the avalanche which we were able to produce by combining various sounds in the wings.

Rautendelein dug me out of the mass of rocks, and here took place her first meeting with Heinrich. At this moment they fell in love with each other. Heinrich, fully recovering his senses, tells in a breathless voice of the disaster that has overtaken him, that he had wanted to cast a tremendous bell (an idea, a religion) which might ring out to all the world and tell it of happiness. But the bell was too heavy, and when men began to hang it up, it fell down, destroying everything in its path, and its creator Heinrich fell with it. Night descends with all the little sounds of the hills, and the far echo of human voices. A pastor, a teacher and a villager are coming in search of the great master, but the Wood Sprite, whose howl echoes threateningly in the hills, has taken them off the road and is leading them to the Devil's Dell. The howling of the Wood Sprite and the human voices come nearer and nearer while there is a long pause on the stage. At that time this was a novelty that forced people to speak about it.

Down below in the trap, as if far away in the valley, appear the lights of lanterns, dots of light that became larger and larger before the eyes of the spectators as they approached. This gave the little stage the appearance of tremendous depth, and also realism of distance. Now, the Wood Sprite leaps from stone to stone down the high cliff to the brook, runs across the fallen tree, leaps to a high platform, then to another, and howling, disappears from the stage while his voice dies out in the distance. Meanwhile humans issue from the trap, and they are also forced to move along with the help of gymnastics, to climb over cliffs, rising and descending again, or disappearing in the trap in order to rise from it in another place, squeezing through between two cliff sides, and at last crossing the brook in the darkness.

Seeing the red light in Wittichen's cavern, the pastor commands her in the name of God to come out. And now from the cavern, preceding Wittichen crawls a threatening shadow and after it Wittichen herself, with a stick, illuminated by the red glare of the light. At the demand of the pastor she shows him Heinrich who lies at her feet, and whom the humans carry back to the valley. There rises a fog. In its formless clouds there appear unclear silhouettes, of creatures who slept under the stones and who now awake. These are elves who, weep for the fate of the sun-god Baldur. Filled with new hope for the future, they circle in an endless dance, rising to the cliffs and coming down from the heights to the accompaniment of wild cries, howls, whistling and a full orchestra of the sounds of the hills.

Heinrich is carried home to his wife who is terribly grief-stricken. He lies dying on his bed while his wife runs for help. Into the empty house comes a woman in a peasant's dress, with carefully hidden hair and strange, transparent eyes. She takes care of the dying man, and runs into the open door of the kitchen which is soon illuminated by the red light of the hearth. There is the sound of dishes. The shadow of Rautendelein is seen moving in the kitchen, now and then there are glimpses of herself running past the door with loose golden hair which makes her look like a beautiful witch. With short, animal-like movements she swiftly looks into the sick-room, into the face of the sick man, and runs back to the kitchen to finish preparing a magic draught. At last she makes the sick man drink it, and he sees a beautiful dream, a boat that glides somewhere, into a beautiful shore, and he rises and wants to go into the beautiful world that calls to him, together with Rautendelein. But on the threshold he meets his wife, who reminds him of the earth, of their past love, of their children, and begs him not to leave them. But the master, in the grasp of his new idea, denies all of them and goes back to the hills to his new and fateful Muse.

In the hills, in the free and rare air, with a wide horizon before him, inspired by his beautiful Rautendelein, Heinrich dreams again of doing something great and superhuman. Only in his sleep the echoes of the old nightmare appear and a monster who has come swimming over the mountain lake, presses him down, and with his threatening " Bre-ke-ke-ke-kex " tells him of the destruction that awaits him.

His beautiful super-earthly life is broken in on by the tiresome pastor, with his dead and unconvincing morals, and his quotations from the Holy Writ. With hardship he has climbed so far in order to try for the last time to return the talented heretic to the bosom of the church. The new dream of Heinrich seems to the pastor to be so terrible and blasphemous that he runs away from the hills to the valley, from where there can be heard the voices of humans who are cursing Heinrich. They crawl up with sticks and pitchforks to kill the enemy of the church, but Heinrich beats them back and disdainfully throws masses of stone down on them. At last Heinrich makes a smithy, and gnomes and other unclean beings are hired to toil over an unheard-of human bell. Hunchbacked, cross-eyed, crooked and deformed creatures, under the blows of the red hot iron staff of Heinrich, bending to the ground beneath heavy loads, carry up and down tremendous metal parts which are forged in the hellish smithy. The red-hot masses of metal, black, sooty smoke, the forge, red as hell itself, tremendous bellows which blows up sparks of fire, terribly ringing blows of the hammer against melted silver, the noise of falling masses of silver, the cries of Heinrich create on the stage a hellish factory.

To-day the work is especially obstinate and hot, for the bell is already moulded and soon its long-expected ringing will be heard in the whole world. And it rang out with such terrible power that human ears and nerves could not hold the elemental sound. Heinrich runs from it in terror. Vainly Rautendelein tries to retain him. Man is not able to conceive that which is only open to superhumans and gods. Again Heinrich falls. Again, with his hopes broken, he is in the dell where he met his beautiful dream and inspiration, Rautendelein, who weeps above the babbling brook. He goes away. She remains grief stricken with a crowd of sad elves, who weep for the lost hero and for the dream that will never be realized on earth. Rautendelein marries the Nickelmann.

The material given by the poet in the play is rich enough for any stage director's fantasy. I must confess that at the time the play was produced, I had already learned to make use of the floor of the stage; talking in contemporary language I was an experienced constructor. I will try to explain what I mean. The frame of the opening of the stage plus the floor of the stage create three dimensions, height, width and depth. The artist draws sketches on paper or canvas that have only two dimensions and often forgets the depth of the floor of the stage, that is, the third dimension. Of course in his drawing he expresses it in perspective, but he does not consider the measurements of the stage. Transferring the flat sketch to the boards, the fore-stage shows a tremendous space of theatrical, dirty, flat and empty floor. The stage begins to resemble a simple concert platform on which one can stand before the footlights and declaim and move, as far as variety and expression in the vertical standing body of the actor can go. Such a position limits greatly the scale of plastic pose, movements, and actions. Because of this, the interpretation of the spiritual life of the rôle becomes paler, less expressive and less variegated. And the stage director who could in this sense help the actor with his *mise en scène* and grouping, is also half-bound by the mistakes of the artist, who has substituted for the sculptural shaping of the floor boresome, flat and dirty boards. Under such conditions the actor must, standing alone before the prompter's box, without any help from the stage director or the *mise-en-scène* fill with himself all the stage, place in himself alone the entire play and only with the help of living over, mimetics and plastics limited to a tremendous degree, bare the subtle and complex soul of a Hamlet, a Lear or a Macbeth. It is hard to centralize on one's self the attention of a crowd of a thousand undisciplined spectators.

Oh, if there were actors who could fulfil the simple *mise en scène* of standing near the prompter's box! What a joy that would be and how it would simplify the business of the theatre. There would have been no need of the artist, but — there are no such actors in the world. I went to watch the greatest actors to explain to myself how many minutes they, standing on the fore stage before the footlights, without any outside help, could centralize on themselves the attention of the crowd. I also watched how variegated their poses, movements and mimetics were. Practice showed me that the maximum of their ability to hold the attention of a crowd in a strong and impressive scene is seven minutes. This is tremendous! The minimum, during an ordinary scene, is one minute. This is also much! Further on, they no longer have the variety of expressive means. They are forced to repeat themselves, and that weakens attention, until the next passage which renews new methods of interpretation and the attention of the spectator. Notice that this happens with a genius. Then what happens with ordinary actors, with their home-made methods of play, with their round flat pancake of a face, with arms that do not bend, with a body that is petrified with strain, with feet that do not stand but stamp in one place? Can they hold the attention of the spectator long? And it is they who love more than any one else to stand on the fore stage with a dead, unexpressive face, and a body that is simply exhibited. It is they who try to be as near the prompter as they can. And they pretend to fill the whole stage with themselves? To hold all the attention of the audience all of the time? But they never succeed. This is why they are so nervous, and whirl like eels, afraid, that the public may grow bored. More than all they must bow to the

stage director and the artist and beg that the constructor prepare for
them a comfortable floor which might help them, together with the aid
of the director and the artist, to interpret those spiritual subtleties of
a rôle which they cannot interpret themselves with their home-made
methods. What business have I, an actor, with the fact that behind
me hangs a drop curtain painted by a great artist? I don't see it, it
does not inspire me, it does not help me. Just the opposite; it only
forces me to be as talented as the background against which I am standing and which I do not see. Often this wonderful backdrop only interferes with me, for I have not agreed with the artist beforehand,
and in the majority of cases we pull in different directions. Better give
me one good armchair around which I will find an endless series of
methods for the expression of my emotions. Give me a stone on which
I may sit down to dream or lie in despair or stand high in order to be
near the sky. These palpable objects seen by us on the stage are much
more necessary and important for us actors than colorful canvases that
we do not see. Sculptural things live with us and we with them, while
painted backdrops hang behind us and live separately from us, for there
is no connection between us and them.

This art of the constructor which helps the actor to reveal his inner
life was known to me at that time and I knew how to use it.

"The Sunken Bell" gave tremendous possibilities to the director-
constructor. Judge yourself. The first act — hills, chaos, stones,
cliffs, trees and waters where all the unclean creatures of the fairy tale
abide. I prepared such a floor for the actors on which they could not
walk at all.

"Let them creep," I thought, "or sit on stones; let them leap on
the cliffs or balance and climb the trees; let them descend into the trap
so as to climb back again. This will force them, and myself among
them, to get used to a new *mise en scène,* and to play in a way that was
new to the stage, without standing near the footlights, for there was
nothing there to stand on; without triumphal operatic processions, with-

out the raising of arms. And I made no mistake. As a stage director I not only aided the actor but called forth without his will new gestures and methods of play. How many parts gained from this *mise-en-scène!* The leaping Wood Sprite that was played excellently by G. S. Burdzhalov, the swimming and diving Nickelmann, played beautifully by Luzhsky and Sanin, Rautendelein leaping along the cliffs, played by Andreieva, elves born of the mist, Wittichen squeezing through the cleft in the hills, all this by itself made the rôles characteristic and colorful and awoke the imagination of the actor. Justice demands that I acknowledge this time a great step forward as a stage director.

As far as my acting was concerned, it was an altogether different story. All that I could not do, all that I should not do, all to which I am not called by nature made the chief substance of the rôle of Heinrich. Lyricism in that sweet effeminate sentimental way in which I then falsely understood it, romanticism which neither I nor any actor outside of a real genius could express simply, meaningfully and nobly, and at last pathos in strong places in which my stage director's hokum did not help me — all this was far above my strength and my ability. And when an actor wants to do something that is impossible for him to do he falls into the same old trap of outer mechanical stencils, for the stage stencil is the fruit of artistic impotence.

In this rôle, with moments of great climax, I learned more strongly and clearly, more coarsely and stagily and confidently, to stencil all that was beyond me and what I had not yet reached. New harm from not understanding by true *emploi,* a new stop in the development of my art, a new violation of my nature.

But ——

Admirers who always interfere with the correct self-appraisal of an actor again rooted me in my mistake. True, many friends, whose opinion I valued, kept a sad and much-meaning silence. But this only made me try more to believe in flattery, for I was afraid to lose faith in myself. And again I light-mindedly explained their silence by jealousy or intrigue. But nevertheless there was a gnawing pain within me which caused dissatisfaction. Let me say in my defence that it was not the self-love of a spoiled actor that made me so self-confident. Just the opposite; continual secret doubt of myself, panicky fear of losing faith in myself, without which there would not be courage enough to go out on the boards and meet the crowd face to face — this is what forced me to force myself to believe that I was successful. The majority of actors are afraid of the truth not because they cannot bear it, but because it can break in the actor his faith in himself.

The play was crowned with extraordinary success. It was given not only in the club, but later in the Art Theatre, into whose repertoire it was carried over.

CHAPTER XXVI

I FIRST saw Tommaso Salvini in the Imperial Great Theatre where he played almost all Lent with his Italian troupe. The play itself was "Othello." I don't know what had happened to me, but due to my absence of mind or to the insufficient attention I paid to the visit of the great genius, or because I had been mixed up by the visits of former celebrities, like Possart for instance, who did not play Othello but Iago, I was attracted more in the beginning of the performance by the actor who played Iago and thought him to be Salvini.

" Yes, he has a good voice," I told myself. " He has good material in him, a good figure, the general Italian manner of play and declamation, but I see nothing extraordinary. The man who is playing Othello is no worse. He also has fine material in him, a wonderful voice, diction, manners, height."

I treated coldly the ecstasies of the *cognoscenti*, who were ready to faint at the first sentence uttered by Salvini. It seems that the great actor did not want to attract all the attention of the audience to himself in the very beginning of the play. If he had wanted to do so, he could have done it with one moment of genial silence, as he did in the Senate scene immediately after. The beginning of this scene brought forth nothing new, except that I was able to examine the figure, costume, and make-up of Salvini. I cannot say that they were in any way remarkable. I did not like his costume at that time, nor later. Make-up? I don't think he had any on at all. There was the face of the man himself, and perhaps it was unnecessary to make it up. There were his large, pointed mustaches, his wig that looked too much like a wig, his figure, too large, too heavy, almost fat, great eastern daggers that dangled at his waist and made him look stouter than he was, especially when he donned a Moorish cloak and hood. All of this was not much typical of the soldier Othello.

But ——

Salvini approached the platform of the doges, thought a little while, concentrated himself and, unnoticed by any of us, took the entire audience of the Great Theatre into his hands. It seemed that he did this with a single gesture — that he stretched his hand without looking into the public, grasped all of us in his palm, and held us there as if we were ants or flies. He closed his fist, and we felt the breath of death; he opened it, and we knew the warmth of bliss. We were in his power, and we will remain in it all our lives, forever. Now we understood who this genius was, what he was, and what we were to expect from him. It appeared that in the beginning his Othello was not Othello, but Romeo. He saw nothing and nobody but Desdemona, he thought of nothing but of her, he believed her boundlessly, and we wondered how Iago could ever change this Romeo into the jealous Othello. How am I to transfer to you the strength of the impression Salvini made? Let me speak in images, it will be easier.

Imagine that I come to a sculptor, a superman, a god, mighty and tremendous, and ask him:

" Show me Venus of Milo."

The divine sculptor, conscious of the importance of what is going to happen and of what he is going to show me, takes an enormous mass of heated metal. Knowing clearly each line, curve, hollow of the sublime foot, the sculptor god presses, crushes, and bends the formless mass with his mighty fingers, without fearing to burn himself. In his hands appears the tremendous and wonderful foot of a woman, the most beautiful, the most correct, the most classic of all female feet. There is nothing in it that can be changed. It is a law unto eternity. The sculptor god unhurriedly places in front of you a complete part of the future statue, the beauty of which you already begin to fore-know. He has no care whether the sculptured foot is to your liking, whether it creates an impression or not. What he has made exists. It is. If the onlookers are mature enough they will understand; if not, the gates of Eden are closed to them. Continuing the mystery he has begun, the sculptor god labors with even greater repose on another divine foot, on the torso. But here for a moment his repose leaves him. The tender bosom of a woman, modelled from the hard metal, suddenly grows soft in his hands and begins to lift gracefully as if in the act of breathing. The sculptor god stops work and is lost in ad-miration. His face is kind, his smile soft like that of a lovesick boy. The beautiful torso of the woman seems to be light, so light that it rises as of itself, although it is of the hardest metal. On the head of Venus the great sculptor works long and with enthusiasm. One feels that he loves the nose, the eyes, the mouth, the lips, and the swan neck of the divine head.

Now all is ready!

Here are the legs — one! Here is the torso, the arms — two! Here is the head. He places it upon the torso — three!

Look, Venus is alive!

I knew her in my dreams, but never saw her in reality, never thought that she could exist in real life, that she could be so simple, so natural, so light, so airy and so tremendous. She has been poured now into a strong monumental bronze but she still remains a super-human dream, although one can touch her, sense her with the hands, although this dream is so heavy that one cannot lift her. We could never think, looking at the heavy rough metal, that she could so easily reach the heights. It seems that the heavy bronze breathed clouds of unseen ether which at first made us drunk and then carried us to spheres alien to human consciousness.

The creation of Salvini on the stage was a bronze monument. One part of it, like the foot of Venus he molded in the monologue before the Senate. In other scenes and acts he molded the rest of the parts. Put together, they made a deathless monument of human passion, of jealousy, composed of a Romeo-like love, of endless trust, of hurt love, of noble horror and wrath, and of inhuman revenge. Salvini showed each part molded in bronze, although at the beginning they seemed to us to be so diffuse, so unseizable, so dim — as though they were decomposed in the transparent ether of our dreams. And how many more untranslatable feelings and remembrances this rough and heavy bronze created! The Othello of Salvini is a monument, a law unto eternity which can never change.

Our famous Russian poet, K. D. Balmont, has said somewhere, " One must create eternally, once and forever."

Salvini created eternally, once and forever.

Having opened for a moment the gates of paradise in his monologue before the Senate, having showed for the duration of one second at his meeting with Desdemona what trustfulness and boyish love were possible for the courageous and no longer young soldier, Salvini closed for a time the sublime gates of his art, closed them intentionally. He had made sure of our trust in him at one stroke, and like trained dogs that sit on their hind legs and watch the eyes of their trainer we fell hungrily on those places and words of the rôle which Salvini commanded us to notice and to remember.

But in one place he momentarily whipped us up, evidently so that our attention might not weaken. That was in the scene on Cyprus where he made short work of Cassio and Montano. He looked at them so terribly with his tremendous eyes, he lifted his curved scimitar, making it flash in the air, turned it, and lowered it with such Eastern ease and swiftness, that we understood at once how dangerous it was to play with him and what Othello really was:

> For since these arms of mine had seven years' pith
> Till now some nine moons wasted, they have used
> Their dearest action in the tented field.

We were also made to understand why

—— little of this great world can I speak
More than pertains to feats of broil and battle.

The curtain rose on the third act. The scenery was of the most banal operatic design, in the old style of the Great Theatre, and we were disappointed until Salvini appeared on the stage to admire, play, and exchange tenderness with his Desdemona. Now it seemed that two young people in love with each other were on the stage; now that he was an old man tenderly caressing the hair of his granddaughter; now he was the good humored husband created for the purpose of being forever deceived by women. How he disliked to occupy himself with his affairs and part from Desdemona. How long were their farewells, and how their eyes talked for them and they made mysterious cabalistic signs to each other that expressed their hidden secrets. And then, when Desdemona left him, Othello still followed her with his gaze so that poor Iago found it hard faring to distract the attention of the general from his young wife and concentrate it upon himself. It seemed that to-day Iago would reach no results with Othello, who was too much in love with Desdemona. Looking sidewise at his papers of business, idly playing with a goose-feather pen, Othello was in too good spirits to enter with his soul into tiresome affairs. He wanted to be idle, he gossiped with Iago. Have you ever seen a general waste time with his orderly? This close domestic is a familiar of all the secrets of his master; often his counsel is heard with respect, although at most times it is a subject for amusement. Othello loved to jest in his merry moments with his kind, loyal, and loving Iago, his domestic, his familiar. Othello did not know that he was dealing with a demon that hated him and that was seeking cruel revenge.

Iago's first hints about Desdemona only amused Salvini. But this did not stop Iago. He had his plans that led their prey step by step into the pit of jealousy. At first, Othello, as if he struck on a thought that he had never entertained beforehand, lost himself for a moment, but he regained control at once, as his perplexity was laughable in his own eyes. The impossibility of Iago's supposition brings him into even better spirits because he feels that such a thing can never happen to him, — if for no other reasons, — Desdemona is so pure.

But Othello, although he does not know it, is one step nearer to his destruction, and this gives Iago an opportunity to push him down one step more. Othello thinks long and seriously about Iago's new supposition, for it seems to him to be more real and possible than the first. This time he finds it harder to dismiss the thought implanted in him and to return to his former state of bliss. But when he is able to do so, he takes stronger hold of his shaken happiness which has just almost escaped him. Then an even more probable hypothesis rose before Othello. No sooner was he poisoned by it than Iago offered him a new and rather plausible fact, and then its logical development which it was hard to dismiss. Suspicion began to grow into conviction; only the circumstantial evidence was lacking.

This ladder down which Othello descended in the full sight of the spectators from the heights of bliss to the depths of destructive passion, Salvini molded with such clearness, with such merciless logic and such irresistible persuasiveness that the spectator saw all the detailed curves of the suffering soul of Othello and sympathized with him from the depths of the heart. His next meeting with Desdemona no longer called forth his former joy, but a torturing doubt.

If all is a lie, and you are so beautiful and pure, then I have committed a crime before you. I will repent and love you tenfold. But if it is true, as Iago says, that you are as false as you are beautiful, and only hide your spiritual ugliness under the mask of beauty, then you are a viper that the world has never yet seen, and it is my duty to crush you. Where and how am I to find an answer to this question which I must solve now, at once, for I want to kiss you and am afraid to soil myself. I want to love you and am forced to hate you.

This growing doubt Salvini carried to such heights that one feared what was going to happen to him. It was hard to see Othello spring away in evil suspicion from Desdemona when she tried to embrace him and ease his pained head. And in the next instant Othello is repentant and wishes to smooth out the insulting fit that has broken from him despite his better self. He increases his tenderness tenfold, he stretches toward Desdemona to press her to himself again. She approaches him, and again Othello is in doubt and stops her abruptly, to make sure again whether she is not deceiving him. He retreats from her, or rather from his inner struggle and his spiritual doubts.

On his next appearance on the stage Salvini seems to enter as if his inner soul is red-hot, as if burning lava has been poured into his heart, his body is on fire, and he suffers not only mentally but physically also. He seeks some way out of his pain. He grasps hold of anything and everything that might assuage him; he weeps like a child when he says farewell to his army, to his battle steed, to his former life; he tries to express in words the burning pain of his spirit, which we, his audience have lived through with him. But nothing helps him. He seeks respite for his pain in revenge and he throws himself in fury on the only living thing in his presence. He throws Iago to the floor and is on him in one leap, pressing him to the ground, leaps up, lifts his foot above Iago's head to crush it like a snake's, remains in that pause, becomes confused, turns away, and without looking at Iago offers him a hand, lifts him, and falls himself on a couch, crying like a tiger in the desert when he has lost his mate.

At that moment the likeness of Salvini's Othello to a tiger was self-evident. I understood now that even before, in the embraces of Desdemona and in the subtle, feline manners of the speech in the Senate, even in his very method of walking, I had guessed in him the presence of a beast of prey. But this tiger could turn into a gentle child; when he begged Iago to save him from future tortures he was a child that could not bear to be torn by doubts. Even if the very worst had happened he wanted to know it, to be rid of doubt.

The oath of revenge is turned to a ceremony of knighthood in Salvini's Othello; one may think that he is a crusader who is swearing to save the world from the abuse of man's sanctity. In this scene Salvini was monumental.

Salvini is furiously joyful at the finality of proof in the presence of the handkerchief in Cassio's hands. In this he finds the solution of a torturing problem, the answer to a long cankering question. We see what it costs Othello to restrain himself after he has taken a final decision. He is not always successful in restraining himself. For instance, in his scene with Emilia, he could not restrain his hand, which with one tigerish gesture almost tore a piece of flesh out of the side of the procuress, who in Othello's eyes was one most blameworthy. It was even harder for him to control himself in the presence of the Venetian ambassador Lodovico; we saw how the boiling lava rose to his throat and his head until the very time of the catastrophe. For the first time he had struck her whom he had adored and whom he hated now more than anything else in the world.

I will never be able to describe how Salvini stole towards the sleeping Desdemona in the last act, how he was afraid of the folds of his own cloak, which dragged behind him, how he stood admiring the sleeping woman, how he feared and almost ran from his own prey. There were moments when the whole theatre rose like one man in the strain of attention. When Salvini crushed the throat of his beloved, when he threw himself at Iago and killed him with one sweep of his scimitar, I felt again the Bengal tiger in the man's suddenness, agility, energy. But when Othello learned of his fateful mistake, he suddenly became a lost boy who saw death for the first time. And after his speech before his suicide, there talked and acted in him a soldier who had learned to face death all his life, and who is not afraid of it in the last moment of his life.

How simple, clear, beautiful, and tremendous was everything that Salvini did and showed!

But why was it that when I saw Salvini I remembered Rossi and the great Russian actors whom I had seen? Why did I feel that all of them had something in common, something that I seemed to know very well, something I met only in greatly talented actors?

What was it?

I tired myself with thinking, but I could not find the answer.

The relations of Salvini to his artistic duties were touching. On the day of a performance he was excited from the very morning, ate very little, and after dinner retired into solitude and received no guests. The performance would begin at eight o'clock, but Salvini was in the theatre at five, that is, three hours before the performance began. He went to his dressing room, removed his overcoat, and began to wander about the stage. If any one approached him he would talk a little, then leave his companion, sink into thought, stand in silence, and then lock himself in his dressing room. After a while he would issue in his bathrobe or a make-up coat, and after wandering about the stage and trying his voice on some phrase, or rehearsing a gesture or a series of movements necessary for his rôle, he would again retire to his dressing room, put the Moorish make-up on his face and glue his mustaches and beard. Having changed himself not only outwardly, but inwardly he would walk out on the stage again, his footstep lighter and younger than before. The stage hands were beginning to set up the scenery. Salvini tried to talk to them. Who knows, perhaps Salvini imagined then that he was among his soldiers, who were putting up barricades and fortifications against an enemy. His strong figure, his military pose, his eyes attentively fixed on some far-off object seemed to add truth to his supposition. Again Salvini would retire into his dressing room and come out in a wig and the under robe of Othello, then with a girdle and scimitar, then with a turban on his head, and at last in the full costume of Othello. And with each of his entrances it seemed that Salvini not only made up his face and dressed his body, but also prepared his soul in a like manner, gradually establishing a perfect balance of character. He crept into the skin and body of Othello with the aid of some important preparatory toilet of his own artistic soul and body.

Such preparatory work before every performance was necessary for the genius after he had played the part of Othello many hundreds of times, after he had spent ten years in the preparation of the part alone. It was not in vain that he confessed in his reminiscences that it was only after the hundreth or two-hundredth performance that he understood what Othello was and how to play the part well.

Thinking of this genius, I cannot help but remember how our home-grown stars and tragedians appear in the theatre at the time of a performance. They consider it demeaning to appear in the theatre on time. If they are stars the rest can wait for them; it is not worth being stars otherwise. Their glory consists in making the performance late, so that the stage manager may run through the theatre tearing the hair from his head, that the administration may telephone to all possible and probable places looking for them, that the actors in the dressing rooms may sit in perplexity, not knowing what to do — to finish putting on their make-up, or to take it off so as to be able to appear in a hastily improvised play in which the star does not act, and all because of *Caprice*.

But exactly at five minutes to eight the home-grown star deigns to appear in the theatre. The rest cross themselves. They are glad — the performance will take place after all.

He will play!

One, two, three, and the star is costumed, made up, and the sword of Hamlet is at his belt. He knows his business! And everybody around him is in ecstasies.

"This is a real artist! Look at him! He came last, but he is the first on the stage! Young actors — here is an example tc follow!"

But has any one ever asked the home-grown star:

"You managed to dress and make up in five minutes. Let us

grant that that is marvelous. But did you manage to cleanse, dress and make up your soul — and if not then why did you come to the theatre, and why do you play Hamlet? Is it not merely in order to display your graceful legs? And do you think that your legs are the only things that count? Shakespeare carried Hamlet in his soul for years, — do you think that he wrote the play for the sake of your legs? And what is your reason, if you have any, for appearing on the stage at all?

" Come, come, don't drag the wool over our eyes. Do you think we don't understand that there is no man in the world who can pass in five minutes from the sphere of restaurants and vulgar anecdotes into the empire of the superconscious. This requires a gradual, logical approach. You can't rise from the cellar to the sixth floor in one step."

" Well, and what about Kean? " our home-grown star will answer. " Remember, he also arrives at the last moment, when all are waiting in excitement for his appearance."

" That is the theatrical Kean. How much evil he has caused by his example! And was Kean really as he is drawn in the melodrama? If he was, then I don't doubt that he is nervous and shouts before the performance because he has had no time to prepare, because he is angry at himself for his own drunkenness on the day of the performance. Creative nature has its laws, which are the same for Kean and Salvini. Then believe in the example of the living Salvini and not of a dead Kean taken from the pages of a mediocre melodrama."

But no, the home-grown star will always copy Kean and not Salvini. He will always come to the theatre five minutes before the performance is due to begin, and not three hours before, as Salvini did. Why?

In order to prepare something in your soul for three hours, it is necessary to have that something, and the home-grown star has nothing but his talents. He comes to the theatre with a costume in his suit case, but without any spiritual baggage whatsoever. What can he do in his dressing room from five to eight? Smoke? Tell droll tales? That is done much better in the restaurants.

Salvini always hit the bull's-eye with his definitions. For instance he played King Lear in the provinces with a well-known actress. She possessed everything the stage required, ability, figure, a beautiful face, a good voice, gestures, experience. But she did not possess something much more important than all that.

" How do you like her?" Salvini was asked.

" M—ma!—*Il lui manche la poesia,*" answered Salvini. (She lacks poetry.)

At another time during the rehearsal of the last act of " Othello," the role of Lodovico, who appears after the death of Desdemona, was in the hands of a provincial *raisonneur,* who read it apathetically in a thick, churchy bass. Salvini lost his patience and whispered to the stage director:

" *Ditte lui che sa cousine e morte!* " (Tell him his cousin died.)

And to one of our home-grown tragedians, who had lost his voice by drinking, and who asked Salvini what was necessary in order to become a tragedian, Salvini answered:

" You need only three things: voice, voice, and more voice!"

Salvini said this not only to hoarse tragedians but he repeated it at every opportunity, for like Possart, he attached a tremendous importance to the voice in tragic roles.

CHAPTER XXVII

WHAT rôle fitted me least at that time?
What rôle was most harmful to me at that time?
Othello.

But it was of Othello I dreamed, especially since the time I visited Venice. In Venice my wife and I spent livelong days visiting the museums, searching for antique objects, sketching costumes from the frescoes, buying furniture, brocades, and embroidery. I did all this, secretly entertaining the idea of producing " Othello."

I even found Othello himself. In one of the summer restaurants of Paris I met a handsome Arab in his national costume.

" Introduce me to him," I asked my friend the waiter, " and I will leave you a good tip."

In another half hour I was already dining my new friend in a private dining room. Finding that I was interested in his costume, the Arab, without saying a word, undressed to the skin. With the help of the waiter we made the designs of the costume. I learned several bodily poses which seemed to me to be characteristic. Then I studied the Arab's body, his movements and his outer anatomy. Returning to my hotel, I stood half the night before a mirror, putting on sheets and towels in order to make myself into a graceful Moor with quick turns of the head, movements of the hands and the body as graceful as those of a deer, a smooth, royal method of walking, and narrow palms turned towards those who might speak to me.

As soon as I returned to Moscow I began to prepare a production of " Othello." But I was out of luck. One obstacle followed another.

First of all my wife fell sick, and the rôle of Desdemona was given to another amateur actress, but she behaved badly and I was forced to take the rôle away from her in punishment.

" I will rather spoil the production than allow actors' caprices in our good work."

It became necessary to entrust the rôle to a very nice young lady who looked the part, but who had never been on the stage.

" This one will at least work and listen," I reasoned with the despotism that was so characteristic of me then.

Notwithstanding the slight success which we enjoyed with the public, our society was very poor, for our new enthusiasm, the luxury of props, ate up all our profits. At that time we did not even have enough money to hire a hall for rehearsals. These took place in my apartment, in the only room that I could spare.

" This is all for the better," I thought. " The atmosphere of our little Circle will be all the purer for that."

The rehearsals took place every day, lasting till three or four in the morning. The rooms of my little apartment were filled with the tobacco smoke of our actors. It was necessary to serve tea every day. This tired the servant. She grumbled. All these inconveniences and cares my sick wife and I bore without a murmur, to save our enterprise from destruction.

To say the truth, our Circle was not strong enough to provide actors for all the parts in the play. There was no one to play Iago, although every man in the society was tried out. We were forced to invite an experienced actor from the outside. He, like Desdemona, suited his rôle only outwardly; he had a good face, an evil voice and evil eyes. But he was stiff to the verge of despair and was completely devoid of mimetics, which made his face altogether dead.

" We'll get out of this in some way," I said, not without the self-reliance of a stage director.

The play began with the far-off striking of a tower clock. These sounds, so banal now, created an impression in their time. They were followed by the distant splash of oars (we invented this sound also); there was a floating gondola that stopped on the stage, the thunder of chains with which it was fastened to a painted Venetian pile, after which it gracefully rolled from side to side in the water. Othello and Iago began their scene sitting in the gondola, then they passed out of it under the colonnade of the house which resembled the Palace of the Doges in Venice.

In the scene of Brabantio the entire house came to life, the casements opened, sleepy figures looked out of them, servants put on their armor as they came out, picked up their arms and ran in the wake of the abductor of Desdemona. Some entered the gondola which was filled to overflow as it was, and rowed under the bridge, others crossed the bridge on foot, returned for something they forgot, and ran out again. The abduction of the white aristocrat by the blackamoor was given a tremendous meaning in our production.

" Imagine that some Tartar or Persian stole a grand duchess from the palace of the grand duke. What would happen in Moscow? " one of my simple friends who saw the play, told me.

In the Senate, the Doge sat in his traditional seat, in a bonnet and a golden hat. All the senators were in black hats, with wide strips of brocade across their shoulders, and tremendous buttons made of jewels. All who were present at the meeting were in black masks. This was a curious characteristic of the production. Notwithstanding the foolishness of having strangers present at a night conclave, I could not resist putting in this detail, which was noted by me during my journey to Venice; it did not matter that it was not necessary in the play.

How did I say the famous speech of Othello in the Senate? In no way. I simply told a story. At that time I did not recognize the importance either of the word or of speech. The outer image was more important to me. My make-up was not successful, but my figure seemed to do. Poisoned in Paris by my Oriental friend, I copied him.

What is remarkable is that notwithstanding the fact that I was in a costume play, I did not fall victim to the enchantments of the opera baritone. The characteristics of the East built a wall between me and my former bad habits. I had made my own the suddenness of the movements of the Arab, his floating walk, his narrow palm, to such a degree that often I was unable to control these movements even in my private life. They came to me of themselves.

I will stress another detail of stage direction and hokum that was very typical of the time and that helped to cover the faults of the actor. For instance in the end of the scene in the Senate, the senators have left, Othello, Desdemona and Brabantio also. There remained the servants who were putting out the torches, and Iago, hiding like a black rat in a corner. There was complete darkness, which with the aid of two dim lanterns in the hands of the servants gave Iago the chance to hide his dead face. At the same time his fine voice sounded in the darkness better than ever and seemed more threatening than it was. At one stroke I had killed two birds. I hid a fault and showed the best gift of the actor. The stage director helped the actor by hiding him.

In the scenes in Cyprus there was also a novelty for that time. Let us begin by saying that Cyprus is altogether different from Venice, although in the theatre they resemble each other. Cyprus is Turkey. It is inhabited not by Europeans, but by Turks. The extras in the mob scenes on Cyprus were dressed as Turks.

"Why should one not send a blackamoor against blackamoors?" said the same simple friend of whom I have already written.

One must not forget that Othello had come to an island where a revolt had just been crushed. One spark, and the flames would rise again. The Turks look at the Venetians sidewise. The Venetians are not used to ceremonies; even now they do not restrain themselves and conduct themselves as if they were at home. They were drinking in something that looked like a Turkish coffee house, which was built on the fore-stage in the center, where met two narrow Oriental streets which disappeared in a background of hills. From the coffee house there came the sad sounds of a zurna and other Oriental instruments, they were singing and dancing there; one could hear drunken voices. And the Turks walked in groups on the street, looking sidewise at the drunken Europeans, holding their knives ready in their bosoms.

Feeling this atmosphere, Iago invented the plan for his intrigue in a much greater measure than it is usual to show on the stage. His business did not lie in starting a quarrel between two officers who stood in his way. The problem was much greater; it was to make them responsible for a new revolt on the island. Iago knows that all that was necessary for a new revolt was a single spark. He enlarges a single fight between two drunkards into an event, sends Roderigo and runs himself to inform all in the streets of what has happened. And at last he reaches the results he has expected. Crowds of newly revolted Cyprians steal down the two streets to the house of joy to attack the conquerors and destroy them. Scimitars, swords, sticks, glitter above their heads. The Venetians take their appointed battle places on the fore-stage, their backs to the audience, and wait for the attack. At last the two crowds attack the Venetians from both sides, and the fight begins. Othello springs into the thick of it, with a great sword in his hand with which he seems to cut the crowd in two. It was here, in the very pit of death, that one could appreciate his fighting qualities and his courage. And it was here that one could truly appreciate the satanic plotting of Iago.

It is not to be wondered at that the act of Cassio which caused this catastrophe should take on tremendous proportions in the eyes of Othello. It is to be understood that his judgment is strict, his sentence severe. The plot of the play is prepared by the stage director in a large manner. While he could he helped the actor with his production.

Beginning with the third act no hokum on the part of the stage director is any longer possible. All the responsibility falls on the actor. But if I did not have enough of simple restraint and inner creativeness of image for the tragic scene in the third act of "Uriel Acosta" where it was necessary to show the inner struggle between conviction and emotion, between the philosopher and the lover — then where was I to get the much more difficult technique and ability for the role of Othello, where everything is built on the mathematical consequency in the development of the emotion of jealousy, beginning from the most restful state, passing through the almost unnoticeable birth of the passion and on to the very heights of jealousy? It is no light matter to show that growing line of the development of jealousy from the childish trustfulness of Othello in the first act towards the moment of the first doubt and the birth of the passion, and then lead it farther in merciless sequence through all the steps of its growth to its apogee, that is, to beastlike madness. And then, when the innocence of the victim of that passion is undoubted, to cast emotion from the heights to the depths, into the chasm of despair, into the pit of remorse.

All this, fool that I was, I hoped to accomplish with the aid of intuition alone. Of course I was able to reach nothing more than insane strain, spiritual and physical impotence and the squeezing of tragic emotion out of myself. In my strengthless struggle I even lost the little which I had gained in other rôles — which I had seemed to possess since the time of "Bitter Fate." There was no restraint, no control of the temperament, no placing of color; there was only the strain of muscles, the violation of voice and of the entire organism, and spiritual buffers that suddenly grew to all sides of me in self-defence from the problems which I had put before myself and which were too much for me.

To be just, there were places that were not bad in the first half of the play. For instance, the first scene in the third act with Iago, in which the latter casts the first seed of doubt into the soul of Othello; the scene with the handkerchief between Desdemona and Othello, and others. I had enough technique, voice, experience and ability for these scenes, but farther on, feeling my impotence, I thought only of violent effort and created muscular strain. Here was the same feeling of chaos in the emotions and thoughts, strain and self-consciousness with which I had become so well acquainted in the rôle of Peter in " Don't Live to Please Yourself."

There could be no talk about the systematic and gradual growth of emotion. The worst of all was the voice, an organ highly sensitive, that cannot stand strain. Even at rehearsals it had given warning more than once. There was enough of it only for the first two acts, but later it would grow so hoarse that it was necessary to stop rehearsing for several days at a time while a doctor would try his best with it. Only here, when I came face to face with reality, did I begin to understand that for tragedy it was necessary to know something, to be able to do something, that otherwise it would be impossible to give even one performance. The whole secret was in the voice, I decided; it had been placed in my case for singing, and I would place it properly for drama. There was a dole of truth in this, for my voice had been forced inwardly, and I flexed my diaphragm and my throat so that my voice could not reverberate. The rehearsals were stopped for a while. With the obstinacy that was part of me at that time, I began to sing again, and considering that I was experienced enough as a singer, I invented my own system for the placing of the voice for the drama, and I must confess that I reached some good results. It was not that my voice became bigger, but was easier for me to use, and I could now play through not only one or two acts, but the whole play. This was an advance not only in the given rôle but also in my technique for the future.

The work that I did at that time was far beyond my strength. After a long rehearsal I was forced to lie down with a quickened heart, and I would choke as if I had asthma. The production became a torture, but I could not stop it because the expenses had grown very large and it was necessary that they be covered if we did not want to bankrupt our whole society, for there was no place where we could get funds. Besides, my vanity as an actor and a stage manager suffered. I insisted on the production myself, and continued insisting on it when more experienced people tried to persuade me to drop it. Art avenged itself, the theatre taught the obstinate and punished him for his self-reliance. It was a useful lesson.

"No," I thought, lying in bed after a rehearsal with a beating heart and a choking throat, "this is not art. Salvini is old enough to be my father, but he is not sick after a performance, although he plays in the tremendous auditorium of the Great Theatre while I cannot even finish a rehearsal in a little room. And I haven't even enough voice and temperament for the little room. I am losing weight as if I were seriously ill. How will I ever play the part? What evil spirit prompted me to start it? No, it is not so pleasant to act a tragedy as it seemed to me before."

Another failure! At the dress rehearsal in the strongest part of the scene with Iago, I cut his hand with my dagger, blood flowed from his wound, the rehearsal stopped, a doctor came, those present were excited, but what hurt me most was that notwithstanding the deadliness of my play the audience remained completely cold. This hurt me more than anything else. Had a big impression been made by my acting and had I wounded another in the heat of my acting, it would have been said that I had played so strongly that I could not restrain my temperament. This is not good, but it is flattering for an actor to have an uncontrollable temperament. But I had cold-bloodedly wounded a man; it was not my acting, it was human blood that had made the impression. This hurt. Besides, the untoward event pointed impressively to the absence of the necessary restraint. Rumors of the event floated about town, and the news got into the papers. This interested the public, and possibly made them expect more than I could give them.

The production was not successful, and even our beautiful and luxurious stage appointments did not help. They were but little noticed, perhaps because after " Uriel Acosta " scenic luxury became satiating, perhaps because luxurious appurtenances are good and necessary only when the most important things are present with them, — the interpreters of Othello, Iago, and Desdemona. These were completely absent, and the production seemed to have only one good result: it gave a good object lesson to me in my obstinacy, vanity, and ignorance of the fundamentals of art and its technique.

" Don't attempt to play those rôles prematurely which God is kind enough to let you play at the end of your scenic career."

I decided to wait with the playing of tragedy.

But ——

A famous actor visited Moscow. He played Othello, and at his performances the public as well as the press had a good word to say about me in the rôle of Othello. This was enough to set me dreaming again about Hamlet, Macbeth, King Lear, parts that were far beyond my strength in those days, and in which I could only " tear passion to tatters."

There was still another reason that caused the rejuvenation of my former dreams. Rossi himself came to one of the performances of "Othello." The famous actor sat through the performance from the beginning to the end, applauded as the ethics of actors demanded, but did not come back-stage, and asked, as an older man of a younger, that I visit him. In the grasp of spiritual trembling I came to the great actor. He was an enchanting man, remarkably well bred, well read, and well educated. Of course, he had understood everything at once, the idea of the production, the Turkish Cyprus, the hokum with the darkness for Iago, but all this did not surprise him very much or make him enthusiastic. He was against the colorful scenery, the costumes and the production itself, for it took too much of the attention of the spectator away from the actors.

" All these playthings are necessary when there are no actors. A beautiful, wide costume can well cover a pitiful body within which there does not beat the heart of an artist. It is necessary for those without talent, but you do not need it," Rossi sweetened the bitter pill he was preparing for me in a beautiful manner, with wonderful diction and movements of the hands. "Iago is not an actor of your theatre," he continued. "Desdemona '*e bella*' but it is too early to judge her, for she has just begun her career on the boards probably. There remains you."

The great actor fell into a brown study. (And there was enough to think about.)

"God gave you everything for the stage, for Othello, for the whole repertoire of Shakespeare. (My heart leaped up at his words.) The matter is in your hands. All you need is art. It will come, of course —— "

Having said the real truth, he began to embroider it with compliments.

"But where and how and from whom am I to learn that art?" I questioned.

"M-ma! If there is no great master near you whom you can trust, I can recommend you only one teacher," answered the great artist.

"Who is he?" I demanded.

"You yourself," he ended with the gesture he had made familiar in the rôle of Kean.

I was confused by the fact that in spite of all the cues I had given him, he had said nothing to me about my interpretation of the part. But later when I began to judge myself with less prejudice, I understood that Rossi could not have said anything else. Not only he, but even I did not understand my interpretation of the rôle. It all came to the point of finishing the performance without breaking down, of squeezing tragism out of myself, of creating some sort of impression on the spectators, of being successful, of not making a scandal. Can one expect of a singer who is yelling at the top of his voice that he give the most delicate nuances in his singing, that he interpret artistically the songs and arias he is singing? All goes into strength alone, all takes on one hue. Just like painters who smear a fence one given color. They are far removed from the artist who can controlledly and restfully show a crowd his interpretation of a rôle created by himself. For this it is not enough to be simply talented and to have natural gifts; one needs ability, technique, and art. It was this that Rossi had told me, and he could not have told me anything else.

Experience told me the same thing, experience and personal practice in the care I took of my future work, and for my future work.

CHAPTER XXVIII

AFTER I had burned my fingers in "Othello," I found it terrifying to undertake a tragedy, and it was boring to live without Spanish boots and mediæval swords, so I decided to try my mettle in comedy. This motivated the production of "Much Ado About Nothing."

And yet there was still another reason. Let me confess it.

During a visit to Italy, my wife and I had accidentally come upon the mediæval gates of a castle in the park of Turin. A bridge was noisily lowered for us across a water-filled moat, the creaking gates were opened, and we found ourselves in a feudal dream city of the sixteenth century. Narrow streets, houses with colonnades under the hanging roof of which passed pedestrians, a square, an original cathedral, alleys with water basins, the tremendous castle of the lord himself surrounded by its own moat and having its own suspension bridge. The entire town was painted with bright Italian frescoes. Near the gates of entrance were armed soldiers, towers with stairways, entrances, and openings for guns and arquebuses. The entire town was closed in by a toothed wall which was patrolled by a sentry. Crowds of people walked about the town, — citizens, pages, merchants, who always live in this fantastic city and always wear mediæval costumes. Butchers' shops, vegetable shops, fruit shops stretch along all the streets, and above, from the windows of some courtier, hang mediæval breeches and doublet, airing themselves in the sultry air of the street. Passing an armorer's shop you are deafened by the beating of a hammer, and the hot breath of fire singes you. A gloomy priest passes, accompanied by a barefooted friar who is girded by a rope and has a

shaven poll. A street singer intones a serenade. A woman of doubtful appearance calls you to enter a mediæval hostelry, where a whole
ram is being roasted on a spit in a tremendous fireplace.

" The castle is empty, for the master and his family are away," we
were told by the commandant of the soldiers. Here are his barracks,
here is a small kitchen for the soldiers, a large kitchen for the lord,
with a whole steer on the spit hung under the ceiling and waiting to
be lowered into the fire of the tremendous hearth. Here is the dining
room with the two-seated throne of the lord and his lady, with boards
resting on horses instead of tables; here is the inner courtyard from
where one can see the hunting falcons in the highest story beating
their wings and hear their piercing cries. They are being brought to
rest by a hunter in mediæval costume.

We were in the throne room with portraits of the ancestors of the
lord hanging on the walls, with writings of an ethical nature in the
shape of long white tongues seemingly issuing from mouths. In the
bedchamber is a large image. It opens like a door and leads into a
narrow corridor; from the corridor you enter a tower, holding one
round room with a tremendous bed with hangings, the cold stone walls
draped with ribbons, flowers, writings, scrolls of multicolored papyrus.
Here hang breeches, a sword, a cloak. There is great disorder in the
room. It is the dwelling place of a page. We entered the chapel, we
spent some time in the cell of the priest.

After this I began to understand the meaning in Shakespeare's
plays of " Send for the priest " and how he was able to appear in a
moment and raise his hands in blessing. This was because the priest
lived in the same house with the lord, only a room or two removed.
And if you pass the corridor and enter the chapel, why, you can be
married in a moment. He who has been in this castle has felt the
spirit of the Middle Ages.

I decided to live for a time in the feudal city and to gather impressions of the Middle Ages at first hand. It was a pity that strangers

were not allowed to spend the night there, and we remained until we were asked to leave before the main gates were closed.

Since that time, drunk with what I had seen, I looked for a play, not in order to express the poet, not in order to create a beloved image or to interpret an emotion close to the heart of man, or a thought dear to him, but in order to use this excellent material for a production. I did not need scenery and costumes for a play; I needed a play for scenery and costumes. In our age it is a usual occurrence, but in those days it seemed far-fetched and wild. It was with this purpose that I thumbed the pages of Shakespeare, and it seemed to me that my ideas of production were best of all fitted for the comedy of " Much Ado About Nothing."

Besides, there were costume parts — for me and for the others. But I had not thought of one thing — was the rôle of a happy-go-lucky, witty merrymaker fit for a man of my unusual height and figure? I began to think of that only after the rehearsals had already begun.

" One can make two Benedicks out of you," some one told me, " but never one."

How could I find myself in that rôle when everything in it interfered with me? After long tortures it seemed that I had found a way out that was not bad, or rather that was a compromise. I decided to play a clumsy knight, a soldier who must think only of service and hate all women, especially Beatrice. He insults her with premeditation. I hoped to find in outer military coarseness the character of the image. I had already learned to love to hide myself behind a character, but it was a pity that I could not find the character, and for this reason fell again into the quicksands of my old operetta habits, a thing that always happened to me when I did not play a part but myself. The theatrical result is self-explanatory.

From the viewpoint of stage direction I was much more successful. The play found a good home in my mediæval castle. I also felt at home in it. I understood it all; for instance, where the people lived, where the visiting duke Don John and his courtiers intrigued. Right here in the feudal town in one of whose houses they stopped. Where did Borachio and Conrade meet? Why, in the narrow streets of the feudal town. Where were they led? Into the alley near the barracks where Dogberry held court. Where was Claudio wedded? Where did the scandal during the ceremony take place? In the chapel of the castle. Where did Benedick go to challenge Claudio to a duel? To the same house where Don John lived. Where did the masquerade take place? In the inner courtyard, in the narrow corridors, in the throne room, in the dining room. All was clear, natural, cosy, under the hand, just as it was in the Middle Ages.

At that time I thought that the stage director must study and feel the local character of the life of a part and a play in order to show it to the spectator and force the latter to live in that locale as he lived at home. With time I learned the true meaning of so-called realism.

"Realism ends where the superconscious begins." Meanwhile it is enough that I understood the necessity of visiting museums, traveling, collecting books necessary for the productions, — engravings, paintings, and all that pictures the outer life of men, so characterizing the inner life of their spirit. Till that time I loved to collect in all spheres, but from that moment on I began to gather things that bore relation to the theatre and to the business of a stage director.

The usefulness of this production lay also in the fact that I had again proved the importance of characterization in defending myself from harmful, theatrical methods of acting. I thought that the creative road led from outer characterization to inner emotion. As I learned later, this was one of the roads, but not the only one. It was good when the characterization came of itself and I grasped my rôle immediately. But in the majority of cases this did not happen, and I would remain helpless. How was I to make it my own? I thought much and labored much over this problem, and this was useful, since in my search for characterization I looked for it in real life, and when I found it, tried to carry it on to the stage. Before this, in my quest for the methods of acting in a given rôle, I only buried myself in the dust-covered archives of old and lifeless traditions and stencils. In those spiritual warehouses one cannot find inspiration for creativeness. And it is especially there that actors seek stimulants for their inspiration in the majority of cases.

"Seek your examples in life," the great Shtchepkin told us.

The production was very successful — due mostly to the stage direction. As an actor I appealed only to nice and kind high-school girls.

If before, the indifference of the Moscow public drove the actors from the theatre and forced them to think of changing their careers and the necessity of saying final farewells to art, now, after success, there was created a counter trend toward the theatre. The growing popularity teased ambition, and ovations and success became indispensable. They wanted to become honest-to-goodness actors as soon as they could. All became spoiled and the simple amateur accidental performance in the little theatre with small houses and receipts did not satisfy. We needed our own theatre with daily and well-organized performances. The straightforward question of the quickest keeping of my promise, that is, of the creation of our theatre, became more and more pressing. Doubts of the possibility of realizing my plan were heard oftener and sharper. Some of the actors were lured away by other managers. Here Fate helped me again, making me meet the man whom I had sought for a long time. I met Vladimir Ivanovich Nemirovich-Danchenko, who, like me, was poisoned by the same dream. It is strange — I had known him for a long time. He had long been a familiar figure in the theatre, a dramatist and a teacher of dramatic art, a stage director and a critic and an expert, and I, instead of going straight to him, looked for help where I could least hope to find it, among professional managers who knew only how to buy and sell art. The theatre, which performs a cultural mission, demands of the persons engaged in it very much. To be the director of such an establishment one must be a talented expert in his own field, that is, understand art not only as a critic, but as an actor, a stage director, a producer, a literateur, an administrator. One must know the theatre not only theoretically, but practically. One must know the construction of the stage, the architecture of the theatre itself, one must know the psychology of the mob, understand the nature and the psychology of the actor, the conditions of his creative work and life; one must have a wide literary education, tact, sensitivity, breeding, restraint, mind, administrative abilities and much, much more. It is seldom that all these qualities are met with in one person. But they met in Vladimir Nemirovich-Danchenko. He was that director of whom one could dream. It seems that Nemirovich-Danchenko had also dreamed of such a theatre as I imagined and sought a man such as he imagined me to be. We had sought each other for a long time, although it seems that we did not have to look far, for we had known each other for a long time and often met each other, but we had not discovered each other. It was easier for Nemirovich-Danchenko to find me, for I was an actor who appeared publicly, while his stage directing work was shown only once a year at a private performance which not every one could attend.

In the year when Nemirovich had redoubled his quest in the Philharmonic School there was preparing an extraordinary class of graduating pupils. A complete company that seemed to have been hand-picked was being graduated. All of them were more or less fit for the stage, and several had extraordinarily artistic individualities. How could one let such a company, which seemed to be picked by Destiny itself, go? Was it possible to let them disperse to all sides, to the far corners of the provinces? How was one not to make use of them for the creation of the long-awaited theatre!

And at last we met! During the winter we made the closer

acquaintance of each other and of the future actors of our company. Nemirovich visited all the performances of our Society and after each one spoke with me and criticized them with complete sincerity. It can be said in our favor that at that time we were not afraid to hear the truth. He spoke in turn to every actor, put questions to them that were necessary for him for the explanation of the individual nature of each actor. On my side, I was a constant attendant at all the performances of the Philharmonic Society, and in my way did the same thing with his pupils.

In May or in June, 1897, I received a note from Nemirovich-Danchenko, inviting me to a conference in the restaurant " The Slavic Bazaar." We met, and he explained to me the purposes of our meeting. They lay in the foundation of a new theatre, which I was to enter with my group of amateurs, and he with his group of pupils. To this nucleus we were to add chosen professional actors from Petersburg, Moscow, and the provinces. The most important questions before us were these: how far the artistic principles of the chief controllers of the new theatre agreed with each other, what compromises each of them was willing to make, and were there any points in common between us.

The peace conference of Versailles did not consider the world questions before it with such clarity and exactness as we considered the foundations of our future enterprise, the questions of pure art, our artistic ideals, scenic ethics, technique, the plans of organization, the projects of our future repertoire, and our mutual relations.

" Take actor A," we examined each other. " Do you consider him talented? "

" To a high degree."

" Will you take him into the troupe? "

" No."

" Why? "

" Because he has adapted himself to his career, his talents to the demands of the public, his character to the caprices of the manager, and all of himself to theatrical cheapness. A man who is so poisoned cannot be cured."

" And what will you say about actress B? "

" She is a good actress, but not for us."

" Why? "

" She does not love art, but herself in art."

" And actress C? "

" She won't do. She is incurably given to hokum."

" What about actor D? "

" We must pay a great deal of attention to him."

" Why? "

" He has ideals for which he is fighting. He is not at peace with present conditions. He is a man of his ideals."

" I am of the same opinion. Permit me to enter his name on the list of candidates."

Then there arose the question of literature. I felt Nemirovich-Danchenko's superiority to myself at once, and willingly subjected myself to his authority, writing down in the minutes of the meeting that he was to have full power of veto in all questions of literary character.

But in the region of the actor, the stage director and the producer I was far from being so yielding. I had a large fault, which I believe I have cured by this time to a certain extent. Once I became enthused about something, I strained forward to my desire without letting any obstacle hinder me, like a horse in blinders. At such a moment neither rhyme nor reason could stop me. Thanks to my fifteen years of amateur practice, I was quite experienced in matters of stage direction at that time, and Nemirovich-Danchenko was forced to yield me the right of veto in matters of stage direction and artistic production. In the minutes I entered:

" The literary veto belongs to Nemirovich-Danchenko, the artistic veto to Stanislavsky."

During all the following years we held closely to this point of our agreement. One of us would only have to pronounce the magic word *veto,* and our debate would end in the middle of a sentence, the entire responsibility being placed on the shoulders of the one who exercised his right. Of course, we used our power of ultimatum very carefully, and exercised it only in extreme cases, when we were fully convinced that we were in the right. There were mistakes made too, but nevertheless a great deal of good came of the custom we had created. Each of us who was acknowledged to be a specialist in his particular branch had the opportunity to begin and finish his work without any interference. Others, who were less experienced, watched us, and learned what they had not understood at first. In matters of administration and organization I willingly yielded the right of decision to my new comrade, for I saw only too plainly the administrative and organizing powers of Nemirovich-Danchenko.

Besides, it was enough that I did administrative work in my factory and my business office, for I was a director and chairman of a manufacturing and trading company. I was forced to continue this work parallel with my acting and stage direction throughout the whole course of my scenic activities, and right up to the very beginning of the Soviet system. In the business affairs of the theatre I limited myself to an advisory capacity at such times when my business experience could be of use.

The question of finances was also considered at the meeting in " The Slavic Bazaar ". It was decided to elect shareholders from the directors of the Philharmonic Society among whom there were many well-to-do men, and also from the members of the Society of Art and Literature.

In the region of general ethics we agreed at once that before we demanded the fulfillment of all the laws of decency on the part of the actors, it was necessary to place them in human surroundings. Remember in what conditions actors usually live. Often they have not a single corner behind the scenes that they can call their own. Three quarters of the usual theatre is given over to the spectators, who have buffets, tea rooms, coat rooms, foyers, smoking rooms, dressing rooms, corridors for promenades. Only one quarter of the building is given over to the people who work in the theatre. Here there are warerooms for scenery, for properties, for electric apparatus, offices and workrooms.

What space is left for the actor? Several tiny rooms under the stage, without windows or ventilation, always dusty and dirty because no matter how much they are cleaned, the dust from the scenic floor which forms the ceiling of these rooms always eats through the cracks between the boards, a dust that is permeated with dry paint from the scenery, which injures the eyes and the lungs. Remember the furnishings of these so-called dressing rooms: several badly planed boards fastened to the wall by means of T-irons, that are supposed to be make-up tables. A little mirror intended for the use of at least two or three actors, usually bad because it is bought by chance at some glass auction. An old chair no longer usable on the stage. A wooden plank with nails in it instead of a hanger. A wooden door with cracks in the panels. A nail and a rope instead of a lock.

If you look into the kennel of the prompter you are reminded of mediæval inquisition. The prompter in the theatre is sentenced to eternal torture that makes one fear for his life. He has a dirty box lined with dusty felt. Half of his body is beneath the floor of the stage in the dampness of a cellar, the other half, at the level of the stage, is heated by the hundreds of lamps in the footlights on both sides of him. All the dust created at the rising of the curtain or the sweeping of robes across the stage strikes him square in the mouth. And he is forced to speak without stop during performance and rehearsal in an unnaturally squeezed and often strained voice so that he may be heard by the actors alone, and not by the spectators. It is a well-known fact that three quarters of the prompters end with tuberculosis. Everybody knows this, but no one tries to invent a more or less decent prompter's box, notwithstanding the fact that our age is so rich in invention.

The stage and the dressing room, included in the general heating system of the theatre, are usually kept warm only in so far as this is demanded by the needs of the spectator. The temperature of the dressing room is directly dependent on the temperature in the auditorium. Therefore in the majority of cases actors either freeze in their summer clothes or the tights necessary for their parts, or are brought to a point of impotence in the heavy fur coats which they put on in plays like " Tsar Fyodor ". During the time of rehearsals theatres are usually completely unheated. They become colder and colder, what with the carrying in and out of scenery. The tremendous doors that lead from the stage to the street are opened for hours at a time while the stage hands finish their work. Usually they interfere with the beginning of the rehearsals and the actors are forced to breathe frozen air which attacks them directly from the street. Naturally actors are forced to rehearse in their overcoats and rubbers and so bring the mud of the street on the stage. Because there is no place where they can rest between appearances on the stage, they are obliged to wander in the wings, in the cold corridors, in the uncomfortable dressing rooms.

We also spoke of artistic ethics and entered our decisions into the minutes, at times even using aphorisms.

" There are no small parts, there are only small actors."

" One must love art, and not one's self in art."

" To-day Hamlet, to-morrow a supernumerary, but even as a supernumerary you must become an artist."

" The poet, the actor, the artist, the tailor, the stage hand serve one goal, which is placed by the poet in the very basis of his play."

" All disobedience to the creative life of the theatre is a crime."

" Lateness, laziness, caprice, hysterics, bad character, ignorance of the rôle, the necessity of repeating anything twice are all equally harmful to our enterprise and must be rooted out."

My first conference with Nemirovich-Danchenko, which had decisive importance for our future Theatre, began at ten in the morning of one day and lasted till three in the morning of the next day. It continued without a break for fifteen hours, and perhaps even longer. But our pains were rewarded, for we came to an understanding of all fundamental questions and reached the conclusion that we could work together. A great deal of time remained before our theatre was to open, a year and four months, to be exact. Nevertheless we began to work at once. There were many more conferences between us, conferences that did not last fifteen hours as our first one did, but eight or ten hours was our average.

CHAPTER XXIX

W E were faced by a great deal of labor in the preparation of a repertoire for the winter. Besides, we were confronted by a first season of daily performances, which were to be prepared at all costs during the summer months. Where were we to begin working? We had no theatre of our own, for the one we had rented was to pass into our hands only with the beginning of September, and there was not even a room at our disposal for rehearsals. Figuring practically, it was more profitable to conduct rehearsals and pass the summer outside of the city. Happily, one of the members of the Society of Art and Literature, N. N. Arkhipov (later the stage director Arbatov) offered our theatre a good-sized barn on his estate near the summer resort Pushkino, some thirty versts from Moscow. We accepted his offer and remodelled the barn for our needs, — built a stage, a small auditorium, a rest room for the men, one for the women, and added a roofed terrace where the actors might wait for their entrances and drink tea.

At first we had no servants, and all of us, stage directors, actors, and administrators, took care of cleaning the place. Each was forced to take a turn. The first one to be appointed to the task of cleaning and seeing that the rehearsal might take place properly was I. My debut in this rôle was a failure at first, for I filled a samovar empty of water with charcoal, and the samovar melted, leaving us without tea. I had not yet learned to sweep a floor, to handle a refuse shovel, or to remove dust from chairs with any degree of rapidity.

But I managed to create an order of the day which gave our

rehearsals the tone of serious business. First of all I began to keep a chronicle, or rather a book of reports, into which was entered all that had to do with the work of the theatre, — what play was being rehearsed, who rehearsed, what actors did not appear at the rehearsals, who was late and why, what disorder took place, what was to be ordered or made to facilitate the work. The visit of any important guest and all the pleasant and unpleasant happenings of the day were also entered.

The rehearsals began at eleven in the morning and ended at five in the afternoon. Until seven the actors were free to bathe in the river near by, to dine, and to rest, but at seven they returned for the second rehearsal of the day which lasted until eleven at night. In this manner we were able to rehearse two plays each day. And what plays! In the morning " Tsar Fyodor ", in the evening " Antigone ", or in the morning " The Merchant of Venice ", and in the evening either " Hannele " or " The Seagull ". But this was not all. Parallel with the rehearsals in the barn, individual work was being done with one or two of the actors. For this purpose we went into the woods when it was hot and into the caretaker's shack when it was cold. The main part of the work with Moskvin in the rôle of *Tsar Fyodor* took place in the shack. Moskvin would go over his rôle with Nemirovich-Danchenko as soon as the latter arrived from the city, while I was trying out another actor, not quite so suitable for the part. All this work took place in a period of oppressive heat, for that summer was one of the most sultry ever experienced in the locality. To make things worse, our barn had an iron roof. It is easy to imagine to what heights the temperature rose in the rehearsal hall and how we sweated rehearsing the Boyars' bows in " Tsar Fyodor ", the gay dances in " The Merchant of Venice ", and the complicated metamorphoses in " Hannele ".

The actors of the troupe found lodging in the village of Pushkino. Each group established their own household economies. In each group there was one person responsible for cleanliness, another responsible for the food, and a third for the business of the theatre, that is, with informing his group of the slated or deferred rehearsals and the new orders of the directors and administrators. At the beginning, until all the newcomers grew used to each other, there were many misunderstandings. There were even cases when we were forced to part with actors. For instance, at one of the rehearsals two actors who were on the stage quarreled and called each other names that could not be allowed in the theatre and especially at a time when they were fulfilling their allotted tasks. Nemirovich-Danchenko and I decided to punish the actors in question as an example for the rest of the company, and to let the whole troupe pass judgment on them. All the rehearsals were immediately called off. An hour or two after the scandal the whole troupe was called to a meeting; for this purpose men on foot and on horse were sent to look for all of the absent actors. All this was done not without intent, but with the purpose of giving a larger significance to a fact that would serve as an example for the future. When the meeting opened, Nemirovich-Danchenko and I explained to those present the dangerous nature of what had happened, and how it might become a harmful precedent. In other words, the troupe was faced with a definite question: did it want to follow in the footsteps of many other theatres in which the thing that had just occurred was usual, or did the new members of the troupe desire to curtail once and for all the recurrence of acts that would demoralize the venture, and for this purpose punish those guilty of such an act? The actors were much more severe than we had expected. They decided to part company with their guilty comrade who, I may mention, was one of the most prominent persons in the troupe. His leave-taking forced us to re-rehearse almost all the plays that were in process of preparation, in order to train those who undertook his rôles in them. A like incident took place again, but in a milder form, and the new disturber was fined a large sum and given a public scolding, this scolding being repeated by all of the actors in turn. This was a meeting that remained fixed in the memories of the actors, and it did away with all attempts to violate scenic discipline.

Gradually, after closer knowledge of our common work was established, better relationships between the actors were reached. When free of rehearsals the actors engaged in practical jokes. We lived a friendly and a joyful life.

The actors spent their free time in frightening one of the members of the troupe. They first issued rumors that there were ghosts on the estate; one of them had heard knockings and groans at night; another had heard footsteps at a time when all were sleeping; a third affirmed that he had clearly seen a shadow moving in his room. These rumors served to frighten some of the actresses. Once the actor who was to be victimized entered his room, disrobed and was already on the point of falling asleep when an unheard-of thing took place: the towel, the blanket, the pillows flew and crawled to all sides, a chair fell, tables moved, the door of the wardrobe opened. The frightened actor leaped into the corridor in his night clothing. The practical jokers, who were ready for this, entered his room to catch the ghost and hurried to remove the cords and threads that would have compromised them. Of course the actor who was the butt of many such affairs soon found out the source of the seeming miracles, but the continued expectance of new sallies on the part of his tormentors made him nervous. He could not sit down quietly on a chair that seemed to run away from under him; he was afraid to lie down in his bed, for thistles were hidden under the sheets; he was afraid to touch any box in his room for a mouse would almost certainly leap at him if he did so. In a word, the enthusiasm of the practical jokers reached such a stage that we were forced to interfere and beg mercy for the poor actor.

As for myself, I lived on the estate of my parents, some six versts from Pushkino. Daily, at eleven in the morning, I came to the barn for rehearsals and remained there until late in the night. Between rehearsals I rested and dined in the home of one of the actors of the theatre, Serafim Sudbinin, who was later to become a famous sculptor. Thanks to his hospitality, I established my headquarters in his little hut which stood right next to the rehearsal barn. In the same hut the artist Victor Simov was making the models for the scenery which was being prepared in Moscow. Constant companionship with me, the chief stage director, had forced him to make a temporary studio as near to my whereabouts as he could.

When on the 14th of July, 1898, I was traveling to the opening of the rehearsal barn, the horse that drew my carriage became frightened, ran wild, and almost succeeded in destroying the carriage and myself with it. Actors are superstitious. They discussed the fact at length, trying to find out if it boded good or bad luck. Why did the thing happen on the day of the opening? Why had it happened to me, the representative of the new venture? Evidently it was an augury. But in such mysterious matters it is supposed that a misfortune means good luck, and vice versa. And my accident was accepted as good luck for our venture. Soon there was another lucky sign — two of our actors had managed to fall in love and had announced their engagements, and weddings (which are also supposed to bear the character of misfortunes) bring good luck.

It was with such childish methods that the actors prepared themselves for the future which frightened them. We had to be successful, no matter what it would cost us. All of us understood this, as well as the fact that it would be hard to be successful. Outside of the theatre an atmosphere inimical to us was being rapidly created. Individuals in society and the press (which was mostly favorable to us) were trumpeting abroad the failure that awaited us in Moscow. We were dubbed amateurs; it was said that the new troupe had no actors but only luxurious costumes and scenery; the new venture was considered the hobby of a self-deceiving merchant, this last intended to hurt me personally. Many were angry at our declaration that we would produce only ten plays each season, for the other theatres of the city were in the habit of producing a new play every week, and even at that they could not attract enough spectators. And suddenly a group of amateurs appeared and dared to dream of living a whole season on ten plays. (Later we found out that with the careful production of only two plays, "Julius Caesar" and "The Cherry Orchard", we filled our house to its fullest capacity.)

The absence of social, religious and political life in those days forced the newspapers to devote a good half of their space to theatrical affairs. There appeared clever special writers who chose us to be the victims of their irony and witticism. They affirmed for the sake of laughter that we were breeding mosquitoes, flies, crickets and other insects, so that for the sake of realism we might crush some on our foreheads and others on the walls, and force the trained crickets to chirp in order to create an atmosphere of truth to life on the stage. One magazine of very large circulation devoted itself entirely to us; there was not a single page in it that did not have something to say about us. Such treatment on the part of individual persons excited and frightened us, for we did not know the popularizing and advertising value that it brought us. This secret was explained to me by a well-known French critic at a much later date. Studying the history of the foundation of our theatre, he came to the conclusion that we had spent enormous sums for advertising and even supported a whole magazine whose purpose was to scold our well-advertised venture continually. It seems that nothing intrigues the theatre public like unjust attacks in the press. Such advertisement is even better than the advertisement of praise, the French critic told me.

The ill feelings created around us forced us to labor all the more, and our work reached superhuman proportions. It was necessary to coalesce, to unify, to bring to one common denominator all the actors of the troupe, the young and the old, the amateurs and the professionals, the experienced and the inexperienced, the gifted and the gift-less, the spoiled and the untouched. It was necessary to create the whole administration of a complex theatrical organism, it was neces-sary to establish a financial apparatus. The only one who could solve the last problem and steer our ship between all the Scyllae and Charybdae which barred our way was Vladimir Nemirovich-Dan-chenko, who was possessed of an exceptional administrative genius. At first he was forced to occupy himself with this tedious and thank-less task alone.

My work was also hard, but it was much more interesting. It consisted of making all the new members of the troupe acquainted with the chief fundamentals of our art. This was not easy, for at that time I was not yet an authority to the experienced provincial actors to whom the rest of the troupe willingly listened. Of course these men from the provinces preached the very opposite of what Nemirovich-Danchenko and I wanted, for our goal was to destroy the ancient hokum of the theatre. Often these provincial actors told me that our demands could not be fulfilled, or that they were not scenic, or that the spectator would not hear, see, or understand all the nuances on which I insisted; that the stage demanded visualized action, a loud voice, a rapid tempo, and full-toned acting. This "full-toned" acting was understood by many of the actors not in the sense of the fullness of inner emotion and living over the part, but in the sense of the full-ness of shouting, exaggerated gesture and action, and a primitively vulgar delineation of the rôle, fed by animal temperament. At such quarrels with the experienced actors nothing was left to me but to seek the help of my friends, my old comrades in the Society of Art and Literature. I asked them to mount the stage and show the obstinate that my demands could be fulfilled. But when this also failed to per-suade them, I mounted the boards myself, acted and drew applause from those who believed as I did and who had accepted our new scenic faith, and with the help of such success insisted on the fulfilment of my demands. But at times even this did not help. Often I was forced to take even more radical steps to carry through our artistic principles. I would leave the obstinate actor in peace, and redouble my efforts with his stage partner. To the latter I would give the most interesting of the *mises en scène,* and help him with all that a stage director could help an actor, work with him after rehearsals, and let the obstinate one do whatever he wished. Usually his desire was to stand in front of the prompter's box, looking across the footlights at the spectators, exchanging compliments with them, and becoming obsessed by the drunkenness of declamatory speech and theatrical poses. I confess that I even sank to the extent of intriguing in order to teach the obstinate a lesson. I helped him to stress all the ancient conventionalities which he called tradition. In answer to the speech of the experienced actor sung with false pathos, I taught his partner to reply simply and according to the inner contents of the words. Simplicity and truth at once betrayed the obstinate actor.

At last my preparatory work was given an examination. This was the rehearsal at which the play was presented before the whole troupe, the stage directors and the friends of the theatre for the first time. At this rehearsal the old, obstinate, experienced actors failed completely, while their younger comrades received many compliments. This sobered the obstinate actors. I remember that after one such rehearsal which saw the brilliant failure of an experienced actor, he was so shaken by what had happened that he came to my home near Pushkino on a troika in the middle of the night and awakened me. I came out in my night clothes and we talked far into the dawn. At last he was listening to me like a scholar that had failed at an examination, and he swore that he would be obedient and attentive in the future. After this I was able to tell him all that I found necessary to say, all that I could not say so long as he entertained a feeling of superiority toward me. At other moments, when it was necessary to bring all to one common denominator, I was saved by the despotism of stage direction that I had learned from the methods of Kronek with the Meiningen Players. I demanded that the actors obey me, and I forced them to do so. True, many of them performed what I directed them to do only outwardly, for they were not yet ready to understand those directions through the medium of emotion. But what was I to do? I could see no other means, for we were faced by the necessity of creating a complete troupe and a new theatre with new tendencies in the space of a few months.

As the reader knows, I had brought into the new venture no unusually large baggage of artistic knowledge and experience. But Nemirovich-Danchenko had contributed his large artistic erudition and experience. Together there was *something* that was of the nature of a valuable impetus to an art beginning to turn cold in the mold of routine. Of course, it was impossible to dream of molding all of our actors into a new form in the space of several months. Therefore my chief problem lay in the preparation of the performance itself, so that the presentation might amaze the spectator of itself and enjoy at least a material success. They were right who said that in those days we had scenery and costumes but no actors. Our actors were too green to allow us to build our success on their shoulders. It was necessary to invent something so as to hide the actors for the time being by the luxuriousness of costumes, decorations, scenery, properties and a production that might dazzle the spectator. Behind the shelter of this the actors were to be given time to grow and to form. This is why the leit-motif of our first productions was the success of scenery, costume, and the work of the stage directors, which was pushed into a preëminent position.

While Simov was making of himself a real theatrical artist, I, as the chief stage director, was forced to enter into all the details of costumes and scenery. Luckily, Simov was a rare exception among the artists of that period, for he was interested not only in painting in the theatre, but in the play itself, its interpretation, and its qualities from the actors' and stage director's viewpoints. This helped him to enter into the very soul of the theatre. He also understood the dire necessity of helping the inexperienced actors by means of the production. Together with him we sought those means which might for the time being direct the attention of the audience away from the actor, and change its usual demands for conventionality and theatricality to which it had become used, to something better. I denied, deny, and will deny theatricality in that bad sense in which it is usually understood. I recognize not the theatricality, but the scenic quality of that which takes place in the theatre. To create that which is scenic and to get rid of moldy theatricality — that was our greatest care at the time. In approaching this goal we were not afraid of using any means to destroy the unnecessary, dead branches of the tree of the theatre.

For instance the orchestra, with its polkas and castanets before the rise of the curtain on a tragedy. What relation has such cheap music to " Hamlet " ? It does not help, it only interferes with the play, as it creates an altogether different atmosphere in the auditorium than the play demands. It can be said that serious music of the same tone as the play can be used. Why not? But it would cost too much, and besides, music would have to be written for every play separately. And where was one to find a composer who understood the conditions and the demands that the play made on music? These are altogether different than in the opera or the symphony, and it was therefore necessary to create a composer of the new type. We made a trial in this direction also, ordering special music as an overture to " Tsar Fyodor ". The overture was excellent musically, but it did not help our dramatic purposes. The result was that for the first time in Moscow music was completely banned during the intermissions between the acts.

There was still another question. Why those wings of bright and unbearable red which were used in front of the footlights and only killed the effects of other colors necessary in the theatre? And the red wings, as well as the curtain with the painted golden tassels and velvet curtainlets, followed in the wake of the music. Instead of them there were used folded draperies of a warm but subdued hue that would not kill the effects of the colors of the artist on the stage.

CHAPTER XXX

THE business of producing plays at that time was at very low ebb. First of all, almost no one was interested in the history of costume, no one made collections of ancient clothes, or books on costumes, or anything of the sort at all. There were only three styles in vogue in the *costumiers'* shops : " Faust ", " Les Huguenots ", and " Molière ", if one does not reckon our national Boyar fashions.

" Have you some sort of a Spanish costume, like ' Faust ' or ' Les Huguenots ' ? " was the question usually asked of the *costumiers*.

" We have Valentines, Mephistos, and St. Bries of all colors," was the usual answer.

They could not even take advantage of models that were already created for them. For instance, the Meiningen Players, while they were in Moscow, were kind and generous enough to let one of the Moscow theatres copy the scenery and the costumes of one of the plays that they had produced. But it was impossible to recognize the costumes, for every one of the actors for whom they had been made had added his own ideas to the making of the costume, ordering the tailor to add in one place and take away in another, so that in the end all the costumes looked as if they were made for " Faust " and " Les Huguenots ". All of the theatrical tailors had their own traditions and did not even want to look at the books and sketches of the artists, and all novelty and change from the usual in the costume was explained by the lack of experience on the part of the artist. The tailor was the best judge of how to make the costumes.

" I've made plenty of them. Any one with half an eye can see that the artist is doing this for the first time in his life." This was the usual tenor of the tailors' remarks.

However, there were a few among them whom we were able, with a great deal of hardship it is true, to move from their seemingly impregnable position. This happened during the latter part of the existence of the Society of Art and Literature. Since that time, they had managed to create a stencil à la Stanislavsky which was no whit better than the earlier styles of " Faust " and " Les Huguenots ", to such a degree had my instructions been changed in that short period of time. These conditions forced me, as they had done during the existence of the Society of Art and Literature, to undertake the preparation of costumes myself, so that I might find something fresh, something that had not been seen before, something that might " knock the eye of the public out " as we expressed ourselves at that time. I was helped a great deal in this undertaking by the actress M. P. Lilina (my wife) who had fine feeling for costume as well as taste and inventiveness. Besides, the actress M. P. Grigorieva, one of those who was with us during the lifetime of the Society of Art and Literature and is still with us, and who was very interested in questions of costume, offered her aid. There were also other volunteers, relatives and friends, men and women. First of all we began to study the costumes of the epoch of " Tsar Fyodor ", for that was to be our first production. The accepted stencil of Boyar costumes was one that was especially conventionalized. True, there had been attempts to give it new glory in the productions for members of the royal family, for " Tsar Fyodor " was at first not permitted to be played for the general public. But this attempt at rejuvenation expressed itself only in the use of rich materials and finish, which in most cases were far from resembling the costumes of Old Russia and reminded one more than all of fashionable contemporary dress. So far as the style and cutting went, it remained the same that we had come to know as the only product of theatrical tailors. There are nuances in lines and cutting which are never noticed by ordinary tailors, but which are most typical of one epoch of costume or another. They are hard to find; one needs the services of an artist and a connoisseur. It was those secrets, those *je ne sais quoi* of costume that we sought. We read and studied all the books obtainable in Moscow that dealt with Russian costume, we looked for engravings, old armor and monastic and churchly robes, that could be found in the city in rich profusion. We could not copy those archæological models, and we began to look for old embroidery, ancient Russian headdresses, and so forth. I organized an expedition to various cities to visit second-hand dealers and to see peasants and fishermen in the villages, for I knew that the latter kept much that was old and valuable in their trunks. It was there that most of the Moscow antiquaries made their purchases. It was necessary to attack quickly, so that our competitors might have no time to forestall us. The expedition was crowned with success. We brought home a great deal of loot at a rather small price. Then we arranged another expedition to those cities of Russia that are famous for their antiquity, like Yaroslavl, Rostov Yaroslavsky, Troitze-Sergievo, and so on. One of the former members and actors of the Society of Art and Literature, who occupied an important post in the department of railroads and had a private car for his own use, offered this car to our expedition. Part of the troupe, headed by Nemirovich-Danchenko, remained to rehearse in Pushkino while I, the artist Simov, my assistant stage director Sanin, my wife, a *costumière,* and several actors went in search of material. This was a never-to-be-forgotten journey. The private car with the large salon in which we dined every day, the conductor whose duty it was to serve us, the evening dances in the salon, the *petits jeux,* the gymnastics, the serious discussions, the new plans for the future theatre, the exhibition of the materials and objects bought on our journey, the full comfort we enjoyed make a series of unforgettable pictures. At one of the small stations on the line we had our car stopped for a full day and night and gave ourselves over to an enchanting picnic. In this manner we reached the ancient city of Rostov Yaroslavsky (which must not be taken for Rostov on the Don). This interesting city, which enjoys a glorious antiquity, stands on the shore of a large lake. In the center of the city is a large and ancient Kremlin with a palace once inhabited by Ivan the Terrible, that has an ancient cathedral and in it a famous bell tower, known far and wide for its chimes. This antiquity was at one time in a state of half ruin, but, as it often happens in Russia, there appeared a strange and unusual man, who by means of his private fortune did something that was the government's privilege to do. He restored the whole Kremlin of Rostov with its palaces and cathedrals, and we found it in exemplary condition. There he had gathered a large collection of antiquities, embroideries, materials, towels, wall coverings and carpets, which he had bought in the villages and from antiquaries. The name of this remarkable man was Shliakov. He was a simple harness manufacturer and was almost illiterate, but this did not stand in his way of becoming a connoisseur in that branch of archæology which dealt with wall coverings.

Shliakov offered us the keys of the palace and museum, and we lived in the place for a few days, taking down not only the plan of the palace and its rooms, but also sketching all the treasures of the museum. From the purely theatrical desire to gather as much atmosphere as we could in the palace itself we decided to pass a night there. In the darkness of night, with only a candle or so shedding dull light in the corners, we suddenly heard approaching footsteps on the stone flags of the floor. The low door of the chamber of Ivan the Terrible opened and a tall figure in monastic robes bent low in order to enter through the opening. At last the figure squeezed through the doorway and grew to its full height. We recognized one of our comrades. His appearance was unexpected and we suddenly seemed to breathe

the very air of severe Russian antiquity. When our comrade, clad in the museum robes, passed through the long, covered corridor above the arch of the ancient gates, and his candle gleamed in the window, throwing threatening shadows about it, it seemed that the ghost of the Terrible Tsar was walking the flags in the palace.

On the next day it was arranged to have the famous bells in the tower of Rostov ring for us. This was something altogether unheard by us before. Imagine a long, corridor-like tower at the top of the church, its whole length hung with large and small bells of all tones. Many bell ringers ran from one bell to another in order to ring them in the proper rhythm. It was an original performance of an original bell orchestra. Many rehearsals had been necessary in order to obtain the needed rhythm and to teach the men to run from one bell to another in a definite tempo with the perfection essential for the given rhythm.

Having examined Rostov Yaroslavsky, we visited a few more cities, and then sailed down the Volga from Yaroslavl with the current, stopping at the cities on the way to buy Oriental materials, coats and footgear. It was on that part of the journey that all the boots worn to the present day by our actors in " Tsar Fyodor " were bought. Our happy-go-lucky crowd took possession of the whole steamer and set the tone on board. The captain liked us and did not interfere with us. Whole days and almost whole nights all that was heard was laughter: we laughed, the other passengers laughed with us, for we had included the majority of them in our circle. On the night before we left the steamer we arranged a masquerade. All the actors and some of the passengers put on the costumes that we had bought, and sang and played and danced to their hearts' content. For me, the stage director, and for Simov, the artist, this was in a way in the nature of an examination by artificial light of the things bought on living and moving figures in different groupings accidentally meeting and parting. We sat on one side and watched, made our notes and drew plans of how to take advantage of what we saw.

Returning home, we added all the material we brought with us to what we had gathered before. For many hours and even days we sat surrounded by materials, rags, embroideries, and combined the colors, seeking combinations which enlivened the least bright cloths and costumes, and tried, if not to copy, then to catch the tone of the individual pieces of embroidery, the ornaments of the collars of the Boyar costumes, the royal robes, the headgear, and so on. We wanted to leave vulgar and theatrical gilding and cheap scenic luxury; we wanted to find another, simpler, richer finish informed with some of the real spirit of the past. Now and then we were successful, but far from always. Where were we to find materials luxuriant enough for the royal robes? All the excerpts from books, the sketches in museums which we had made while becoming acquainted with the locale and character of the past gave us very fine hints, but we had not found the means and the methods of fulfilling them. This forced me to undertake a new journey — this time to the fair at Nijny Novgorod, where one could often meet with fine old antiquities. I was unusually lucky, for I had hardly arrived in the place where the antiquities were being sold when I found a whole heap of refuse mixed with old things and old clothes. From beneath this heap peered a piece of the same material of which the costume Tsar Fyodor wears in his first appearance on the stage is made. I had found what I had sought so long. It was necessary to get hold of this material at any price. But a group of people was already gathering around the heap, and they seemed to be buyers. From them I found that the whole heap had just been brought from an outlying monastery which was selling its property to stave off poverty. I dug in other parts of the heap — a gold-embroidered female headdress peeped out, one of those worn by the women in " Tsar Fyodor "; in another place was a piece of ancient wood carving; a pitcher protruded from the heap in a third place. It was necessary to act. I decided to buy the whole heap as it lay. It was hard to find the owner of the collection, for it lay without any one watching it and it could easily be taken away. At last I found the monk in charge, bought the whole heap from him for a thousand rubles, and then spent a whole day in digging through it with my own hands, for I was afraid that during the night some one might steal my new-found treasures. It was terrible work, tiring and dirty, and at the end of the day I was exhausted. Nevertheless, during that first day I had saved all that was most important and necessary and had buried the rest in the center for examination on the following day. Sweating and greasy, for the day was of almost tropical heat, I returned to the hotel in a triumphant mood, took a bath, and like the Miser Knight of Pushkin spent the whole night in the examination of my purchases. I returned to Moscow with rich loot, for I brought with me not only costumes, but many other things for the production of " Tsar Fyodor ". There were a lot of wooden dishes for the first scene of the feast of Shuisky, there was carved wood for furniture, Oriental couch covers, and so on. On the stage it is not necessary to create the whole production from the first thing to the last interestingly, luxuriously, or originally. What one needs on the stage are color spots, and it was these color spots that I had found on my lucky journey.

Meanwhile our improvised *costumières* had grown very adept in the creation of the true ancient tone in the costumes and the embroideries. On the stage not all is gold that glitters, and not all that glitters looks like gold. We learned to make the most of scenic conditions and to pass as gold and jewels simple buttons, shells, stones specially cut and prepared, sealing wax, and ordinary rope, which is a perfect imitation of delicate diamond and mother-of-pearl embroidery. My purchases gave us new ideas and in a very little while we began to add imitation work to the costumes as well as real antiquities. Work was in full flow. We had struck on the real path. The new hokum of "blinding the bourgeois" with luxury was found, and it was important, for we were forced for the time being to hide the defects and immaturity of our actors by the splendor of their costumes.

In the other theatres of the time the problems of scenery were solved in a very simple manner. There was a backdrop and four or five wings in arched form. On these were painted a palace hall with entrances, passages, open and closed terraces, a seascape, and so on. In the middle there was the smooth, dirty theatrical floor and enough chairs to seat the dramatic *personæ,* no more. In the spaces between the wings one could see the whole world behind the scenes, a crowd of stage hands, extras, wig makers, and tailors who were promenading and eyeing the stage. If a door were necessary, it would be placed between the wings. It was not taken into consideration that a hole remained above the door. Let imagination add the piece of wall that was lacking. When it was necessary a street with a tremendous perspective of disappearing houses and a tremendous square with painted fountains and monuments was smeared on the backdrop and four wings. Actors who stood near the backdrop seemed to stand much higher than the perspective point of the disappearing houses. The dirty floor of the stage was naked, giving the actors full opportunity to stand in the middle of the stage near the prompter's box, which, as is well known, always attracts the servants of Melpomene.

It was the period of the reign of the luxurious theatrical pavilion, *empire* or *rococo,* painted on canvas. Canvas doors with the cloth shivering when they were closed or opened, and opening and closing of themselves in most cases, especially with the entrances of the stars, who would begin their acting by bowing in appreciation of the ovation with which the public met them.

The question of *mise en scène* and the planning of action on the stage was also solved in a very simple manner in those days. The usual *mise en scène* and scheme of properties, established once and for all for each and every play, was as follows: on the right a sofa, on the left a table and two chairs. One scene of the play would take place near the sofa, the next near the table with the two chairs, the third in the middle of the stage near the prompter's box; then again near the sofa, the table and the prompter's box. A painted red cloth with golden and tremendous tassels, also painted, was supposed to represent rich velvet material and real golden tassels. This had a bent corner beyond which one could see a landscape with mountains, valleys, rivers, seas, cities, villages, forests, parks, fountains and all the other attributes of poesy, prettiness and luxury. Ushers in red waistcoats with golden buttons, in uniforms with epaulets, ran all about the auditorium, making it impossible for the actors to play and for the spectators to hear or understand what was taking place on the stage. The orchestra, unnecessary for any purposes of the play itself, and living its own peculiar intimate musical life in the presence of the audience, was in the most prominent place before the stage and interfered with the actors, the spectators and the performance. Polkas and castanets in the intermissions, the exits of actors with applause, the sudden and unexpected return of heroes who had just died on the stage, endless curtain calls in the intermissions or at the end of the performance — all these ridiculous habits of the time were the changeless accompaniments of each performance.

In our destructive and revolutionary aims, in order to rejuvenate the art, we declared war on all the conventionalities of the theatre wherever they might occur — in the acting, in the properties, in the scenery, the costumes, the interpretation of the play, the curtain, or anywhere else in the play or the theatre. All that was new and that violated the usual customs of the theatre seemed beautiful and useful to us.

Together with plays of a production character, with effective costumes and scenery, it was also necessary to think of the works of contemporary authors, in which welled the life of the generation of that day. In this region also the theatre sought a new approach. For all that was being shown on the stage at that time seemed terrible and ancient to us. True, it was the period when even our best theatre, the Imperial Little, was filled with translations of nice little gay, empty, three-act pieces badly adapted to Russian life. Thanks to the extraordinary gifts of the actors, they were played with polish and to perfection. The talent of the actors hid the faults of the plays, and the majority of the theatre-going public did not understand the poorness of the repertoire that filled the Russian theatres for almost a decade. It was unpleasant to see how the talented Russian actors of that time wasted their genius . The rôle of the rejuvenator of the repertoire from its literary side was undertaken by Vladimir Nemirovich-Danchenko. He began with Chekhov, whose friend he had been for a long time. He was a truly sincere admirer and evaluator of the genius of Chekhov. The following will serve as an illustration.

At that time Nemirovich-Danchenko was one of the best among the younger dramatists. He was considered to have inherited the mantle of Ostrovsky. He had already received half the Griboyedov Prize for one of his plays. The other half of the prize was given to Chekhov for " The Seagull ". But Nemirovich-Danchenko considered this division of the prize unjust. It seemed to him that " The Seagull " was immeasurably higher than the play that he had written. He declined his half of the prize in favor of his rival, whose greater gifts he freely acknowledged. Of course the dream of Nemirovich-Danchenko was to show this play of Chekhov's on the boards of our theatre, for he was convinced that Chekhov had found new paths for the art of the time.

But an obstacle barred the fulfilment of his dreams. " The Seagull " had been produced in one of the theatres in St. Petersburg. Chekhov had been present at the performance and had run away, for the play had failed. In a fit of despair he passed the whole night on the shore of the Neva River, exposing himself to the icy and piercing wind. This was a risky thing for Chekhov to do, for he suffered with tuberculosis. He caught a cold, his illness became more marked, and the doctors sent him to Yalta in the Crimea, where Nemirovich-Danchenko wrote him of our plans about his play. Chekhov did not agree for a long time, but Nemirovich-Danchenko insisted. It cost him a great deal of effort to persuade Chekhov that the play had not died after its failure, but had been shown to the public in the wrong manner. Chekhov could not make up his mind to live over again the tortures that he had undergone in St. Petersburg, but Nemirovich-Danchenko at last succeeded, and permission to produce the play was received.

And here Nemirovich-Danchenko met still another obstacle. Only few people at that time understood Chekhov's play, although now it seems so simple to most of us. It seemed that it was not scenic, that it was monotonous and boresome. First of all Nemirovich-Danchenko began to persuade me, for I, like the others, had found " The Seagull " strange and monotonous after its first reading. My literary ideals at that period were still dangerously primitive. During the course of many evenings Vladimir Ivanovich hammered all the beauties of Chekhov's work into my head. He could talk of a play so well that one had to like it before he was through. How many times in later years both he and I and the theatre as a whole suffered because of this ability of his. He tempts us with his story of a play, and when we meet it face to face, we find that a great deal of what Vladimir Ivanovich told us of the play belonged to him and not to the author of the play.

In this case also, while Nemirovich-Danchenko talked of the rôles and the play, we liked them. But just as soon as I remained alone with the script of the play, I ceased to like it and was bored with it. And it was I who was to write the *mise en scène* and prepare the plans for the play, for at that time I was the only one in the theatre who was closely acquainted with that kind of work. Unconvinced, with chaos in my soul, with the unpleasant perspective of the duty of working on a play which did not interest me, I was allowed to leave Moscow and stay at the estate of one of my brothers, where I was to write the plans and send them to Moscow, from where they were to be taken to Pushkino where the preparatory rehearsals were taking place.

At that time, while our actors were yet untrained, the despotic methods of the stage director were in full force. The stage director of necessity became almost the only creator of the play. Hiding in his study he made a detailed *mise en scène* that agreed with his emotions, his inner sight and hearing. He had no business with the inner emotions of the actor. He thought at that time that it was possible to order others to live and feel according to his despotic will. He gave orders to all and for all places of the performance, and these orders were binding for all of the actors. It was impossible to argue, and besides, there was no one to argue, for the actors were still merely pupils and could not cross weapons with the stage director.

In the stage director's copy of the play everything was written down — how, where, and in what way one was to understand the rôle and the hints of the author, what voice one was to use, how to act and move, where and how to change position. There were special drawings in accordance with the principle worked out at the time for all the business of entrances, exits, and changes of position. There was a description of the scenery, costumes, make-ups, manners, way of walking, methods and habits of the rôles played. I had three or four weeks to perform all this hard and large work with " The Seagull ", and so, instead of resting, I sat in one of the towers of my brother's country home in the Government of Kharkov, from which there opened a monotonous view of the endless steppe with an eternally moving sea of wheat and barley that made me think and

long for the real sea. There was tremendous work before me. I
must confess, that to my amazement, the work seemed very easy.
I saw and felt the play at last, but it was plain to me that what I
had written was not interesting or necessary for the stage. While
I wrote I would say to myself:

" If you want it so much, I will write it, but I don't understand
of what use it is at all."

It was thus I reasoned at that time, being occupied with other and
completely false problems of the theatre. To my amazement, I received a great deal of praise for my work from Pushkino. I was
glad, not so much because Nemirovich-Danchenko praised me, for
he was captivated by the play and might be prejudiced in favor of
my work, but because the actors themselves, who did not like the
play, wrote the same things that Nemirovich-Danchenko did. At
last I received a letter that Chekhov himself, who had been present
at a rehearsal, had endorsed my work. From the same letter I
learned that Chekhov was very much interested in our theatre and
prophesied a large future for it.

" Once cultured people are at its head, and not theatrical mounte-
banks, the theatre cannot but be successful."

These were the words of Chekhov, who was somewhat of a true
prophet. Look at his " Cherry Orchard " which was a true prophesy
of what happened in Russia not so long ago.

Youth, fanaticism, the ability to work, the revolutionary spirit of
our theatre in the sense of artistic rejuvenation also excited Chekhov
and were liked by him.

" It seems that he has grown to like us," they wrote me from
Moscow.

Returning home, I no longer found the theatre at Pushkino. It
was already in the city and was housed in the theatre that we had
rented for the season. I was met by a great disappointment. I remember that when I approached the theatre after my little vacation

I could not control a nervous shiver of excitement. This shiver was the result of the thought — I am going to my theatre, I have a theatre, a stage, dressing rooms, actors, real actors. In this theatre I can create the life of which I have dreamt so long; I can cleanse art of all flotsam and jetsam; I can create a temple instead of a market place. But what was my disappointment when I entered the same Punch and Judy house on which we had declared war.

The Hermitage in Karetny Row was in a terrible state, dirty, dusty, ill-constructed, unheated, with the smell of beer and some sort of acid that had remained from the summer uses of the building. There was a garden near it, and the public was entertained with various divertissements in the open air of the garden, but during rain the entertainment would be carried over into the theatre. Acrobats, cascade singers, pantomimists, clowns, trained animals, and others had left everywhere the vestiges of their bad taste and ill manners The furnishings of the theatre had been intended only for such as they. This could be seen in the choice of colors, in the bad work, in the miserable attempt at luxury, in the posters hung on the walls, in the advertising curtain on the stage, in the uniforms of the ushers, in the choice of food in the buffet and in the entire insulting character of the building and the disorder of the house. We had to get rid of all this, but we had no money for the purpose. We were forced to invent methods of turning the stable into a temple, and of creating an interior that would be bearable for cultured people.

We painted all the walls and the posters on them white. The rotten chairs were covered with decent material; we found carpets and spread them in the corridors which bordered on the auditorium, so as to deaden the sound of footsteps which would interfere with the performance. We took the nasty curtains from the doors and the windows; we washed the windows and painted their frames, hung tulle curtains and covered the worst of the corners with laurel trees and flowers, giving a somewhat cosy appearance to the auditorium.

But no matter how we repaired the old ruin, we could really accomplish nothing. As soon as we cleaned or repaired one fault, another would take its place. I tried to drive a nail into the wall of my dressing room in order to hang a shelf, but the wall was so thin and old that a brick fell out from under the hammer (the dressing rooms were part of an ordinary barn) and a hole appeared in the wall through which the cold air of the street entered the room. Our worst trouble was with the heating of the theatre, for all the chimneys turned out to be spoiled and we were forced to have them repaired at a time when the frosts had already arrived and it was necessary to heat the theatre every day.

This general condition of the theatre brought us a great deal of suffering and many obstacles in the path of our labor. But we did not give up hope and continued to struggle with the obstacles. And they were very serious. I remember that at one of the performances I was forced to tear my costume away from the wall of my dressing room, to which it had frozen, and to put the costume on without warming it. How many of our rehearsals were conducted to the accompaniment of deafening blows on metal chimneys which were being repaired in a hurry only so that they might spoil again on the morrow. The electric wires were also out of order and were being repaired, and the rehearsals took place by candlelight and sometimes in complete darkness. Each day brought its own surprises. Now it came to light that the scenery could not be stored on the stage and it was necessary to build a new barn to hold it; now it was necessary to simplify the *mise en scène,* the production, and the scenery itself, in view of the fact that the stage was not large enough; now I was forced to deny myself some favorite effect because there was not enough light and mechanical apparatus; and now we were forced to make even greater compromises so that the length of intermissions might not overbalance the length of the performance. All this held up our work in the most hurried moment before the opening of the theatre, which was to take place as soon as possible because of the emptiness of our exchequer.

Parallel with all this domestic work went on the administrative work of the theatre. It was necessary to issue preparatory advertisements of the opening of the theatre; it was necessary to give the theatre a name, but as we were only engaged in guesswork as to its future physiognomy, this question hung fire from day to day. The Popular Theatre, The Dramatic Theatre, The Moscow Theatre, The Theatre of the Society of Art and Literature, — all these names were subjected to criticism, and none of them seemed to hold water. The worst of the matter was that there was no time to concentrate and think deeply about the name. All my attention was strained to find out what would be the final result of what we had created. Sometimes I would sit at a rehearsal and feel that one place was too long, and another place not perfected; that a basic mistake in the production interfered with a proper creation of impression. If I had been able to see one of the plays once from beginning to end, everything would have been clear. But this complete, uninterrupted rehearsal could never be attained. First of all the dim lighting did not give me a chance to examine either the groupings or the mimetics of the actors, nor the general appearance of the scenery as a whole. Second, small miscalculations, and the faults of the scenic apparatus stopped the progress of action. Third, the noise of the workmen in the most unexpected moments and places broke all illusion of impression. And there — look, an actor has been late with his entrance, for he has been called aside on important business having to do with the same performance he was acting in, a question of costume perhaps, and now, at the moment most important for me, somebody has come and I myself am called to the office because of necessary business.

Like the tortured Tantalus I tried to reach something that forever escaped me.

At one such moment of my trying to guess the slowly forming sequences of the performance, when I felt that in another instant I would understand what was to be done and in what the secret of correcting the situation lay, I heard the voice of Nemirovich-Danchenko in my ear:

"It is impossible to wait any longer. I propose that we call our theatre The Moscow Art and Popular Theatre. Do you agree — yes or no? It is necessary to decide at once."

Know that if at such a moment a stage director decides on a criminal act, a just judge must look at him with mercy. This is even more comprehensible because at that time it did not matter to me what our theatre was to be called. And without thinking, I gave my consent. But I confess that on reading next day a notice in the papers of the opening of the Moscow Art and Popular Theatre, I became frightened, for I understood what responsibility we had shouldered with the word "Art." My excitement was great after I had conceived this. But God sent me solace. That same day Moskvin was being shown in "Tsar Fyodor" and made a tremendous impression on me. I wept, what with his playing, what with my own emotions, what with joy, what with hope that among us there grew talented men that might become great artists. There was something to suffer for and something to work for.

Time flew. There came the last evening before the opening. The rehearsals ended, but it seemed that nothing had been done and that the performance was not ready. One thought that the incompleted details would ruin the whole production. I wanted to rehearse all night, but Nemirovich-Danchenko insisted on stopping all work and giving the artists time to concentrate and rest before the next evening, October 14, 1898.

I could not leave the theatre. Notwithstanding the late hour, I remained sitting in a box and waiting to see the hanging of the grayish-green curtain, which, it seemed to us, was destined to revolutionize art. I remember that the always happy and optimistic Fyodor Ivanovich Chaliapin, who often visited our theatre in its intimate hours, came in to join me, and together we considered the details of the making of the curtain.

CHAPTER XXXI

I DIVIDE the artistic work of the Moscow Art Theatre into two periods, one from the founding of the Theatre up to 1906, and the other from 1906 up to the present day.

The first period is the continuation of what took place in the Society of Art and Literature when the young and expansive emotion of the amateurs reacted to all that was accidental and in fashion and attracted our attention, carried away our feelings and filled our minds. In these researches of ours there was a great deal of lost motion, there was no system, no base from which to work, no leading motives, no order. We would throw ourselves to one side and then to the other, taking with us all that we had found before. Having tasted the new, we included it in our baggage and carried it in the opposite direction towards some other modish path. On the way we lost what we had gained before. Much in it was changed because of incorrect use. But some of the important and necessary things remained in the secret warehouses of the soul or became one with the conquests of our developing technique.

First of all I will describe the work of the first period of the researches of our Theatre. I will tell of the catastrophe at the end of that period and of the laying of the foundations for the second period. I will never be able to tell of all the details of the tortures and the joys of our researches. I can tell of them in short and general outline only. I will explain the final result to which my labors brought me. Its details are the material of another volume than this. And so, to the story.

[329]

The founding of our new Moscow Art and Popular Theatre was in the nature of a revolution. We protested against the customary manner of acting, against theatricality, against bathos, against declamation, against overacting, against the bad manner of production, against the habitual scenery, against the star system which spoiled the ensemble, against the light and farcical repertoire which was being cultivated on the Russian stage at that time. The best theatres were monopolized by a group of little-gifted dramatists who wrote their empty plays for the benefits of this or that actor and often at his order and under his direction, or took plays from the German or the French, and adapted them for the Russian stage and to Russian life, signing themselves as the adapters of the original writer with the postscript " subject taken from — ".

Like all revolutionists we broke the old and exaggerated the value of the new. All that was new was good simply because it was new. This was true not only of important things, it was true of little things also. For instance, the ushers and ticket sellers in all other theatres wore either evening dress or Court uniform. Ours were to wear a special uniform which resembled that of the Italian Army. Every other theatre had a painted curtain that descended and ascended. Our curtain was made of cloth and parted in the centre. Although the beginning of the performance was marked by an overture, we banished the orchestra entirely after a few performances. We kept music only when the play demanded it. And even then the orchestra was hidden from the eyes of the audience. But the most important thing was that all the other theatres practiced conventionalized theatrical truth, and we wanted another, a real, artistic, scenic truth.

Those who think that we sought for naturalism on the stage are mistaken. We never leaned towards such a principle. Always, then as well as now, we sought for inner truth, for the truth of feeling and experience, but as spiritual technique was only in its embryo stage among the actors of our company, we, because of necessity and helplessness, and against our desires, fell now and then into an outward and coarse naturalism.

I cannot describe all the productions of the Art Theatre. There are too many of them, and they would occupy too much space in my book and too much time and attention on the part of the reader. I must confine myself to the more important productions, to the productions most typical of the various stages through which the development of the art of our Theatre passed. There were many such stages, or rather lines of effort. Like strands in a braid they went apart, came together, were lost in each other, came apart again, came together again. I will try to take each of the important strands out, so to say, and examine it separately. Each strand I will examine represents a long series of related productions.

The first series of productions typical of our creativeness traveled along the line of history and manners. In this series there are plays like " Tsar Fyodor ", and " The Death of Ivan the Terrible ", " The Merchant of Venice ", " Antigone ", and also " Fuhrmann Henschel " and other plays of manners. In this series the stage director was the autocrat of the stage, especially in the first years of the existence of the Theatre. He covered the young and immature actors, of whom many gave great hopes for the future, with the pomp, the outward beauty, the unexpectedness of the production which blinded and amazed the spectator. What else could be done? One was forced to do this first because the demands made on the young actors were so great that they could not fulfil them, and second because the stage director created an outward success, giving time in such manner to the young actors to mature and grow stronger. The fact that we conducted ourselves like fiery revolutionists caused us to be called " wild sectarians "; this behavior was tactless on our part, for it complicated the situation, exciting our enemies and creating larger demands than we were able to meet.

The line of the productions of plays of history and manners was not new and was a continuation of the line begun during my amateur days in the Society of Art and Literature. In the Society such productions were also necessary to serve as screens for the amateurs of the Society. Now the production and the details of history and manners became more artistic and richer in contents. But even now the leading principle was the New for the sake of the New, or, *all that can lead away from the Old is correct.* I confess that often the historical side of the production was used not for the strengthening of the contents of the play, but merely to change the outworn theatrical stencil. Otherwise, we should have welcomed whole-heartedly the stressing of the details characteristic of the contents of the play. Thoughtful stressing is far from being a bad thing. It is a grotesque of a kind. But we were not looking for the most characteristic things. We were looking for the most striking things.

In the realm of the creativeness of the actor exactly the same thing was taking place. Here the problem was not to look like the ordinary stage Boyar, and it hid all the other problems behind its largeness. And to tell the truth, the ordinary theatrical stamp and stencil of the Boyar is the most repulsive of all stencils on the Russian stage. One need only touch it and it envelops the actor from head to foot and creeps into his mind and his heart. It was necessary to defend ourselves against it and to find a new stencil at all hazards. I need not say that this was often accomplished at the cost of the thing that is the very foundation of art, that is, the life of the human spirit. Had we looked attentively into our own souls at that time and asked ourselves by the strength of what we lived while we were on the stage, the answer would have been: " By the strength of the torturing desire to create at all costs a new outward image of history and manners that has never yet been seen on the stage." The contents of the play and all its problems were often forgotten in our search for the outward stencil of the rôles.

" If we could only see the image, see how he walks, talks, laughs, and come to know the quality of his voice," we said to ourselves when we approached the rôle. " If we can find the image, all the rest will come of itself."

" What do you feel? The physically outward image or the fundamental spiritual feeling of the rôle? The idea for the sake of which the poet wrote the play? "

We did not yet put such questions to ourselves.

And again, as at the time of the existence of the Society of Art and Literature, we donned all sorts of costumes, footgear, stuffing, to feel the image of the body; we glued on noses, beards, mustaches, we put on wigs, hoping to strike accidentally on the things that we did not as yet know and for which we were painfully searching. With the same goal in mind we examined photographs, we visited art galleries, seeking to find a hint that could intuitively help us to attain the desired outward image. Our creativeness was based on accident. A long series of rehearsals was spent in the search of such accidents. One would find a new manner of talking and try to bind it to the text, the action, and the *mise en scène* of the stage director. Now and then we were successful to a degree, and tried to make our discovery the basis for the further development of the rôle. But you must not conclude that the passage from the outward to the inward was our only method. No, even then we understood that it was far from being the best. But what could we do when the more correct inner approaches were still closed to us, and we had not yet found the key that would unlock the doors of the soul of the rôle? Passing from the outward to the inward we were often successful in piercing some of the mysteries, and then we would strike on the inner line of the development of the rôle. There would be a spark and then the flame of real feeling and a miracle.

But was it right to base our creativeness on accident, on our own abilities and talents, on the theory of chance? We played the image.

All of us who took part in the work understood very well that our first performance would place all our future on the turn of one card. On that evening we would either pass through the gates of art, or they would be shut before our very faces, and I would have to remain a merchant and a manufacturer and the chairman of the most boring business conferences for the rest of my life. All these thoughts were especially poignant on the day of the opening. My worry was increased by my sense of helplessness. My business of stage directing was done, it was behind me; the matter lay in the hands of the actors now. Only they could bring the performance to life, and I could do nothing more than stand, suffering and helpless, in the wings. How could I sit in my dressing room when the stage had become the ground of a battle between life and death? It is not to be wondered at that I wanted to take full advantage of the last moment of my active part in the production just before the curtain rose. I had to impress the actors for the last time.

Trying to kill in myself the deadly fear of what was to come, trying to look courageous, happy, and convinced of success, I turned to the actors before the last bell for the curtain with words of encouragement. It was not a good thing that my voice broke now and then from irregular breathing. In the very middle of my speech the orchestra on the other side of the curtain thundered into the overture and drowned my words. Deprived of the possibility of talking, there was nothing left for me to do but to begin to dance so as to give vent to the energy that was boiling in me and that I wished to instill into the actors who were soon to face the public. I danced, singing to myself, shouting out encouraging sentences, with a face that was white and deathlike, with frightened eyes, with broken breath, with convulsive gestures.

" Constantin Sergeievich, leave the stage! At once! Don't annoy the actors! " I heard the hard, commanding voice of the actor Alexandrov, in whose hands the entire administration of the performance had been placed. He had and still has exceptional abilities in such matters, a knowledge of the psychology of actors and ingenuity and authority at decisive moments.

My dance stopped on a half movement. Driven away and insulted, I walked away from the stage in shame and locked myself in my dressing room.

" I have given so much to the production, and now, at the most important moment, I am driven away as if I was an unnecessary stranger."

Don't pity me. My tears were the tears of an actor. We are sentimental men, we actors, and we love to play the part of injured innocence not only on the stage, but in life also.

Later on I came to appreciate Alexandrov's decisiveness for what it was worth.

The curtain of our Theatre rose first on the tragedy " Tsar Fyodor," written in a somewhat cinematographic manner. The author illustrates with great logicalness every passing moment of the plot. At the time the play was written this was considered to be necessary on the stage. Modern taste considers too much detail bad in the theatre, and at present we play " Tsar Fyodor " in shortened form.

The first scene was that of a feast in the home of Prince Shuisky to which he has invited his friends for the purpose of signing a demand that the Tsar divorce the Tsarina. The feasts of Boyars had old and outworn stencils on the stages of Russia. It was necessary to avoid these stencils at any and all costs. Therefore, true to my revolutionary principle, " the New at all costs," I placed this scene " on the roof " as the actors said. The left side of the stage was turned into a covered terrace with large wooden columns in the Russian style. It was separated from the footlights by a balustrade, which hid the lower halves of the bodies of the Boyars who sat and stood behind it. This gave a certain piquancy to the scene. The right half of the stage pictured the roofs of Moscow, the towers and the domes of the mediæval city losing themselves in perspective. This gave a great deal of atmosphere and picturesqueness to the setting, and the terrace, which was only half as wide as the stage, did away with the employment of any great number of supernumeraries. If the feast had been shown on the whole stage, it would have looked but thin with the small number of extras we had at our disposal, due to our poverty.

The covered terrace twisted backstage around a corner of the house and was lost in the wings. At the turning point there sat many of the actors and supernumeraries, creating movement and gravitation from the stage to the wings, and giving an illusion of distance and free space to the whole scene.

The colorful costumes of the Boyars and the representatives of the common people; the servants with great platters on which rested geese and shotes and large pieces of beef, and fruits and vegetables; the barrels of wine that were rolled in on the stage; the wooden goblets and dishes that I had brought from Nijny Novgorod; the slightly drunken guests; the beautiful Princess Mstislavskaya who passed as hostess among the guests with a great winecup; the noise of happy and of serious discussions, and later the long line of the signatories to the demand — all of this was new and unusual at the time we first produced the play.

In contrast to this picture there was the life of the court with its etiquette, its museum costumes, cloths, throne, ceremony. I will not describe the scene of the quarrel and peace-making between Shuisky and Godunov, for we have shown it in our performances in Western Europe and America. But there were scenes that we did not show, like the one in which Shuisky is led to prison and execution at the order of Godunov, and which takes place on a bridge outside the city. From the first wing on the left which pictured the highway, a log bridge was thrown to the last wing on the right where it descended to earth again. Under the bridge one saw a river, sailboats, rowboats. On the bridge was an endless procession of the most variegated figures dressed in the costumes of the ancient provinces of central Russia. At the entrance to the bridge sat beggars, and a blind minstrel sang a song written for the purpose by the famous Russian composer, Grechaninov. This was sung to rouse the passersby against Godunov. The crowd stopped, listened, grew in proportions, and reached a warlike mood, inflamed by the fiery supporter of the Shuiskys, the centenarian Kuriukov. When the Shuiskys appeared, surrounded by guards, there was a pitched battle. The guards had the better of it. Weeping women kissed the hands and feet of the national hero, bidding him farewell, and he uttered his last words on earth to them.

In the production of " The Death of Ivan the Terrible " in 1899, the line of the plays of history and manners was drawn with even more of its faults and excellencies. Here too was the shielding of the actors by the stage director, with great care to create something new, with the amazement of the spectator, with the overacting of the outward image, with the approach to the inward through the outward, and with great reliance on accident and talent.

Alexei Tolstoy's " The Death of Ivan the Terrible " is the first part of a trilogy, the second part being " Tsar Fyodor " and the third " Boris Godunov." Notwithstanding the many faults of the production, there were in it some successful places which are deserving of remembrance. For instance, the first scene, which takes place in the Duma. It is early morning. All is dark. A low palace room, oppressive and gloomy as the whole reign of Ivan. The mood is churchlike, like the mood before early mass, when figures of worshippers with concentrated faces meet in the gloom, moving slowly, their gestures still reminiscent of their dreams, their voices hoarse and sleepy. Quiet talk. The men stand in small groups, in little circles. They think rather than talk. The mood is one of worry. The meeting is slow and unbusinesslike. No one can come to any decision.

The situation is a dilemma. Ivan has abdicated his throne, there is no one to replace him, and all are so terrorized that they cannot even decide to go to beg the Tsar to reconsider his decision and to return to the throne. Light begins to break through the gloom. The first ray of the sun passes through a little window above and falls on the head of the young Boyar, Boris Godunov. He seems to be enthused and delivers a wonderful speech that encourages the whole gathering, and the Boyars go to beg the Tsar to remain on the throne.

The next scene takes place in the bedchamber of the remorseful slave of God, the Tsar Ivan. The Tsar finishes his prayers. He is tortured by sleepless nights, he is in the garb of a monk that contrasts with the burning candles, the shining gold, and the precious stones of the prayer niche. Through the low door one can see the tall black figure that performs the last of the hundreds of genuflections for the night in a condition of extreme exhaustion. Bending low, he comes in through the arched door, with a deathlike face and dull eyes, and falls strengthlessly in a chair near the bed. Light begins to glimmer in the windows. He hears the Boyars coming. He undresses hurriedly and lies down on the bed in one shift, playing the dying man. The Boyars approach his bed on the tips of their toes, like men sentenced to death, their heads lowered. They surround his bed on all sides, silently sink to their knees, bow, touching the floor with their foreheads, and lie motionless on the floor. Ivan does not move, pretending that he sleeps. There is a torturing pause. Then a careful, cunning word from Godunov. The prayers of the Boyars. The capricious Tsar refuses to accede to their wishes for a long time, then consents, but on terrible conditions. From beneath the coverlet there is protruded his thin white foot. He rises from his bed with difficulty. He is helped and clad in his royal robes; they put the crown on his head and give him his scepter. The tired, almost dead, dried-up old man grows visibly into the old Ivan the Terrible, with the eyes and the nose of an eagle. In a quiet but piercing voice he declares death sentence on Shuisky, who has dared not to appear to beg him to return to the throne. There is the ringing of bells. The royal procession passes into the cathedral to pray. Sternly and powerfully in their wake walks one of the wisest and most cruel of the kings of all time, Tsar Ivan the Terrible.

CHAPTER XXXII

T HE line of the fantastic includes such plays as " The Blue Bird " and " The Snow Maiden ".

The fantastic on the stage is an old passion of mine. If there is beautiful fantasy in a play, I confess that I am ready to produce the play for the sake of the fantasy. For fantasy is interesting, beautiful, amusing. It is my rest, my little joke, which is now and then so necessary to the actor. It is not in vain that the French song has it:

> " *Le temps en temps il faut*
> *Prendre un verre de Clicquot.*"

And for me the fantastic is a glass of foaming champagne. This is why I took such joy in the production of " The Snow Maiden " and " The Blue Bird ". One must not forget that in " The Snow Maiden " there is exceptionally beautiful Russian epos, and in " The Blue Bird " an artistically interpreted symbol.

It is engaging to invent something that has never happened in life, but is nevertheless a truth that lives in men and nations forever. " The Snow Maiden " is a fairy tale, a dream, a national legend, written in remarkable and sonorous verse by Ostrovsky. One can even believe that Ostrovsky, who has always been called a realist and a dramatist of manners, had never written anything but beautiful poetry and was interested only in romanticism, when one reads " The Snow Maiden ".

Let me sketch a few moments of its production, — for instance, the prologue, which takes place on a mountain covered with snow

[340]

drifts and overgrown with trees and bushes. The bushes are thickest below, near the footlights. Winter and frosts have deprived them of their leafage, and now their dry, black branches crackle and wheeze and mix with each other in the gusts of the rushing wind. From the forestage to the very end of the backstage there is a continually rising incline that is as wide as the stage itself, with all sorts of rising and falling platforms. All this is piled with great stuffed bags that portray the uneven surface of the snow. The snow lies in masses on the trees and on the bushes, bending them to the ground with its weight.

From the distance there comes the singing of a great crowd. These are the inhabitants of a happy village in the kingdom of Berendey come to celebrate Whitsuntide in their pagan fashion and carrying its straw image. The merry crowd of singing and dancing children, old men and women, roll down the mountain side, rise and dance around the straw image which they later carry away to another place to burn. Only a few pairs of lovers are left to do all their love-making before the great fast days come, and they cannot have enough of kissing among the snowbound trees. But now they too run away with laughter and with noisy play. A solemn silence falls on the mysterious forest, the wind grows stronger, bringing a snowstorm, and soon in the distance there is heard a sea of incomprehensible sounds. Grandfather Frost is coming. One can hear his gigantic voice from far away and the wild answers of the beasts and trees and spirits of the forest.

Meanwhile, on the very forestage, where the bushes stretched their bare boughs, there is the waving of hundreds of fingers, the boughs beat against each other; there is crackling, wheezing, moaning, and a whole family of wood sprites come to life. They had been hidden in the bushes, or rather, they were the bushes. Now they seem to rise from the heart of the earth itself, grow to their full height, run about, as if looking for some one on the forestage. These wood sprites made the appearance of a forest that had come to life and created an altogether unexpected scenic effect which frightened the women who sat in the first rows of the auditorium.

The fantastic is good only when the spectator does not understand at once how the effect is created. And this time it was hard to guess at once that the bushes along the forestage were nothing but supernumeraries in costumes.

An awakened bear stuck his head out of a cave and crawled out amidst the running wood sprites, black and tremendous and furry against the white background of the snow. The illusion was complete and it was impossible to guess how such a lifelike animal was made on the stage. It was not in vain that the actor who sweated in the bearskin that was well formed with wire, had long studied his rôle in the zoölogical garden, watching the life of bears in their cages. The snowdrift hid the bottom part of his body and his legs, and the human figure could not be noticed at all because those parts that might have betrayed themselves were covered with white fur and became one with the background.

Meanwhile the noise grew to larger and larger proportions in the distance. In order to judge of the noise created, I will take the reader backstage with me. Imagine the entire cast, actors and supernumeraries, chorus men, musicians, stage hands, office help, and many of the administrators of the theatre in full meeting. Each of them was given three or four peculiar instruments. These were whistles, castanets, and other machines, many of them invented by ourselves, for the purpose of making peculiar noises. Almost a hundred persons, each playing on three or four of these instruments, made up our orchestra. Some of them were even able to use their feet, pressing down specially arranged boards which cracked and sang like ancient trees. When the forte of this orchestra reached its highest note, a snowstorm composed of white confetti blown by large ventilators was let loose on the stage from the top of the right wing. Back of this were long streamers of many-toned tulle that were fastened at one end to sticks. Amidst this snowstorm there rolled down from the mountain in the embrace of his little, enchanting daughter, Snow Maiden in a white fur coat and a white fur hat, the tremendous figure of Grandfather Frost in a colossal white hat with a tremendous white beard, dressed in the costume of an Eskimo decorated in the Eastern style with many-colored fur. With a wild shout he rolled down to the forestage, then arranged himself on a snowdrift and read a wonderful and poetic monologue in his thundering voice and with unrestrained temperament, the while his mischievous daughter played with the black bear, rode astride his broad back, and rolled with him in the snow.

CHAPTER XXXIII

CONTINUING to react almost youthfully to all new movements, we struck out in our researches towards the fashionable influence of symbolism which had just risen on the horizon of art, but we did not forget to take with us all of our former baggage, that of history and manners and that of the intuition of feelings, all of our experiences and the new and very important literary influence which Nemirovich-Danchenko cultivated in our Theatre.

Among the plays and productions in the symbolic sequence I count the works of Ibsen (with the exception of " The Enemy of the People "), the works of Maeterlinck (who, although he does not consider himself a symbolist, was felt by us to be an impressionist), Knut Hamsun, and some others.

It is a hard nut to crack — the Symbol. It is successful when it has its source not in the mind, but in the inner soul. In this sense symbol and grotesque are alike. It is necessary to play a rôle hundreds of times, to crystallize its essence, to perfect the crystal, and in showing it, to interpret the quintessence of its contents. The symbol and the grotesque synthesize feelings and life. They gather in bright, courageous and compressed form the multiform contents of the rôle. We could not create such a symbol at the time I am speaking of for many reasons. First because of our artistic inexperience; second because of the lack of the necessary technique; third because we had not yet played each rôle hundreds of times nor carried it to compactness and depth compressed by the symbol; and fourth and last,

[344]

we could not create a true symbol in the works of Ibsen because they are alien to the soul of the Slav.

Chekhov did not like Ibsen as a dramatist although he placed Ibsen's talents very high. He thought him dry, cold, a man of reason. And Ibsen's white horses in "Rosmersholm" seemed to us to be creatures of dry reason, although I am certain that to the Scandinavian this symbol is as near as the chariot of Elijah and its thundering passage across the sky on the stormy Day of Elijah is to the Russian. But, more's the pity, I was not a Scandinavian, and I never saw how Ibsen was played in Scandinavia. Those who have been there tell me that he is interpreted as simply, as true to life, as we play Chekhov. We also longed for this, but we were too clever when we played Ibsen to reach the results of Chekhov's simplicity and depth. We could not play his works as if they were plays of manners, nor could we play them as if they were plays of the intuition of feelings. In our productions of Ibsen things and sounds did not live on the stage as they did in our productions of Chekhov. We portrayed him with care, but that was due to the fact that Nemirovich-Danchenko was a great student of Ibsen and knew how to interpret, explain, express, and feel him. But the rest of us were merely echoes. True, among the actors there was now and then a case of extreme exception. For instance, at the dress rehearsal of "Hedda Gabler" I was enthused and carried away by the last scene of Lövborg before his suicide. The mad flight of genius excited me, and I ceased to be clever and gave myself over to intuition. But one moment does not make a rôle.

True, "Brand," produced by Nemirovich-Danchenko and Luzhsky, bore another character, it was less of a cold and formal symbol. But this production was made after 1906, and I am now speaking only of the period prior to that year.

Our relations to Ibsen were best of all characterized by Chekhov. After he was told that the old veteran of the Russian stage, Artem, whom he loved very much, would play one of the chief rôles in "The Wild Duck", Chekhov was plunged in thought and said nothing. Artem was completely unfit to play any part in any of Ibsen's plays. He was a typical Russian, with all the peculiarities, good qualities and faults of the Slavic nature, which often seem wild and ridiculous when seen amid the circumstances of alien life.

Once when Chekhov was sitting on the shore of a river, waiting for the fish to bite (he was an inveterate fisherman) he suddenly and unexpectedly began to laugh so loudly that the entire river echoed in answer.

"What is the matter, Anton Pavlovich?" his friends asked him.

"Listen," he answered. "Artem can never play Ibsen."

We also laughed.

"What are you laughing at? You are laughing at yourselves!"

Another series of productions and plays followed the line of the intuition of feelings, which I still consider to be the only true one. In this series I would include all the plays of Chekhov, many of the plays of Hauptmann, "Trouble from Reason", the plays of Turgenev, Dostoyevsky, and others. How was it that we struck on this line, and in the plays I have mentioned, and not in others?

Why does a man fall in love with one woman, and not with another who may be richer, more beautiful and kinder than the first? Apparently there was something in these plays which entered our souls and called forth creativeness on the line of the intuition of feelings. What was it?

There are plays which on first sight do not display their depths. After reading them you say:

"Good. But there is nothing extraordinary, nothing amazing. Everything is just where it should be; we know what it is, it is true, but it is not new."

Often first acquaintance with such plays is disappointing. It even seems that there is nothing to say about them after they are read.

The plot and the subject can be summed up in two words. Rôles? There are many good rôles, but there are none that would attract the ordinary actor to want to play them. The other rôles are little ones; they can be written on one sheet of paper. One remembers individual words, a few scenes. — But strange, the more one gives freedom to his memory, the more one wants to think about the play. Some places, resuscitated in memory, force you, because of their inner strength, to think of them and of other places, and at last of the play in its entirety. Having read it again, you make new discoveries. Playing one and the same rôle five hundred and more times, you discover something new in it at every performance, as though within the play there is hidden an unfathomable spring of creativeness, or a flower that spreads about it the perfume of pure poetry.

Everyday cares, politics, economics, the larger part of general social interests — these make the kitchen of life. Art lives higher, observing from the height of its birdlike flights all that takes place beneath it. It makes concrete and synthesizes all that it sees.

There are plays written on the simplest of themes, which in themselves are not interesting. But they are permeated by the eternal, and he who feels this quality in them perceives that they are written for all time.

Chekhov is a writer of such plays. Read him in the kitchen of life, and you will find nothing in him but the simple plot, mosquitoes, crickets, boredom, gray little people. But take him where art soars, and you will feel in the everyday plots of his plays the eternal longings of man for happiness, his strivings upwards, the true aroma of Russian poetry, in no smaller measure than it is felt in Turgenev. There you will understand the talented work of Treplev, and in his rules of the theatre you will recognize a great deal that is important for the art at all times, something like what Hamlet says in his scene with the actors. There you will understand that Astrov and Uncle Vanya are not simple and small men, but ideal fighters against the terrible realities of the Russia of Chekhov's time. There you will notice that Chekhov's plays are accompanied by the continuous laughter of the audience, which never rings so often and so loud and so clear as it does in his plays, for Chekhov himself was one of the men who are in love with life, and greatly. When he and his heroes forget the sad reality of life, he is normal, healthy and courageous. But when the plot of the play drags him and his heroes into the sad and dark life of the eighties of the last century, then the happy laughter of the men in love with life serves but to make clearer the hardships that were borne in Russia by the great men who became heroes in the days of revolution. I cannot believe that a man like Astrov would remain unrecognized at a moment of national uplift in Russia. Sonia and Uncle Vanya came to life and the Serebriakovs and Gaievs perished together with that epoch which no one could criticize and condemn like the same Chekhov whom present innovators, who have painted themselves in new colors, consider a dead letter in the drama. I know of no greater idealism than that which believes in a better future although it is surrounded by hopeless circumstances. And all the plays of Chekhov are permeated and end in a faith in a better future on the part of the fatally ill, talented and life-loving poet, whose own life was as hard as that of his heroes.

Not Chekhov alone; Ostrovsky and Gogol also fall into opprobrium when they are judged and analyzed in the kitchen of life. " Gogol is funny! " they say in the kitchen, and they do not notice the tears that shine through the laughter of the poet. " Ostrovsky is amusing! " they say about the great dramatist, and do not notice the grand and epic serenity of the man and his works.

Those who speak of the nonage of Chekhov have not yet grown to understand him. Works like Chekhov's outlive the generations of men, notwithstanding that the subjects treated in them are old and no longer fashionable. Chekhov's *what* may be dying, but Chekhov's *how* has not yet begun to live as it should in our theatres and in our art. The Moscow Art Theatre is famous because of Chekhov, but has it taken from him what he himself and through the medium of Treplev said about art? Has what he said been realized? In Russian dramatic art there were many important chapters, beginning with Volkov, passing through Shtchepkin, Gogol, and Ostrovsky, and finishing with Chekhov. But his chapter is far from ended. First there must be born some one to create a new chapter, but meanwhile those who want to live by the light of the eternal in art must understand, and what is most important of all, feel all the eternal which Chekhov has given to the theatre of the world and to the art of the theatre. It is impossible to pass over Chekhov if one is to go on with the creation of new art.

This line, which I called the line of the intuition of feelings, we reached at that time unconsciously, accidentally, for reasons unknown to us, and we still follow it. In it I will search for new seeds to sow for the coming generations. Let what is fashionable be created, — there is in it also a great deal of the beautiful and the useful. Let us enthuse over it, but let us not forget the eternal; let us not forget those lighthouses of art which must be kept in order; let us, like the Vestals, keep the fires always burning in those lighthouses. And the last of these belongs to Chekhov.

One can wander from the highway and go far into the woods to gather flowers and pick berries, but one must not forget the whereabouts of the highway; one must not go too far from it, or one may be lost.

It will be said that all I say about Chekhov and the eternal which is hidden in him is not new. It touches not only him, but every other great poet of the theatre, even Shakespeare, Sophocles, Ibsen, — all those who fill their plays with great thoughts and feelings. Why, then, do I not include their plays in the series of plays created in our Theatre on the line of the intuition of feelings along which we were led by Chekhov?

I cannot answer this, or rather I can answer this with guesses. Chekhov may be nearer, more contemporary to us than the others. Perhaps it was because of this that we felt him more deeply. But there are rôles and plays in Shakespeare which I cannot read without a shudder. Yet why can I express my perceptions of Chekhov but cannot express my perceptions of Shakespeare? And can many of the famous actors interpret the essence of the great English dramatist? I know many actors who specialize in distorting the works of Shakespeare and other great tragedians. They even call themselves Shakespearian actors. But I will say:

"Do the exact opposite of what they are doing if you want to interpret that essence of Shakespeare and of the art of which we are now speaking, which binds us with the most delicate, tender and cobweblike threads to the souls of those poets whom we incarnify along the line of the intuition of feelings." Apparently it is not the inner feeling itself, but the technique of its expression that prevents us from doing that in the plays of Shakespeare which we are able to do to a certain degree in the plays of Chekhov.

That is the only solution. We have created a technique and methods for the artistic interpretation of Chekhov, but we do not possess a technique for the saying of the artistic truth in the plays of Shakespeare. This is what interferes with our living him over, and forces us to act him, to declaim, to falsify, to pretend, and to achieve nothing.

Chekhov discovered to us the life of things and sounds, thanks to which all that was lifeless, dead and unjustified in the details of production, all that in spite of our desires created an outward naturalism, turned of itself into living and artistic realism, and the properties that surrounded us on the stage took on an inner relationship with the soul of the actor. Chekhov, like no one else, was able to create inward and outward artistic truth. This is why he was able to say the truth about men. This could not be said if they were surrounded on the stage by falsehoods. Chekhov gave that inner truth to the art of the stage which served as the foundation for what was later called the Stanislavsky System, which must be approached through Chekhov, or which serves as a bridge to the approach of Chekhov. Playing Chekhov, one is not forced to search for the feeling of truth, which is such a necessary element of the creative mood.

CHAPTER XXXIV

"THE SEAGULL"

I HAVE already said that after my first acquaintance with Chekhov's "Seagull" I did not understand the essence, the aroma, the beauty of his play. I wrote the *mise en scène,* and still I did not understand, although, unknown to myself, I had apparently felt its substance. When I directed the play I still did not understand it. But some of the inner threads of the play attracted me, although I did not notice the evolution that had taken place in me.

The rôle of the fashionable writer Trigorin, the literary antipode of the talented Treplev who is his rival in the love of Nina Zarechnaya, the heroine of the play, a young, naïve, provincial girl, was somehow beyond my powers. Yet nevertheless I was in the play, I was bound to it innerly, and together with the other actors sincerely gave myself up to the mood that was being created on the stage. The Chekhov mood is that cave in which are kept all the unseen and hardly palpable treasures of Chekhov's soul, so often beyond the reach of mere consciousness. This cave is that vessel in which is hidden the great riches of Chekhov. One must know how to find the place where it is hidden; one must be able to find the vessel itself, that is, the mood; one must know how to open it, in order to perceive what it is that makes Chekhov's art so unescapable. Apparently there are many ways to the hidden riches, to the entrance into the soul of the play, the rôles, and the actors who play them.

Nemirovich-Danchenko and I approached the hidden riches each in his own way, Vladimir Ivanovich by the literary road and I by the road of the actor, the road of images. Vladimir Ivanovich spoke of the feelings which he sought or foresaw in the play and the rôles. I could not speak of them and preferred to illustrate them. When I entered into a debate of words I was not understood and I was not persuasive. When I mounted the stage and showed what I was talking about, I became understandable and eloquent. True, often these varied approaches to the play interfered with the work and the rehearsals and caused long discussions which passed from debates of a detail to debates about principles, from the rôle to the play, from the play to art, from art to its fundamentals. There were even quarrels, but these quarrels were always of artistic origin and they were more useful than dangerous. They taught us that very essence which we seemed to foreknow in its general outlines, but not in concrete, systematic and clear rules. We seemed to be digging tunnels from two opposite sides towards one central point. Little by little we approached each other; now only a thin wall separated us; now the wall was broken and we could easily pass from the literary to the artistic and unite them for the general procession of the actors along the way that we had found. Once we found that inner line of the play, which we could not define in words at that time, everything became comprehensible of itself not only to the actors and the stage directors, but to the artist and the electrician and the *costumier* and all the other co-creators of the production. Along this line of inner action, which Chekhov has in a greater degree than any other dramatist, although until this time only actors are aware of it, there was formed a natural force of gravity towards the play itself, which pulled all of us in one direction. Much was correctly guessed by the interpreter of the play, Nemirovich-Danchenko, much by the stage directors, the *mise en scène,* the interpreters of the rôles (with the exception of myself), the scenic artist, and the properties.

Simov understood my plans and purpose of stage direction and began to help me marvelously towards the creation of the mood. On the very forestage, right near the footlights, in direct opposition to all the accepted laws and customs of the theatre of that time, almost all the persons in the play sat on a long swinging bench characteristic of Russian country estates, with their backs to the public. This bench, placed in a line with some tree stumps that remained from a destroyed forest, bordered an alley set with century-old trees that stood at a measured distance from each other. In the spaces between their trunks, which seemed mysterious in the darkness of night, there showed something in the form of a proscenium that was closed from sight by a large white sheet. This was the open-air theatre of the unsuccessful and unacknowledged Treplev. The scenery and properties of this theatre are poor and modest. But listen to the essence of his art and you find that it is a complete grammar for the actor of to-day. Treplev speaks of real art in the midst of night, amidst the trees of a damp and ancient park, waiting for the rising of the moon. Meanwhile from the distance there comes the trivial racket of a fashionable and tasteless waltz that changes at times to an even more tasteless but melodious Gipsy song played by Treplev's mother, a provincial actress. The tragedy is self-evident. Can the provincial mother understand the complex longings of her talented son? It is not at all amazing that he runs away from the house to the park so often.

To the accompaniment of tasteless conversation and jokes, the domestic spectators take their places on the long bench and the tree stumps, their backs to the public, very much like sparrows on a telegraph line. The moon rises, the sheet falls, one sees the lake, its surface broken with the silver gleams of the moon. On a high eminence that resembles the base of a monument, sits a grief-stricken female figure wrapped in manifold white, but with eyes that are young and shining and cannot be grief-stricken. This is Nina Zarechnaya in the costume of World Grief, the long train of which, like the tail of a snake, is stretched over grass and undergrowth. The wide cloth was a courageous gesture on the part of the artist, a gesture of deep contents and beautiful generalized form. How talented is this Treplev with the soul of Chekhov and a true comprehension of art.

Nina Zarechnaya is the cause of the failure of Treplev's talented play. She is not an actress, although she dreams of being one so as to earn the love of the worthless Trigorin. She does not understand what she is playing. She is too young to understand the deep gloom of the soul of Treplev. She has not yet suffered enough to perceive the eternal tragedy of the world. She must first fall in love with the scoundrelly Lovelace Trigorin and give him all that is beautiful in woman, give it to him in vain, at an accidental meeting in some low inn. The young and beautiful life is deformed and killed just as meaninglessly as the beautiful white seagull was killed by Treplev because of nothing to do. Poor Nina, before understanding the depth of what she is playing, must bear a child in secret, must suffer hunger and privation many years, dragging herself through the lower depths of all the provincial theatres, must come to know the scoundrelly attentions of merchants to a young actress, must come to know her own giftlessness, in order to be able in her last farewell meeting with Treplev in the fourth act of the play to feel at last all the eternal and tragic depth of Treplev's monologue, and perhaps for the last and only time say it like a true actress and force Treplev and the spectators in the theatre to shed holy tears called forth by the power of art.

The conditions under which we produced " The Seagull " were complex and hard. The production was necessary to us because of the material circumstances of the life of our Theatre. Business was in a bad way. The administration hurried our labors. And suddenly Anton Pavlovich fell ill in Yalta with a new attack of tuberculosis. His spiritual condition was such that if " The Seagull " should fail as it did at its first production in Petrograd, the great poet would not be able to weather the blow. His sister Maria Pavlovna warned us of this with tears in her eyes, when, on the eve of the performance, she begged us to postpone it. You can judge of the condition in which we actors played on the first night before a small but chosen audience. There were only six hundred rubles in the box office. When we were on the stage there was an inner whisper in our hearts:

"You must play well, you must play better than well; you must create not only success, but triumph, for know that if you do not, the man and writer you love will die, killed by your hands."

These inner whisperings did not aid our creative inspiration. The boards were becoming the floor of a gallows, and we actors the executioners.

I do not remember how we played. The first act was over. There was a gravelike silence. Knipper fainted on the stage. All of us could hardly keep our feet. In the throes of despair we began moving to our dressing rooms. Suddenly there was a roar in the auditorium, and a shriek of joy or fright on the stage. The curtain was lifted, fell, was lifted again, showing the whole auditorium our amazed and astounded immovability. It fell again, it rose; it fell, it rose, and we could not even gather sense enough to bow. Then there were congratulations and embraces like those of Easter night, and ovations to Lilina, who played Masha, and who had broken the ice with her last words which tore themselves from her heart, moans washed with tears. This it was that had held the audience mute for a time before it began to roar and thunder in mad ovation.

We were no longer afraid of sending a telegram to our dear and beloved friend and poet.

Illness prevented Anton Pavlovich Chekhov from coming to Moscow during the season. But in the spring of 1899 he arrived with the secret hope of seeing " The Seagull " and demanded that we show it to him.

"Listen, it is necessary for me. I am its author. How can I write anything else until I have seen it?" he repeated at every favorable opportunity.

What were we to do? The season was over, the theatre was in the hands of strangers for all of the summer, all our belongings had been taken away and stored in a small barn. In order to show Chekhov a single performance, we would have had to go through almost the same amount of preparatory work as we did for the beginning of the whole season, that is, we would have had to hire a theatre and stage hands to unpack the scenery, the properties, the costumes, the wigs, and to bring them to the theatre, to collect the actors, to rehearse the play, to put in the necessary lighting system, and so on. And as a result of all this, the special performance would be a failure. It would be impossible to arrange it in a hurry. The inexperienced actors, not being used to the new stage, would lose themselves completely, and that would be the worst thing that could happen, especially in a Chekhov play. Besides, the auditorium of a theatre hired by chance would be devoid of all furniture, as the latter would be in the hands of cabinet makers and upholsterers during all summer for renovation. The play would have no appeal in an empty theatre. And Chekhov would be disappointed. But the words of Chekhov were a law to us, and once he insisted, it was necessary to fulfil his wishes.

The special performance took place in the Nikitsky Theatre. It was attended by Chekhov and about ten other spectators. The impression, as we had expected, was only middling. After every act Chekhov ran on the stage and his face bore no signs of any inner joy. But as soon as he saw the backstage activities, he would regain his courage and smile, for he loved the life of the theatre behind the scenes. Some of the actors were praised by Chekhov, others received their full meed of blame. This was true of one actress especially, with whose work Chekhov was completely dissatisfied.

"Listen," he said, "she can't act in my play. You have another actress who could be much finer in the part, who is a much better actress."

"But how can we take away the part once the season is over?" we defended ourselves. "That would amount to the same thing as if we threw her out of the company. Think what a blow that would be. She won't be able to bear it."

"Listen, I will take the play away from you," he summed up in a severe way, almost cruelly, surprising us by his hardness and firmness. Notwithstanding his exceptional tenderness, delicacy and kindness, he was severe and merciless in questions of art and never accepted any compromises. In order not to anger and excite the sick man, we did not contradict him, hoping that with time everything would be forgotten. But no. Unexpectedly, when no one even dreamt that he would say it, Chekhov would repeat:

"Listen, she can't act in my play."

At the special performance he seemed to be trying to avoid me. I waited for him in my dressing room, but he did not come. That was a bad sign. I went to him myself.

"Scold me, Anton Pavlovich," I begged him.

"Wonderful! Listen, it was wonderful! Only you need torn shoes and checked trousers."

He would tell me no more. What did it mean? Did he wish not to express his opinion? Was it a jest to get rid of me? Was he laughing at me? Trigorin in " The Seagull " was a young writer, a favorite of the women — and suddenly he was to wear torn shoes and checked trousers! I played the part in the most elegant of costumes — white trousers, white vest, white hat, slippers, and a handsome make-up.

A year or more passed. Again I played the part of Trigorin in " The Seagull " — and during one of the performances I suddenly understood what Chekhov had meant.

"Of course, the shoes must be torn and the trousers checked, and Trigorin must not be handsome. In this lies the salt of the part: for young, inexperienced girls it is important that a man should be a writer and print touching and sentimental romances, and the Nina Zarechnayas, one after the other, will throw themselves on his neck, without noticing that he is not talented, that he is not handsome, that he wears checked trousers and torn shoes. Only afterwards, when the love affair with such " seagulls " is over, do they begin to understand that it was girlish imagination which created the great genius in their heads, instead of a simple mediocrity. Again, the depth and the richness of Chekhov's laconic remarks struck me. It was very typical and characteristic of him.

CHAPTER XXXV

AFTER the success of "The Seagull" all the theatres of Russia began to demand Chekhov's work and began negotiations with him for the production of his other play, "Uncle Vanya". Representatives of various theatres visited him at his home and Anton Pavlovich conducted his business with them behind closed doors. This confused us, as we also wanted to produce his play. But one day Chekhov returned home angry and excited. It seems that one of the administrators of a theatre to which he had long promised his play and with whom he was forced to conduct negotiations, had unknowingly insulted the famous writer. Possibly confused by the presence in his office of a world-famous personality, and not knowing what to say in his confusion, he had asked Anton Pavlovich:

"And what are you doing now?"

Chekhov, greatly surprised, answered him:

"I write stories and novelettes, and sometimes plays."

I don't know what happened after that, but at the end of the interview Chekhov was handed a report from the Repertoire Committee of the theatre in which there were many flattering words about his play, which was accepted for production in the theatre, on one condition, however, — that the author change the end of the third act, in which the indignant Uncle Vanya shoots Professor Serebriakov.

"It is impossible to think," read the report, "that an enlightened, cultured man like Uncle Vanya could shoot on the stage at a person with a diploma, that is, Professor Serebriakov."

Chekhov reddened with indignation at the foolishness of the report and at once broke out into prolonged and happy laughter when he quoted the above sentence, which later became historical. Only Chekhov was able to laugh unexpectedly at a time when laughter was the last thing expected from him.

We were inwardly triumphant, for we felt that we were in for a holiday, that the fate of " Uncle Vanya " had been decided in our favor. And, of course, in the end the play was given to us, which made Anton Pavlovich himself very happy. We began to work at once. It was first of all necessary to take advantage of the presence of Anton Pavlovich in order to have him explain what he wanted as the author of the play. It may seem strange, but he could not talk about his own plays. Feeling as if he were being questioned himself by a judicial examiner, he would grow confused, and in order to find a way out of the strange situation and get rid of us, he would take advantage of his usual statement:

" Listen, I wrote it down; it is all there."

Or he would tell us, " Listen, I will never write plays again. I received for ' The Seagull ' just so much. . . ."

And he would take a five-kopek piece from his pocket, and showing it to us, would roll with long laughter. We could not control ourselves either and laughed together with him. Our conversation would lose its business character for the time being. But after waiting some time, we would renew our questions until at last, in a word dropped by accident, Chekhov would hint to us of an interesting thought or some characteristic trait of his creations. For instance, we talked of the rôle of Uncle Vanya himself. It is accepted that Uncle Vanya is a member of the landed gentry who manages the estate of the old Professor Serebriakov. It would seem that we had not far to look. The costume and the general appearance of a landed gentleman are known to all, high boots, a cap, sometimes a horsewhip, for it is taken for granted that he rides horseback a great deal. It was so that we painted him to ourselves. But Chekhov was terribly indignant.

"Listen," he said in great excitement, "everything is said there. You didn't read the play."

We looked into the original, but we found no hint there unless we were to reckon several words about a silk tie which Uncle Vanya wore.

"Here it is, here it is written down," Chekhov tried to persuade us.

"What is written down?" we were in amazement. "A silk tie?"

"Of course. Listen, he has a wonderful tie; he is an elegant, cultured man. It is not true that our landed gentry walk about in boots smeared with tar. They are wonderful people. They dress well. They order their clothes in Paris. It is all written down."

This little remark uncovered the drama of contemporary Russian life: the giftless, unnecessary professor enjoys life. He has a beautiful wife, he enjoys scholarly fame which he has not deserved, he is the idol of St. Petersburg; he writes foolish, learned books which his mother-in-law, old fool that she is, reads like the Bible. In the burst of general enthusiasm even Uncle Vanya himself is under his influence for a while, accepting him in the light of the Petersburg rumors about him, considering him to be a great man, and working unselfishly for him on the estate in order to support his fame. But in the end it is seen that Serebriakov is a blown-up soap bubble who occupies a post in life that he has not earned, while the talented Uncle Vanya and his friend Astrov are forced to rot in the darkest corners of the provinces. One wants to call the real doers and workers to the source of power and to throw the giftless and famous Serebriakovs from their high posts. From that time on, Uncle Vanya became for us a cultured, soft, elegant, poetic, fine type of man, almost like the unforgettable and enchanting Petr Ilyich Tchaikovsky.

When the rôles in the play were being distributed, many interesting things took place. Without taking into account the number of actors and the number of rôles in the play, Chekhov wanted his favorite actors to play all the parts in the play. Otherwise he threatened:

" Listen, I will rewrite the end of the third act, and send the play to the Repertoire Committee."

But Chekhov seldom finished the sentence without beginning to laugh and infecting us with his pure, childlike laughter also.

CHAPTER XXXVI

THE JOURNEY TO THE CRIMEA IN 1900

ALL this was in the springtime of our theatre, its rarest and most joyful moment. In 1900 we were going to visit Anton Pavlovich in the Crimea — it was our first guest journey, it was our début on the road. We were the heroes of the day, not only in Moscow, but in Crimea also, in Sevastopol, in Yalta. We said to ourselves:

" Anton Pavlovich cannot come to visit us because he is sick, but we are going to visit him, because we are in the full bloom of health. If Mohammed does not come to the mountain, the mountain comes to Mohammed."

The actors, their wives, their children, the children's nurses, stage hands, property men, *costumiers* and *costumières,* wigmakers, several carloads of properties and scenery moved from cold Moscow to meet the sun of the South. Take off your fur coats, take out your summer clothes, your straw hats! It does not matter that you will freeze a day or two — you will be warm when you arrive. We were to travel two days and nights. A whole railroad carriage was in our hands. All this makes one happy and joyful when one is young and spring is in the air. I cannot describe the practical jokes, the ridiculous scenes, the comic telegrams which we sent to our friends while on our way, the choral singing and the solo singing, the new friendships, the anecdotal events of that journey. And before us was hope, success, glory, which we, so to say, were already drinking on credit.

Here at last was Bakhchisarai, a warm spring morning, flowers, the bright costumes of the Tartars, their picturesque headdress, the sun. And here was white Sevastopol also. There are few cities in the world more beautiful than Sevastopol. White sand, white houses, chalk mountains, blue sky, blue sea with white foam on the waves, white clouds and a blinding sun. But after a few hours the sky was covered with dark clouds, the sea blackened, the wind rose, there was a rain with snow in it, and the never-ending sound of a threatening siren. It was winter again. And poor Anton Pavlovich was supposed to make a sea journey from Yalta in such weather to see us. But we waited for him in vain; we looked for him on the arriving steamer in vain. Chekhov had not come, but there was a telegram from him. He had had an attack of illness again, and he was not sure that he could come to Sevastopol.

The summer theatre in which we were to play stood gloomily on the shore of the sea, its doors boarded up. The boards had not been taken off all winter, and when the doors were opened in our presence and we entered, it seemed to us that we had suddenly been transplanted to the North Pole, such was the coldness and dampness that greeted us. Daily the young company of our actors met on the square in front of the theatre before rehearsals. The well-known critic Vassiliev was with us. He had come to write correspondences to Moscow.

"This was the way Goldoni traveled with his own press representatives."

All of us were dressed in our best spring clothes, and all of us were freezing.

But now there came Easter. And with it, unexpectedly, arrived Chekhov. He came to the meetings of the theatre in the city gardens, that took place of mornings. Once, having heard that we were looking for a doctor to attend our sick artist Artem, whom Chekhov loved very much, Anton Pavlovich cried out in a hurt tone of voice:

"Listen, I am the doctor of this theatre."

He was very proud of his medical calling, much more than of his talents as a writer.

"My real profession is medicine, but I sometimes write in my spare time," he would say very seriously. And a moment had not passed when he himself would begin to laugh, almost rolling with merriment. He attended his beloved Artem, for whom he later specially wrote the part of Chebutikin in "The Three Sisters" and Firs in "The Cherry Orchard." He prescribed valerian drops for Artem, the same prescription jestingly made by his Doctor Dorn in "The Seagull."

The night of the first performance arrived. We showed Chekhov "Uncle Vanya." The performance was unusually successful. The author was called before the curtain scores of times. This time Chekhov was satisfied with the performance. He saw our company for the first time in the real production of a public performance. In the intermissions he would come into my dressing room and praise me, and at the end he made only one remark about the scene where Astrov goes away.

"He whistles. Listen, he whistles! Uncle Vanya is crying, but Astrov whistles!" Again, I could not get any more out of him. But, knowing the laconical nature of his remarks and their deep meaning, I broke my head in thought over the new problems that he had placed before me.

"How is that?" I said to myself. "Sadness, hopelessness, and merry whistling?"

But his remark came to life of itself during one of the later performances. Believing in what Chekhov said, I whistled. What was going to happen? I felt at once that the whistle was truthful, that Astrov must whistle. He has lost his faith in men and life to such an extent that in his distrust of them he has become a cynic. Men cannot hurt or insult him in any way at all. But luckily for Astrov, he loves nature and serves it in idea, without thought of reward; in planting forests he believes that he feeds the rivers, which, without him and those like him would run dry.

THE JOURNEY TO THE CRIMEA

At the time of our visit to the Crimea, Anton Pavlovich was most enthusiastic about Hauptmann's "Lonely Lives." He saw it for the first time and he liked it more than any of his own plays.

"He is a real dramatist. I am not a dramatist. Listen, I am a doctor."

After the performance of "Lonely Lives" Chekhov showed a great deal of attention to one of the actors of our group, Vsevolod Meierhold, who in his turn could not find words to express his admiration of Chekhov and Chekhov's writings. He played the leading parts of Treplev in "The Seagull" and Johannes in "Lonely Lives."

From Sevastopol we went to Yalta, where we were awaited by the whole literary world of Russia, which seemed to have come especially for the purpose of seeing us in the Crimea. Bunin, Kuprin, Mamin-Sibiriak, Chirikov, Stanyukevich, Yelpatyevsky, and the new sensation, Maxim Gorky, who lived in the Crimea because of weak lungs, were all there. Besides the writers there were many actors and musicians, among them the young and much promising Rakhmaninov, who admired Chekhov insanely as a writer and a personality. It was here that we first met Gorky, whom we tried to persuade to write plays for us. Once of an evening, sitting on the terrace and listening to the sound of the Crimean waters, he told me in the darkness of his dreams about a new play which he later called "The Lower Depths". In the first draft the leading part was that of a lackey from a well-to-do house who was more fond of the collar of his dress shirt than of anything else in the world, for it was the only thing that bound him to his former life. The lodging house was close, its inhabitants cursed, the atmosphere was poisoned with hate. The second act finished with an unexpected raid by the police. At the tidings of the raid the whole anthill came to life, trying to hide stolen goods. In the third act came the spring, the sun; nature bloomed again; the inhabitants of the ill-smelling lodging house came out into the clean air to work on a farm; they sang songs under the sun and in the open air, forgetting their erstwhile hate of each other.

Daily, at a certain hour, all the actors and writers met at the summer dwelling of Chekhov, where lunch would be served. The hostess was the only sister of Anton Pavlovich, our common friend, Maria Pavlovna. The head of the table was occupied by Chekhov's mother, a lovely old lady, liked by everybody. After listening to the stories of the success of Chekhov's plays, she, notwithstanding her great age, wanted to go to the theatre, not to see us, of course, but a play of her son's. On the day of her going to the theatre, having come before lunch, I found Anton Pavlovich in great excitement. It seems that his mother had taken out an ancient silk dress and wished to put it on for her visit to the theatre. Anton Pavlovich was in terror.

" Mother in her silk dress wants to see the play of her Antosha. Listen, that must not happen."

And right on the spot, after his heated exclamations, he would fall into happy, enchanting laughter, because the picture of his mother in her silk dress, applauding her son, who has written a play and comes to the theatre to bow to the public, seemed very funny to him. " And the theatre pays me for this — so much! " And laughingly he took three kopeks from his pocket.

At the daily meals in Chekhov's house there was much talk of literature. These discussions of the best of specialists discovered to me many important and interesting, — especially for the stage director and actor, — secrets, of which the dry pedagogues who teach the history of literature are not even aware. Chekhov tried to persuade everybody to write plays for the Art Theatre. Some one mentioned that one of Chekhov's stories could easily be dramatized. The book was brought and Moskvin was forced to read the story. His reading impressed Anton Pavlovich to such a degree that from that time on he forced Moskvin to read something after dinner daily. This is the

THE JOURNEY TO THE CRIMEA

secret of how Moskvin became the sworn reader of Chekhov's stories at all charitable and other concerts later on.

Our journey to the Crimea came to an end. In reward, Chekhov and Gorky promised each to write a play for us. Speaking between ourselves, that was one of the chief reasons why the mountain had come to Mohammed.

CHAPTER XXXVII

NOW, after the success of both of Chekhov's plays, our Theatre could not get along without a new play from his pen. We began to attack Anton Pavlovich to have him fulfil the promise he gave us in the Crimea to write us a new play. We were forced to tire him with our continual questions and hints. It was hard for him to have us continually beating at the gates of his soul, it was hard for us to force ourselves to violate his will. But there was nothing else for us to do. The fate of the Theatre from that time on was in his hands; if he gave us a play we would have another season, if he didn't the Theatre would lose all of its prestige. Unhappily the health of Chekhov seemed to be on the wane. The freshest news from his quarters came from Olga Kipper from the Crimea. — Strange! — We began to suspect her. — She knew altogether too much about everything that was going on in Yalta — of the state of health of Chekhov, of the weather in the Crimea, of the progress of work on the play, of the coming or not coming of Chekhov to Moscow.

"Aha," said we, Petr Ivanovich and I.[1]

At last, to the pleasure of all, Anton Pavlovich sent the first act of the new play, still unnamed. Then there arrived the second act and the third. Only the last act was missing. Finally Chekhov came himself with the fourth act, and a reading of the play was arranged, with the author present. As was our custom, a large table was placed in the foyer of the theatre and covered with cloth, and we all sat down

[1] A quotation from Gogol's "The Inspector-General".

around it, the author and the stage directors in the center. The atmosphere was triumphant and uplifted. All the members of the company, the ushers, some of the stage hands and even a tailor or two were present. The author was apparently excited and felt out of place in the chairman's seat. Now and then he would leap from his chair and walk about, especially at those moments when the conversation, in his opinion, took a false or unpleasant direction. After the reading of the play, some of us, in talking of our impressions of the play, called it a drama, and others even a tragedy, without noticing that these definitions amazed Chekhov. One of the speakers, who had a self-evident Eastern accent and tried to display his eloquence, began to speak of his impressions with pathos and the common vocabulary of a tried orator:

" Although I do not agree with the author in principle, still — "

Anton Pavlovich could not survive this " in principle." Confused, hurt, and even insulted, he left the meeting, trying to go out without being noticed. He succeeded, for we had not understood what had happened, and least of all could explain the cause that had made him leave us. Afraid that it was his state of health that had forced him to leave the Theatre, I went at once to his home and found him not only out of spirits and insulted, but angry. I do not remember ever seeing him so angry again.

" It is impossible. Listen — ' in principle ' ! "

At first I thought that the flatness and the out-of-place use of the commonplace phrase and the vulgarity of pronunciation had made Anton Pavlovich lose his patience. But the real reason was that he had written a happy comedy and all of us had considered the play a tragedy and even wept over it. Evidently Chekhov thought that the play had been misunderstood and that it was already a failure.

The work of stage direction began. As was the custom I wrote a detailed *mise en scène,* — who must cross to where and why, what he must feel, what he must do, how he must look, — things that are considered strange, superfluous and harmful at the present time, but which were unavoidable and necessary at that time because of the immaturity of the actors and the swiftness of production.

We worked with spirit. We rehearsed the play, everything was clear, comprehensive, true, but the play did not live; it was hollow, it seemed tiresome and long. There was something missing. How torturing it is to seek this something without knowing what it is. All was ready, it was necessary to advertise the production, but if it were to be allowed on the stage in the form in which it had congealed, we were faced with certain failure. And then what would happen to Anton Pavlovich? And what would happen to the Theatre? Yet, nevertheless, we felt that there were elements that augured great success, that everything with the exception of that little something was present. But we could not guess what that something was. We met daily, we rehearsed to a point of despair, we parted company, and next day we would meet again and reach despair once more.

"Friends, this all happens because we are trying to be smart," some one suddenly pronounced judgment. "We are dragging the thing out, we are playing bores on the stage. We must lift the tone and play in quick tempo, as in vaudeville, without any foolishness."

We began to play quickly, that is, we tried to speak and move swiftly, and this forced us to crumple up the action, to lose the text of our speeches and to pronounce our sentences meaninglessly The result was that the play became worse, more tiresome, from the general disorder, hurry and flying about of actors on the stage. It was hard to understand what was taking place on the stage and of what the actors were talking. The prevalent mistake of beginning stage directors and actors is that they think that the heightening of tone is the quickening of tempo; that playing in full tone is loud and quick talking and strained action. But the expressions the " heightening of tone ", " full tone ", " quickening of tempo " have nothing to do with the actor and all with the spectator. To heighten tone means to heighten the mood of the audience, to strengthen the interest of the spectator in the performance; to quicken tempo means to live more strongly and intensively and to live over all that one says and does on the stage. And in talking and acting so that the spectator does not understand either the words or the problems of the actors, all that the actor really accomplishes is the letting down and lowering of the interest of the spectator in the performance and the general tone of his spiritual state of being.

At one of our torturing rehearsals the actors stopped in the middle of the play, ceased to act, seeing no sense in their work and feeling that we were standing in one place and not moving forward. At such times the distrust of the actors in the stage director and in each other reaches its greatest height and threatens to cause demoralization and the disappearance of energy. This took place late at night. Two or three electric lights burned dimly. We sat in the corners, hardly able to restrain our tears, silent, in the semigloom. Our hearts beat with anxiety and the helplessness of our position. Some one was nervously scratching the bench on which he sat with his finger nails. The sound was like that of a mouse. Now again there happened to me something incomprehensible, something that had remained a secret to me ever since an analogous happening during the rehearsals of " The Snow Maiden ". Apparently the sound of a scratching mouse, which must have had some meaning for me at an early period of my life, in conjunction with the darkness and the condition and the mood of the entire night, together with the helplessness and depression, reminded me of something important, deep and bright that I had experienced somewhere and at some time. A spiritual spring was touched and I at last understood the nature of the something that was missing. I had known it before also, but I had known it with my mind and not my emotions.

The men of Chekhov do not bathe, as we did at that time, in their own sorrow. Just the opposite; they, like Chekhov himself, seek life, joy, laughter, courage. The men and women of Chekhov want to live and not to die. They are active and surge to overcome the hard and unbearable impasses into which life has plunged them. It is not their fault that Russian life kills initiative and the best of beginnings and interferes with the free action and life of men and women.

I came to life and knew what it was I had to show the actors. I had to show them what was to be done on the stage and how. And they also came to life. We began to work; it was clear to everybody that the dress rehearsal was not far away at last. Olga Knipper still had some trouble with her part, but Nemirovich-Danchenko worked privately with her. At one of the rehearsals something seemed to open in her soul and her rôle began to progress excellently.

Poor Anton Pavlovich did not wait, not only for the first night, but even for the dress rehearsal. He left Russia, giving his failing health as an excuse for going. I think there was another reason also — his anxiety over the play. This suspicion of mine was borne out by the fact that Chekhov did not leave an address where we could telegraph him of the reception of the play. Even Olga Knipper did not know where he had gone. And it seemed —

But Chekhov had left a viceroy in the person of a lovable colonel who was to see that there should be no mistakes made in the customs of military life, in the manner and method of the officers' bearing in the play, in the details of their uniforms, and so on. Anton Pavlovich paid a great deal of attention to this detail of his play because there had been rumors that he had written a play against the army, and these had aroused confusion, expectation, and bad feelings on the part of military men. In truth, Anton Pavlovich always had the best of opinion about military men, especially those in active service, for they, in his own words, were to a certain extent the bearers of a cultural mission, since, coming into the farthest corners of the provinces, they brought with them new demands on life, knowledge, art, happiness, and joy. Chekhov least of all desired to hurt the self-esteem of the military men.

During the dress rehearsals we received a letter from Chekhov abroad, but again there was no mention of his address. His letter stated, " Cross out the whole speech of Andrey and use instead of it the words ' A wife is a wife '." This was typical, for it gives a good picture of the laconism of Chekhov. In the original manuscript Andrey delivered a fine speech which defined wonderfully and censured strongly the prosiness and smallness of many Russian women. Till marriage they kept alive in themselves a bit of poetry and femininity. But once married, they wore dressing gowns and slippers at home, and rich but tasteless clothes outside. The same dressing gown and the same tasteless clothes were apparent in their spiritual life and relationships. Is not this whole thought of Chekhov expressed without the use of unnecessary words in the secret meaning and the undercurrent of his short sentence, so full of helplessness and sadness: " A wife is a wife " ?

CHAPTER XXXVIII

OUR Moscow season ended with a great ovation intended for all the artists of our company. In later years, these Moscow ovations grew to be a custom before our yearly journey to Petrograd and even took on the form of special ritual. They were only overshadowed by the ovation we received when we moved to our new theatre in the Kamergersky Alley, where our revolving stage was shown for the first time to our Moscow audiences.

It was with a great deal of fear, and only because of economic necessity, that we undertook our first journey to Petrograd in 1900. Our fear was due to the fact that there had always been a great deal of intellectual enmity between the two capitals of the country. The new capital considered Moscow to be a provincial town and itself one of the cultural centers of Europe. All that was of Moscow was a failure in Petrograd and vice versa. The Moscovites lost little love on the bureaucrats of Petrograd with their formalism and cold affectedness. They lost no love on the city of Petrograd itself, with its fogs, its short and gloomy days, its long winters and its white summer nights. Moscow was proud of its dry frosts, of the bright glitter of white snow under the winter sun, of its hot, dry summers.

It is not remarkable that we expected the same show of antagonism towards the visiting Moscow theatre. But we were badly mistaken. Both society and press, with but a few exceptions, received us very hospitably. We were fêted by the most diverse classes of society. The most memorable occasion was a large dinner in the tremendous hall of Contin. The best orators of the time, Anatoliy Koni, S. A. Andreievsky, Kotliarevsky, Karabchevsky, greeted us with speeches interesting in content and talented in form. Koni assumed the rôle of a severe legal procurator (at that time he was the procurator of Petrograd). In a dry, official tone, turning to Nemirovich-Danchenko and myself, he said:

" The accused will rise."

We rose from our chairs.

" Gentlemen of the jury, you have before you two criminals who have committed a cruel deed. With forethought and malice they have killed the well-known, well-beloved, respected, honored, and ancient — (after a comic pause) — routine. (Again the serious tone of the attorney). The murderers have mercilessly removed from it the ancient cloak of the clown; they have broken out the fourth wall and have shown the intimate life of men to the crowd; they have destroyed theatrical lies and have put in their stead truth, which, as it is well known to everybody, is like poison to old routine."

In his peroration he turned to all who were present, and in the name of justice begged them to show no mercy in their sentence, to wit: " Sentence the two of them, and all of their artists, to life imprisonment — in our hearts."

Koni ended his speech in this unexpected manner, after an artfully managed pause, during which his face lost its severe expression, and assumed a kind and tender mask.

Another of the orators, Karabchevsky, unexpectedly announced that:

" A theatre has come to visit us, but to our complete amazement, there is not a single actor or actress in it."

It seemed that he was beginning to criticize us.

" I do not see a single shaven face," he continued, " nor any curled hair burned by daily application of the hairdresser's irons; I hear no artfully sonorous voices; I see no actorlike manner of walking, no theatrical gestures, no false pathos, no waving of hands, no strained animal temperaments. What kind of actors are they? And where are their actresses? I do not hear their rustling skirts, their backstage gossip and intrigues. Where are their painted faces, their drawn eyebrows, their beaded eyelashes, their whitewashed foreheads and hands? What kind of actresses are they, anyway? In this theatre there are no actors and no actresses, but men and women who deeply believe — " The rest was lost in compliments.

The third orator, Professor Kotliarevsky, talked from the historical point of view, considering us to be the heirs and followers of Shtchepkin.

In that time of political unrest — it was but a little while before the first revolution — the feeling of protest was very strong in all spheres of society. They waited for the hero who could tell the truth strongly and bravely in the very teeth of the government. It is not to be wondered at that the image of Doctor Stockman became popular at once in Moscow, and especially so in Petrograd. "The Enemy of the People" became the favorite play of the revolutionists, notwithstanding the fact that Stockman himself despised the solid majority and believed in individuals to whom he would entrust the conduct of life. But Stockman protested, Stockman told the truth, and that was considered enough.

On the day of the well-known massacre on Kazansky Square, "The Enemy of the People" was on the boards of our Theatre. The average run of spectators that night was from the intelligentsia, the professors and learned men of Petrograd. I remember that the orchestra was filled almost entirely with gray heads. Thanks to the sad events of the day, the auditorium was very excited and answered even the slightest hints about liberty in every word of Stockman's protest. In the most unexpected places of the play the thunder of applause would break in on the performance. The performance was more political than artistic. The atmosphere in the theatre was such that we expected arrests at any minute and a stop to the performance.

Censors, who sat at all the performances of " The Enemy of the People " and saw to it that I, who played Doctor Stockman, should use only the censored text, and raised trouble over every syllable that was not admitted by the censorship, were on this evening even more watchful than on other occasions. I had to be doubly careful. When the text of a rôle is cut and recut many times it is not hard to make a mistake and say too much or too little. In the last act of the play, Doctor Stockman, putting into order his room, which has been stoned by the crowd, finds in the general chaos his black coat, in which he appeared at the meeting on the day before. Seeing a rent in the cloth, Stockman says to his wife:

" One must never put on a new coat when one goes to fight for freedom and truth."

The spectators in the theatre connected this sentence with the massacre in Kazansky Square, where more than one new coat must have been torn in the name of freedom and truth. Unexpectedly my words aroused such a pandemonium that it was necessary to stop the performance, into which a real mob scene was interpolated by impromptu. There had taken place the unification of the actor and the spectators who took on themselves the rôle of the chief actor in the theatre, that same mob action of which so much is said by the theoreticians of art. The entire audience rose from its seats and threw itself towards the footlights. Thanks to the fact that the stage was very low and there was no orchestra before it, I saw hundreds of hands stretched towards me, all of which I was forced to shake. The younger people in the audience jumped to the stage and embraced Doctor Stockman. It was not easy to establish order and to continue with the play. That evening I found out through my own experience what power the theatre could exercise. From that evening on many attempts were made to drag our Theatre into politics, but we, who knew the true nature of the Theatre, understood that the boards of our stage could never become a platform for the spread of propaganda, for the simple reason that the very least utilitarian purpose or tendency, brought into the realm of pure art, kills art instantly.

Thanks to our success in Petrograd, we established close relations with that city, and after the end of our Moscow season each year brought our productions to the northern capital, either at Easter or during Lent. Not only the private, but even the imperial theatres of Petrograd opened their doors to us willingly, and that was considered a great honor at that time. We mostly played at the Mikhailovsky Theatre, where we were preceded by a French troupe with Guitry, Feraudy, Coquelin and Sarah Bernhardt at its head.

The popularity of our Petrograd seasons was so great that all the tickets for all the performances would be sold long in advance of our coming to Petrograd. Six months before we would undertake our yearly journey we would receive orders for seats. When tickets were placed on sale in Petrograd great crowds of students, professors, government employees, court nobility, officers and other people kept bivouac for days and nights on Mikhailovsky Square until their turn came to buy tickets, warming themselves at bonfires. They met and parted from us in a very touching manner, turning the occasions into street parades and thundering hurrahs that we heard long after our train would pull out of the station, bound for Moscow. The last performance of the Petrograd season was the beginning of our summer rest. Right after the performance we usually made a journey to the islands on the Neva. There can be nothing more terrible or more beautiful than spring in Petrograd. A good Petrograd spring is poetical, aromatic. Warm sea air, early greenery, the beginning of the white nights, spring flowers, nightingales.

On one such night we met on the islands the old and famous operetta singer, Alexander Davidov, who was known as the greatest interpreter of Gypsy songs in Russia. In his prime one could not hear him without weeping, there was so much soul and temperament in his singing. It was not for nothing that the famous tenor Mazzini loved to hear him. But Davidov had become old, he was a ruin, he had no voice left. Yet his glory still lived. The young people among us who had never heard the old man on the stage, but had heard so much about him, begged him to sing something for them that they might be able to tell their children that they too had heard the famous Davidov. We wakened the owner of a café, made him open his restaurant and make us some coffee, and here the famous old man, with the hoarseness of age in his voice, sang, or rather declaimed musically several love songs that made us weep. He showed his great art even in the semimusicianly sphere of the Gypsy song. Besides this, he forced me to think of that secret of sound and word in musical declamation which was known to him, but not to us, who were the servants of the word. Peace to the ashes of the talented old man! This was the last time I saw him, for soon afterwards he died.

CHAPTER XXXIX

D URING some years our theatrical season did not end in Petrograd, but would be carried over into one of the great provincial cities like Kiev, Odessa, or Warsaw. These journeys to the South, the sea, the Dnieper or the West were very much to our liking. The expansivity of Southerners is known to everybody.

The same things that happened in Moscow and Petrograd were repeated again. Written resolutions, crowds of people, overcrowding and catastrophes near the box office, ceremonious meetings and farewells, the rain of flowers and all the other attributes of success were ours. They even arranged a *folie journée* for us, that is, they hired a large steamer, the lower cabins of which hid a military band, a Rumanian orchestra, a chorus, soloists. These hidden delights appeared unexpectedly to the joy of everybody on the deck during the journey and added their spice to the happiness of the occasion. We would dance on the deck in the heat of the day to the sounds of the military band, or the steamer would stop near a large meadow on the shore of the river and we would institute open-air festivals with all sorts of athletic contests and games, and processions with music. Then we would board the steamer again and sail further to examine the wonderful ancient monastery in Kiev and its remarkable ikons. Here the end of the season would be celebrated with a triumphant dinner in the city park after the performance which lasted long past midnight. We were up far into the dawn. The rising sun opened a landscape of indescribable beauty to our eyes, a landscape with a far horizon where, like a twisting snake with shining scales, ran the legendary Dnieper.

We walked on the shore of the river and the gates of the old palace were opened to us. We were in a Turgenev-like atmosphere, with ancient flower beds, alleys, summerhouses and benches. One place in the palace park we recognized as the scenery of the second act of Turgenev's " A Month in the Country ", with which we had just ended our season in Kiev. Here there were also benches for spectators. The entire surrounding begged for a performance in the open air, in the midst of nature. We were asked to repeat the second act of the play. We consented and began our improvised performance with a great deal of aplomb. My turn also came, and now Knipper-Chekhova and I, as we are supposed to do in the play, walked along a long alley-path, repeating our text, and then sat down on a bench, according to our usual *mise en scène,* and — I stopped, because I could not continue my false and theatrical pose. All that I had done seemed untrue to nature, to reality. And it had been said of us that we had developed simplicity to a point of naturalism! How far we are from simple human speech, how conventional we saw to be what we had become used to do on the stage, considering our scenic truth to be real truth. Theorists will say, " This is as it must be ", and they will develop a whole theory and read a thesis on relative truth, on scenic conventionality. They might be right in their own way, in theory, but if they had been in my place on that occasion so important for me, at that performance in the dawn, they would have understood that the trees, the air, the sun hinted to us of such real, beautiful and artistic truth which cannot, because of its æstheticism, be compared to that which is created in us by the dead wings of a theatre. Let the artist who paints the scenery for the stage be great, but there is another, all-powerful Artist who acts in mysteries and ways unknown to us on our superconsciousness. This artistic truth, hinted to us by nature, is incomparably more æsthetic and more beautiful, and what is even more important, more scenic than that relative truth and theatrical conventionality with which it is the habit to limit theatrical creativeness. At that time I realized it completely, and more than once in my further activities in the Theatre I came to see the truth of what I had realized.

In Odessa our farewells almost ended in a catastrophe, and our art almost descended into the depths of the political kitchen. This was at a time when one of the usual pre-revolutionary moments fell on the city. The atmosphere was filled with electricity. The police were very active. When we left the theatre in which we had been playing we found ourselves surrounded by a tremendous mob of Southerners with fiery temperaments. They carried us with them along the streets to the wonderful sea boulevard of the city and along the boulevard to the hotel where we were stopping. This was done to the accompaniment of outcries, loud singing, sudden stops and speeches of a revolutionary character. At the end of the boulevard towards which we were being carried a patrol of police awaited the crowd. As we approached the patrol, the atmosphere about us became even more electrified than before. In order to avoid a catastrophe, we, the actors, began *pourparlers* with the police and begged them to wait a little before they dispersed the crowd by force and to trust us to do the thing by persuasion. They consented. Then we turned to the crowd with gratitude for the honor they had shown us and which would long remain in our memory.

" Do not darken this wonderful evening for us," we begged them, " with an unpleasant finale, with a report in the police station, arrests, and a fight. Let us part as friends and go to our homes with pleasant memories of our meeting."

We bade farewells and departed. Only a small group of young people remained. When I came into my room, I could hear the cries of men in the distance. Apparently something was going on outside, but in the darkness that enveloped the street one could not tell what it was.

Some of our actors and stage directors had gathered a certain amount of knowledge and experience. They began to dream of a larger independence than the one the Theatre could give them. My first assistant, A. A. Sanin, received an invitation from the Imperial Alexandrinsky Theatre in Petrograd, and the actor Vsevolod Meierhold, together with a few others of our troupe, established an enterprise in the provinces on the model of the Art Theatre and produced plays from our repertoire and according to our *mises en scène*. These productions enjoyed a tremendous success in the provinces.

Our first performance of " Tsar Fyodor " was visited, almost accidentally, by Savva Timofeievich Morozov, the rich manufacturer of whom I have written in the beginning of this book. His appearance in the theatre is deserving of notation, for this remarkable man was fated to play the important and honorable rôle of a Mæcenas who not only was able to bring material sacrifices to the altar of art, but who could also serve art faithfully, unselfishly and without any love of self, ambition or the thought of personal gain.

Morozov saw the performance and decided that it was necessary to help our Theatre. The chance to do this arose almost at once, for notwithstanding our artistic success, the material progress of the Theatre was far from satisfactory. There was a loss that grew with each month. Our sinking fund was spent and it was necessary to call a meeting of our shareholders and ask them to sacrifice more money. It was a pity, but the majority of them found it impossible to do so because of the lack of private means, despite their warm desires to help the Theatre. The crisis was almost catastrophic.

Unexpected by any of us, Morozov suddenly came to the meeting and offered to buy up all the holdings of the shareholders. They consented, and from that time on, Morozov, Nemirovich-Danchenko and I remained the only owners of the Theatre. Morozov financed it and undertook to supervise its business affairs. He entered into their smallest details and began to love the Theatre to such an extent that he gave all of his free time to it.

Being a born artist, he naturally wanted to take an active part in the artistic work of the Theatre also. He undertook the supervision of the electric lighting of the stage and the auditorium. He spent the summer in Moscow, being unable to leave the city because of his business affairs. He lived in a luxurious house on Spiridonovka, the same house that served as the headquarters of the American Relief Administration at the time of the Russian Revolution. As soon as his family would leave for the country, he changed the parlor of his home into a laboratory for his scenic experiments and the trials of various systems and methods of electrical lighting were made there prefatory to their introduction into the Theatre. The great bathroom of the mansion was turned into a chemical laboratory in which were prepared lacquers of various tones and colors for the painting of electric bulbs and glass, so that more artistic tones of stage lighting could be achieved. Trials of all sorts of electric effects which demanded a space were made in the large garden that surrounded the house. Morozov was not afraid of hard work, and dressed in working apparel, labored side by side with the electricians and smiths, astounding specialists with his knowledge of electricity. With the beginning of the season Morozov would enter on his duties as the supervisor of the lighting in the Theatre, and he placed his department on a very high footing, a thing far from easy to accomplish, considering the bad condition of the wiring and machines in the rented Hermitage in Karetny Row.

Notwithstanding his multitudinous business interests, Morozov visited the Theatre at almost every performance, and when he could not do so, he kept in touch with the Theatre by telephone in order to be fully aware of what was afoot not only in the lighting department, but in every branch of the complex theatrical mechanism. Morozov was touching in his enthusiasm, in his unselfish devotion to art, in his overwhelming desire to help the Theatre in every possible way. I remember that once the scenery and properties of a play that had been announced could not be arranged properly and in time for the performance. Because there was no time to remake the scenery, we were forced to cover its faults as much as we could, and all of us began to search for props that could be used, in the mass of theatrical effects in the storage rooms. Even the directors were engaged in the work, and with them Savva Timofeievich. It was touching to see him, the president of countless banks, institutions, societies, with an extraordinary position in the trade world, climbing ladders to hang draperies and pictures, and carrying furniture, in the guise of a simple stage hand. At that moment my liking for him became deeper and more tender.

On coming to know better all the good qualities of Morozov, we brought him nearer to the purely artistic side of the Theatre. And this was done not because he controlled the financial nerves of the Theatre, but because he evinced much taste and understanding in the fields of literature and artistic creativeness. Problems of the repertoire, of the distribution of rôles, of the examination of the faults of the performances and their production were solved with the aid of Morozov, who proved himself a useful worker in this field also. But Morozov showed most self-sacrifice and devotion and love for the Theatre when the question of hiring a new building for the Theatre could no longer be avoided or delayed.

Morozov undertook to settle this question himself, and he settled it according to his own nature, in a broad and generous way. He built us a new theatre with his money, or rather, a new and excellent stage with all its necessary accoutrements, leaving the auditorium as it was and merely renovating and repairing it. All for art and the actor — that was the motto that controlled his actions. In this manner he did exactly the opposite of what is usually done when a theatre is built. Usually three quarters of the money is expended on the foyer and the various rooms used by the audience, and only one quarter on art and the actors. Morozov spared no expenses for the stage and its paraphernalia, for the dressing rooms of the actors, but as far as the auditorium and the foyer were concerned, he finished them with extraordinary simplicity. A high wooden panel with cloth in frames; above the panel portraits of great writers, poets, actors and artists; along the panel wooden benches with cushions, white walls with a slightly dark border — that was the foyer, simple, modest, without one spot of color. The auditorium was finished in seasoned oak and the balustrades of the boxes and balconies, the furniture, the doors, the embrasures and panels were made of the same wood. The walls were also white, with hardly noticeable borders, without any bright spots or gilding. All the other rooms for the use of the audience were finished in the same style. This was done so as not to tire those sitting in the auditorium and to save all the color spots and effects for the stage. The rebuilding of the theatre was completed in several months.

Morozov, in order to be always present to oversee the work, refused a well-earned rest for the summer and lived the whole time in a small room near the theatre office, in the midst of noise, dust, and cares. He was willing to substitute these for the fields and woods of his numerous country estates. You must agree that only a large love and devotion to our Theatre could have made him act as he did. He spent special love on the stage and its lighting. According to the plans that we had worked out in common, he built a revolving stage which at that time was rare, even abroad. This stage was much better perfected than the usual type of revolving stage, in which only the floor revolves. Morozov built a stage with a complete revolving substage beneath it. A tremendous trap was made in the stage which could be sunk with the aid of electricity in order to serve as a river or a mountain chasm. The same trap could be lifted, so as to make a terrace or a mountain platform. The lighting system was the best obtainable at that time, and included the newest reflectors and apparatus made in Russia or abroad. It was worked by means of an electrical keyboard which controlled the entire lighting of both stage and auditorium. There were many other perfections with which it is not the province of this book to deal.

CHAPTER XL

THE general unrest and the coming revolution brought to the boards of our Theatre a series of plays that mirrored the social and political mood of discontent, protest, and dreams of a hero who would bravely tell the truth.

The censorship and the police administration were at the 'ght of their activity, the blue pencil made endless journeys across the text of the plays, crossing out the slightest hints that might evoke unrest or the breaking of the peace. There was fear that the theatres would became the arena for propaganda. And to tell the truth, attempts were made in that direction.

But true art fades whenever it approaches tendential, utilitarian, unartistic paths. In art tendency must change into its own ideas, pass into emotion, become a sincere effort and the second nature of the actor. Only then can it enter into the life of the human spirit in the actor, the rôle, and the play. But then it is no longer a tendency, it is a personal credo. The spectator can make his own conclusions, and create his own tendency from what he receives in the theatre. The natural conclusion is reached of itself in the soul and mind of the spectator from what he sees in the actor's creative efforts. This is a necessary condition, and it is only when such a condition is present that one can think in the theatre of producing plays of a social and political character. Were we in the possession of such creative conditions?

We knew that Gorky was writing two plays. He had told me of one in the Crimea, — it had no name as yet. The other was called

"Small People". We were interested in the first, for in that Gorky had chosen the life of the people he loved, those "creatures that once were men" who created his fame as a writer. We insisted that Gorky finish his first play at once so that we might open our new Theatre, built for us by Morozov, with its production. But Gorky complained about the persons of the play and could not finish it.

"You see, the trouble is that all these people of mine have surrounded me, and are crowding me and themselves, and I can't get them to take their proper places or make peace between them. The devil take them! They talk, talk, and talk, and they talk so well that it is a pity to stop them, by God. My word of honor!"

"Small People" became ripe for production before the first play. Of course, we were glad to get this play too, and decided to open our new theatre with its production. The trouble was that we had no actor who could take the part of Teterev, a contra basso from the church choir of a provincial town, who was the hero of the play. The rôle demanded a brightly colored individuality and a thundering voice. Among the pupils of our school there was one who undoubtedly fitted the part. He had the necessary voice, he had served in a church choir, and later sang in one of the suburban restaurant choruses. Baranov, — that was the name of the pupil whom we cast for the part of Teterev. He was undoubtedly talented, very kind-hearted, but at the same time a drunkard and completely uncultured. It would have been hard to explain to him the literary subtleties of Gorky's play. But in the rôle of Teterev, as we were able to see later, his barbarism did him a great favor. He took all that Teterev says and does in the play for the gospel truth. Teterev became for him a real person, a hero and ideal, and thanks to this, the tendencies and thoughts of the author recreated themselves in the soul of the actor. It would have been impossible to reach such seriousness and sincerity in one's relation to the situations in the play and the thoughts of the rôle portrayed by the use of any technique. What made it possible in the case of Baranov was his child-like naïveté. His Teterev was not theatrical, he was a real choir singer, and the spectator felt this at once and appreciated it at its true worth. The rest was in the hands of the stage director.

The season of 1901-1902, during which " Small People " was in preparation, was reaching its close, but the play was not yet ready for the general dress rehearsal with which we usually fixed the play in our minds. If it were not fixed in time, everything would be forgotten and we would have to begin the work all over again. Therefore, notwithstanding all obstacles, we decided to hold the dress rehearsal in Petrograd, where we usually ended our season. The time was one of unrest, and the police and the censors watched every step we made, for the Art Theatre, thanks to its new repertoire, was considered to be too radical, and Gorky himself was under the sur-veillance of the police. At the beginning the powers that were did not want to allow the production of the play at all. But due to the good offices of some influential persons, among whom was Count Witte himself, we at last received permission to stage a private per-formance before an audience consisting of official persons who were actively concerned with politics and censorship. All of official Petro-grad, beginning with the grand dukes and the ministers and includ-ing representatives of the censorship committee, the police and other governmental departments, were present in the Mikhailovsky The-atre where the production was staged. The vicinity of the theatre and the theatre itself was guarded by a special cordon of police, and mounted gendarmes were stationed in the square before the theatre. One could think that these preparations were being made not for a general dress rehearsal but for a general battle.

Count Witte did more than any one to secure permission for the production. At last the permission was received, but many changes were made by the censors in the text of the play. Among them some were of a very curious nature. For instance, the words

" the wife of the merchant Romanov " were supplanted by the words
"the wife of the merchant Ivanov " for the name Romanov smelled
of a hint at the reigning house.

The play was successful. Baranov in the rôle of Teterev was
more successful than the play. He was a product of the soil, a
second Chaliapin. Society ladies wanted to make his acquaintance.
He was led into the auditorium. He was surrounded by Princesses.
He flirted with them. The scene was almost indescribable. On the
next day the papers praised him to the skies. In this praise he found
his destruction. The first thing he did after reading the reviews
was to buy a top hat, gloves, and a fashionable coat. Then he began
to curse Russian culture roundly.

" All we have is ten or eleven newspapers. And in Paris or London," he said, " there are five hundred, five thousand."

In other words, Baranov was sorry that only ten or eleven newspapers praised him, and that were he in Paris, there would have
been five thousand reviews of his acting. This, from his point of
view, was the real meaning of culture.

Baranov's tone changed. Soon he began to drink. He was cured
and pardoned, because he was a genius in his way. He began to live
an exemplary life. But as he went on playing the rôle of Teterev
and his success grew, he became more and more spoiled. He was
guilty of inaccuracies, he took advantage of his illnesses, and once
he failed to come to the Theatre at all. We were forced to bid him
good-by. He walked the streets of Moscow declaiming puffed-up
verses and monologues in a thunderous voice and roaring in mighty
vocal crescendoes. Policemen led him to police stations. At times
he would visit us in the Theatre. He was welcomed kindly, he was
fed, but he never asked us to take him back into the Theatre, saying:

" I understand that I am not worthy of it."

Later on one of us met him on the highway dressed in under-
clothes, and at last he disappeared. Where is he now, the dear, tal-

ented tramp with his childlike heart and brain? Most probably he
has perished — from too much glory, not being able to survive success. Peace to his dust!

We received the second play from Gorky, which he called " The
Lower Depths of Life ", but later changed to " The Lower Depths "
on the advice of Nemirovich-Danchenko. There was a difficult problem before us, — a new author, a new style, a new tone and manner
of writing on the part of the author and playing on the part of the
actors, and a new and peculiar romanticism and pathos that bordered
both on theatricality and propaganda.

" I can't bear to see Gorky come out on the pulpit like a clergy-
man and read his apostolic letters to his congregation in a churchy
manner," said Chekhov about Gorky at one time. " Gorky is a
destroyer, who must destroy all that deserves destruction. In this
lies his whole strength, and it is for this that life has called him."

Our natures were alien to Gorky's wide gestures, to his revelatory
thoughts, to his sharp aphorisms, to his destructive flights, and to
his peculiar pathos. One must be able to say Gorky's words so
that the phrases live and resound. The instructive and propagand-
istic speeches of Gorky, even those like the one about Man, must be
pronounced simply, with sincere enthusiasm, without any false and
highfaluting theatricality. Otherwise a serious play will become a
mere melodrama. It was necessary to make our own the peculiar
style of the tramp, and not to exchange it or mix it up with the accepted type of theatrical vulgarity. In the tramp there must be
breadth, freedom, a nobility that is all his own. It was dangerous
to assume the usual declamatory tone. All this was important to me
not from the viewpoint of social and political movements and tendencies, but from the viewpoint of the innovator, for whom all that
was new was important mostly because it was new.

It was necessary to enter into the spiritual springs of Gorky himself, just as we had done in the case of Chekhov, and find the cur-

rent of the action in the soul of the writer. Having made our own a part of the Gorky soul, we would have the right to speak, to interpret the contents, the thoughts, the plot of the play, to act simply, without any unnecessary strain or effort, without the necessity of persuading some one, of propagating something, — and the spectator would not be bored in looking at us and listening to us; he would find it pleasant to believe us all of the time, for the spiritual content of Gorky and of ourselves would justify and round out the tendential parts of the play and the empty moments of the performance, which, under other circumstances, might become specifically theatrical stuffing and nothing else.

How were we to enter into the soul of the new dramatist and his play?

Again Nemirovich-Danchenko and I approached both author and play, each in our individual manner. Vladimir Ivanovich, as was his wont, gave a masterly analysis of the play. Being a writer, he knows all the secret approaches of literature which serve him as short cuts to creativeness. I, as was my habit at the beginning of all work, was in a helpless muddle, running from the local color to feeling, from feeling to the image, from the image to the production. I even bothered Gorky, looking for creative material. He told me how he wrote the play, where he found his types, how he wandered in the first part of his life, how he met the originals of the characters in his play. From Gorky I ran to those "creatures that once were men", who furnished him with material for his writing.

We arranged an expedition, in which many of the actors in the play, Nemirovich-Danchenko and I, took part. Under the leadership of the writer Giliarevsky, a connoisseur of the life of tramps, who always helped them with money and advice, we went by night to the Khitrov Market. This was a large section of the town which housed tramps exclusively. Their religion was freedom, their sphere — danger, burglary, adventure, theft, murder. All this created around them an atmosphere of romanticism and a peculiar savage beauty which we were seeking at that time. But we were not in luck. It was hard to get permission from the secret organizations of the Khitrov Market. A large theft had taken place that night and the entire Market was in a state of siege. Patrols of armed gunmen were stationed in various places. They would stop us in the endless underground passages, demanding to see our passes. In one place we had to steal by unseen or disaster would have overtaken us. After we had passed the first line of defence our progress became easier. We walked freely along continuous dormitories with numberless board cots on which lay crowds of tired people that resembled corpses, — men and women. In the very centre of the underground labyrinth was the local university and the intelligentsia of the Market. They were people who could read and write, and who at that time were occupied in copying parts for actors. These copyists lived in a small room. They proved themselves kind and hospitable, especially one of them, a well-educated man with fine hands and a delicate profile. He spoke many languages. He was an ex-officer of the guard, who had lost all his property and who had fallen to the depths. For a time he had been able to resume a decent life, to marry, to secure a good position, to wear a uniform.

" I would like to show myself in this uniform in the Khitrov Market," he thought one fine day.

He forgot the idea rapidly. But it returned again and again. Once, when he was commandeered to Moscow, he appeared in the Khitrov Market, astounded all of its inhabitants, — and remained there for the rest of his life, without any hope of ever getting out.

All these people received us like welcome guests whom they had known for a long time. And, in reality, they knew our names and patronymics, for they often worked for us, copying our rôles, and trying to please their favorite actors. As soon as we entered, vodka and sausage appeared on the table and a feast began. When we told them that we intended to produce a play about people like them, they were so touched that they began to weep.

"What honor is ours!" cried one of them.

"What is there so interesting in us that they want to show us on the stage?" another wondered naïvely.

Their talk ran to the theme that when they would stop drinking and become decent people and leave this place, they would —

One of them especially spoke about his past. His only souvenir of it was a little picture cut out of some illustrated magazine which portrayed an old father showing a check to his son, while the mother stood aside and wept. Simov did not like this picture. This was a signal for the breaking out of chaos. The living vessels full of alcohol came to terrible life; they grasped bottles, sticks, tabourets, and attacked Simov. Another moment, and he would have been killed, but Giliarovsky thundered out a quintuple oath, astounding not only us by the complexity of its construction, but even the denizens of the depths. It is impossible to swear in any other language so picturesquely as in Russian. The copyists turned to stone from the unexpectedness of the oath and the enthusiasm and æsthetic satisfaction it brought them. Their mood changed at once. There was mad laughter, applause, ovations, gratefulness and congratulations for the inspired composition of the curse, which perhaps saved us from death.

The excursion to the Khitrov Market, more than any discussion or analysis of the play, awoke my fantasy and my creative mood. There was nature which one could mold to his desire; there was live material for the creation of men, *mise en scène,* images, models and plans. Everything received a real basis and took its proper place. Making the sketches and the *mise en scène,* or showing the actors any of the scenes, I was guided by living memories, and not by invention or guesswork. But the chief result of the excursion was the fact that it forced me to feel the inner meaning of the play.

"Freedom at any cost!" that was its meaning for me. That freedom for the sake of which men descend into the depths of life and become slaves. But they become slaves of their own will, and can remove their yoke at any time, only to put it on again and become slaves once more. It is said that the play is tendentional, that it has social and political notes. Be it so! For me, the actor, the play is — *freedom* — and the spectator is free to draw his own conclusions from our scenic life.

In this condition, "with a wide open soul", as we Russians say, it was easy for us to understand and feel the remarkable direction of the play by Nemirovich-Danchenko.

But alas, all this was true only in part of me in my rôle of Satin. Within me I understood and felt all this; it traveled from my soul to my tongue, from my soul to the dynamic centers and periphery of my body that truly reflected the unseen inner life of the rôle. But in the moment of outward appearance there took place a movement towards my habitual theatricality, and I began to play not the rôle, but its result, the tendency, the idea, the gospel of Gorky. I over-acted romanticism and fell into ordinary theatrical pathos and declamation. In my search for the creative mood I moved now along the line of feeling — but did not live it over intuitively — or along the line of the symbol and reached the most commonplace portrayal of tendency, the embraces of the coldest theatrical pathos and falsity. This went on for a very long time, till that memorable moment of my life when before me there opened some of the mysteries of creativeness. But of these later.

The production was crowned with tremendous success. There were endless curtain calls for the actors, the stage directors, and for Gorky himself. It was very funny to see him appear for the first time on the stage, and stand on the boards with a cigarette in his teeth, smiling and lost, and not knowing that he was supposed to bow to the audience and to take the cigarette out of his mouth.

"Just see, my little brothers, this is success, by God, my word of honor," Gorky seemed to be saying to himself. "They are clapping, really. They are yelling! There's a wonder for you!"

Gorky became the hero of the day. He was followed in the streets. Mobs of admirers, especially of the fair sex, gathered about him. In the beginning he was confused. He would approach them, pulling at his rusty, cropped mustache, and running his strong fingers through his long hair or throwing his head back so as to clear his face and forehead of the mass of hair that fell over it, — trembling, distending his nostrils, hunching his body in confusion.

"Brothers," he would say to us, smiling guiltily, "you know — somehow, it is not comfortable — really — my word of honor! — Why do they eye me like that? I am not a singer or a dancer. — Who would ever have thought it! — By God! — My word of honor — "

But his funny confusion and peculiar, bashful manner of speech intrigued and attracted admirers more and more. Gorky's personal attraction was strong. He had his own beauty of plastics, freedom and ease. There is an imprint in my visual memory of his fine pose when he stood on the shore of Yalta, waiting for my steamer to leave. Carelessly leaning against bales of baggage and supporting his little son Maxim, he looked thoughtfully into the distance, and it seemed that in another moment he would rise from the shore and fly into the boundless blue in the wake of his dreams.

CHAPTER XLI

SMALL PEOPLE " was to be followed by Lev Tolstoy's " The Power of Darkness ". Continuing to play the new for the sake of the new, we could not make peace with the theatrical stencil of the Russian mujik or the opera stencil of what might be called *le paysan*. For one who knows the village and Russia, for one who understands what is village darkness and what is its power, it would be an insult to see one of the mujiks of Tolstoy in slippers and with ribbons in the hair. At the present time one cannot believe that an actor could go out on the stage in such a manner in a peasant play, but at the time I am writing about it was a common occurrence.

The scenery and the productions of such plays in general was in the same spirit. We declared war on such an interpretation of peasant plays. We wanted to show the real mujik, and not only the costume, but also the inner physique of his soul. But the result was not what we wanted. We could not give the spiritual side, we had not reached the stage where we could interpret that yet. In order to fill the void, as is always the custom in such cases, we exaggerated the outward and external side of manners. This remained unjustified innerly, for lifeless objects, properties, and sounds began to bulge out of the general scheme. This resulted in naked naturalism. And the nearer it was to reality, the more ethnographical it was — the worse it was for us. There was no spiritual darkness, and therefore the outward and naturalistic darkness proved unnecessary. It had nothing to round out and illustrate. Ethnography choked literature and the art of the actor.

"THE POWER OF DARKNESS"

If we were not able to create something new of an inner nature, we were successful in creating more than was necessary in the sense of scenery and costumes, and I can say with certainty that the stage had never yet seen such a real village as we showed. We made an expedition for the purpose of studying village life to the estates of Stakhovich in the Government of Tula, the place where the action was supposed to have transpired. We lived there for two weeks and visted the nearest villages. Both Simov, the artist, and Grigorieva, who took care of the costumes in the Theatre, were with us. We studied the buildings, and made plans of them, of the natural geography and topography of the courtyards, barns, outhouses, and main structures on the estate. We studied the customs, the marriage ceremonies, the run of everyday life, the details of husbandry. We brought back with us from the village clothes, shirts, short overcoats, dishes, furniture. Not only that — we also brought two living specimens of village life with us, an old man and an old woman. Both proved to possess talents for the stage, especially the woman. They were to direct the play from the viewpoint of village customs. After several rehearsals they knew the text of all the rôles without the help of the prompter. Once, when the actress who played Matryona was ill, the old woman took her place in the rehearsal. The work of the peasant woman made a tremendous sensation. It was she who showed for the first time on the stage the real Russian village, in all its spiritual darkness and power. When she gave Anisya the powder with which the latter was to poison her husband, when she put her crooked hand in her bosom, seeking there for the little package of poison, and then quietly, in a business-like way, as if not understanding the depth of her villainy, explained to Anisya how to poison a man gradually and secretly, the cold sweat broke out on our foreheads. The son of Lev Nikolaevich, Sergey Lvovich, was present at this rehearsal and he was in such ecstasy over the old woman's playing that he tried to persuade us to give her the part of Matryona in the performance. His proposal was tempting. After a talk with the actress who had played Matryona, she consented to give the part to the old woman. There was only one insurmountable difficulty. In the scenes where Matryona was supposed to be angry or to scold some one, the old woman did not use Tolstoy's text and made much of her own text which was composed of such oaths that it was certain that the censorship would never allow them on the stage. No matter how much we begged her that she should not do it, it was impossible to convince her that she could get along on the stage without vulgarity. In her opinion this was impossible for a true village type. There was still another circumstance — she interpreted the inner and outer contents of Tolstoy's tragedy so fully, truthfully, and in such bright colors, she justified each of our naturalistic details of production to such an extent that she became unreplaceable to us. But when she left the stage and the regular actors of the company were on, their spiritual and physical imitation betrayed them. This was true of all except Butova, who played Anisya, and who had fine feeling for the village, its power and its darkness. The old woman and Butova created an unforgettable duo. So much the worse for the rest of the cast. The real peasant woman broke it up.

With a breaking heart I was forced to exclude the old woman from the list of actresses, for she still continued to swear. I transferred her to the crowd which gathered in front of the house of Peter, the husband whom Anisya poisoned. Here, too, the appearance of the old woman gave away the imitation of the other actors. I hid her in the back rows, but the one note of her weeping covered the exclamations of all the rest in the scene. Then, not being able to part with her, I invented a special pause for her sake, during which she was to cross the stage, droning a song and calling some one in the distance. The sound of the old and weak voice was possessed of such breadth and gave the spirit of the Russian village with such veracity that it was impossible for any one of us to appear on the stage after her exit. We made a final trial. We did not let her come out, but made her sing in the wings. But even this was dangerous for the actors. Then we made a phonograph record of her voice, and her song provided a background for the action without breaking up our ensemble.

It was with pain that we denied ourselves her great but unapplied talents. But the experiment did not pass in vain for me. I convinced myself by experience and saw my conviction justified many dozens of times that naturalism on the stage is only naturalism when it is justified by the inner experience of the actor. Once naturalism is justified, it either becomes necessary (especially in Tolstoy's plays, for Tolstoy loves things and the details of human life more than all other authors) or it is simply unnoticed, thanks to the inner display of the emotions of the actor and the complete mixing of inner and outer life. I would advise all theoreticians who do not know this from their own experience to see their words justified on the stage itself, as I did. They were right in what they said about us, for our unjustified naturalism was a mistake. It did not have the desired success, nor did I in my rôle of Mitrich, notwithstanding that for its sake I pasted bumps on my forehead and disfigured my hands, feet, and all my body in order to look like a mujik. This unjustified imitation only made things worse. I did not feel anything, neither the soul nor the body of Mitrich. I played in false tones and was only a stage caricature.

The naturalistic line in this production did not become one with the more important line of the intuition of feelings.

The production of " The Enemy of the People " and the rôle of Doctor Stockman should be included in the series of plays that fell under the social and political mood, because in those days " The Enemy of the People " had not only artistic but social meaning and was to a great extent the expression of the time. It is not remarkable that the play at once came under the surveillance of the censor and the police. Not a single performance took place without ovations that resembled demonstrations.

But I personally, the interpreter of the chief rôle in the play, never, not even for one moment, felt the presence of tendency or politics in my life on the stage, and the demonstrations that accompanied the performances only interfered with me. I was carried along by an altogether different line of action in the play, — the love of Stockman for *truth*. I was wrathful in the play at the people that I had loved once, while I looked at them through the eyes of Stockman's soul. I sincerely sympathized with Stockman and understood his feelings when his eyes saw the rotten souls of the men who had once been his friends. I feared in those moments — for Stockman or for myself — I don't remember. I felt and understood that with each succeeding scene I became more and more lonely, and when, at the end of the performance I at last stood alone, the final sentence of the play " He is the strongest who stands alone " seemed to beg for utterance by its own power.

In my actor's perceptions I felt myself more at home on the stage in the rôle of Stockman than in any other rôle in my repertoire. In it I instinctively followed the line of the intuition of feelings. For me Stockman was not a politician, not an orator at meetings, not a *raisonneur,* but a man of ideals, the true friend of his country and his people. He was the best and purest citizen of his motherland.

From the intuition of feelings on my part the result was a performance of a social and political meaning. From the intuition of feelings I passed naturally to the inner image with all its peculiarities and details : the short-sighted eyes which spoke so eloquently of his inner blindness to human faults, the childlike and youthful manner of movement, the friendly relations with his children and family, the happiness, the love of joking and play, the gregariousness and attractiveness which forced all who came in touch with him to become purer and better, and to show the best sides of their natures in his presence. From the intuition of feelings I went to the outer image, for it flowed naturally from the inner image, and the soul and body of Stockman-Stanislavsky became one organically. I only had to think of the thoughts and cares of Stockman and the signs of short sight would come of themselves, together with the forward stoop of the body, the quick step, the eyes that looked trustfully into the soul of the man or object on the stage with me, the index and the middle fingers of the hand stretched forward of themselves for the sake of greater persuasiveness, as if to push my own thoughts, feelings and words into the soul of my listener. All these habits came of themselves, unconsciously, and quite apart from myself. From where did they come?

From where? The creative ways of nature are beyond human ken. Who would ever think that I found the make-up and the outer image of the rôle of General Krutitsky in Ostrovsky's " Enough Stupidity in Every Wise Man " in the general appearance of an old house, standing somewhat askew in an older courtyard, and seemingly swollen and overgrown with mossy side beards! From this house ran out little old men in undress uniforms, with many unnecessary papers and projects à la General Krutitsky under their arms. All this together brought me in some mysterious way to the make-up of my rôle in Ostrovsky's comedy. And in the rôle of Stockman also the material for the outer image was taken unconsciously from memories.

A few years passed and I still played Stockman, and little by little I found accidentally the sources of many of the elements of the inner and outer images. For instance, in Berlin, I met a learned man whom I had often met before in a sanatorium near Vienna, and I recognized that I had taken the fingers of Stockman's hand from him. It is very possible that it was really so. Meeting a famous musical critic I recognized in him my manner of stamping in one place in the rôle of Stockman. I only had to assume the manners and habits of Stockman, on the stage or off, and in my soul there were born the feelings and perceptions that had given them birth. In this manner, intuition not only created the image, but its passions also. They became my own organically, or, to be more true, my own passions became Stockman's. And during this process I felt the greatest joy an artist can feel, the right to speak on the stage the thoughts of another, to surrender myself to the passions of another, to perform another's actions, as if they were my own.

"You are mistaken, you are animals, yes, animals," I said to the crowd at the public lecture in the fourth act of the play, and I said this truthfully and sincerely, for I was able to assume the viewpoint of Stockman himself. And I found it pleasant to say this and to feel that the spectator, who had begun to love me in the rôle of Stockman, was excited, and angry at me for the tactlessness of arousing my enemies with too much sincerity.

My double, the actor and stage director that resided in me, understood well indeed the scenic effect of such misunderstanding between the actor and the spectator. It called out in both of them sincere passions, truthful living over of the moment, lively sympathy, and therefore I wanted all the more to say my speech as sincerely as it was given me, so that the spectator might be more excited than he was, that he might be all the angrier at Stockman and love Stockman all the more for his childlike truthfulness.

Playing a rôle in a play that was one of the series of social and political productions, I struck on the line of the intuition of feelings and forgot the politics in the play, which became all the stronger because of it. Traveling along the line of the intuition of feelings, I perceived instinctively the characteristic thread of manners in the rôle. The symbol of the rôle discovered itself by its own power. Perhaps in our art there exists only one correct path — the line of the intuition of feelings! And out of it grow unconsciously the outer and inner images, their form, the idea and the technique of the rôle. The line of intuition at times absorbs into itself all the other lines, and grasps all the spiritual and physical contents of the rôle and the play. I had experienced this even before, at the time I created the rôle of the uncle in "The Village Stepanchikovo". There too, the more sincerely I believed his impossible naïveté and goodness of heart, the more tactless his actions became, the more the spectator was excited by his tactlessness, the more misunderstandings there were, the stronger did the spectator love the hero for his childlike trustfulness and spiritual purity. There too the line of the intuition of feelings absorbed all the other lines of the rôle, and the creative goal of the author and the tendency of the play were created not by the actor but by the spectator, as the result of all that he saw and heard in the theatre.

In the rôle of Stockman I unconsciously reached all that I could not consciously reach in the rôle of Satin. In Stockman I did not think of politics and tendency, and they created themselves. In Satin I thought of the social and political importance of the play, and that did not pass over the footlights. What road was one to take in the approach to a social and political play? One must himself live with the thoughts and feelings of the rôle and act in concordance with them. Just as logical action causes reaction, so artistic creativeness causes to appear the idea of the play and its tendency. Let the spectator formulate it himself.

All that concerns the actor is to create the artistic action.

CHAPTER XLII

I T is decided that we are to produce Shakespeare's 'Julius Cæsar '," Nemirovich-Danchenko said to me entering my room and decisively putting his hat on the table.

" When will we produce it? " I wondered.

" At the beginning of the coming season," answered Nemirovich-Danchenko.

" But when will we manage to make the plan of production, the scenery, and the costumes? If not to-day, then to-morrow all of us are going on our summer vacations," I continued in amazement.

But when Nemirovich-Danchenko talks as confidently as he did on that occasion, it means that he has sat up more than one night with a pencil in his hand developing the plan of a production and examining all the possible details of the work in every branch of the large theatrical mechanism.

The choosing of a play for the repertoire of our Theatre is very much like the experience of great birth pangs. And in the year in question this process was harder than usual. It was already May; it was time to go on our yearly journey to St. Petersburg, and no one knew as yet what the work for the next season was to be. There was no time to debate; it was necessary to agree with Nemirovich-Danchenko and to begin doing all that was possible.

The journey to St. Petersburg was put off, Nemirovich-Danchenko and Simov went to Rome to gather material, and a regular office was established in the theatre to take care of the preparatory work. We established a series of departments at the head of which were responsible persons and their assistants, all from the roster of the actors and stage directors. These departments were housed in the foyer of the theatre and the rooms adjoining it. One of the departments took care of the literary side of the play, and its text, its changes and cuts, its translation, its comparison with other texts of the same play, and researches in foreign and domestic publications, criticism and so on. Anther department took care of all that treated of the locale, the social conditions of life, the customs, buildings, and usages of the time of Cæsar. A third department took care of the costumes, their sketches, their cutting, their material, its buying and dyeing. A fourth department took care of weapons, armor, and properties. A fifth department of the material for sketches, the making of scenic models, a sixth department of music, a seventh of the ordering and the performance of all that was decided upon, an eighth of the rehearsals of the actors, a ninth of the mob scenes and supernumeraries. The tenth department was administrative and reviewed the work of the other nine departments.

A military discipline was proclaimed in the theatre, and all the actors, the members of the administration and the workmen were mobilized. No one was to refuse to work on any pretext whatsoever. Those of the mobilized who were not occupied in the theatre itself were sent to visit museums, to learned specialists of antique culture, to private collectors, to antiquaries, and were to find material and bring it to the proper departments for examination by the actors, stage directors and artists. All the persons and institutions that were approached by the Theatre through its representatives responded to our approaches, and sent us their priceless publications, rarities, armor, and so on. One can say with confidence that all the rich material possessed by Moscow was used by us in our researches. Still richer material, brought by Nemirovich-Danchenko from Rome, completed our collection.

Thanks to our organization, we were able to collect in several weeks as much as it would have taken us more than a year to collect under ordinary circumstances. Much of which we cannot even dream at present could be gotten before the war. For instance, those members of the properties commission who were sent to the stores took a tremendous amount of material of various qualities and colors and brought it to the theatre in trucks. The materials were hung on the stage on specially prepared frames. They were lighted by the footlights, the side lights and the top lights and spots, singly and in various combinations, and examined from the auditorium. The more effective pieces of cloth were laid aside for further use in the proper departments. The color scale of the costumes was chosen with special attention and care, and no matter what groups of actors met on the stage, they always created a bouquet of harmoniously chosen colors.

After his return from abroad, Nemirovich-Danchenko took charge of the entire production, and the rest of us helped him. I, on my part, began first of all to work out with the artist the construction of the scenery, and the floor plan that would give room for the rich *mises en scène* of the stage director. Simov prepared the sketches. Each set of scenery was to have its scenic originality and its peculiarity, not only in the sense of color and design, but also in the sense of the stage director's construction of the plan of the stage and the *mise en scène*. This *je ne sais quoi* (I use this term in order to avoid the unpleasant and untrue word *hokum,* which would make small my idea of scenery) was to be found in the first place. Let me explain by an example.

On a comparatively small stage with a comparatively small number of extras we were to show the passing of the large army of Brutus going into battle. In the same scene there appears for the purpose of *pourparlers* before battle, Brutus' enemy, Antony. His armies, ready to give battle, are seen in the distance. The action takes place in a great valley with a wide horizon comfortable for the coming

together of masses of people. With the help of a backdrop horizon
and a painted perspective we were able to attain the desired impression of distance. But thanks to the conditions imposed by the perspective, we could not place any life-size figures in the back of the
stage, and would have to transfer all of them to the forestage. Then
where were we to show the army of Antony? We could not understand from the model set of scenery alone how to approach all the
problems that faced us, how to arrange the passages, giving them
the least possible amount of space in order to create the impression
of large masses of people with a small body of extras. For this
purpose the roughly made model is put on the stage, and its contours
are followed and created on the stage proper out of any properties
that come under hand. Having done this and tried the passage of
the army, we came to understand that it would make only a doll-like
impression. It was necessary to deceive the public. A trial showed
that it was much better to show the passing warriors not in their full
height, but only down to their waists, that is, their heads and the
upper parts of their torsos. It was even better if these passing men
would disappear and appear again. The illusion becomes greater
when the passing of the armies takes place behind the trunks of trees
or behind out-butting cliffs. All that was hinted in the rough recreation of the model on the stage was repeated on the stage again.
Taking advantage of the great trap on our stage, which, when lowered
formed a great crack in the floor, we reached the effect of having the
armies appear and disappear to appear again. At the same time
that the armies passed, other extras moving behind them carried a
forest of spears, increasing the illusion of numbers in the crowd.
This piece of hokum had still another profitable point; it gave us
the possibility of costuming the extras only so far as their heads
and torsos were concerned, for their legs were not seen. The spaces
between the cliffs through which the movements of the passing armies
could be seen could always be widened or narrowed without disturb-

ing the illusion. The extras passed along the trap, and circling the backdrop, appeared again before the public. The result was an endless procession of passing warriors obtained with the use of comparatively few extras. While the extras passed behind the backdrop, tailors managed to put new details on their armor; that is, they changed helmets, donned other cloaks, and thus gave the illusion of a new detachment of soldiers, who were as yet unseen by the public. This effect was very profitable materially and scenically, but required many rehearsals.

The same small number of extras allowed us to create convincingly the effect of a street crowd in the first act. The construction of the floor and the motives for the scenery of the first act were brought from Rome by Simov and Nemirovich-Danchenko. We were able to make use of the great trap in creating the impression of a street disappearing under a hill. In its depth the effect of a moving crowd was created in the same manner as the movement of the armies, and a whole cross-section of the life of ancient Rome was shown on the stage. Rows of stores stretched from the forestage into the trap and were lost in the movement of the crowd. Merchants stood in front of them, calling in the buyers; here and there was seen the shop of an armorer where swords, shields and armor were in the process of forging, and in the necessary places the ringing of the hammers in the shop covered the talk of the crowd. The street passed along the whole width of the stage and disappeared in the wings, while on the right an alley with a typical Italian stairway poured into it from the hills. In this way the citizens moved towards each other, up and down and along the stage, and their movements on meeting created a garish and lifelike picture of Roman street life. At the point where the street rose from the trap to the stage, was the shop of a barber, where Roman patricians met and engaged in conversation, as we do in our clubs. Above the shop on a typical flat roof there was a little garden with a bench. From there the people's tribunes delivered their speeches, stopping the mob which crowded the forestage for the time being.

Matrons, with slaves who carried their purchases following them, passed along the stage. They were respectfully greeted by the dandies from the barber's shop, who, after the matrons passed, hurried to call in the courtesans who were on the streets.

Up from below on the street that ran along the stage came the procession with Cæsar and Calpurnia. When it reached the center of the stage it was stopped by the soothsayer. Cæsar, triumphantly recumbent on his litter, and Calpurnia reclining in tender ease on hers, became anxious. Behind them appeared Brutus and his supporters. He followed the procession with a sorrowful gaze. He was surrounded by citizens who stretched toward him written petitions and complaints against their ill-treatment. I must not forget one rather anecdotal occurrence which shows eloquently the necessity of the strict training that must be given to the most insignificant of extras. I played Brutus. Once one of the extras who was to hand me a petition did not appear in the theatre on time. Nemirovich-Danchenko, who followed the performance from the wings, called over one of the free extras, who in private life was a clerk in one of the municipal institutions, and asked him to hand me the necessary paper. With a walk typical of the manners of a clerk who approaches his superior, the messenger approached me, and making a completely modern bow, said very clearly, " Constantin Sergeievich, Vladimir Ivanovich ordered me to give you this," and stretched out the property Roman tablets towards me. Of course my mood changed at once, and all the plotting emotions which I had created with such hardship in myself for the interpretation of the rôle were changed to one single effort to prevent myself from laughing in the poor clerk's face.

We studied costumes, their cutting, and the methods of wearing them and carrying armor by the application of ancient plastics. We were forced to make not only a theoretical, but a practical acquaintance with these plastics. For this purpose there were made for rehearsal costumes, cloaks, togas, sandals, and other articles of ancient dress, which we put on and wore for many days in the theatre. Not only did we rehearse in these cloaks and togas, but we worked on the production while wearing them. In the intimate life of the theatre there was created a cross-section of antique social life, and the performer of every rôle in it gathered real experience in the wearing of the costumes of the period. This experience taught us a great deal which one cannot learn in books, or from theories or drawings. I tried to systematize all that feeling and experience hinted to me to create a scheme of movements, of conscious manners of handling a cloak and its folds, of gathering the folds in the closed hand; and then I shared with the others the results of what I achieved. By personal experience they grew used to what they were taught theoretically. In the region of plastics we created a scheme of movements and gestures which were borrowed from ancient statues and frescoes. Each one of us, so to say, drew them through himself, that is, he revivified them and justified them by his personal sensations. In the region of plastics we found some fundamentals which were useful to me not only in " Julius Cæsar ", but also in my further experiments and researches.

CHAPTER XLIII

THE LAST YEAR WITH CHEKHOV

IN the autumn of 1903 Anton Pavlovich came to Moscow in very
ill health. Nevertheless, he was present at almost all the
rehearsals of his new play, the name of which he could not yet
decide upon. Once of an evening he telephoned me to come to him on
business. He was sick and could not leave the house. To visit Anton
Pavlovich was a rare happiness. I dropped all my affairs and rushed
to see him. He was very high-spirited, notwithstanding his illness.
Apparently he did not wish to speak of the business on hand at once,
but to leave it for the very end, just as children like to leave sweets
for the very end of a meal. Meanwhile we all sat at the tea table and
laughed, because it was impossible not to laugh in Chekhov's presence. But tea finished, Anton Pavlovich led me to his study, closed
the door, sat down in his traditional corner of the divan, and made me
sit before him. But even then he did not begin with the business on
hand at once, still keeping it for dessert. Meanwhile he was trying
to persuade me that some of the actors did not fit their parts and
should be replaced by others.

"But of course, they are wonderful actors," he tried to soften his
criticism.

I knew all that was said was only a prelude to what he really
wanted to say. Anton Pavlovich was a man of the theatre and knew
that parts could not be changed in a play which was trembling on the
threshold of its first night. At last we came down to business. Anton
Pavlovich made a pause, during which he seemed to chew on what he
wanted to tell me. He could not control his lovable smile, which was

even triumphant at that moment, notwithstanding the fact that he tried in every way to be serious.

"Listen, I have found a wonderful name for the play. A wonderful name," he declared, looking directly at me.

"What is it?" I was excited.

"Vishneviy Sad" (The Cherry Orchard), and he rolled with happy laughter.

I confess that I did not thoroughly understand the reason for his gladness, for I found nothing unusual in the name. But I was forced to put on the appearance that his discovery had made an impression on me, and at the same time I wanted to find out from Chekhov what it was that excited him in the new name of the play. But here I stumbled on one of the strange traits of Chekhov. He could not philosophize and explain what he had created. And so he explained the beauty of the name "Vishneviy Sad" by repeating in various ways and with various intonations and color in the voice:

"Vishneviy Sad. Listen, it is a wonderful name. Vishneviy Sad. Vishneviy — "

His intonations made me understand that he was talking of something beautiful, tenderly loved, and this inner meaning of the name was reflected not in the name itself but in the intonation of Anton Pavlovich. I carefully gave him a hint of this. My words saddened him, the gladness and triumph left his face, and our conversation lost life.

Several days, perhaps a week, passed after this meeting. Anton Pavlovich felt better and began to go out. Once, during a performance, he came into my dressing room and with a triumphant smile sat down at my side near the make-up table. He loved to watch actors put on their make-up and costumes. If we looked at him at such moments we could do without a mirror, because the expression of his face told us at once whether we drew a successful or unsuccessful line on our faces.

" Listen, not Vishneviy, but Vishnéviy Sad," he stated triumphantly and became all laughter.

At first I did not even understand of what he was speaking, but
Chekhov lovingly repeated the word, stressing the tender sound of
" e " in the word as though he were trying to caress with its help that
former beautiful life which was no longer necessary, which he himself
lovingly and with tears was destroying in his play. This time I understood the great and yet delicate difference. Vishneviy Sad is a commercial orchard which brings in profit. Such an orchard is necessary
to life even at the present. But Vishnéviy Sad brings no profits. It
hides in itself and in all of its flowering whiteness the great poetry of
the dying life of aristocracy. The Vishnéviy Sad grows for the sake
of beauty, for the eyes of spoiled æsthetes. It is a pity to destroy it,
but it is necessary to do so, for the economics of life demand it.

All remarks, which had to be dragged out of Anton Pavlovich by
main force, seemed to be rebuses. He did not like to make them, and
he would always hide from the eyes of the stage directors who haunted
him. If any one came to a rehearsal and saw Anton Pavlovich mod-
estly sitting somewhere in the back rows, he would never have believed
that this was a great poet and the author of the play. No matter how
hard we tried to make him sit down at the stage directors' table, so
that it might be easier to consult him, our efforts were in vain. We
would make him sit down at the table, and he would begin to laugh.
It was impossible to understand what made him laugh, whether it was
the fact that he had become a stage director and sat at such an important table, or that he was inventing means of deceiving the stage
directors and disappearing from their ken.

" I wrote it," he would answer to our questions; " I am not a stage
director, I am a doctor," and he would hurry to get away and hide
himself in some dark corner.

Comparing the manner in which Chekhov conducted himself at
rehearsals with the manner in which other authors conducted them-

selves, I cannot help but wonder at the extraordinary modesty of the great man and the boundless vanity of the little writers. One of them, for instance, when I suggested that a long-winded and false-sounding monologue in his play be shortened, told me with complete belief and the anger of the insulted in his voice:

" Shorten it, but do not forget that you will be held responsible by history."

But when we dared to suggest to Anton Pavlovich that a whole scene be shortened, the whole end of the second act of " The Cherry Orchard," he became very sad and so pale that we were ourselves frightened at the pain that we had caused him. But after thinking for several minutes, he managed to control himself and said:

" Shorten it."

Never after did he say a single word to us about this incident. And who knows, perhaps he would have been justified in reproaching us, because it may very well be that it was the will of the stage director and not his own which shortened a scene that was excellently written. After the young people left Varya with a great deal of noise, Sharlotta came on the stage with a rifle and lay down in the hay, singing some popular German song. Hardly able to move his feet, there entered Firs, lighting matches, looking in the grass for the fan dropped by his mistress. There takes place a meeting of two lonely people. They have nothing to speak about, but they so want to speak, for a human being must speak to some one. Sharlotta begins to tell Firs of how she worked in her youth in a circus and performed the *salto mortale*, in those very words, which, in our version she says in the beginning of the act when on the stage with Epikhodov, Yasha and the maid. In answer to her story, Firs talks at length and randomly about something that cannot be understood that happened in the days of his youth, when somebody was taken somewhere in a wagon accompanied by sounds of squeaking and crying, and Firs interprets these sounds with the words cling-clang. Sharlotta does not understand anything in his story, but catches up his cue so that the one common moment in the lives of these two lonely people may not be disturbed. They cry " Cling-Clang " to each other and both laugh very sincerely. This was the way Chekhov ended the act.

After the stormy scene with the young people, such a lyric ending lowered the atmosphere of the act and we could not lift it again. I suppose that it was mainly our own fault, but it was the author who paid for our inability. What would a newly baked celebrity have done in the place of Chekhov?

CHAPTER XLIV

IS it necessary to describe the production of "The Cherry Orchard"? We have played it so often in Europe and America. But I will say some things about it, not for the sake of following the line of the evolution of the Moscow Art Theatre in it, but in order to tell of the last year in the life of Chekhov and of his death which had a tremendous importance in the life of our Theatre.

The production of "The Cherry Orchard" was accomplished with great hardships. The play is delicate, it has all the tenderness of a flower. Break its stem and the flower dries, its odor vanishes. The play and the rôles live only when the stage director and the artist dig deep enough to reach the secret treasure house of the human spirit in which is hidden the chief nerve of the play. In my great desire to help the actors I tried to create a mood around them, in the hope that it would grip them and call forth creative vision. In those days our inner technique and our ability of reacting on another's creative soul were very primitive. I took all the bypaths I could think of. I invented all sorts of *mises en scène,* the singing of birds, the barking of dogs, and in this enthusiasm for sounds on the stage I went so far that I caused a protest on the part of Chekhov, who loved sounds on the stage himself. The form in which he expressed his disagreement with me was very interesting.

" ' What fine quiet,' the chief person of my play will say," he said to some one so that I could hear him. " ' How wonderful! We hear no birds, no dogs, no cuckoos, no owls, no clocks, no sleigh bells, no crickets.' "

That stone was intended for my garden.

Nemirovich-Danchenko and I did not think that the production would be ripe at its first performance. And meanwhile, until the play was produced, it risked becoming boresome. The success of the play was necessary at all costs, for the health of Anton Pavlovich was in a precarious condition. So we decided to take advantage of the jubilee of Chekhov's literary activity and to stage the first night of the play on that day. Our reckoning was simple. If the actors were not able to put the play over, its failure of great success could be blamed on the unusual conditions of the jubilee evening which would not fail to draw the attention of the spectators away from the actors to the author. But the appointed date was very near and the play was not yet ready. Besides, I had to think of a present for Anton Pavlovich. This was a hard question to settle. I visited all the antiquaries in Moscow, hoping to find something, but outside of some very fine embroidered cloth I found nothing. As there was nothing better, we decorated the jubilee wreath with this cloth. " At least," I thought, " we will present him with something of artistic value."

But Anton Pavlovich never forgot this gift.

" Listen, this is a wonderful thing, it must be kept in a museum," he upbraided me after the jubilee.

" Tell me, Anton Pavlovich, what should we have given you? " I asked in my confusion.

" A rat trap," he answered seriously, after thinking for some time. " Listen, mice must be destroyed." Here he began laughing himself. " Korovin sent me a beautiful present, a beautiful one! "

" What was it? " I became interested.

" Fishing poles."

None of the other presents he received pleased Chekhov, and some of them angered him with their banality.

" Listen, one shouldn't give a writer a silver pen and an ancient inkwell."

" Well, what should one give? "

" A piece of rubber pipe. Listen, I am a doctor. Or socks. My wife doesn't attend to me as she should. She is an actress. And I walk around in torn socks. ' Listen, little soul,' I say to her, ' the big toe of my right foot is coming out.' ' Wear it on your left foot,' she answers. It can't go on that way — "

And he rolled with happy laughter.

But at the jubilee he was far from happy. It seemed that he foresaw his own end. After the third act he stood deathly pale and thin on the right side of the stage and could not control his coughing while gifts were showered on him and speeches in his honor were being made. Our hearts grew small in us. Some one in the audience cried loudly that he should sit down. But he drew his brows together and stood throughout the duration of the jubilee, over which he laughed so innocently in his works. Even on that evening he could not control his smile. One of the best-known professors in Russia began his speech almost with the same words with which Gaiev greeted the old clothespress in the first act of " The Cherry Orchard."

" Dear and much respected (instead of saying clothespress, the professor used Chekhov's name) — I greet you — "

Anton Pavlovich looked sideways at me (I had played Gaiev) and a villainous smile passed over his lips.

The triumph was a really triumphant occasion, but it smelled of a funeral. Our souls were heavy within us.

The performance itself enjoyed but a mediocre success and we blamed ourselves for not having portrayed much that was in the play.

Chekhov died without ever seeing the real success of his last flowerlike play.

The spring of 1904 approached. The health of Anton Pavlovich became worse and worse. There appeared dangerous symptoms in the region of the stomach and there were hints of tuberculosis of the colon. A council of doctors decided to send Chekhov to Badenweiler.

He began to prepare to go abroad. All of us tried to see him as often as it was possible. But his health often stood in his way of seeing us. Notwithstanding his illness his love of life did not leave him. He was very interested in the production of Maeterlinck, which was at that time in rehearsal. It was necessary to keep him informed of the course of work, and to show him the models of the scenery and explain the *mise en scène*.

He himself was dreaming of writing a play of a character altogether new to him. Really the theme of his proposed play was not very Chekhov-like. A husband and his friend love the same woman. The common object of their love unites them and their jealousy of each other creates complex interrelationships. The end is that both go on a polar expedition. The scenery of the last act portrays a large ship crushed amid icebergs. The play ends with both friends seeing a white vision slipping over the snow. Apparently this is the shade, soul or symbol of the woman they both love, who has died while they were away. This is all that could be found out from Chekhov about the play he never wrote.

Chekhov was in reality a practical joker and a schoolboy in spirit. During the unrest of pre-revolutionary days Chekhov was riding in an open cab with a large pumpkin in his hands in which there were supposed to be specially prepared pickles. This pumpkin was wrapped in paper and bound with ropes. On the way it became clear that the pickles were not those that Chekhov liked.

" Cabby, stop," Chekhov commanded, as the carriage approached a policeman.

" Take this," he said with decision in his voice to the policeman, giving the latter the heavy, round package.

" You can start, cabby."

The horse moved forward, and Chekhov turned towards the policeman, and pointing to the package, cried, " It is a bomb! "

The policeman remained in an almost petrified pose, holding the pumpkin carefully away from him, while Chekhov and his friends were loudly laughing a good distance away.

During the very middle of spring rehearsals, before the end of the season, Anton Pavlovich invited me and several of the actors from our Theatre, some relatives and friends, to supper. Apparently some ceremony was in preparation. Perhaps he had finished a new play? We were somewhat mystified by the fact that the supper was to take place not in Chekhov's home, but in Vishnevsky's. But we explained this by saying that it was hard for Anton Pavlovich to raise all his household up, especially as he did not feel very well himself.

We met at the appointed hour and waited for Chekhov. An hour passed. The supper was growing cold. We called by telephone, but no one answered from Chekhov's home. We were beginning to become afraid that something out of the way had happened. But here there arrived a telegram from Chekhov and Olga Knipper, asking us to wish them a happy honeymoon. In order to be rid of ceremony, Chekhov had decided to gather all his friends and relatives in one place while he married Olga Knipper at another, and to leave for their honeymoon on the Volga and the Oka without unnecessary farewells.

CHAPTER XLV

THERE took place a small event, which, however, made a very strong impression on me. When we were producing an evening of Maeterlinck, and I needed a sculptured figure of the dead pastor, the spiritual leader and shepherd of the helpless blind for Maeterlinck's " The Blind ", I called in one of the sculptors of the fashionable modernistic trend to make the statue. He came to look at our stage model and our sketches. I told him of my plans for the production, which, I may say, were far from satisfactory to me personally. The sculptor, using a very rough form of statement which was fashionable among the newly-born innovators in art at that time, declared to me that for such a production as ours we needed a sculpture made of " tow ". Then he departed without even the formality of a farewell. This vulgar incident made a very strong impression on me at the time, not because of the man's insulting impudence, but because I felt the presence of truth in what he said, and because I began to feel more poignantly that our Theatre had run into a blind alley. There were no new roads, and the old roads were being rapidly destroyed. Anton Chekhov's light was dying, it was clear that he was not fated to remain long in our midst, and that the new play of which he was dreaming would not see the footlights. Oftener and oftener he would repeat:

"I have written a great deal already, a whole library, in fact. I am not a dramatist. Hauptmann is a dramatist, and Naidenov."

This continual talk of his was a bad sign. Feeling his own weakness, he tried to avoid all mention of his new play by the use of a jest.

At the same time, as a shareholder in the Theatre, he considered himself obligated to work for it. Nevertheless only a few of us thought about the future. The Theatre was successful, we could hardly house our audiences, everything seemed to augur success, but the few of us who understood our real position were eaten by the worm of doubt. It was necessary to do something to the Theatre, to all the actors, to one's own self as a stage director who had lost his perspective and as an actor who had turned to stone inwardly. I felt that I appeared on the stage empty of all inner content, accompanied only by outer theatrical habits, without inner enthusiasm. Under such conditions art becomes mere craft, mechanical playing, torture. No, it would have been better to pave the streets than to continue as I was doing.

Again there came that period of research during which the New becomes the only goal. The New for the sake of the New. Its roots are sought not only in your own art, but in others also, — in literature, in music, in painting. I would stand before a painting of Vrubel's or of some other modernist's, and according to my stage director's and actor's habit squeeze myself into the frame of the painting in thought, try to enter into it, so as to become infected with its mood and become physically accustomed to it, not from without, but from within, — so to say from Vrubel himself. But the inner content expressed in the painting is indefinite; it is not palpable to the consciousness; it is felt only at rare moments of inspiration, and once felt, it is soon forgotten. In these superconscious moments of inspiration it seems that you let Vrubel travel all through you, through your body, your muscles, gestures, poses, and these begin to express the inner being of the painting. You remember what you have found physically, you try to carry it to the mirror and with the help of the latter to reassure yourself of the lines expressed by your body, but to your amazement you find only a caricature of Vrubel in the glass, the old, hateful, and outworn operatic stencil.

And again you go to the painting, and again you stand before it and feel that you are expressing its inner content in your own way, but this time you examine yourself on the witness stand of your own emotions, you look at yourself with your inner eyesight, and alas, you recognize again the old and hateful operatic acquaintance. At best, you catch yourself imitating the outer form of Vrubel's lines, forgetting the inner being of the painting. At those moments you feel yourself to be a musician playing on a spoiled musical instrument, a paralytic who tries to express a beautiful thought, whose voice and tongue, against his will, create only coarse, unpleasant and repulsive sounds. No, you say to yourself, the problem is beyond your strength, for the forms of Vrubel are too spiritual, unmaterial, and abstract. They are too far removed from the real, well-fed body of contemporary man, whose lines are changelessly fixed once and forever. You cannot cut your shoulders off in order to slope them as they are sloped in the painting; you cannot lengthen your arms, your legs, your fingers; you cannot turn out the waistline as the artist demands of you.

In other and courageous moments, you decide differently. No, you say to yourself, the cause is not that our body is material, but that it is not trained, it is not malleable, it is not expressive. It is accustomed to the demands of everyday life, and for the sake of that life has made certain necessary forms its own for the expression of everyday feelings. But for the abstract or high experiences of the poet and their scenic expression, there exists a whole archive of dusty, worn-out, and obsoletely fixed stencils with theatrical procession instead of walking. In us there are two types of movement and gestures, one normal, natural and lifelike, used in everyday life; the other abnormal, unnatural, non-lifelike, used to imitate something that you cannot feel. This type of movement and gesture is borrowed from Italian singers, bad paintings, illustrations, and postcards. Can one interpret the beauty of Vrubel which consists in superconscious uplift, in noble abstraction from the life of the human spirit, by means of these vulgar forms?

Then I went to sculpture, seeking in it roots for the new art of the actor, but the results and the conclusions were the same. I went to music, trying to reflect its sounds by my body and my movements, and I was persuaded again that all of us were poisoned by the ballet and the opera.

"My God!" I cried to myself. "Is it possible that we, the artists of the stage, are fated, due to the materiality of our bodies, to the eternal service and expression of coarse realism and nothing else? Are we not called to go any farther than the realists in painting went in their time? Can it be that we are only forerunners in scenic art?

"And what about the ballet in the shape of its best representatives, Taglioni, Duncan, Pavlova? It has separation from the materiality of the body. And what about the gymnasts who fly like birds from one trapeze to another? You never even believe that they have a body. That means that with us too there can be that separation from the body. It *must* be found and developed."

And again in the silence of night there began the examination of the body, that resembled the work I did in my youth in my paternal house.

I also began to pay attention to the voice, which we had long ago forgotten. Is the sound of human speech so material and coarse that it is not able to express that which is abstract, uplifted, and noble? For instance there was Chaliapin, who rose higher and higher in world-wide fame at that time. Had he not reached what we were seeking in drama?

"Yes, but that was in the opera, in music," the voice of doubt rose within me.

But cannot conversational speech be musical?

I tried to speak prose and declaim verses, and here again I met my hateful acquaintance, the theatrical declamatory stencil. The more I sought for purity of sound, the more there was of vocal acrobatics which tried to take the place of the long and vibrating musical note of my search. I got rid of it and tried to speak plainly, but the result was simple everyday speech. One could not speak of ideal love, of universal sorrow, of the mysteries of being, of the Eternal, in the voice that resulted.

But in moments of inspiration, when, due to reasons unexplainable to us, one feels not the conception of the words themselves, but the deep meaning that is hidden in them, one finds the simplicity and nobility for which one has searched. In such minutes the voice reverberates and there is musicalness of speech. Whence does it come? That is a secret of nature. She alone can make use of the human apparatus as a talented virtuoso uses his musical instrument. She alone can draw a strong sound from the voiceless. Let me tell a story in point.

One of our actors was entirely devoid of a scenic voice. His voice was weak and hardly audible from the stage. Neither singing nor any other artificial means helped him. Once, when he and I were walking in the Caucasus, we were attacked by sheep dogs. My comrade shouted so loud in his fright that he could be heard a mile away. He had a very strong voice, but only nature could control it.

"This means," I said to myself, "that the secret of the voice lies in feeling an emotion. Once that is felt, the voice comes of itself."

And I tried to feel my emotions and to inspire myself, but this only caused a squeezing in the throat and spasms in the body. I tried to enter into the very being of words, but the result was the heavy, deep speech of a learned ninny.

During this period of researches I met again with Vsevolod Meierhold, who had at one time been an actor in the Moscow Art Theatre. During the fourth year of our existence he had left us for the provinces, where he organized a theatrical company, repeating our productions in the beginning, but later creating his own productions on the bases developed in our Theatre. Like me, he sought for something new in art, for something more contemporary and modern in spirit.

The difference between us lay in the fact that I only strained toward the new, without knowing any of the ways for reaching and realizing it, while Meierhold thought that he had already found new ways and methods which he could not realize partly because of material conditions, and partly due to the weak personnel of his troupe. Kind fate again brought me into touch with the man who was most necessary to me at the given time in my researches. I decided to help Meierhold in his new labors, which, as it seemed to me then, agreed with many of my dreams at the time.

But in what form and where were we to realize our dreams? First of all they demanded full realization in laboratory work. For this there was no place in the Theatre with its daily performances, its complex duties and its severely economical budget. We needed a special institution, which we named very happily The Theatrical Studio. This was neither a ready-made theatre nor a school for beginners, but a laboratory for more or less mature actors.

The work of the creation of the Studio occupied most of my time. I repeated again all the mistakes I had made during the founding of the Society of Art and Literature. It would have been best to have the Studio of the most modest proportions, without giving it an opportunity to widen its work at the beginning, and keep it in bounds until time, work, and experience would help it stand firmly on its own feet. But enthused by the fact that a very fine house was being rented at a rather low price, and believing again in the old fable that a theatrical enterprise is most profitable when it has a large auditorium for its audiences, I decided to hire a theatre for the Studio. With this I made the expenses of the new enterprise ten times what they should have been. There was the necessity of remodelling the entire house, and the hiring of a large body of men to take decent care of the theatre. And the young painters, with Sapunov and Sudeikin at their head, enthused by the new idea, offered their costly services for the decoration of the Studio, — costly because their young and unleashed imagination passed all bounds of the practical, so that they even painted the parquet floor of one of the foyer rooms in green color. I confess that it was very beautiful, but alas, all the wooden flags of the floor became warped, and it was necessary to lay a new flooring.

There were many other interesting and beautiful ideas in decoration, but it would have been more practical to spend our money on the stage itself rather than on the decoration of a house that was not ours, out of which we could not have made a decent theatrical foyer, no matter how hard we tried.

Just as at the time of the Society of Art and Literature, many departments were added to the Studio. The musical department was in the hands of Ilia Sats and several other talented composers. Dissatisfied with the usual orchestral instruments, which fall far short of representing all sounds, they occupied themselves in the search of new instruments with which to enrich orchestration. " Is not the sound of a shepherd's pipe which we hear in the quietness of a summer morning when the sun rises, beautiful? " they said. " Is not this sound necessary in music? What orchestra instrument can yield a sound even comparable to it? The oboe, the clarinet yield sounds that are factory made, sounds in which one does not feel the presence of nature." They examined various other national and ancient instruments like the lyres on which blind men accompany themselves when they sing psalms or songs of Alexei the Man of God, and Caucasian and Negro instruments with their specific sounds which do not appear in the modern orchestra. It was decided to arrange an excursion over all Russia to assemble a complete troupe of unrecognized musicians and actors from among the common people, to provide for a concert, to bring something new into music and art.

The excursion took place, many interesting subjects were found and even brought to Moscow, — things and people that had never even been heard of before. There was an altogether exceptional shepherd virtuoso on the pipe who could shame in the strength and musicalness of sound the wind instruments of the orchestra, retaining the naïveté and aroma of fields and woods in his playing. There was an unusual trio, a mother and two children with most remarkable voices, the high soprano of the little girl, the alto of the boy, and the contralto of the mother, who could continue the sounds of her voice without any breathing intervals, exactly like an accordion. One could never notice when she breathed. I had never seen such a thing before in all my life.

There were fairy-tale tellers and *diseurs* who half-chanted, half-declaimed their wares. There were women mourners who, with the help of rather original cadences and vocal changes and scales, wept for the dead at funerals. There was one altogether extraordinary person, whose æsthetics lay open to question, but whose genius and originality were beyond any doubt. This was a selfmade *diseur* who imitated a man who was drinking from grief. Sobbing, and beating his breast, with wails and shrieks of despair and tears, he told sad stories of his beloved, of his brother who died on the field of battle, of his friend, of the mother who left her children and gave herself over to debauch. The tears flowed in torrents from his eyes; his temperament grasped the soul — one could not see his unusually strong but unæsthetic livings over without shuddering and tears.

It is a pity that it was impossible to show the new troupe to the public, as all these new artists either did not come or ran away when they did come, for the First Revolution had arrived almost simultaneously with the opening of the new Studio.

Instead of keeping in check all the attempts of the young enthusiasts, I was enthused by them myself, and even helped them in their enthusiasms. The new ideas were of tremendous interest to me. It is but natural that my example infected others.

There was a search for capitalists, and while we were waiting for them, there was the expenditure of money in reliance on the profits of the future. Many losses were made in advance, and a part of the troupe gathered. There was no capitalist, and all the expenses of the Studio fell on my shoulders, notwithstanding the fact that the larger part of the debt I had incurred in the Society of Art and Literature still remained unpaid. I was consoled by the fact that the budget was rather modest, figuring on a loss of fifteen thousand during the first year, with the condition that in the following years this loss was to be returned a hundredfold. As is usual in like cases, the budget seemed reassuring and open to no doubt.

A whole company of young actors was gathered, who came from Moscow and Petrograd. Among them were the now famous Pevtsov and Kostromskoy.

The rehearsals took place in Pushkino, just as at the founding of the Moscow Art Theatre. I built a barn that was almost a replica of the old one, took the actors out to the village for all of the summer, advanced them money, and left Moscow and its environs for the season, in order to become acquainted with the results of the work when I returned. It seemed to me then that complete independence was needed by the young actors in order to assure success. If I interfered with their work before the time was ripe I would only frighten them. My presence and authority might oppress and violate their young imagination, the will and the power of the stage director and the actors. After coming to know hints of what would be ready for me at my arrival, I could, with the help of my experience, lay the foundations of their young art. But the most important reason why I held myself at a distance from the new Studio and left Moscow was because my plans did not call for the hanging of two theatres about my neck instead of one, and the troubles that would be resultant on the doubled weight of direction this would entail.

During all summer I received reports of the rehearsals and letters in which I was informed of the new principles and methods of performance developed in the Studio. They were original, but would they prove acceptable in practice?

The principle of the new Studio, to express it in as few words as possible, was that realism and local color had lived their life and no longer interested the public. The time for the unreal on the stage had arrived. It was necessary to picture not life itself as it takes place in reality, but as we vaguely feel it in our dreams, our visions, our moments of spiritual uplift. It was this spiritual state that was to be portrayed scenically, just as it was portrayed by the painters of the new school on their canvases, by the musicians of modernism in their compositions, and by the newly arrived poets in their poetry. The works of these painters, musicians, and poets had no clear outlines, no definite and finished melodies to express exact thoughts. The strength of these works lay in the combination and complementarity of colors, lines, musical notes, and the euphony of words. They created a mood that infected the audience subconsciously. They issued hints which forced the spectator to create in his own imagination.

Meierhold knew how to talk of his dreams and thoughts and found rare words for their definition. From the reports and letters I understood that we agreed in our fundamentals, and that we sought for one and the same thing. This was that impressionism which had already been established in the other arts, but had not yet been applied in ours.

Now, judging by the letters, the young Studio was able to introduce impressionism in the theatre and find a beautiful and conventionalized scenic form for its expression.

"But perhaps these letters and reports are simply the result of enthusiasm and self-deception," I doubted. "They may be accepting an imitation for the real thing. Perhaps they think that outward acting which does not come from inner experiences but simply from the eye and the ear, acting which is simply a photograph of the painting and the sound they have before them, is the real new principle of acting? It is easy to deceive ourselves in our sphere of art; it is easy to take craftsmanlike theatrical emotion for the inspiration of the true artist. It is no little task to carry over to the stage those principles which were created in painting, music, and the other arts that had gone so far ahead of us. Will the speaking voice ever be able to express those delicate nuances of emotion which are heard in the orchestra and its instruments? Will our material and definite body be able to take on the unexpected contours and lines we see in modern painting?"

I saw no means for the creation of the things I felt in my own imagination, nor for what I saw in the paintings of Vrubel, heard in the new music and read in the new poetry. I did not know how to incarnate on the stage those delicate shades of feeling which were hardly expressed in the much more developed medium of words. I was helpless as actor and stage director and impotent to bring to life the things that interested me no less than they interested Meierhold. I was afraid to violate the spiritual and creative apparatus of the actor. I thought that tens and hundreds of years and a whole new culture were necessary to make us actors pass the road that had already been passed by the other arts, before we could satisfy the demands made on us by the public, made, in my opinion, before their true time.

Not having at hand the new actor who had passed the many preparatory stages and reached the highest spheres of technique, I was clearly conscious of only one thing. We were to learn, learn, learn, work, work, work, in order to catch up with the progress of the other arts. Perhaps our contemporary scenic culture would create new actors able to kill or hide the materiality of their bodies so as to increase their spiritual creativeness. But as it was, we had no such actors. What is worse, we did not even know the means and methods for their creation and education.

So how could the young actors, so young that they were almost pupils, conquer the hardships before them, hardships that were too difficult for great and finished actors, for masters of the art and its technique?

If they would teach me, I would be sincerely happy and grateful.

In other and more courageous moments of hope, I believed that every generation had something of its own that could not be seen by the eyes of the generation that preceded it. Who knows, perhaps that New which was part and parcel of the young generation was the thing for which we of the older generation had sought with such difficulties in our art. Perhaps that which we could not find, which we could only desire, was normal to them. If so, then there could be nothing amazing in the fact that they should find the technique and the methods which would allow them to kill the materiality in them, and to live a disembodied, spiritual and creative life on the stage, a life of which we could only dream.

Though all the attempts of the Studio were to be crowned with failure, still it could accomplish important results, even if those were only of a negative nature. That is, it would show not what ought to be done, but what ought not to be done.

"Even that would be useful," I consoled myself. "It does not matter if the young people deceive themselves or if they even cause themselves some harm. During one summer they will not have time to make a complete break between inner emotion and outward incarnation, the two things that must always be closely related in the case of any true actor."

Debating with myself in the foregoing manner, I gave all the encouragement I could to the researches of the Studio in the letters I wrote to the younger people.

The autumn came on, and I returned to Moscow. The Studio showed the results of its summer's work in the rehearsal barn in Pushkino. It did not show the plays in entirety, but only chosen scenes which were most characteristic of the problems of the innovators. There was a great deal that was new, interesting, and unexpected. There were beautiful groupings, effective light spots, the ingenuity and talented imagination of the stage director.

I confess that I looked at the dress rehearsal with great interest and left it somewhat reassured.

Again I let the young people have all the freedom they wanted. They continued their work in Pushkino, and I began my usual labors in the Moscow Art Theatre, awaiting news of another general rehearsal. But no invitation came, time passed, our financial conditions imperatively demanded the quickest possible opening of the new theatre of the Studio, for our actual expenses had long ago left the budget far behind.

At last there was a dress rehearsal of Maeterlinck's " The Death of Tintagiles ", Hauptmann's " Schluck and Jau ", and several one-act plays by other writers. After seeing the rehearsal everything grew clear in my mind. The young and inexperienced actors were strong enough, with the help of the stage director, to pass before the public in the small scenes, but when they attempted to play in a drama of great inner contents and subtle character drawing, and all this in a conventionalized form accepted by the body and the mind, but not by the heart, the young people showed their childish helplessness in all its sincerity. The talented stage director tried to hide the actors with his work, for in his hands they were only clay for the molding of his interesting groups and *mises en scène,* with the help of which he was realizing his ideas. But there was not even enough to show the stage director's technique, ingenuity, and planning, for the actors were too young in their art. The stage director could only demonstrate his ideas, principles, researches, ingenuities, but there was nothing that could give life to them. And without that, all the interesting plans of the stage director turned into dry theory, into a scientific formula that caused no inner reaction in the spectator.

I was convinced again that between the dreams of the stage director and their realization there is a tremendous distance, and that the theatre is first of all intended for the actor and cannot exist without him. For the new art new actors were necessary, actors of a new sort with an altogether new technique. There were no such actors in the Studio, and the sad fate of the institution was clear to my mind.

The only way out was to create a studio for the stage director and his labors of production. But at that time I did not overlove the stage director in the theatre. He was interesting to me only in so far as he helped the creativeness of the actor and not at all in his manner of hiding the actor's faults. The studio of the stage director, wonderful though it might be, did not answer my needs and dreams of that time, especially if it is taken into consideration that I was beginning to be disappointed in the scenic work of painters, in canvas, in paint, in cardboard, in the outward means of production, and in the hokum of stage direction. All my hopes were pinned on the actor and on the development of a solid foundation for his creativeness and his technique.

It was dangerous to open the Studio in the incomplete shape in which it was at the time, dangerous, as it seemed to me, for that very idea for the sake of which it was organized, and which was as dear to me as it was to Meierhold. A good idea, badly shown, dies for a long time. Not to open the theatre, that is, not to show publicly what had been done, was also impossible, because of purely financial reasons. The position we were in was tragic. To add to all this the First Revolution broke about us. The citizens of Moscow had no time to think of the theatre. The opening of the new enterprise, in view of the march of events, would be delayed for a long time. If it were laid off for a very long time, I could not liquidate the enterprise so as to pay everybody for their work, and so I was forced to make a hurried liquidation of the Studio, after paying all who were engaged in its work an advance that covered the entire winter season that followed. The result was an accumulation of debts which I spent all the years following to repay.

And then it became clear that a Moscow season was impossible even for the main group of the Moscow Art Theatre.

CHAPTER XLVI

OUR Theatre had run into a blind wall. We renewed " The Seagull " with Meierhold, who had returned to us, in the rôle of Treplev, and then produced a new play of Gorky's called " The Children of the Sun ", which, although written about the pre-revolutionary period through which we were passing, was composed in the oldest and least interesting tones. The majority of the company were glad that the Studio had failed, for the Theatre had been jealous of my activity in the Studio. With the liquidation of the Studio I returned completely to the Theatre.

"Stanislavski tried, burned his hands, and now he understands that he can't get along without us actors."

Meanwhile Nemirovich-Danchenko and I clearly saw that we were at a crossroads; that it was necessary to freshen both ourselves and the company; that we could not remain in Moscow, not because the threatening revolution and the general mood of the country was in our way, but because we did not know where to go and what to do. The only way out was to make a journey abroad.

And here came along an event that gave us the necessary push and furnished a mask for the real cause of our journey. Before the first night of the Gorky play rumors spread through the city that the elements of the Right, who were called the Black Hundred, considering our Theatre too extremely Left and Gorky an enemy of the Motherland, were preparing to attack us during the first performance. The first-night audience was anxiously awaiting some sort of promised scandal.

[439]

In the last act of the play there is a revolt at the time of a plague on the stage. Over the fence of the house where the chief persons of the play lived, supernumeraries dressed as flour carriers, their clothes stained white, leaped on the stage, and the spectators thought this so lifelike that they took the supernumeraries for the Black Hundred which was supposed to attack the Theatre. On the stage, according to the text of the play, there was heard a shot, and Kachalov fell.

" They have killed Kachalov!" some one shouted in the audience. There was a tremendous noise; revolvers suddenly appeared in the hands of most of the spectators. Somebody hurried to drop the curtain. Then it was raised again. To quiet the audience Kachalov walked to the footlights, making joyous gestures to show that he was not hurt. All of us ran to the stage, shouting to quiet the audience, but it was impossible to stop the panic. Many women fainted, others had hysterical fits; the couches in the foyers were covered with their bodies. Most of the spectators left, cursing the Theatre; the others remained to see the end of the play, demonstratively silent and refraining from applause. The play was a complete failure. This tragi-comic event served in part to explain the cause of our intended journey abroad. It seemed to illustrate the impossibility of a continuance of the season in Moscow.

Soon there flared up the First Revolution of 1905-1906. Our performances stopped for the time being, we locked ourselves in our homes, the actors organized a self-defense, and headed by the inspector of the theatre and his helper, guarded the Theatre day and night. A little later the shooting in the streets stopped, but the state of siege still continued. The city authorities forbade the inhabitants to go out on the streets after eight in the evening.

To settle the question of our journey abroad, the entire Direction of the Theatre met in my apartment and spent the whole night there. The married men came with their wives, for they were afraid to leave them at home. It was necessary to settle the question of going abroad at once, and to send an advance man to Berlin to hire a theatre and order the scenery, for we were forbidden to take any scenery from Moscow with us. Those who remained in Moscow were to get the money and to organize the journey. The meeting lasted all night and even after the guests went to sleep and put out the candles, for the electricity would not work. No one could sleep and the debates about the conditions of the journey did not cease till morning.

After a few days the actor Vishnevsky went abroad as the advance man of our company, and on January 24, 1906, the entire company, and I with my wife and children, went to Berlin by way of Warsaw. Our journey through Russia was spent in painful anxiety. In Warsaw, where we arrived late at night, we were advised not to travel through the city from one station to the other, but to take advantage of a train that circled the city. It was said that revolutionary bands were abroad in the city. On the next day we crossed the border and could afford to forget the nervous strain that we had undergone during the three previous months of danger and revolution.

In Berlin we were met by beautiful weather. In the daytime it was possible to walk in fall coats, although it was the end of January. Because of a marriage in the German imperial family, the city was filled to overflow, and instead of stopping at a hotel, we were forced to rent an apartment which had just become free after a theatrical club left it. We found place in its rooms and began housekeeping, Nemirovich-Danchenko and his family, I and mine, Vishnevsky, Knipper, and so on. I cannot say that there was much comfort, but it was all new and original, and we were very happy.

At first the Germans treated the Russians, and us also, in a manner that could not be called hospitable. The stage hands in the theatre had a rather naïve conception of Russian art. I suppose it seemed to them that we were Eastern acrobats. Some one even wondered that we had not brought with us any trapezes, ladders, ropes, or walking wire. The scenery we had ordered was not half ready, for the scenic designers and painters were doing rush orders for American theatres. No one took any notice of Russians.

We were saved by our own stage hands, who had come together with us from Moscow, who had created our Theatre together with us, who loved our Theatre, who were raised on the same milk of art that we had imbibed. They showed themselves in their full glory. In several nights of concentrated work, for the theatre was occupied by another troupe in the daytime, four stage hands did what we could not get from a whole factory for the period of a month. Even here there were obstacles. In order to have the right to work on the stage at night we were forced to pay the regular stage hands of the theatre overtime wages for work they never did. We picked our supernumeraries from among the Russian emigrants in the city. Due to the fact that after the Japanese war and the revolution, the treatment of Russians abroad was almost disdainful, it was our mission to try to uphold, in so far as we could, the reputation of Russia. First of all it was necessary to amaze everybody with discipline and the love for work. The actors understood the circumstances, and their conduct was exemplary.

Our rehearsals went on, with short breathing spaces, from early morning to late night in an order that was unknown to the theatre in which we were forced to play. Soon there arose legends about our backstage life and work. The relations towards us became better, but they were still far from ideal.

We got along without the services or the guarantee of a manager and worked at our personal risk. The insufficiency of material means and experience did not allow us to conduct an advertising campaign which was necessary in the great city. Our placards, painted by Simov, had artistic value, but they were not coarse or striking enough to have any advertising value. Besides, it seems that there were not enough of these placards, for I personally, although I traveled a great deal about the city and looked for them, was able to find them only once amid the gaudy advertisements of commercial establishments.

Nevertheless, the theatre was filled on the first night. But beginning with the second performance, the theatre was half empty. We opened with " Tsar Fyodor ". At that time our Theatre was cutting a window from Russia to Europe. We were risking our reputation, not only in Europe, but in Russia also, for if we had suffered failure at that time, which was so hard for our motherland, the Russians would never have forgiven us. Besides, what could we do if we returned to Russia without any money, for all that we had was spent before we raised the curtain on the first night in Berlin.

I will not describe the nervousness of the actors and the sharpness of the backstage atmosphere during the first performance. But even before the curtain rose, the stage hands were congratulating us. For what? It seems that that fine old veteran of the German stage, the favorite of all Berlin, the famous and remarkable actor Haase, had come with his wife to the theatre. They were a very honorable, ancient, and charming couple. We were told that their coming was a sign of good luck, for the old people, because of their extreme age, came to the theatre only on the most extraordinary of occasions. Apparently our performance was being viewed, if not by the great public, then by the very cream of Berlin intelligentsia.

A storm of applause greeted us after the first short scene of " Tsar Fyodor ". And when the curtain rose on the second scene, in which the scenery does not change, but the general picture is completed by a large number of Boyars in fine costumes, and by the patriarch and hiero-monk (played by Kachalov and myself) the applause was renewed and redoubled. The success of the performance grew with each act. Our old friend and favorite, the famous German actor, Barnay, visited us in our dressing rooms, and at the end of the performance there were flowers, and curtain calls, and success. The entire working staff of the theatre changed their relations towards us.

Instead of the former disdain there was almost adoration. From that time on it was easier for us to play in a theatre that was not ours.

Notwithstanding the progressive growth of our artistic success, the material affairs of the Theatre were in very bad shape, and we barely had money to pay the modest expenses of our company. We needed an increase in advertisement, but we had no money to pay for it. Extraordinary and exceptional criticisms, that reached the proportion of enthusiastic panegyrics, helped us temporarily, for they turned the attention of the rather small part of the theatrical public to us. The crowd knew nothing of us as yet. The Berlin press was at that time at the very zenith of its excellence. First of all, it could not be bought. The theatre not only spent nothing on it, but could not even send complimentary tickets to the newspapers, for according to the customs of the city, the tickets were bought by the newspapers for cash. We were amazed at the knowledge of Russian literature and life displayed by the critics. At times one could imagine that the criticisms were written by Russians. When I asked one of the journalists how they produced such remarkable critics I was told of a very clever and purposeful method used in Germany. They let a young critic, he told me, always write an article full of praise. Any one could blame a thing, but it took a specialist to praise it.

The newspapers that were to decide our fate abroad were awaited by us with great trembling and trepidation. Let me illustrate. Early in the morning, as soon as the papers were brought, my wife and I were awakened by the actors who lived with us. Forgetting all convention, a crowd of them, with the papers in their hands, tore into our bedroom, some in coats, others in bathrobes, others in dressing gowns, with triumphant, excited faces. A wife of one of the actors, who knew German very well, translated the reviews literally to this strange assemblage. From them it seemed that we had taken Berlin by storm. But the success of "Tsar Fyodor" and the plays of Chekhov, Gorky, and Ibsen in the newspapers helped but little in the finances of the theatre. These were in a very bad way. More than praise was needed to fill the theatre.

One of the performances of " Tsar Fyodor " was attended by the wife of the Crown Prince, who had been a Russian Grand Duchess. Apparently she had told the German Empress of it, for the latter also visited the theatre. A few days later I sat in the office of the theatre. The telephone rang. I asked:

" Who is speaking? "

" Der Kaiser," I heard in the receiver.

I thought I had not heard aright. I called a German who was standing near me and asked him to continue the conversation, for I was not very sure of my own German. The Kaiser, having heard the stories of his wife and daughter-in-law about the production of " Tsar Fyodor ", wanted to see it himself, but he had only one free evening and another play was slated for performance. He was asking us to substitute " Tsar Fyodor ". There could be no better advertisement for the theatre than the Kaiser's attendance, and we agreed to his demand at once, remembering what we had been told — " If the Kaiser comes, you won't have enough place for the audience." And now, without any work on our part, Wilhelm himself wanted to come to see us. An hour later narrow red ribbons with the announcement of the fact that the change in the program was at the Kaiser's bidding were already pasted across our posters. This was the custom in Berlin at that time.

Returning to the theatre a few hours later, I could not approach it, for the entire street was filled with automobiles and carriages. And an hour or so later all the tickets for the performance were sold, and a " standing room only " sign, so dear to the heart of every man of the theatre, was hanging prominently in the foyer. The first rows of the orchestra were reserved for the actors of the Imperial theatres. They came even from the neighboring cities. The Russian ambassador, as was his custom, was late. Nemirovich-Danchenko and I were therefore forced to meet Wilhelm. He appeared in a Russian uniform and turned to us at once, calling us by name.

" I have seen Savina in the rôle of Vassilissa, the wife of Ivan the Terrible. ' Tsar Fyodor ' seems to be a continuation of that play. In what year did the son of Ivan the Terrible reign? "

The question was put so unexpectedly that we could not answer it at once. Wilhelm forestalled us and himself gave us the dates of the reign of Fyodor. Apparently our names, and the historical facts about the play were given him before he came to the theatre, and he took advantage of that with the dexterity of an actor. Add to this simplicity and temperament. He was a very energetic, thick-set man of no great height, with rather large freckles on his face and ordinary mustaches combed slightly upward, but far from the exaggerated manner in which they are drawn in his portraits. He sat in the most prominent seat in his box, surrounded by his entire family, and behaved very naturally, squirming about and asking questions almost every moment of those sitting around him, or leaning from his box towards the orchestra to make mimic signs of approval to the actors from his theatres who sat below him. During intermissions he applauded demonstratively. He was either a very enthusiastic man or a very good actor.

During intermissions we were called to the imperial box, and he asked us a series of questions about the theatre in a very businesslike way. His questions were so much to the point and betrayed such knowledge of the stage that they forced me to believe that he had some counselor behind the scenes with him all the time. At the end of the performance, when the audience had already left the theatre, the emperor and the oberintendents of many imperial theatres still remained in the box, asking questions about our Theatre. We told them in detail of our theatrical life and work from A to Z, while the Kaiser interrupted us now and then and turned to his attendants, pointing out to them the things we had and they did not have. The best idea of the impressions of the Kaiser can be gotten from the memoirs of one of his attendants, who writes:

March 19, 1906. Dinner took place at half-past six, because their majesties went to the Berliner Theatre to see a performance of the Moscow Art Theatre given in Russian. The program of the evening was Alexei Tolstoy's drama, "Tsar Fyodor Ivanovich", in which is pictured a terrible epoch of Russian history, the end of the rule of the House of Rurik, about the year 1608. The performance made on me the very strongest impression that I have ever received in the theatre. The acting reaches such artistic heights that one forgets one is in a theatre, and one lives over the soul-shaking historic events. All that is theatrical is absent. The actors have displayed the creative power of individual personalities as it is given only to the greatest perfection of dramatic art to portray. The scenery, the stage direction, the *mise en scène,* the costumes, were without fault, but they only filled out the impression made by the drama, without supplanting it as often happens in the imperial theatres, more's the pity. In one word, all bathos was forgotten, there was not a single theatrical gesture, all was pure truth and perfect art. The poor, weak-minded Tsar Fyodor was touching in the midst of the terrible struggle of the two contending factions and called out the deepest of sympathy. Although one does not understand a single word, the performance is so engrossing that one completely forgets the words and lives over the tragedy together with the actors.

The Kaiser acknowledged, as he said himself, only tragedy and historical plays. As if to make up for this the Crown Prince preferred the plays of the new dramatists, who at that time were Ibsen, Chekhov and Gorky. The Prince was present in the imperial box at almost every one of our performances.

As it had been prophesied, the visit of Wilhelm to our Theatre did its work: the receipts became larger, and Berlin began to talk about us. At the end of our guest season, which lasted some six weeks, our success was not only artistic, it was material. We were dined and honored by the German actors, by societies, by individuals, and by the Russian colony. But what made the greatest impression on us were two dinners given in honor of our Theatre.

One of them took place in the small apartment of Haase, and the other in that of Gerhardt Hauptmann. Usually dinners are given in restaurants or hotels, so as not to put out those who give them, but in a special case that calls for more than usual hospitality, a reception and a dinner is given at home. Haase was so enthused by our performances that he invited all of theatrical Berlin into his little home, a man and woman from each of Berlin's most important theatres. The result reminded me of Noah's Ark. At this gala occasion there were also present actors of the Meiningen troupe who had come to Berlin to rehearse a play for the jubilee of the old Duke of Meiningen. Knowing of my admiration for the Meiningen Players, Haase wanted to please me by introducing me to the actors who had given me so much pleasure in their time. In countless speeches we exchanged mutual thanks and after dinner I was put into an armchair in the corner of a small room and the actors sat down around me. I was to tell them step by step, detail by detail, the entire course of our creative work. This difficult and psychologically complex labor was performed in German, which I had managed to forget by that time. It is not to be wondered at that some of my turns of speech caused friendly laughter to enliven my audience. I retain a grateful memory of this reception tendered me by the great German actor and his wife. His kindness went even further. Not long before his death Haase sent me photographs of himself in various rôles with very touching dedications and a very friendly letter. I answered him, but I think that my letter did not find him among the living.

The other reception and dinner which I have mentioned also has its story, which I will touch only because it has to do with a great writer with whom I have had the great happiness and honor to become acquainted, and who made a very powerful impression on me. Hauptmann attended all of our performances. The first one he saw was " Uncle Vanya ". The influence of Hauptmann on Russian literature and his love for it are well known. It was at our performances that

Hauptmann first became acquainted with Russian dramatic art. I was told that during the intermissions, Hauptmann, notwithstanding his timidity, expressed rather loudly his opinion of Chekhov and the Theatre, and the opinion was flattering to both. After the performance Nemirovich-Danchenko and I went to see the great writer to bear witness in person of our respect for the man whose plays we had been the first to produce on the Russian stage. We found complete chaos in his little apartment. His wife, from whom, rumor had it, he drew the type of Rautendelein in " The Sunken Bell ", and the rôle of Pippa in " And Pippa Dances ", was very much interested in orchestral music, and, if I do not make a mistake, in conductorship. They were expecting some sort of musical rehearsal apparently, for one room was completely occupied by music stands. Because of the lack of space the orchestra flowed over into the study of the writer, from which the music seemed to strive to drive out the literature.

Hauptmann reminded us by something in his bearing of Anton Chekhov. Besides, he resembled Anton Pavlovich in his modesty, timidity and laconism. It is a pity that our conversation could not be very long, variegated, or eloquent, first because we were confused in Hauptmann's presence, and second because our German was not strong enough for literary and artistic discussion. Hauptmann said that he had always dreamed for his plays of such acting as he saw in our Theatre, without unnecessary theatrical strain and conventionality, — simple, deep, and rich in content. Specialists had told him that such acting was impossible because the theatre had its own demands and conventionalities. Now, at the sunset of his literary activity, he saw at last what he had always dreamed of. He was doubly sorry that we had not brought one of his plays in our repertoire. We answered that one does not bring coal to Newcastle.

CHAPTER XLVII

A MONG Russian actors there exists a custom of celebrating the end of each winter season. This season lasts from August until the beginning of the Great Fast (about the middle of February). During the Great Fast all the theatres are closed, as the tenets of the Greek Orthodox Church make the seven weeks of the fast a time of prayer and fasting. The only performances allowed during that period were those in foreign languages, and all Russian actors remained without work. These enforced vacations were considered in the nature of a holiday and they were opened by a gala performance to make up for the hard work of the week that preceded the holiday, when actors appeared on the boards twice each day.

It is the Russian habit to eat cabbage at the time of the Great Fast, and the holiday performance was therefore called a Cabbage Party. However, cabbages were distributed at this party only as souvenirs.

Our Theatre remained true to the tradition and arranged a whole series of such Cabbage Parties, out of which in due time there developed the Chauve-Souris of Baliev.

The forerunner of the Cabbage Party, the so-called " evening of joy " for the delectation of the young actors and pupils of the Theatre took place even as far back as 1901, in the rehearsal barn on the Bozhedomka, in the same place that was once the famous park of the Hermitage with its several theatres, and its other features, which I have already described in an earlier portion of this book. But now the park was destroyed; the place was covered with houses. There we built a barn with a stage of the same dimensions as that of the theatre we were building in the Kamergersky Alley. There was no auditorium in this barn, but there was a large room with a balcony, and here sat the stage directors and examined or rebuilt the scenery that was being prepared for the theatre in the Kamergersky Alley. It was in this barn that we arranged an impromptu evening of amusement in 1902.

On the stage, which was divided in half, there was a Punch and Judy show on the left, with its own curtain, where the actors performed all sorts of impromptu numbers. On the right half of the stage was a paling to which seemed to be glued a Russian *traktir* or tea house, like the one of which Bubnov dreams in " The Lower Depths ". In the so-called auditorium there was a multitude of unexpected effects. The heat, the crowding, the lack of air were beyond description. During the evening there were invented and gathered on the spot various costumes; plays were acted impromptu on the Punch and Judy show stage and were crowned with a success that is rare in the real theatre.

Ivan Moskvin played the part of a servant in the Punch and Judy show, a part that consisted in doing as little as he possibly could. He lifted and lowered the curtain, not always in time, so as to spoil the effect of the numbers; he helped the jugglers and gave them the things they did not need or he betrayed the secrets of their tricks; in tragic places he would come on the forestage and begin to laugh very loudly, or he would weep at the funniest efforts of the actors. He created a character sketch that was later used by Chekhov in the making of the rôle of Yepikhodov in " The Cherry Orchard ".

Reflecting the great enthusiasm for wrestling there was the parody of a wrestling match. A Frenchman wrestled with a Russian. The Frenchman, graceful, thin, in tights and female pantaloons, was Kachalov; the healthy Russian cabman in a shirt with rolled-up sleeves was Gribunin. Of course there was no wrestling but only a burlesque, the grotesque of the funny sides of the bought decisions of the wrestling jury and the crooked methods of the wrestlers themselves. Moskvin in his tactlessness gave all of this away to the audience. There was a mind reader who cleverly laid bare the secrets of the Theatre. There was so much laughter that one of the spectators fell ill. It was necessary to stop the performance for a little while, but this only served to increase the laughter tenfold.

In 1908, on the day of the decennial jubilee of the Theatre, the fourteenth of October, a like evening of impromptu entertainment was arranged in the Theatre itself, on its large stage, after a reception and its attending ceremonies. This was perhaps the most successful and the happiest evening of amusement ever arranged by the Theatre.

In 1903, to please Chekhov, who seemed to have premonitions of his threatening end and wanted to enjoy himself for the last time, another comical evening was arranged to meet the New Year. There was a supper in the lower foyer of the Theatre; in the upper foyer the younger people danced, and the stage was turned into a Punch and Judy show and auditorium for the public, among whom was Anton Pavlovich, who did not want to occupy the seat of honor reserved for him, and lost himself somewhere in the back rows. The most unbelievable things took place that night. There was a wrestling match between the tremendous and powerful Chaliapin dressed as an Oriental, and the little, short-legged Sulerjitsky, of whom I will say a great deal in the following chapters. Then both wrestlers sang Little Russian songs. Four Vienna grisettes, Moskvin, Gribunin, Luzhsky, and the actor Klimov from the Little Theatre sang a quartette composed of the following impossible words:

" Ich bin zu mir spazieren haus "

and danced a cascade jig.

On the ninth of February, 1910, there took place the first Cabbage Party with paid admissions, the proceeds from the sale of the tickets to aid the more needy among the actors of the Theatre. This evening and others like it which were of almost the same character, were also arranged impromptu during the hardest week in the life of the Russian actor, the week before the Great Fast. They worked everywhere, in the dressing rooms, in the corridors, in every corner, during performances, in the intermissions, and for nights at a time. It is hard to imagine the amount of energy the Theatre spent and the results reached during the short period of work. The work done was equal to the staging of a Shakespearean play in fifteen or twenty scenes. Add to this the decoration of the Theatre and the auditorium, of all the corridors, and all of the five foyers in the building.

The night between Sunday and Monday in the first week of the Great Fast as well as the whole day of Monday changed the Theatre so that it was hard to recognize it. All the chairs of the orchestra were carried out and their places were occupied by tables, at which those who had paid admission ate supper. The waiters were the young actors and pupils who were not engaged in the performance proper. Under the tables were hidden various electrical effects. The balconies of the Theatre were decorated with painted tapestries and garlands; from the ceiling hung lanterns; each of the tables had a little colored lamp that created a fine atmosphere when the theatre was darkened. In the upper balcony were hidden two orchestras, one of string instruments, another of wind. Tremendous baskets filled with serpentine and confetti, with whistles and toy balloons were also held in readiness.

At eight in the evening the public would enter the theatre and sit down in the proper places. The lights would go out and the auditorium would be gradually plunged into darkness. Giving the audience just enough time to get used to the darkness, the auditorium would suddenly be invaded by a sea of variegated sounds. The trumpets blared, the drums beat, the string instruments sang on their highest notes, the wind instruments wheezed, the cymbals rang, the thunder machines of the Theatre roared through the whole house, all the instruments for the torture of the ear that the Theatre possessed were used to their utmost. Together with this bacchanale of sound all the projectors of the Theatre were turned on the public. The audience was blinded, while from every corner of the auditorium flew confetti and serpentine, and hundreds of little balloons of all shapes and colors floated above the secene of mad revelry. These were tied to threads, and during the evening they swung above the heads of the guests or burst and fell, adding to the garish gaudiness of the picture.

After this was over there began a program on the stage. For instance, a tremendous cannon would be rolled out. Little Sulerjitsky would walk out after it, dressed in a peculiar uniform made of leather and oilcloth. He delivered a long speech, parodying the English language. An interpreter would explain that Sulerjitsky was about to try to reach Mars. For this he would be placed in the cannon and shot into the air. There came his wife. There was a touching and tear-stricken scene of parting, also in pseudo-English. Here, unexpected by all including myself, who as the stage director of the Cabbage Party had examined all the numbers on the program on the eve of the performance, there appeared in the background a mysterious figure in a female bonnet and Natasha's red coat from " The Three Sisters ". The figure was lost in spasmodic weeping as it looked at the brave Englishman, and hid its tears in the fur collar of its cloak.

" Who is it? " I asked in amazement.

" Apparently it is the secret sweetheart of the Englishman, who. because of the presence of his wife, does not dare to say farewell to her lover in this, perhaps the last moment of his life."

It was Moskvin, who played ten different parts on that evening, and who could not come into the auditorium and see the program.

He wanted to see the number with the cannon, and he invented the following ingenuity—to assume the rôle of the Englishman's sweetheart and in that manner see the number, also completing the ludicrous picture.

The fearless hero was approached by Kachalov and Gribunin, also dressed as strange artillerists. They had just cleaned and oiled the cannon, and now, with small oilers in their hands, they approached the hero and began to oil his costume so that he might slip into the cannon the easier. Up in the balcony a large hoop covered with white paper was ready to receive the adventurer. All was ready. The farewells were over. The brave man delivered his final speech before his long journey. He was lifted to the mouth of the cannon and pushed in. Then Kachalov and Gribunin loaded the cannon with powder, lit the end of a long stick, and carefully put the fire to the gunwick. The audience, and especially the ladies, covered their ears, afraid to hear the thundering shot. But to the amazement of all, the shot of the cannon was not louder than the explosion of a toy pistol, although both the artillerists who fired it fell from the shock and the auditorium was filled with Sulerjitsky's terrible cry. The paper circle was torn and in the hole was the figure of brave Colonel Sulerjitsky. The military orchestra played a triumphant *touche*. All this was so unexpected by the public that some seriously averred that they had seen Sulerjitsky fly through the air and some were really mystified as to how the effect was achieved. In reality, Sulerjitsky, while the cannon was being loaded, made his way by short cuts to the top story and gave the signal for the firing of the cannon.

And here is another number that created a sensation. On our stage we have a revolving circle. We made a low barrier around the circumference of this circle. In the background there was a panorama of a circus filled with people. Also in the background was the entrance for the artists of the circus, and a circus orchestra on a balcony above it. In the corridor behind the entrance crowded the circus attendants in red uniforms and white tights and black boots. Among them was I in the rôle of the ringmaster, in white breeches, in black shiny boots, with a coat that had a standing collar thrown about my shoulders, in a top hat slightly askew for more effect, with a large nose, black mustaches, and thick black eyebrows. On the edge of the revolving circle was put a stationary wooden horse on which danced Burdzhalov in the costume of a bareback rider, leaping through paper hoops. Those who held these hoops stood on the floor proper of the stage, while the flirtatious rider and the horse revolved together with the revolving circle.

Then there came the number of the ringmaster himself, who showed a trained stallion to the audience. For this number I removed my coat and appeared in a black frock coat and white gloves. All the circus attendants in their red uniforms arranged themselves in rows, the orchestra played a triumphant march, I entered, bowed to the public and walked around the circle. Then the chief equerry approached me, gave me a whip and I cracked it (I learned this art during several weeks of hard practice before the Cabbage Party) and the trained stallion, played by one of the best-known actors of our Theatre, would fly out into the arena.

There is more than one reason why the actor, when he is not working in the theatre, tries to spend his time as pleasantly as he can. Labor in a strained and nervous atmosphere often creates sharp feelings, and actors naturally want to meet under other conditions that dissolve their nervousness, — over a cup of tea or wine, at an entertainment, or in serious conversation. Others, who are temporarily deprived of interesting scenic work, wish to act something somewhere, and they seek for the opportunity. Others, who have no families, no home atmosphere, who are tortured by solitude, want to create a home and a family for themselves. Still others, for whom the work of the real theatre is too hard and serious, seek for easy and quick success, which is given them by the light genre of the cabaret. These are the conditions that gave birth to a sort of club or amusing meeting place for the actors and other workers of our Theatre. But the most important bit of impetus given to the creation of the Chauve-Souris was the appearance of two men who were masters in the sphere of the jest, the satire, the miniature, and whose talents shone brightly in that sphere. They were Nikolai Tarassov and his friend Nikita Baliev, with whom life brought us into touch at a critical moment during our journey to Berlin, when both gave memorable help to our Theatre. Once met, the Theatre did not part from them for a long time. In the Chauve-Souris both showed their unusual gifts, Baliev as *conférencier* and Tarassov as a subtle wit, a writer, a dramatist, and a poet.

On the twenty-ninth of February, 1908, in the house of Pertsev near the Temple of the Savior, in a small, comfortable, but poor cellar, the Chauve-Souris saw the night of its birth. The date of the opening forced us to celebrate its birthday only once each four years. The satires, burlesques and grotesques of the establishment were very new to Moscow. People tried to come to the cellar all the more because it was hard to be admitted. At the beginning only actors and artists could come in. Perhaps those were the best days of the young establishment. There was a cascade of wit, of unusual jests, of talentful numbers, and the unexpected discovery of some talented men and women.

CHAPTER XLVIII

THE BEGINNINGS OF MY SYSTEM

THE eve of great events surrounded us in its thunder clouds. The death of Chekhov tore out a large part of the heart of our Theatre. The illness, and then the death of Morozov, tore out another part of that heart. Dissatisfaction and anxiety after the failure of the Maeterlinck plays and the catastrophic demise of the Studio on Povarskaya, dissatisfaction with myself as an actor, and the complete darkness of the distances that lay before me, gave me no rest, took away my faith in myself, and made me seem wooden and lifeless in my own eyes.

It was in this condition that I went to spend the summer of 1906 in Finland. After I arrived, I would spend my mornings on a cliff that overlooked the sea, taking stock of all my artistic past. I wanted to find out where all my former joy in creation had vanished. Why was it that in the old days I was bored on the days when I did not act, and that now I was happy on the days I was free from work? It was said that it could not be different with a professional who played every day and who often repeated the same rôles, but this explanation did not satisfy me. Apparently the professionals of whom this was said did not love their rôles and their art. It would have been better for them to clerk in a bank or in a shop. The explanation would only fit some mechanical trade. But a rôle and art can never become tiring. Duse, Yermolova, Salvini, had played their great rôles many times more than I had played mine, but this did not stand in their way of making those rôles more perfect with every repetition. Why was it then that the more I repeated my rôles the

[458]

more I sunk backward into a stage of fossilization? Examining my past step by step, I came to see clearer and clearer that the inner content which was put into a rôle during its first creation and the inner content that was born in my soul with the passing of time were as far apart as the heaven and the earth. Formerly all issued from a beautiful, exciting, inner truth. Now all that was left of this truth was its wind-swept shell, ashes and dust that stuck in the niches of the soul due to various accidental causes, and that had nothing in common with true art. For instance, there was my rôle of Doctor Stockman in " The Enemy of the People ". I remembered that when I played it at first it was easy for me to assume the viewpoint of a man with pure intentions, who sought only for the good in the souls of others, who was blind to all the evil feelings and passions of the little men who surrounded him. The perceptions that I had put into the rôle of Stockman had been taken by me from living memories. I had seen with my own eyes the destruction of one of my friends, an honest man whose inner conscience would not permit him to do what was demanded of him by the great of this world. On the stage, during the playing of the rôle, these living memories used to guide me, and always and invariably awoke me to creative work.

But with the passing of time I had forgotten the living memories, I had even forgotten the feeling of truth which is the fundamental element, the awakener, the mover and the lever of the spiritual life of Stockman and the leit-motif of the entire play.

Sitting on a bench in Finland and examining my artistic past, I accidentally struck on the feelings of the Stockman long lost in my soul. How was it that I could have lost them? How could I have gotten along without them? But how well I remembered every movement of every muscle, the mimetics of the face, legs, arms, body, and the slitting of the eyes that belonged to a short-sighted man.

During our last journey abroad, and in Moscow before that journey, I had mechanically repeated these fixed appurtenances of the rôle and the physical signs of absent emotion. In some places I had tried to be as nervous as possible and even exalted, and for this purpose I had made quick, nervous movements. In other places I had tried to look naïve and in order to do so had achieved childlike and innocent eyes by technical means; in still other places I had exaggerated the manner of walking, the gestures typical to the rôle, and the outer results of an emotion that was long dormant. I copied naïveté, but I was not naïve; I moved my feet quickly, but I did not perceive any inner hurry that might cause short quick steps. I had played more or less artfully, copying the outer appearances of experiencing my part and of inner action, but I had not experienced the part or any real necessity for action. From performance to performance I had merely made a mechanical habit of going through all this technical gymnastics, and muscular memory, which is so strong among actors, had powerfully fixed my bad theatrical habit.

In the same manner I examined other rôles, trying to make head and tail of the living material from which they had been created in their time, that is, in my own memories of the experiences that had been the awakeners of creativeness. I examined in my memory all those places of the rôles and those moments of creativeness which had come to me with a great deal of pain; I recalled the words of Chekhov and Nemirovich-Danchenko, the advice of stage directors and comrades, my own creative pains, and separate stages in the process of the birth and development of my rôles. I reread the notes in my artistic diary which rebuilt in my mind all that I had experienced during the process of creativeness. I compared all this to what remained in my soul, and I was amazed. God, how my soul and my rôles were disfigured by bad theatrical habits and tricks, by the desire to please the public, by incorrect methods of approach to creativeness, day after day, at every repeated performance!

What was I to do? How was I to save my rôles from bad

rebirths, from spiritual petrification, from the autocracy of evil habit and lack of truth? There was the necessity not only of a physical make-up but of a spiritual make-up before every performance. Before creating it was necessary to know how to enter the temple of that spiritual atmosphere in which alone it is possible to create.

With these thoughts and cares in my soul, I returned after a summer's rest to begin the season of 1906-1907 in Moscow.

During one performance in which I was repeating a rôle I had played many times, suddenly, without any apparent cause, I perceived the inner meaning of the truth long known to me that creativeness on the stage demands first of all a special condition, which, for want of a better term, I will call the creative mood. Of course I knew this before, but only intellectually. From that evening on this simple truth entered into all my being, and I grew to perceive it not only with my soul, but with my body also. For an actor, to perceive is to feel. For this reason I can say that it was on that evening that I " first perceived a truth long known to me ". I understood that to the genius on the stage this condition almost always comes of itself, in all its fullness and richness. Less talented people receive it less often, on Sundays only, so to say. Those who are even less talented receive it even less often, every twelfth holiday, as it were. Mediocrities are visited by it only on very rare occasions, on leap years, on the twenty-ninth of February. Nevertheless, all men of the stage, from the genius to the mediocrity, are able to receive the creative mood, but it is not given them to control it with their own will. They receive it together with inspiration in the form of a heavenly gift.

Not pretending at all to be a god and to hand out heavenly gifts, I nevertheless put the following question to myself:

" Are there no technical means for the creation of the creative mood, so that inspiration may appear oftener than is its wont? " This does not mean that I was going to create inspiration by artificial means. That would be impossible. What I wanted to learn was how to create a favorable condition for the appearance of inspiration by means of the will, that condition in the presence of which inspiration was most likely to descend into the actor's soul. As I learned afterward, this creative mood is that spiritual and physical mood during which it is easiest for inspiration to be born.

"To-day I am in good spirits! To-day I am at my best!" or "I am acting with pleasure! I am living over my part!" means that the actor is accidentally in a creative mood.

But how was one to make this condition no longer a matter of mere accident, to create it at the will and order of the actor?

If it is impossible to own it at once, then one must put it together bit by bit, using various elements for its construction. If it is necessary to develop each of the component elements in one's self separately, systematically, by a series of certain exercises — let it be so! If the ability to receive the creative mood in its full measure is given to the genius by nature, then perhaps ordinary people may reach a like state after a great deal of hard work with themselves, — not in its full measure, but at least in part. Of course the ordinary, simply able man will never become a genius, but it will help him to approach and in time to become like the genius, of one school with the genius, the servant of the same art as the genius. But how was one to reach the nature and the component elements of the creative mood?

The solution of this problem had become the "regular enthusiasm of Stanislavski", as my friends expressed themselves. There was nothing that I left undone in order to solve the mystery. I watched myself closely, I looked into my soul, so to say, on the stage and off. I watched other men and actors, when I rehearsed my new parts or their new parts with them. I also watched them from the auditorium. I performed all sorts of experiments with them and myself. I tortured them; they grew angry and said that I had turned the rehearsals into an experimental laboratory, and that actors were not guinea pigs to be used for experimentation. And they were right in their protests. But the chief object of my researches remained the great actors, Russian, and foreign. If they, oftener than others, almost always walked the stage in the midst of a creative mood, whom was I to study if not them? And that is what I did. And this is what I learned from what I saw: in Duse, Yermolova, Fedotova, Savina, Salvini, Chaliapin, Rossi, as well as in the actors of our Theatre when they appeared to best advantage in their rôles, I felt the presence of something that was common to them all, something by which they reminded me of each other. What was this quality, common to all great talents? It was easiest of all for me to notice this likeness in their physical freedom, in the lack of all strain. Their bodies were at the call and beck of the inner demands of their wills.

The creative mood on the stage is exceptionally pleasant, especially when it is compared with the state of strain to which the actor is subject when the creative mood is absent. It can be compared to the feelings of a prisoner when the chains that had interfered with all his movements for years have at last been removed. I luxuriated in this condition on the stage, sincerely believing that in it lay the whole secret, the whole soul of creativeness on the stage, that all the rest would come from this state and perception of physical freedom. I was only made anxious by the fact that none of the actors who played with me, or the spectators who saw me play, noticed the change which I believed had taken place in me, leaving out of consideration the few compliments I received about one or two poses, movements and gestures that I had stressed.

After the production of "The Drama of Life" I was free of new rôles and the work of stage direction until the end of the season of 1906-1907. Playing my old parts, I continued my researches, my experiments, my public exercises and the study of the problems of the theory and the technique of our art. The habit of free physical creative mood on the stage grew stronger little by little, became dynamic, and gradually assumed the character of second nature.

And then, like Doctor Stockman, "I made a new discovery." I began to understand that I felt so pleasantly and comfortably on the stage because my public exercises centered my attention on the perceptions and states of my body, at the same time drawing my attention away from what was happening on the other side of the footlights, in the auditorium beyond the black and terrible hole of the proscenium arch. In what I was doing I ceased to be afraid of the audience, and at times forgot that I was on the stage. I noticed that it was especially at such times that my creative mood was most pleasant.

There was one fact that made me very happy. At one of the performance given by a visiting star in Moscow, I watched his acting very closely. In my capacity of actor, I felt the presence of the creative mood in his playing, the freedom of his muscles in conjunction with a great general concentration. I felt clearly that his entire attention was on the stage and the stage alone, and this abstracted attention forced me to be interested in his life on the stage, and draw closer to him in spirit in order to find out what it was that held his attention.

In that moment I understood that the more the actor wishes to amuse his audience, the more the audience will sit in comfort waiting to be amused, and not even trying to play its part in the play on the stage before it. But as soon as the actor stops being concerned with his audience, the latter begins to watch the actor. It is especially so when the actor is occupied in something serious and interesting. If nobody amuses the spectator there is nothing left for him to do in the theatre but to seek himself for an object of attention. Where can that object be found? On the stage, of course, in the actor himself. The concentration of the creating actor calls out the concentration of the spectator and in this manner forces him to enter into what is passing on the stage, exciting his attention, his imagination, his thinking processes and his emotion. That evening I discovered the greater value of concentration for the actor. Besides, I noticed at that performance that the concentration of the actor reacts not only on his sight and hearing, but on all the rest of his senses. It embraces his mind, his will, his emotions, his body, his memory and his imagination. The entire physical and spiritual nature of the actor must be concentrated on what is going on in the soul of the person he plays. I perceived that creativeness is first of all the complete concentration of the entire nature of the actor. With this in mind, I began the systematic development of my attention with the help of exercises I invented for that purpose. I hope to dedicate more than one chapter of my next book to these.

I looked at another great visiting star in his great rôles. He pronounced the introductory words of his part. But he did not strike directly on true emotion, and yielding to the mechanical habit of the theatre, fell back on false pathos. I looked at him carefully and saw that something was taking place in him. And really, he resembled a singer who used a sounding fork to find the true note. Now it seemed that he had found it. No, it was a trifle too low. He took a higher note. No, it was too high. He took a note a little lower. He recognized the true tone, came to understand it, to feel it, placed it, directed it, believed in it, and began to enjoy the art of his own speech. He *believed!*

The actor must first of all believe in everything that takes place on the stage, and most of all he must believe in what he himself is doing. And one can believe only in the truth. Therefore it is necessary to feel this truth at all times, to know how to find it, and for this it is unescapable to develop one's artistic sensitivity to truth. It will be said, " But what kind of truth can this be, when all on the stage is a lie, an imitation, scenery, cardboard, paint, make-up, properties, wooden goblets, swords and spears. Is all this truth? " But it is not of this truth I speak. I speak of the truth of emotions, of the truth of inner creative urges which strain forward to find expression, of the truth of the memories of bodily and physical perceptions. I am not interested in a truth that is without myself; I am interested in the truth that is within myself, the truth of my relation to this or that event on the stage, to the properties, the scenery, the other actors who play parts in the drama with me, to their thoughts and emotions.

The actor says to himself:

" All these properties, make-ups, costumes, the scenery, the publicness of the performance, are lies. I know they are lies, I know I do not need any of them. But *if* they were true, then I would do this and this, and I would behave in this manner and this way towards this and this event."

I came to understand that creativeness begins from that moment when in the soul and imagination of the actor there appears the magical, creative *if*. While only actual reality exists, only practical truth which a man naturally cannot but believe, creativeness has not yet begun. Then the creative *if* appears, that is, the imagined truth which the actor can believe as sincerely and with greater enthusiasms than he believes practical truth, just as the child believes in the existence of its doll and of all life in it and around it. From the moment of the appearance of *if* the actor passes from the plane of actual reality into the plane of another life, created and imagined by himself. Believing in this life, the actor can begin to create.

Scenic truth is not like truth in life; it is peculiar to itself. I understood that on the stage truth is that in which the actor sincerely believes. I understood that even a palpable lie must become a truth in the theatre so that it may become art. For this it is necessary for the actor to develop to the highest degree his imagination, a childlike naïveté and trustfulness, an artistic sensitivity to truth and to the truthful in his soul and body. All these qualities help him to transform a coarse scenic lie into the most delicate truth of his relation to the life imagined. All these qualities, taken together, I shall call the *feeling of truth*. In it there is the play of imagination and the creation of creative faith; in it there is a barrier against scenic lies; in it is the feeling of true measure; in it is the tree of childlike naïveté and the sincerity of artistic emotion. The feeling of truth, as one of the important elements of the creative mood, can be both developed and practised. But this is neither the time nor the place to speak of the methods and means of such work. I will only say now that this ability to feel the truth must be developed to such an extent that absolutely nothing would take place on the stage, that nothing would be said and nothing listened to, without a preparatory cleansing through the filter of the artistic feeling of truth.

If this was true, then all my scenic exercises in loosening the muscles as well as in concentration had been performed incorrectly. I had not cleansed them through the filter of spiritual and physical truth. I took a certain pose on the stage. I did not believe in it physically. Here and there I weakened the strain. It was better. Now I changed the pose somewhat. Ah! I understood. When one stretches himself in order to reach something, this pose is the result of such stretching. And my whole body and after it my soul, began to believe that I was stretching towards an object which I needed very much.

It was only with the help of the feeling of truth, and the inner justification of the pose, that I was able more or less to reach the loosening of the muscles in actual life and on the stage during performances.

From that time on all my scenic exercises in the loosening of muscles and in concentration passed under the strict control of my feeling of truth.

CHAPTER XLIX

BY 1906 there had appeared on the theatrical horizon the great artistic figure of my friend and comrade, Leopold Antonovich Sulerjitsky, or as all of us who knew him called him, "Dear Suler". This remarkable man of exceptional talent, or rather talents, who played a large part in our Theatre and in the history of Russian art, deserves that we yield him our attention for some time.

Imagine a little man with short bow legs that resembled the letter O, of powerful physical build and unusual strength, with a handsome, enthusiastic and always lively face, with clear, laughing eyes, with delicate lips, mustaches and a beard *à la* Henri Quatre, with a high voice of enchanting timbre in singing, with a purely southern color, especially on his high *Do*. The altogether exceptional temperament of Sulerjitsky brought life and passion into every enterprise he undertook. His talents displayed themselves in all fields. He was not only a fine singer with a good manner of singing and great musicalness; he was also an artist trained in the School of Painting and Modeling, full of a promise of accomplishment in his youth, who had supplanted art with a life devoted to ideals, and who had not reached his true stature as a painter. He was a gifted writer, one of his works being the book "To America with the Dukhobors", which was famous in its time. Manuscripts that remained after his death bear witness that he had literary talent of the first water. He was a wonderful orator who could be persuasive and effective; a self-taught scholar of great knowledge, although he received a very negligible amount of education in his childhood; a well-known revolutionist who fulfilled dangerous missions at the dictates of his party. Disappointed in politics, he became a fiery Tolstoyan, and a very close and trusted friend of the great man. For a long time he copied the manuscripts of the great writer, and in the evenings he would sing for Tolstoy and tell him stories of his wanderings.

And really, his whole life was a poetic fairy tale. It was hard to resist his interesting stories. What had he not been in his time — a fisherman in the Crimea setting out to the open sea in wild winter weather, fearlessly giving himself over to the fury of the elements; a sailor who had made several journeys around the world; a shepherd; a tramp who had walked the roads accepting any and all sorts of work that fickle fate sent him; a painter who was once ordered to paint a carriage, although he had no idea of how to paint carriages and relied only on the knowledge of color that he had attained in his days in the School of Painting and Modeling. The result was a scandal — the paint on the carriage cracked and peeled, and Sulerjitsky ran away in disgrace, without receiving a penny for all his work.

When his time came to serve in the army, he, under the influence of Tolstoyan teachings, refused to become a soldier. For this he was tried and sentenced to solitary confinement. Then it was decided that he was not normal and he was forced to live in an insane asylum, which almost caused him to lose his reason. Then he was exiled to the fortress of Kushka in Asia at a time when a fever deadly to all but the aborigines raged in the district. On the way, one of the officers under whose control he had been exiled held him up for a time, under all possible pretexts, so as to save the life of the exile. Here there took place a romance which is described very beautifully in one of his unfinished stories.

In Kushka, Sulerjitsky was already prepared to die, when General Kuropatkin, who visited the fortress, freed him. He traveled on horseback, alone, over the steppes of Turkestan. At nights he was more than once surrounded by packs of jackals, his horse fell sick, he was hardly able to reach human habitation.

When he returned from exile, Tolstoy entrusted him with the leadership of a large party of Dukhobors who were emigrating from the Caucasus to Canada. There was very little money on hand, and it was necessary to charter an old steamer and with the help of the Dukhobors make it fit for a long and risky voyage. Suffering through many storms, almost wrecked on more than one occasion, losing many of the party on the way from sickness, hunger and weakness, the steamer reached America at last. In Canada, Sulerjitsky lived for a year or two with the Dukhobors, conducting negotiations with the government as the representative of the peasants, leading the peasants and teaching them how to begin their new life. Life in a tent, hard cares, harder work, all this left a mark on his health. I wonder if the rich Dukhobors in Canada know of this, or whether they know that his family and his two children are at present suffering need, hunger and cold in Moscow.

Having arranged the life of the Dukhobors in Canada, Sulerjitsky received a request from Tolstoy to take over another party of emigrants, which had become stranded on the Island of Cyprus. Here Sulerjitsky fell sick with yellow fever, which left its mark of destruction on his health. When he became well again, he led the Dukhobors to Canada, and helped them to settle in their new fatherland.

When he returned to Moscow, Sulerjitsky happened to come to our Theatre. At that time he was altogether penniless, and reminded one of a sparrow, with the one difference that the sparrow has its nest, and he did not even have a corner of his own, for, because of his political activities, he had lost his right to live in Moscow. He was under the control of the police and when the imperial family visited Moscow he would be sent not only out of the city, but out of the province. In ordinary times he lived secretly in the hut of a railroad watchman beyond the limits of the city. He came to our Theatre often, and after the performance he would sleep on the boulevards, dressed in a sailor's blouse and pea coat.

Later, when he became acquainted with all of us, the actors invited him to pass the nights at their homes. It often happened that an actor would come home, open his door, and trip over something that lay on the floor in the darkness of the corridor. Sulerjitsky had come in a short time before and gone to sleep on a carpet in the hall, for his clothes were unclean and he did not want to soil the apartment. He was cleaned, washed, and fed, and passed the night now with one, now with another of the actors, bringing liveliness, laughter, joy, and life with him. The stories and the singing would last long into the wee hours.

We in the Theatre came to love him so much that it seemed that he had become one of us, that he belonged to the Theatre. He did not have any definite work, but he was always quietly doing something for the Theatre. He was present at rehearsals; if it were necessary to move scenery he was on the spot; if it were necessary to make props, to sew costumes, to rehearse for some one, to go over a rôle with some one, to prompt, Sulerjitsky was *Figaro ci, Figaro là*. I grew very close to him and we became the nearest of friends.

At last Sulerjitsky married and was forced to drop his wandering life, for which he longed the rest of his days. Happily his wife also proved to be an exceptionally fine human being and knew now not to enchain his freedom.

CHAPTER L

I WAS not inspired by middling success. Just the opposite; there was in my soul a remnant of dissatisfaction with myself. And I felt myself facing a blind wall where I was pushed by the process of the evolution of our art. Nevertheless, I did not yield myself to despair. Perhaps I foreshadowed subconsciously the coming of something, and this supported the courage in me. Besides, the repertoire of the coming season was successfully put together, and this encouraged me in the continuation of my work. The following plays were slated for the new season in the theatre: Griboyedov's " Trouble from Reason ", one of the classic peaks of Russian comedy; Knut Hamsun's " Drama of Life ", with a Scandinavian symbolic and impressionistic tendency very fashionable at the time; Ibsen's philosophical tragedy " Brand ", and finally a play by the young Russian dramatist Naidenov, a favorite of Chekhov's, written in old tones. This was a rich and variegated repertoire in all directions and to all tastes.

The most interesting of these productions for me was " The Drama of Life ". This play is one of Hamsun's trilogy, " At the Gates of the Kingdom ", " The Drama of Life " and " Sunset Glow ". In " The Drama of Life " everything is unreal. It seems that the author himself looks on everything that takes place through the eyes of his hero, the talented Kareno, who is living through the climacteric moment of his creative life. He is writing a chapter about justice, and for this purpose he needs a glass tower as near the sky as possible, for that chapter cannot be written on earth. Kareno symbolizes the dream of the artist, Teresita, who loves him, womanly passion. The "red rooster has begun to sing in her", that is, her blood has spoken. The limping postman, the ugly Quasimodo, who loves Teresita, symbolizes animal passion. The father of Teresita, squeezing profits out of his estate, symbolizes miserliness. The beggar Teu, with a hand always stretched out to receive alms, symbolizes justice. The urge of the poet Kareno towards the heights struggles with the fleshly passions and earthly desires of the other people in the play. It is a pity that the dreams born under the glass dome of the tower cannot come to life upon earth. People set fire to the tower, it is destroyed, and with it the creation of the poet who has dared to dream of the divine on earth.

Around this tragedy of the human spirit swirls the life of the earth. Teresita, in a fit of love, madly plays on the piano, and in an attack of insane jealousy puts out the lantern in the lighthouse in order to sink the ship on which her rival is traveling to her love. The growing greed of the father forces him into insanity. An epidemic rages at a fair among the stores filled with masses of manufactures, with buyers and tradesmen who call in the crowds, amidst mad music and madly whirling carousels, and its victims fall dead without stopping for a moment the insane dancers of the fair. Like threatening signs amidst this emotional chaos are the entrances and exits of ghostly musicians, the appearance of the beggar Teu, northern lights in the winter sky, the thunder of underground hammer blows in the quarry where gigantic workmen cut marble for the father of Teresita. In these moments life seems to be a nightmare.

It is a play of great talent which demands exceptional temperaments, a different and specialized form of acting; it is a picture painted in bold colors, with definite stripes of red, white, and black, without any half tones or shadows. Each of the persons in the play moves fatally along the path of his passions, without the slightest excursion into this or that byway, to his human or superhuman goal, and perishes without reaching it.

It was in this production that I first consciously applied all my attention as a stage director and actor almost entirely to the inner character of the play and its rôles. And in order that nothing might stand in its way, neither stage directors' *mises en scène* nor actors' methods of stage portrayal, all the gestures, movements and changes of position on the part of the actors were completely done away with, for at that time they seemed to us to be too material, bodily, and realistic. And in those days we sought only unseen, unembodied passion that was naturally born in the soul of the actor. We thought that for its interpretation the actor needed only his face, his eyes, and mimetics. Let him live over in immovability and with the whole strength of his temperament the passion entrusted to him.

The sketches of the scenery were in character with the general plan of the production. They were painted in large and sharply separated planes and stripes of primary colors; the hills were very hilly, the tree trunks very perpendicular, and the lines of the river flowing in the distance very straight.

It was in such manner that the outer and inner interpretation of the production of the play were planned. It is a pity that between the plan and its execution, as is the case between theory and practice or a dream and its coming true, there was a large difference. The dreamers, the Karenos among us, were struggling with the real conditions of life in the theatre. We also tried to build glass towers as near heaven as possible, and our towers tumbled to the earth. Life showed me again by a living example that it is easy to dream and create theories in art, but it is hard to practice them. It would seem that there was nothing simpler than naked passion and nothing else. But the simpler the thing is, the harder it is to do. The simple must have a great deal of content. Bare of content it is as useless as a nutshell without meat. The simple, in order to become the most important and move itself forward, must contain in itself the entire gamut of complex life phenomena.

How is one to create real passion, and not its surrogate, not its ugly theatrical imitation?

"Talent and inspiration are necessary," many will say. This is a commonplace and time-eaten phrase, and not the answer to the question. Besides talent, an inner spiritual technique is necessary; without it one cannot find true psychological and physiological approaches to the soul of man for the natural and conscious birth of a superconscious creative impulse in it. Until art will learn how to create subconscious passions consciously all will remain as of old, and because of the lack of better means, the stage director will squeeze emotion out of the actor, urging him ahead as if he were a horse that cannot move a great load from its place. "More, more," the stage director will cry. "Live more strongly, give me more of it! Live the thing over! Feel it!"

At one of the rehearsals of "The Drama of Life" one of my assistants, squeezing emotion out of an actor, suddenly found himself straddling the back of the tragedian. The actor tore passion to tatters, chewed the floor with emotion, and the stage director sat on him and beat him to encourage him. In truth those were the tortures of creation.

Each actor squeezed out of himself the passion that he was ordered to create; one the uplifted urgings of the poet, another animal excitement and temperament, a third love and jealousy, a fourth greed. Each one did it for himself, for they were not connected with each other, and acted each in his own way, without dependence on the meaning of the text which was pronounced mechanically, according to habit. Passion was squeezed out for the sake of passion; what was necessary was not the words and thoughts, but only concepts, only the sound of words. With the help of these sounds they imitated a non-existent passion. It is natural that with such a violation of nature, living emotion hid within its secret sources as soon as it was approached by the direct route and forced to do something it was not able to do. Hiding deep in the soul, the frightened emotion sent out in its stead a regiment of ordinary theatrical stencils and the over-anxious muscles tried to supplace the absent emotions by overstrain. Physical strain was considered to be strength, and the general strained condition inspiration.

And when we introduced the immovability sketched in the general plan of the production, the violation became complete. It spread throughout the whole body and face, passed to the vocal apparatus and created cramped stops in it. This made the face petrify and lose its mimetics; the register of the voice came down to five notes; the intonation became monotonous. In order to revivify the dulled voice and speech, we used the oldest methods of conventionalized theatrical declamation. The result was that our quest for the new brought us to the oldest and deadest methods of our ancestors, to those same methods that were laughed out of court by Hamlet in his speech to the actors. Instead of naked passion there was a bad conventionality, instead of art there was trade. Nature always avenges the violation and the breaking of her laws.

Yet nevertheless, notwithstanding all these failures, the production of " The Drama of Life " was interesting and new, for we had introduced conventions of the method of production new for those days. For instance, the principle of low relief. Gigantic figures of workmen with shovels and pickaxes in poses that were reminiscent of the sculptures of Meunier were placed along a long stone wall. A fine effect was made by the scenery and *mise en scène* of the fair with a mob of Chinese shadows. The tents of the tradesmen, made of oiled linen, were a fine screen for the silhouettes of the actors in the mob scenes, who moved behind the linen in the light of a reflector that threw their shadows on the screen, or who walked in front of the screen. The tents with the shadows were placed on platforms that rose above each other on the backstage. Thanks to this placing, the whole crowd was visible and seemed ghostly. Like shadows they madly whirled on carousels and seemed to lose themselves upward, like great winds. The hellish music of a hand organ followed them. No less effective was the storm of sound and music on the sea during the scene of the shipwreck. The silent appearance of the mysterious figure of the beggar Teu was picturesquely threatening. These colorful spots in the spirit of the then existing revolutionary tendency in the theatre gave the original production a sharpness unknown before that time.

The conquerors in the production were all its creators except the most important, that is, the actors. The painter carried for the first time that fashionable tendency that enthused the more advanced wing of the contemporary artists to the stage. The musicians did the same in their sphere. The stage director sensed several new methods of production, despite the fact that we consciously tried to hide that side of our collective work at the time. Perhaps it was the very nature of the theatre, perhaps it was the imperfection of the art of the actor, perhaps it was the backwardness of the actors themselves that moved the stage director into the limelight. Only the actors found nothing new in their sphere.

But that was not all. In the pursuit of the new they had lost the little that they had found so far, and returned to the old, but this old was done by them badly, amateurishly, without the restraint and technique of the creators of the conventional method. Dilettantism made itself felt. But as it often happens in the theatre, the failure of the actors was hidden by the successful performance of the other workers in the theatre. The actors were protected by the other artists, who with them created the production under the common shelter of the theatre. The mood created by the scenery was written down as coming from the actors; the original costumes and make-ups were written down as created by the actors; the fine and original musical accompaniment was written down as a new manner of the vocal expression of emotion.

How many productions in the theatres of all time can be mentioned where giftless actors hid behind an artistic stage director. How many times the background overcame the most important thing in the theatre, the play of the actors.

This time too the general impression of the whole performance was pleasing. It seemed that the theatre had found its new path. One must be a great connoisseur and specialist in our art to differentiate the work of every co-creator of a performance and to judge it at its real value. But the crowd meets the actor face to face during the performance, and therefore it is the actor alone who receives plaudits and encouragement. The other co-creators who hide in the wings of the theatre often remain forgotten by the audience.

The liberal half of the audience, those of the left, with the sharpness and courage so characteristic of them, applauded the actors in "The Drama of Life" madly, and cried, "Death to realism! Down with crickets and mosquitoes! Long live the Left! All praise to our best theatre!"

At the same time, the more conservative half, that of the right, hurt and insulted, hissed demonstratively and exclaimed, "Shame on the Art Theatre! Down with the decadents! Long live the old theatre!"

The success of the production was scandalous. Only innovators are proud of such success. But the first attempts at something new remain almost always misunderstood and misevaluated. There appear other people who borrow the new and show it to the general public in popular form, reaping the laurels that do not belong to them. This time the same thing happened, but not in the sphere of the actors' art, for there the actor moved backwards and not forwards. We felt ourselves to be of secondary and not primary importance; we were in the rôle of "assistants." It was very like a certain event in my early youth, when I was in the lowest grades of the gymnasia. We children envied the eighth-class men who had arranged a holiday with dancing, food, and sweetmeats. We watched through a door-crack to see how our elders amused themselves, and we wanted to arrange the same sort of a holiday, but did not know how to begin. We were forced to ask for help from our elder comrades. They agreed kindly, brought a round dozen of helpers with them, and began the arrangements. The end was that they and their helpers occupied the tables and devoured the sweetmeats while we waited on them. When we protested, they said:

"Grow up first, learn, and think of holidays and parties only after that."

Having eaten and danced, the guests thought it necessary to thank us as their hosts, but this thankfulness was more in the nature of irony. The same irony permeated the applause and curtain calls and the honorable hissing which fell to our due at a performance in which we were only waiting men. We had played the part of school-boys. Without having learned the elementals, we wanted to have what belongs of right only to eighth-class students in other arts, that is, the painters and musicians. Their arts are at least eight classes ahead of ours. Hundreds of generations ago they created funda-mentals for themselves, and they are still developing them. They continue in the quest of newer and newer paths. Through failure they conquer positive results, advancing step by step.

But our art has not yet passed its road to Calvary and yet it has long ago rested on the small laurels of its conventionalized and long-dormant technique, which has turned into a trade. The major-ity of actors are interested not in their art, but in rôles. To them it is important not to create, but simply to find out how to play certain parts so as to increase their repertoire. All their calculations are made on inspiration and on the talent which is given by chance to only a few happy men. Denying laws, fundamentals and technique, they are proud of the utter absence of these in the art and think that this negation on their part is a symptom of true talent. The majority of them are ignoramuses, who think themselves greater than everybody else. They must still learn, but all they think of are the wreaths of easy success. With the exception of some outstanding geniuses and a few self-taught men, we have no real art or technique. Without being aware of it ourselves, we are still laying the foundations of a craft and not an art. In the best of cases we are talented or untalented dilettanti, who play well or ill, but only accidentally. We are so backward that we cannot march step in step with other arts, but due to our inexperience we try to reach the level of those arts, notwithstanding the great distance that separates us from them. One cannot leap from the first story to the eighth, one cannot pass directly from the first class to the eighth without a gradual ascent or a systematic approach. One cannot demand of a schoolboy that he pass an examination for a doctorate. He will not pass it. Neither did we pass when we were required to produce that which was reached naturally and gradually by the practitioners in other arts.

It is only through a strongly developed outer and inner technique that one can reach immovability without strain, the complete concentration of one's inner life on the stage, the ability to fire one's passion and show it in its nakedness without theatrical methods and with the help of imagination and creative effort. This is the greatest demand that can be made of a great and finished actor. It is natural that we proved ourselves helpless and unprepared to meet the demand made on us. Like helpless children, we caught the hem of our grandmother's skirt, seeking in its pockets the few remaining old stencils of the past that rested in the archives of our art.

The performance had aroused many discussions and caused many articles to be written, and many lectures to be delivered. There were discussions of the literary value of the play, of the work of the stage director, artist and composer, but there was not a single word about the actors, except some lines in the reviews where it was said that this actor played his part well or that actor played his part badly, while the rest successfully aided the ensemble. The production had only one good thing about it — it showed me in practice the complete inadequacy of our art and of our actors, who were to be taught from the very beginning in their art and made to create fundamentals for it. In this sense I consider the production of " The Drama of Life " a historical turning-point in my artistic activity. From that moment on my work and my attention were devoted almost completely to the study and teaching of inner creativeness. Taking into consideration my natural fault, the passionate and direct character of my questings, and changing my front, I put on a pair of opaque spectacles and forgetting and ceasing to love the outward in art, I became interested only in inner technique.

The production of " The Drama of Life " also marked the first appearance in our Theatre of two exceptionally gifted men, who were fated to play a large part in the work of our Theatre. The first of these was Sulerjitsky, who had decided to become a stage director and wanted to learn at my side. He worked in the production of " The Drama of Life " as my closest assistant. The other was the musician and composer Ilia Sats, who tried to write music for the drama for the second time in his life. His first trial had been made in the studio on Povarskaya, where he wrote the music for Maeterlinck's " The Death of Tintagiles ", which was not fated to see the footlights. I think that for the first time in the history of the theatre, Sats showed an example of how music for the drama was to be written. Before beginning his work, Sats was present at all the rehearsals, taking a stage director's interest in the learning of the play and the development of the plan of production. Initiated into all the nuances of our work, he understood and felt no worse than we in what place in the play, and to help whom, that is, the stage director in the general mood of the play or the actor who lacked certain elements for the interpretation of certain parts in his rôle, or for the sake of displaying the fundamental idea of the play, his music was necessary. Then he included the quintessence of the rehearsal work in his musical theme and the chords that were the chief material of his composition. He wrote the music at the very last moment, when it was impossible to wait for its completion any longer.

The process of writing it took the following form. He asked his family to lock him in one of the remotest rooms of his apartment and not to let him out until the music would be completely written. His desire was fulfilled to a dot and his door was opened only three or four times a day so that food could be brought to him. During several days and nights sad and solemn melodies and chords were heard from the room of the willing prisoner, or one heard his cries, or a very ridiculous and affected declamation, from and through which he apparently approached the musical theme. Then for days at a time everything was deadly still, and his family thought that he was weeping, that something had happened to him, but they were afraid to knock at his door, for any commerce with the outer world at such moments threatened to kill all desire to create in Sats. He showed the finished work to me and Sulerjitsky, who was an accomplished musician. Then, after the orchestration was completed, he rehearsed the musicians and played the music for us again. Here there took place long operations that must have been unbearable for the composer, during which all that was unnecessary for the drama in his music was amputated. After this Sats would lock himself in again and rewrite his music, then he would rehearse the musicians again, and would be subjected to a new operation, until at last we reached what we wanted. This is why his music was always a necessary and organic part of the production. It might have been more successful or less successful than the music of other composers, but it was always different from theirs. The music for " The Drama of Life " was one of the chief glories of the production.

As for Sulerjitsky, I shall have a great deal to say of him in the description of the further development of our Theatre, and I will only mark here his entrance into the work, and the beginning of his beautiful activity. My memories of my work with this remarkable man are filled with deep and true pleasure.

Our Theatre, or rather, its art, was in a blind alley. Our researches stopped, and it was only necessary to make head and tail of the material that was on hand, to arrange it, to re-evaluate it, to put it together and to look at our balances to see that we were completely bankrupt.

We needed a new beginning. We needed new bases and foundations justified by knowledge and the laws of nature. Each stone of these bases was created, tried, and cut through years of effort, and then went into the building of the so-called Stanislavsky System, which at present has already reached definite form. It will be asked:

"Can there exist a system for the creative process? Has it really got laws that have been established for all time?"

In certain parts of the system, like the physiological and psychological, such laws exist for all, forever, and in all creative processes. They are indubitable, completely conscious, tried by science and found true, and binding on all. Each actor must know them. He does not dare to excuse himself because of his ignorance of these laws, which are created by nature herself. These conscious laws exist for the purpose of awaking another and higher superconscious region of creativeness. This latter is outside of our comprehension, and we are helpless in our consciousness when we attain it. It is ruled by inspiration. It is that miracle without which there can be no true art, and which is served by the conscious technique of the actor which I tried to establish.

THE SUPERCONSCIOUS THROUGH THE CONSCIOUS! That is the meaning of the thing to which I have devoted my life since the year 1906, to which I devote my life at present, and to which I will devote my life while there is life in me.

CHAPTER LI

THE artist paints his sketches in oils. All his tones and lines harmonize. The deep azure of the sky, the light tone of greenery with the vague outlines of foliage that seem to become one with the boughs of the nearest trees, the tree tops illuminated by the sun, seem to melt away in the air about them. All this gives a charming atmosphere to the sketch. It is painted on canvas or on paper, which have two dimensions only, length and width, but — on the stage there are three dimensions, for the stage has the depth of its floor with many planes which are expressed only in perspective on the smooth surface of the artist's sketch.

When the artist's sketch is transferred to the stage, it is necessary to force this third dimension — that is depth — upon it. Not a single sketch, especially one of the character of a landscape, can stand up under this operation. The smooth, even, unified azure sky of the sketch is divided into five or more planes on the stage. The cut parts of the sky hang in rows, beginning with the forestage and reaching the backdrop, each placed according to mathematically measured plans, and remind one of nothing so much as long towels painted blue. In theatrical parlance these are called flies. And oh, what heavenly theatrical flies they are! Notwithstanding their seeming etherealness and transparency, they cut off the tops of church towers, trees, roofs, houses, if these are carelessly placed behind the flies and their heavenly azure. Each of the flies hangs opposite a batten (a long metallic box with many electric bulbs). One batten burns more brightly, another less, the azure tone of each of the flies naturally changing but not

DISAPPOINTMENTS

becoming one with the tones of the other flies and clearly distinguish-able from them. This convention disparts the unity of the theatrical sky. In order to do away with the blue towels of the flies, scenic artists exercise all of their ingenuity. For instance, they throw boughs with greenery across the whole width of the stage. The result is a series of arboreal arches which hang in rows on every plane of the stage. The flies, instead of being azure in color, become green. But they still remain where they are.

The sketch of the scenic artist has neither flies nor wings nor card-board bushes nor earthen mounds and ditches. But on the stage, with its third dimension, they cannot be avoided. The wings and the card-board bushes are cut out, so to say, one by one, from the sketch, and placed on the stage as separate and independent entities. For instance, the sketch has a tree and behind it a corner of a house in perspective, followed by hayricks. It becomes necessary to separate them from each other and to manufacture several flats which are placed one behind the other on the stage, one made to resemble the tree, the other the corner of the house, the third the hayricks. Or you see trees and bushes on the sketch. It is hard to see where the tree is separated from the bush. The softness of gradation is as charming in the sketch as it is in nature. But on the stage it is altogether different. The theatrical flat, torn away from the sketch and having become an inde-pendent part of the scenery, has its own sharp and definite outline of cardboard or wood. The coarseness of the wooden contours of foli-age is a bad and typical characteristic of the theatrical flat. The charming delicacy of the scenic artist's sketch is always uglified on the stage.

But there is even a greater evil. The third dimension, that is, the depth of the stage and the scenery, places the artist face to face with the terrible floor of the stage. Its soiled boards can be covered with painted canvas, but only when there is no dancing or ballet in the play in question. But what can one do with the tremendous, smooth, and tiresome surface? One can only destroy it by building platforms and traps. But do you know what it means to build a whole floor during a short intermission? Think how much longer it makes the performance. But let us grant that it has been done. How is one to hide on the floor the mathematically placed planes of the stage with their straight lines of wings and cardboard or wooden flats? One must have great ingenuity and a thorough knowledge of the stage in order to wrestle with the obstacle and to hide it both in the sketch and on the stage.

But there are yet other hardships. The artist's sketch is done in juicy, bright, living oils, or in tender water colors, or in guache, while scenery is done in bad glue paint and the man for whom it is done always demands that there should be as much glue as possible in the paint, for otherwise the paint will peel from the scenery and lose its freshness and newness, and the dust of it is poisonous for the lungs and the throat. Thanks to all these conditions of the stage when taken together it is often very hard to recognize the sketch of the artist in the completed scenery, or the scenery in the sketch. And no matter what the artist might do, he will never be able to conquer materiality and coarseness in stage scenery.

The theatre, and its scenery as such, is a convention, and cannot be anything else.

But does it follow from this that the more there is of this convention the better and not worse it is? And are all conventions good and permissible? There are good and bad conventions. The good conventions may not only be left as they are, they may even be welcomed, but the bad conventions must be destroyed.

Good theatricality is a convention; it is Scenism in its best sense. All that helps the play of the actor and the performance is scenic. The chief aim of the performance is first of all the reaching of the fundamental goal of creativeness. Therefore that convention which helps the actor and the performance to create the life of the human spirit of the play and its characters on the stage is good and scenic.

This life must be convincing. It cannot flow amidst palpable lies and deception. The lie must become or seem to be the truth on the stage in order to be convincing. The truth on the stage is something in which the actor, the artist and the spectator believe sincerely and implicitly. Therefore convention, in order to be accepted as such, must have a shadow of truth on the stage, that is, it must be truthlike, and the actor and the spectator must believe in it.

Good convention must be beautiful. But the beautiful is not that which theatrically blinds and amazes the spectator. The beautiful is that which uplifts the life of the human spirit on the stage and from the stage, that is, emotions and thoughts of the actors and the spectators.

The production of the stage director and the playing of the actors may be realistic, conventionalized, modernistic, naturalistic, impressionistic, futuristic, — it is all the same so long as they are convincing, that is, truthful or truthlike; beautiful, that is, artistic; uplifted, and creating the true life of the human spirit without which there can be no art.

Convention which does not fulfil these requirements must be branded as bad convention.

Wings, the stage floor, cardboard, glue paint, scenic planes in the majority of cases help to create bad, unconvincing, false and ugly scenic convention, which interferes with the creation of the life of the human spirit on the stage and turns the temple of the theatre into a Punch and Judy show.

All these bad theatrical conventions of scenery spoil the sketch of the artist, which is also conventional, but conventional in the good scenic sense of the word.

Let places of amusement make peace with bad theatricality. But in the real Theatre a death sentence must be pronounced once for all on bad theatrical conventions.

Of late the cult of theatrical convention without any difference as to its quality is considered fashionable and in good taste. Theatrical convention, both in the play of actors and in the production of plays, is considered by the wise innovators in the light of pleasant unsophistication. These men, creating only with the mind, try to be naïve and believe in what they call their childlike lack of taste.

In the time I write about we argued differently. Losing faith in the theatrical means of production, and declaring war on bad theatricality, we turned to good theatrical convention, hoping that it would take the place of the bad convention that we hated. In other words, we needed new principles of production for the continuance of our theatrical labors. We needed a new quest for Art.

Some principles of production about which long articles are printed in newspapers and magazines, about which learned themes are read, and which are put forward as almost the fundamentals of the new movement and considered a turning point and a discovery in art, are in reality the results of simple accident, or are called forth by the most practical necessities. It seemed to me, in the days about which I am writing, that all scenic means and methods of production found and invented at that date had already come to the end of their rope. Where were we to look for new ones? Were we to found a special studio for researches in scenery? I had no money for it, for I was still indebted over my ears after my attempt with the Studio on Povarskaya. Instead of a lasting studio, we were forced to make use of a temporary, traveling workroom. We decided to do as follows: to call those interested in questions of production to my house on a certain day, and to have all sorts of material ready for us to work on, paper, cardboard, paint, pencils, drawings, books, paintings, sketches, clay for modelling, pieces and samples of materials of variegated colors and tones and textures. Each one was to try to express in one model form or another what he was dreaming of, — a trap in the stage, new architecture for the theatre, a new principle of scenery or of its component parts, a costume, or an original combination of colors, a simple theatrical trick perhaps, a new scenic possibility, or a method and style for a new production.

Only a few enthusiasts came to the first meeting. Among them were my friend Sulerjitsky, the artist Yegorov, who worked in the Theatre at that time, the actor Burdzhalov who was a technician by specialty, and I. We all appeared at the appointed time completely empty, without a creative idea, even without a definite problem to solve. We were all disappointed by the old, which had grown tiresome, but no one knew what to put in its place. These conditions interfered with the proper development of our work at the beginning. The hardest thing of all is to begin creative work, to find a goal, a foundation, a ground, a principle, or even a simple scenic piece of hokum and to be enthused by it. Enthusiasm, even the very smallest, may become the beginning of creativeness. Until one feels it, one knows that he is not standing on firm ground. It was necessary to look for something, but we did not know how and where. One squeezed creative thoughts and feelings out of one's self, one wandered up and down the room, one began to do something but did not finish it, was disappointed and stopped. We combined materials of various hues, we drew the divisions of the scenic floor, we tried to take advantage of some accident and use it as a starting point in the hopes of finding an important scenic principle. We worked dispiritedly.

I needed a piece of black velvet, but it had disappeared, although we had seen it just before. We began to look for it and opened boxes, drawers, but could not find it. When we stopped at last we saw that the piece of black velvet was quietly hanging in the most noticeable place of passage in the room. Why had we not seen it before? The answer was simple. Because a larger piece of black velvet was hanging on the wall directly behind it. Black was not seen against black. More than that, the piece of velvet covered the back of a chair and the chair was turned into a tabouret. We did not understand at first where the back of the chair disappeared and from where the unfamiliar tabouret had appeared in my room.

Eureka! The new principle was found.

But to say the truth it seemed new only because it was very old and well forgotten by everybody. That black is not seen against black is not great news. It is the principle of every camera obscura. There is not a single panoptical room where men, furniture and things have not appeared and disappeared suddenly before the very eyes of the spectator. How did it ever happen that such a practical and comfortable principle had not been used on the stage until that time? And it is useful and necessary in the theatre, in the fantastics of " The Blue Bird ", for instance, which, because of the imperfection of theatrical mechanics, we did not know how to produce. We began to understand that the new principle could simplify many technical problems and metamorphoses in Maeterlinck's play, and once this was so, then our dreams would be realized and we could produce " The Blue Bird ", which we had begun to love very much.

The new discovery enthused me so much and its results seemed to be so important, that my imagination began to play, my mind to work, and there appeared instantaneous and oft-repeated enlightenment. This does not come often, and it must be made use of whenever it comes. I ran into my study in order to bring order into the thoughts and emotions that were aroused in me and to write down the things that I might forget in other and everyday moments of life.

Columbus was not as excited when he discovered America as I was at that time. I believed in the great importance of this discovery, long known to everybody, implicitly.

Only think, we had found a background, which, like a piece of black paper, could give the stage the appearance of having only two dimensions, width and height, for with the presence of the black velvet, which would cover the whole stage, its sides, its ceiling and its floor, the third dimension would disappear entirely, and the velvet would pour itself into one plane. On such a tremendous black sheet one could draw in various paints and lights all that the human mind could conceive. At the top of this great black plane, on its sides, on its bottom, it was possible to show the faces or the entire figures of actors, and whole sets of scenery which could disappear before the very eyes of the spectator or appear when a section of the black velvet was moved aside. It would be possible to make thin figures out of stout ones, sewing pieces of black velvet to the sides of the actors' costumes and so seeming to cut away all that was unnecessary. It would be possible to perform painless amputations of legs and arms, hide the body, cut off the head, by simply covering the amputated parts with black velvet.

After the evening of research I have just described, our attempts at the production of " The Blue Bird " received an altogether new direction. In a room hidden from the eyes of the curious we arranged a large camera obscura, and there the original group of inventors made a series of endless experiments. We discovered many new scenic possibilities and effects. We considered ourselves to be great inventors, but alas, our hopes were greater than the results we accomplished. The dream, the theory, is much easier than practice. In reality many things are altogether different than in theory. The disappearance of a set of scenery and its appearnace in various parts of the stage, now on the left, now on the right, now at the top, now at the bottom — was not that a discovery?

But when we carried our trials to a large stage we understood that this piece of hokum had too much hokum about it. A trick like that could be used in some revue, but not in a serious play, for it is too effective in the theatrical sense. There appeared a new disappointment. When we saw the scenery made of black velvet, and the entire portal of the stage turned into a gloomy, sarcophagal, awful, and airless distance, we seemed to sense the presence of death and the grave on the stage.

Isadora Duncan, who happened to be in the theatre at that time, cried out in terror, *" C'est une maladie! "* and she was right.

" Well," we consoled ourselves, " we will carry our principle through in other colors of velvet."

But alas, this principle worked only with black velvet, which absorbs all rays of light, and thanks to this quality kills the third dimension on the stage. Other shades of velvet do not accomplish this, and the third dimension thrives among them as it does in the midst of customary scenery.

But fate took care of us. It sent us Andreiev's play, " The Life of Man ".

" This is where we need this background," I cried out, after reading the play, and I was not mistaken.

When I ask myself why my researches ended in a catastrophe, although there were found many truths that helped me later to know the free road of creativeness, I see that all these truths were merely separate elements of my art. But separate elements of art can fulfil the purposes of creativeness no more than separate elements of the air can serve man for breathing.

CHAPTER LII

ANDREIEV was an old friend of our Theatre. Our friendship began in the long ago when he was a journalist and signed his theatrical reviews with the pseudonym " James Lynch ". After becoming famous as a writer and dramatist, Andreiev was very much hurt by the fact that not a single one of his plays had been included in the repertoire of our Theatre. But this time everything was favorable to the inclusion of his new play, " The Life of Man", in our repertoire, although it was out of character with all the other plays that we had produced. There was an opinion extant at that time, an opinion which it is impossible to overthrow, that our Theatre was a realistic theatre only, that we were interested only in local color, and that all that was abstract and unreal was uninteresting to us and unreachable by us. And yet, who had been the first to produce plays of the latter character in Russia? Who was it who was really interested in the quest and creation of the abstract? But once an idea gets into the mind of the public, it is hard to dislodge it. In reality, at the time of which I am writing, I was interested only in works of an abstract nature and sought for means and methods for their scenic interpretation. It was not my fault that our art was so backward that it had not yet grown to be able to take care of abstract plays. I could not make peace with the fact that transcendent human emotions were falsified by the coarse conventions of mediocre scenic craft. For it is true that the noble flights of the human spirit have nothing in common with the exaggerated declamation of stentorious voices, with highfaluting theatrical style, with vocal acrobatics, with

[493]

the triumphant and conventional movements of the actor, and with all the other coarse methods of theatrical performance.

Andreiev's play came exactly at the right time, and answered all of our demands. The manner of its outward performance was already found. I speak of the black velvet, in which I still believed at that time. True, I found it hard to be forced to show the new scenic invention in "The Life of Man", and not in "The Blue Bird", for which it had been intended. But thinking that the sphere for the use of velvet would be much greater than it was proven to be in reality, I decided that the new principle could be used in many productions. And the dark background fitted Andreiev's play exactly. The gloomy genius of Andreiev, his pessimism, were the true complements of the mood created by black velvet on the stage.

The little life of man in Andreiev's play can take place only in gloomy blackness, in deep and fearsome endlessness. Against such a background the terrible figure of Some One in Gray seems even more ghostly than it is. It is seen, and yet it somehow seems that it is not seen. There is felt the presence of some one whom you can hardly delineate and who gives the whole play a fatal and fateful shading. In such surroundings, where one may speak of the Eternal, one must place the little life of man and give it the appearance of accidentality, ghostliness, evanescence. In Andreiev's play this life is not even life, but only the scheme of life, the general outline of life.

I reached this by having the scenery made out of ropes. These, like lines in a drawing, marked the contours of a room, windows, doors, tables, chairs. Imagine a black piece of paper with the scenery drawn on it in white lines. On the stage one felt a fearsome and endless depth behind these lines. It is natural that the people in this schematic room were to be not people, but merely the schemes of people. Their costumes were also outlined. Some parts of their bodies were covered with black velvet which became one with the background and seemed not to exist at all. In this schematic life there is born a schematic man, who is welcomed by the schemes of his parents, relatives, and friends. The words pronounced by them express, not living joy, but simply its formal report, in the shape of the customary exclamations used in coarse human parlance for the given occasion. They are uttered not by living voices but seemingly with the help of phonograph records. All this foolish life is born unexpectedly from the darkness of the background before the eyes of the spectators and disappears just as unexpectedly in that darkness. People do not enter through doors and do not exit through them, they appear unexpectedly on the forestage and disappear in the endless space of the darkness in the background.

The rope scenery of the second scene, that of the youth of man and his wife, was suggested in the more joyful lines of rose tone. The actors also gave more signs of life. The tempo of the love scenes and the impudent challenge thrown by the young man at Fate reached the stages of ecstasy at times. But the life that had barely flamed up in youth dies in the third act in the midst of conventional society. The large ballroom, which bears witness of the luxurious life and richness of the man, is drawn in a rope outline of golden color. A ghostly orchestra of musicians with a phantom conductor, the dead, lifeless dances of two whirling females, and on the forestage before the footlights a row of deformities, — old women, old millionaires, rich old maids, bridegrooms and ladies. The gloomy black and gold riches, the loud colors of the dresses of the women, the dead black evening coats, the dull, self-satisfied, immovable faces. — I may mention that among these was Nikita Baliev, so well known in America at the present time.

" How beautiful! How luxurious! How rich! " the guests exclaimed lifelessly.

In the fourth scene the life which has hardly begun is already rolling downwards. The loss of an only child breaks down the strength of the aged couple. In a moment of despair they call on

Some One in Gray, but he is expressively silent. Then the crazed father attacks him with his fists, but the mysterious figure melts in the endless distance and the man and the woman remain with their sorrow, unaided by higher powers.

The death of the man, who is drinking himself into forgetfulness at an inn in the last scene of the play, is a continuous nightmare. Black figures in long cloaks, like rats with tails, crawling across the floor, their cronelike whispering, coughing and grumbling create horror and fearful premonition. Then along the forestage rise single and massed figures of drunkards and disappear in the darkness. They growl with drunken voices, they gesticulate in despair, or they remain in drunken immovability, like nightmare visions. Their cries sound for a moment in the darkness, and then are lost, leaving behind them the indefinite sighs of drunken breathing. At the moment of the death of Man, a multitude of tremendous human figures that reach the ceiling grow from nowhere; there is a bacchanale of flying and creeping deformities, which symbolizes the death agony. Then there is a last terrible, ringing blow which pierces to the very marrow of the bones, and the life of Man is ended. All disappears, the Man himself, the shadows, the drunken nightmare. Only in the bottomless and endless darkness there again grows the tremendous figure of Some One in Gray, which pronounces in a fateful, steely, and unescapable voice, once and forever, the death sentence of all humanity.

We were able to reach all these effects with the help of the black velvet, which played a tremendous part in the entire performance. The play and the production were very successful. It was said that the Theatre had discovered new paths in art. These paths, as is always usual in scenical revolutions on the stage, did not go any farther than the scenery. As far as the art of the actor was concerned, it only repeated what we had found long ago in the " Polish Jew " and " Hannele " for the appearance of shadowy figures. Were we successful in finding and creating in ourselves and in the performance the gloomy soul of Andreiev, the true mysticism which we sought on the stage at that time, the retreat from realism and the entrance into the spheres of the abstract? Justice demands the confession that we did not reach these artistic goals. Having cut ourselves away from realism, we had, as is usual, struck a simple theatrical stencil, which was exceptionally comfortable and useful to us, and which the actor mistook for real life and experience. Our only gain in comparison with other innovators was that not all of our stencils were borrowed from our forefathers. There were some that we created ourselves.

Again the work of the actor was mixed up in the mind of the public with the work of the other scenic creators, and it was decided that a great deal that was new had been discovered in the sphere of the actor also, that we actors had created a new era. But even specialists cannot differentiate in the general ensemble of a performance the work of each of its individual and collective creators. The creation of an era in the art of the actor does not consist in inviting an artist of modernistic inclination and ordering him to sketch original sets of scenery; it does not consist in thinking out a new ingenuity of production in the midst of which the actor can stencil his rôle with the help of prediluvian methods of acting. This is far from creating a revolutionary performance. There is the new, good, and perhaps even the revolutionary setting designed by the artist, and with it, the oldest, most outworn, mediocre acting which is mistakenly accepted for creativeness, art, the true living over of the part by the actor and real emotion.

It is but natural that, notwithstanding the success of the production, it did not satisfy its creators.

CHAPTER LIII

MAETERLINCK entrusted his play to us on the recommendation of some Frenchmen, personally unknown to me, who had seen some of the productions of our Theatre. Other theatres, including those in the motherland of the poet, considered the production of the play too expensive.

When we became acquainted with the play, we saw that in order to produce it not as a simple fairy tale, but as something more serious, that is, so that the hokum spread throughout the play might not strike the spectator as being of the theatre theatrical, we needed the permission of the author to soften some of the scenes in the play. We could have written a letter to Maeterlinck, but we were faced by the impossibility of treating the technical side of the question in a mere letter, and for a while we thought of sending him a detailed report. In the end I decided to send him the speech I delivered to the actors before the first rehearsal. Maeterlinck grew interested in my speech and began a correspondence with us, at the same time giving us carte blanche to make all the changes in the play which seemed necessary to us. Until the end of the season of 1907-1908 we worked over his play, dreaming of producing it without hateful and irritating theatricality. This forced us to make some very important changes, and we thought it necessary to see the author in person before we acted. In the summer I decided to go to see him, for he had sent me a very pleasant invitation to visit him. At that time he lived in his castle about six hours by rail from Paris.

I was very anxious to know how Maeterlinck lived on his estate.

Was it a real château he lived in? Was the manner of life he led simple or complex? Was I to take my evening clothes with me, or were my everyday clothes sufficient? Then there was the question of baggage. Would one valise be enough? Would it not be strange to appear with a load of baggage? However, when I started, I had a great amount of gifts, candy, and other baggage with me. I was on pins and needles in the railroad carriage. I was going to visit a famous writer, a philosopher, and it was necessary to prepare a wise, or at least a clever phrase for use at our first meeting. I did invent something, and I confess that I wrote down the pompous result of my ingenuity on my cuff.

At last the train approached the station. I got off. There was not even a single porter on the station. Outside there were several automobiles, the chauffeurs crowded near the little entrance gate. Weighted down with a mass of packages, which fell from my hands, I approached the gate. Some one asked me to show my ticket. While I was rummaging in my pockets, my packages flew to right and left about me. At this critical moment I heard the voice of one of the chauffeurs calling me:

" Monsieur Stanislavski? "

A clean-shaven chauffeur of advanced years, gray, handsome, of fine carriage, strongly built, dressed in a gray coat and a chauffeur's cap, helped me to gather my belongings. My coat fell from my shoulders. He picked it up and threw it carefully over his arm. Then he led me to an automobile, sat down in the driver's seat, and placed me next to him.

" Now I will take you to my home."

Who was it? I was well acquainted with the portrait of Maeterlinck. This man did not at all resemble it. For some reason I decided that the man was a relation of Maeterlinck, or of the author's wife. But when we began to travel with the rapidity of lightning, making our way with unbelievable skill among the children and poultry of the village street, I was completely persuaded that my companion was a real chauffeur. Never before in my life had I traveled with such speed. I had no time to admire the beautiful Norman landscape around me; I was choked and deafened by the air that rushed to meet us. At one of the turns we almost crashed head on into a wagon, but my chauffeur managed to avoid hitting the horse with unbelievable artfulness and almost spilled me from my seat. We began to talk. We were forced to jerk our words at each other. We spoke of Maeterlinck and his wife, the actress Georgette Leblanc, and I said that I supposed my companion liked automobiles more than anything else in life. He explained that at the beginning it was very pleasant to ride in the automobile, but that later on one got tired of it.

I kept stealing random looks at him. Who was he? When the automobile was climbing a hill, I was at last able to ask him:

" Who are you, sir? "

And my answer was, " Maeterlinck."

I threw up my hands and did not know what to say. For a long time both of us loudly laughed. Alas, the phrase I had so carefully prepared could not be used. It was all for the better, for the simple and unexpected manner of our meeting had brought us quickly close to each other.

We approached the estate, which was situated in a thick forest and had tremendous monastic gates. Great sculptural groups were arranged in a deep niche near the gates, like actors on a stage. The ancient gates creaked in opening for us, and the automobile, which seemed an anachronism in these surroundings, entered the gates and then passed beneath a grandiose arch where in the olden times were made famous Norman liqueurs. The place was an abbey; no matter where one turned, one saw the remnants of several centuries of a life that had already disappeared. Many of the buildings were in ruins, others were still intact. We rode up to the main building of the abbey, which at one time had been the refectory. I was led into a tremendous hall filled with sculptures, a hall with arches, columns and a great stairway. Here our coats were removed, and from above, in a beautiful Norman robe, there descended, greeting me with the words, "How are you, Monsieur Stanislavski?" Mme. Maeterlinck, a very pleasant hostess, and a very clever and interesting conversationalist.

In several rooms to the right of the great hall, which were modernly comfortable, were the dining and sitting rooms. If one went up the stairway one saw a long corridor where the cells of the monks used to be in the old days. This corridor was walled in by an enfilade of many rooms. Here were the bedroom, the study of Maeterlinck, and other rooms for which a modern use could be found. Here took place the intimate domestic life of the family. Then, passing a series of libraries, chapels, and halls, whose beauty I have no words to describe, one entered a large room which faced on a terrace. As the room was in the shade, it must have been the place where Maeterlinck worked in the daytime.

I cannot forget the nights passed in the round tower which once housed an archbishop. The mysterious noises of the whole sleeping monastery, vague crumblings, exclamations, shrieks imagined in the night, the tower clock, the footstep of the watchman — all this seemed to be bound up with Maeterlinck himself. So far as his private life is concerned I must lower the curtain, for it would be very immodest to describe something that was opened for me only by happy accident. I can only say that Maeterlinck is a charming, kind, and joyful host and companion. For days at a time we spoke about art, and he was very glad to know that actors were entering so deeply into the very being, meaning, and analytical study of their craft. He was especially interested in the inner technique of the actor.

The first days of my visit were spent in conversations of a general nature and in getting acquainted with each other. We walked a great deal. Maeterlinck always carried a little Monte Cristo rifle with him. In a little brook he caught some special sort of fish. He told me of the history of his monastery, making head and tail of the tumult that had taken place in the abbey in the course of many centuries. In the evening we were preceded by candelabra and would pass in procession along all the halls and corridors of the abbey. Our loud steps on the stone flags, the antiquity about us, the gleaming candles, the mysteriousness of all about us created a very unusual mood in me. But it seemed to be very natural that Maeterlinck lived in such a place. In the far-off sitting room we drank coffee and talked. His dog would scratch at the door. He would let it in, saying that Jacquot had returned from his café, that Jacquot had been in the neighboring village where he was living through a little romance, but at a stated hour returned to his master. The dog would leap to his knees and an enchanting conversation would begin between dog and master. It seemed to me that the dog understood him. Jacquot was the prototype of the Dog in " The Blue Bird ".

To end these running reminiscences of the wonderful days I passed with Maeterlinck and his wife, let me say a few words of how Maeterlinck behaved towards the entire plan of the production of his fairy tale. At the beginning we spoke a great deal about the play itself, of the characteristics of the parts, of what Maeterlinck himself wanted in the play. And here he expressed himself definitely and in an extraordinary manner. But when the discussion reached the problems of the stage director, he grew confused and could not imagine how the thing could be done on the stage. I was forced to explain the whole thing to him in images and to show him some of my ideas in production by domestic means. I played all the parts for him. And it was pleasant to deal with such a talented man, for he grasped easily what I had to say to him. Usually a theatrical pedant demands that his slightest directions be obeyed. But Maeterlinck, like Chekhov, was not so severe in his demands. He was easily carried away by what he liked, and his imagination willingly traveled in the directions I suggested. He was hurt only by one thing. He had thought that children, and not trained actors, must appear in his play. Our Theatre looks at this question in the light of the exploitation of child labor.

In the daytime Mme. Maeterlinck and I would dream of the production of " Aglavaine and Selysette " and " Pelleas and Melisande ".

In various corners of the estate we found the well of Melisande, the tower of Selysette, and many other natural sets for the plays, and we even decided to produce one of the plays on the estate. Later on Mme. Maeterlinck was able to bring our dreams to life when she produced " Pelleas and Melisande ".

At last Maeterlinck put me into the automobile again, and he and his wife took me to the station, but this time by another road. We bade fond adieus to each other, and Maeterlinck promised to come to Moscow to see our production of " The Blue Bird ".

Time flew. The decennial jubilee of the Art Theatre was before us. No matter how hard we tried to avoid a formal occasion, we could not get away from it. It took place, notwithstanding that it coincided with the death of one of the most beloved and talented artists of the Russian stage, Alexandr Pavlovich Lensky. The jubilee began with the rising of a thousand-headed crowd in honor of and in gratefulness to the dead man. One man was being taken to the graveyard, others were being honored in life.

Against the background of the gray curtain with the seagull, which was hung on the very backstage, the representatives of various deputations sat in an amphitheatric semicrcle. In the center near the footlights was a platform for the orators. Near it was a larger platform for the groups who came with congratulations. Here was also a piano. From the stage to the orchestra there was a wide, carpeted stairway, and in the middle of the auditorium was still another platform with a tremendous table for the expected gifts. Of these there were so many that they were laid not only on the platform and the table, but along the footlights and the stairway. Representatives of all the theatres and cultural institutions came to celebrate with us; there were speeches, reading, poetry, singing and dancing. Fyodor Chaliapin sang a musical letter from Rakhmaninov, who was away in Dresden. It was a talented musical jest, which Chaliapin interpreted inimitably and gracefully.

"Dear Constantin Sergeievich," he sang, "I congratulate you from the depth of my heart and my soul. All these ten years you walked forward and forward and found 'The Blue Bird',," he continued to the church motif of "Many Days" with the playful accompaniment of the polka that Sats had written for "The Blue Bird." The church motif, interwoven musically with the light polka, provided amusing divertissement.

At the end of the jubilee, which will always remain in our memories, we went to accompany the body of Lensky to its last resting place.

When the solemn ceremony was over, we returned to the Theatre, where the younger actors had arranged an impromptu evening of amusement and laughter.

CHAPTER LIV

A T about this period, 1908 or 1909, I do not remember the date exactly, I came to know two great geniuses of the time who made a very strong impression on me, — Isadora Duncan and Gordon Craig. I appeared at Isadora Duncan's concert by accident, having heard nothing about her until that time, and having read none of the advertisements that heralded her coming to Moscow. Therefore I was very much surprised that in the rather small audience that came to see her there was a tremendous percentage of artists and sculptors with Mamontov at their head, many artists of the ballet, and many first-nighters and lovers of the unusual in the theatre. The first appearance of Duncan on the stage did not make a very big impression. Unaccustomed to see an almost naked body on the stage, I could hardly notice and understand the art of the dancer. The first number on the program was met with tepid applause and timid attempts at whistling. But after a few of the succeeding numbers, one of which was especially persuasive, I could no longer remain indifferent to the protests of the general public and began to applaud demonstratively.

When the intermission came, I, a newly baptized disciple of the great artist, ran to the footlights to applaud. To my joy I found myself side by side with Mamontov, who was doing exactly what I was doing, and near Mamontov was a famous artist, a sculptor, and a writer. When the general run of the audience saw that among those who applauded were well-known Moscow artists and actors, there was a great deal of confusion. The hissing stopped, and when the public saw that it could applaud, the applause became general, and was followed by curtain calls, and at the end of the performance by an ovation.

From that time on I never missed a single one of the Duncan concerts. The necessity to see her often was dictated from within me by an artistic feeling that was closely related to her art. Later, when I became acquainted with her methods as well as with the ideas of her great friend Craig, I came to know that in different corners of the world, due to conditions unknown to us, various people in various spheres sought in art for the same naturally born creative principles. Upon meeting they were amazed at the common character of their ideas. This is exactly what happened at the meeting I am describing. We understood each other almost before we had said a single word. I did not have the chance to become acquainted with Duncan on her first visit to Moscow. But during her second visit she came to our Theatre and I received her as a guest of honor. This reception became general, for our entire company joined me, as they had all come to know and love her as an artist.

Duncan does not know how to speak of her art logically and systematically. Her ideas come to her by accident, as the result of the most unexepected everyday facts. For instance, when she was asked who taught her to dance, she answered:

"Terpsichore. I danced from the moment I learned to stand on my feet. I have danced all my life. Man, all humanity, the whole world, must dance. This was, and always will be. It is in vain that people interfere with this and do not want to understand a natural need given us by nature. *Et voilá tout,*" she finished in her inimitable Franco-American dialect. Another time, speaking of a performance of hers that was just over, during which visitors came to her dressing room and interfered with her preparations, she explained:

"I cannot dance that way. Before I go out on the stage, I must place a motor in my soul. When that begins to work my legs and arms and my whole body will move independently of my will. But if I do not get time to put that motor in my soul, I cannot dance."

At that time I was in search of that very creative motor, which the actor must learn to put in his soul before he comes out on the stage. Evidently I must have bored Duncan with my questions. I watched her during her performances and her rehearsals, when her developing emotion would first change the expression of her face, and with shining eyes she would pass to the display of what was born in her soul. In remembering all our accidental discussion of art, and comparing what she did to what I was doing, it became clear to me that we were looking for one and the same thing in different branches of art. During our talks about art, Duncan continually mentioned the name of Gordon Craig, whom she considered a genius and one of the greatest men in the contemporary theatre.

" He belongs not only to his country, but to the whole world," she said, " and he must live where his genius will have the best chance to display itself, where working conditions and the general atmosphere will be best fitted to his needs. His place is in your Art Theatre."

I know that she wrote a great deal to him about me and our Theatre, persuading him to come to Russia. As for myself, I began to persuade the Direction of our Theatre to invite the great stage director to come so as to give our art a new impetus forward and to pour more yeast into the dough at the time when it seemed to us that our Theatre had broken through the blind wall before it at last. I must pay full justice to my comrades. They discussed the matter like true artists and they decided to spend a large sum of money in order to advance our art.

We gave Gordon Craig an order for the production of " Hamlet ". He was to work both as artist and stage director, for he was both, and in his younger years had been an actor in Henry Irving's company and had enjoyed a great deal of success. His artistic heritage was also of the best, for he was the son of the great Ellen Terry. It was from her that he must have inherited his temperament which differentiated him from the cold-blooded sons of Albion and brought him very near to the wide nature of the Russian.

On a day of crackling frost, dressed in a spring coat and wearing a felt hat with large brim, with a long scarf about his neck, and without a cent in his pocket, Craig came to Moscow and stopped in the best hotel in the city, taking a room with a bath, in which I found him splashing about in icy water. First of all it was necessary to dress him warmly for the winter in our Russian way, for otherwise he risked becoming a victim of pneumonia. We found a fur coat, a fur hat and felt boots among the costumes of " Trouble From Reason " and Craig used these while he was in Moscow. He looked so original in these clothes that he attracted general attention on the streets of the city.

This amused the talented stage director greatly and he soon came to feel himself at home in Moscow and especially in our Theatre. He was very friendly with my friend and assistant Sulerjitsky. They felt the presence of talent in each other and were never separated after their first meeting. They were very picturesque when seen together, both always joyous and laughing, Craig with his large figure, long hair, beautiful and inspired eyes, in a Russian hat and a merchant's fur coat, Sulerjitsky with his short, small figure in a short Canadian coat and a conical fur hat. Craig spoke an Anglo-German jargon, Sulerjitsky an Anglo-Ukrainian patois, and this gave rise to a mass of *quid pro quo* anecdotes, wordplay and laughter.

When I made the acquaintance of Craig in his Adamic costume, lying in an icy bath at the time of a twenty-five degree frost, I felt as if I had known him for a long time. The discussion of art that began between us seemed to be the continuation of a discussion that we might have been having the very day before. In his bathrobe, with his long, wet hair, he heatedly explained to me his beloved fundamental principles, his original researches in the quest of a new art of movement.

He showed me sketches of this new art in which lines and clouds and stones and something that resembled tree trunks created an unceasing impetus upward, and one believed that out of this there would come some still-unknown and new art. He spoke of the indubitable truth that it is impossible to put the human body side by side with flatly painted canvas, that sculpture and architecture and objects of three dimensions are needed as the background for the body of the actor. He admitted painted canvas only at the further end of architectural passages on the stage. The excellent sketches he had made for his former productions of " Macbeth " and other plays, and which he showed me at that time, no longer answered his needs. He, like myself, had begun to hate theatrical scenery. What he needed was a simple background for the actor, out of which one would be able however to draw an endless number of moods with the help of lines and light spots.

Further, Craig said that every work of art must be made of dead material, stone, marble, bronze, canvas, paper, paint, and fixed forever in artistic form. According to these fundamentals, the living material of the actor's body, which endlessly changes and is never the same, was not useful for the purposes of creation, and Craig denied actors, especially those of them who had striking or beautiful individuality and who were not of themselves artistic creations — like Eleanora Duse or Tommaso Salvini, to take two instances. Craig could not bear the usual behavior of actors and especially actresses.

" Women," he said, " ruin the theatre. They take a bad advantage of the power and influence they exercise over men. They use these evilly and bring intrigues, favoritism and flirtation into the realm of art."

Craig dreamed of a theatre without men and women, without actors. He wanted to supplant them with marionettes who had no bad habits or bad gestures, no painted faces, no exaggerated voices, no smallness of soul, no worthless ambitions. The marionettes would have cleansed the atmosphere of the theatre, they would have given a high seriousness to the enterprise, and the dead material from which they were made would have given Craig an opportunity to hint at that Actor who lived in the soul, the imagination, and the dreams of Craig himself.

But, as it became clear later on, the denial of actors did not interfere with Craig's enthusiasm for the slightest hint of true theatrical talent in men or women. Feeling it, Craig would turn into a child, leap in joy from his chair, propel himself headlong at the footlights, the long mane of his graying hair thrown in disorder about his face. When he saw the absence of talent he would become angry and dream of his marionettes again. If he could have been given Salvini, Duse, Yermolova, and Chaliapin, and instead of giftless actors an ensemble of marionettes made by himself, I believe that he would have been happy and considered all his dreams fulfilled.

These discrepancies of Craig's often interfered with the understanding of his fundamental artistic desires and especially of the demands he made on actors.

On becoming acquainted with our Theatre, its actors, and the conditions that surrounded our work, Craig agreed to become a stage director in the theatre and accepted service for a year. He was entrusted with the production of "Hamlet", and he left at once for Florence to prepare his sketches and his plans.

After a year passed, Craig returned with a complete plan for the production of "Hamlet". He brought with him the models of the scenery and the interesting work began. Craig supervised everything and Sulerjitsky and I became his assistants. We were joined in our work by the stage director Mardjanov, who pretended to be an innovator in the theatre, and who later founded the Free Theatre in Moscow. In one of the rehearsal rooms which had been given over entirely to Craig, there was built a large model reproduction of our stage. This was lit by an electric system that was an exact copy of what the production would have on our real stage, not a single detail of any effect being overlooked. Craig placed the models of his scenery on this small stage and experimented with lights. Having no faith, just like me, in the usual theatrical methods and means of production, in wings, flies, and flat scenery, Craig refused to have anything to do with them, and turned to the use of simple convex screens which could be placed on the stage in endless combinations. They hinted at architectural forms, corners, niches, streets, alleys, halls, towers, and so on. These hints were aided by the imagination of the spectator, who in this manner became one of the active creators of the production.

The materials of which Craig was to make his screens were not yet definite to us, they were to be, so to say, organic, that is, as near nature as possible, and as far from being artificial as we could have them. Craig agreed to use stone, fresh lumber, metal, or cork. As a compromise, he admitted rough country linen and burlap, but he would not listen to any talk of a paper imitation of all these natural and organic materials. Craig disdained all factory-made and theatrical falsification. It seemed that nothing simpler than the screens could be imagined. There could be no better background for the actors. It was natural, it did not hurt the eyes, it had three dimensions, just like the body of the actor, it was picturesque, due to the endless possibilities of lighting its architectural convexities which gave freedom of play to light, half tone, and shadow.

Craig dreamed of having the entire performance take place without intermissions or the use of the curtain. The public was to come to the theatre and see no stage whatsoever. The screens were to serve as the architectural continuation of the auditorium and were to harmonize with it. But at the beginning of the performance the screens were to move gracefully and their lines were to take on new combinations. At last they were to grow still. From somewhere there would be light that would give them a new picturesqueness, and all present in the theatre were to be carried away in their dreams to some other world which was only hinted at by the artist, but which became real by virtue of the colors of the imaginations of the spectators.

When I saw the sketches of scenery that Craig brought with him, I knew that Duncan had been right when she told me that her friend was great not when he philosophized about art, but when he took brush in hand and painted. His sketches explained his artistic dreams and problems better than any words. The secret of Craig, however, was not in painting, but in his wonderful knowledge of the stage and of scenic nature. Craig was first of all a genius as a stage director.

He also brought with him models of the screens, which he placed on the large model stage. Talent and artistic taste were expressed in the combinations of the corners of lines and the methods of lighting the scenery with light spots and rays which Craig threw over the architectural lines, the corners and the forms of the convex screens. Figures cut out of wood represented the actors. Sitting at a table and explaining the play and the *mise en scène,* Craig moved the figures on the stage with the help of a long stick and actually demonstrated all the movements of the actors on the stage.

While he was doing this, we followed the inner line of the development of the play, and directed by it, tried to explain the motives of the change in position on the part of the figures and entered these motives in our copies of the play. When we read the very first page of the play it became evident that the Russian translation often interpreted the intaglio of the inner meaning of Shakespeare incorrectly. Craig showed this to us with the help of a whole English library on the subject of "Hamlet" which he had brought with him. Very large misunderstandings took place because of the untrue translation. One of these held our work back for two or three days. In the scene between Hamlet and his mother before the murder of Polonius and the appearance of the ghost of Hamlet's father in the chamber of the Queen, the mother asks her son:

"What shall I do?"

And Hamlet answers her:

" Let the blunt King tempt you again to bed."

Usually this answer of Hamlet's was explained in the following sense: that he, having lost faith in his mother, and being certain that she cannot be saved, becomes ironical. Proceeding from this interpretation, the actress who played the mother often painted her as a woman who is sunk in sin. But as Craig insisted, Hamlet treats his mother with the tenderest of love, respect, and care till the very end, for she is not bad, but simply light-minded and spoiled by the atmosphere of the court. The words of Hamlet which seem to invite his mother to further debauch Craig explained as a purely English finesse of Shakespearean speech that gave the words themselves a negative meaning. This is why Craig understood the rôle of the mother not as a negative but as a positive image.

This is not the only example of our misunderstandings. I could quote many other instances where during our linear examination of the translation we found many misinterpretations of places that overturned the old Russian interpretation of the character of the entire play.

Craig widened to a great extent the inner contents of Hamlet. To Craig, Hamlet was the best of men, who passed like Christ across the earth and became the victim of a cleansing sacrifice. Hamlet was not a neurasthenic and even less a madman, but he had become different from other people because he had for a moment looked beyond the wall of life into the future world where his father was suffering. After he came to know the life of tortures and suffering on the other side, the actuality of life changed in Hamlet's mind. He looked deep into earthly life in order to solve the mystery and the meaning of being; love and hate, the conventionalities of court life, began to mean altogether different things to him, and problems too difficult for a simple mortal which were placed before him by his murdered father brought him to confusion and despair. If all could be settled by the murder of the new King alone, Hamlet would not have tarried a minute, but the crux of the matter·lay not only in the murder of the King. In order to lighten the sufferings of his father it was necessary to cleanse the entire court of evil; it was necessary to carry fire and sword throughout the whole kingdom, to destroy the harmful, to repulse the old friends with rotten souls, like Rosencrantz and Guildenstern; to save those pure of soul like Ophelia from earthly ruin and immure her, safe at last, in a monastery. It was necessary to think that Hamlet, as the best and most suffering man on earth, raised to heaven after his earthly deeds, would there meet his liberated father. These inhuman tortures made Hamlet some sort of superman in the eyes of the simple mortals who lived the humdrum life of the court among the little cares of life; a man unlike any other, and therefore insane. Speaking of the court, Craig understood the whole world.

This widened interpretation of Hamlet showed itself in the outward side of the production also. Craig's ideas of Hamlet displayed themselves in a monumentality, in a largess of measure, in a generality and simplicity of decorative production. The divine right, the power, the despotism of the King, the luxury of court life were treated by Craig in a color of gold that approached naïveté. For this he chose simple gilt paper very much like that used to decorate Christmas trees, and pasted it on all the screens used in the court scenes of the play. He was also very fond of smooth, cheap brocade, in which the golden color always preserves the imprint of childish naïveté. The King and Queen sat on a high throne in golden and brocaded costumes, among the golden walls of the throne room, and from their shoulders there spread downwards a cloak of golden porphyry, widening until it occupied the entire width of the stage and fell into the trap. In this tremendous cloak there were cut holes through which appeared a great number of courtiers' heads, looking upward at the throne. The whole scene resembled a golden sea with golden waves. But this golden sea did not shine with bad theatrical effect, for Craig showed the scene by dimmed lights, under the slipping rays of projectors that made the gold glitter in places with terrible and threatening glow. Imagine to yourself gold covered with black mourning tulle. It was a picture of royal greatness as Hamlet saw it in his torturing visions, in his extreme solitude after the death of his father.

Craig's production showed in this scene of the play the mono-drama of Hamlet. He sat on the forestage, near the stone balustrade of the palace, sunk in his sorrowful thoughts, and he visualized the foolish, licentious, and unnecessary luxury of the court life of the King he hated. Add to this scene, so remarkable for its imagination and mystic impressionism, the impudent, threatening, piercing fanfares of brass instruments with unbelievable dissonances, which proclaimed to the whole world the criminal greatness and hypocrisy of the King who rose to the throne. These fanfares, as well as the rest of the music used in the production of Hamlet, were written with exceptional success by Ilia Sats, who, according to his custom, was present at our rehearsals and took part in the work of stage direction before he began to write.

Another unforgetable scene of Hamlet in Craig's production disembowelled the entire inner contents of the pictured moment. Imagine a long, endless corridor, beginning from the first wing on the forestage and passing in a semicircle to the last wing of the backstage on the other side of the stage, where the corridor was lost in the tremendous building of the palace proper. The walls rose so high in the air that their tops could not be seen. They were covered with gilt paper and lighted by the inclining rays of projectors. In this long and narrow golden cage the black and suffering figure of Hamlet, silent and solitary, paced in melancholy, reflected in the golden mirror of the walls of the corridor. From beyond the corners it was watched by the golden King and his courtiers. Along the very same corridor the golden King passed with his golden Queen.

Here also entered, noisily and triumphantly, the crowd of court actors in bright theatrical costumes, with long feathers in their caps, who marched evenly and plastically, with theatrical effect, to the sounds of flutes, cymbals, hautboys, piccolos and drums. The men in the procession carried brightly painted chests with costumes, and parts of gaudily painted scenery. They personified the beautiful and joyful art of the theatre; they gladdened the heart of the great æsthete and filled with joy the poor and suffering soul of Hamlet. Craig looked at the actors through the eyes of Hamlet. At their entrance Hamlet showed himself to be the young enthusiast that he was until the death of his father. With special joy he greeted his dear guests; amid the everyday life of the court their coming brought him for a moment the wonderful relaxation of art, and he grasped it with avidity, in order to find rest from his spiritual suffering. Hamlet was just as artistically excited in his scene with the actors in their backstage kingdom amid the putting on of make-up and the donning of costumes to the accompaniment of the rattling and tuning up of some musical instruments. Hamlet was a friend of Apollo, and this was his true sphere.

In the play within the play Craig unfolded a great picture. The forestage was turned by him into a stage for the play actors. The deepest backstage was something in the shape of an auditorium. The play actors were separated from their stage audience by the tremendous trap that we have on our Moscow stage. Two great columns marked the proscenium of the stage within the stage. From it to the trap ran steps, and from the trap to the backstage other steps which led to the high throne where the King and Queen presided. On both sides along the walls sat several rows of courtiers. They, as well as the King and the Queen, were dressed in shining gold costumes and cloaks, and resembled bronze statues. The court actors mounted the forestage in their gaudy costumes, with their backs to the footlights and the audience, and their faces to the King and Queen, and performed their play.

Meanwhile, hiding from the King behind one of the columns on the forestage, Hamlet and Horatio watched the King from a point of vantage. The King and his golden courtiers were plunged into darkness, only now and then a wandering ray of light fell on a golden costume. But Hamlet and Horatio and the court actors on the forestage were in full and glaring light that gave wide play to the rainbow costumes of the comedians. When the King trembled, Hamlet, like a tiger, threw himself into the depths of the trap towards the King and his courtiers. In the darkness there was a confusion, a scandal; the King ran through the bright swath of light on the forestage, followed by Hamlet, who leaped after him, a bloodthirsty beast on the track of his prey.

Not a whit less solemn was the final scene of the duel that was furnished with many platforms at different heights, steps, columns, the King and Queen on their great throne in the backstage, and the duellists on the forestage below. There was the garish grotesque of the costume of Osric the courtier, the hand-to-hand conflict, death, the body of Hamlet stretched on a black cloak. Far beyond the arch a veritable forest of spears moving in all directions, and the banners of Fortinbras, who was approaching; he himself, like an archangel, mounting the throne at whose foot lay the bodies of the King and Queen; the solemn and triumphant sounds of a soul-gripping funeral march; the slowly descending and gigantic banners that covered the black body of Hamlet with their white folds, showing only the dead and happy face of the great cleanser of the earth who had at last found the secrets of life on earth in the arms of death. So did Craig picture the court that had become Hamlet's Golgotha.

Hamlet's personal life ran its course in another atmosphere, informed with mysticism. The very first scene of the play realized that life. Mysterious corners, passages, strange lights, deep shadows, moon rays, court sentries, unfathomable underground sounds at the rise of the curtain, choruses of variegated tonalities becoming one with underground blows, the whistling of the wind, and a strange, far-off cry. Meanwhile from among the gray screens that were the walls of the castle emerged the ghost who wandered in his search for Hamlet. He was hardly noticeable, for his costume was of the same color as the walls. At times he was altogether unseen, then he appeared again in the halftone of the light of a projector. His long cloak dragged behind him. The cries of the sentries frightened him, and he seemed to fade into the niches of the walls and to disappear.

In the other scenes that took place at the sentry posts of the palace Hamlet and his comrades hid in deep embrasures, waiting for the appearance of the ghost. Again the ghost slipped along the wall, becoming one with it, and the spectator, like Hamlet himself, hardly guessed at the ghost's presence. The scene with the ghost took place at the very highest point of the palace wall, against the background of a clear moonlit heaven which later began to redden with the first glow of the rising sun. The ghost led his son here to be farther away from the hell where he suffered and nearer to the heaven whither his spirit was straining. The transparent cloths covering the dead body of Hamlet's father seemed to be ethereal against the background of the moonlit sky. But the black figure of Hamlet in its heavy fur cloak bore strong witness of the fact that he was still chained to the material and terrible world of grief and suffering and vainly strove to guess the hardly palpable hints of unearthly being and life beyond the grave.

This scene, and many others, were informed with the anxiety of mysticism. There was even more of that in the scene of the monologue of " To be or not to be ", which was designed by Craig, but which we were unable to realize according to his plans. In his sketch Craig expressed himself in the following manner. There was a long palace corridor, gray and gloomy, that had lost in the eyes of Hamlet its former royal golden glow. The walls were blackened, and hardly noticeable shadows crept up these walls from beneath. These shadows personified the earthly life that had become hateful to Hamlet, the frozen horror that took hold of Hamlet after the death of his father and especially after he had for a moment gazed into the next world. It is of his earthly life that he said with horror and disgust, " To be," that is, to continue to live, to exist, to shudder, to suffer and to torture himself. The other side of Hamlet was pictured on the sketch by a bright swath of light in the sunny rays of which appeared and disappeared the silvery figure of a woman who tempted Hamlet to come to her. This was what Hamlet called, " Not to be," that is, not to exist in this unworthy little world, to go out of it, to die. The interplay of darkness and light was to symbolize the struggle in Hamlet between death and life. All this was wonderfully pictured in the sketch, but I, as the stage director, could not bring it to life on the stage.

Having told us of all his dreams and plans of production, Craig left for Italy, and Sulerjitsky and I began to fulfil the ideas of the chief stage director and initiator of the production.

This moment saw the beginning of our tortures.

What a tremendous distance there is between the scenic dream of an artist or a stage director and its realization upon the stage. How coarse are all the existing scenic means of incarnification. How primitive, naïve, and impotent is scenic technique. Why is the human brain so inventive in matters that touch the killing of one man by another, or in questions of well-fed comfort in everyday life? Why is it that the same mechanics are so coarse and primitive where man strives to satisfy not his personal bodily needs but his best spiritual longings which rise from the purest æsthetic depths of the artistic soul? In this region there seems to be no inventiveness. The radio, electricity, light rays, create wonders everywhere but not in the theatre, where they could find a completely exceptional use in the sense of beauty and forever banish from the stage disgusting glue paint, papier maché and properties. May a time come when newly discovered rays will paint in the air the shadows of color tones and the combinations of lines. May other rays light the body of man and give it that indefiniteness of outline, that disembodiment, that ghostliness which we know in our waking and sleeping dreams. Then, with a hardly seen ghost in the image of a woman we will be able to realize Craig's conception of Hamlet's " To be or not to be ". But with the use of ordinary theatrical means the interpretation suggested by Craig looked like a piece of hokum on the part of the stage director, and for the hundredth time reminded me of the helplessness and the coarseness of theatrical means of production.

Knowing of no one outside of Isadora Duncan who could have realized the image of bright death, finding no scenic means for the showing of the dark shadows of life as they were drawn in the sketch, we were forced to deny ourselves Craig's plan for the production of " To be or not to be ".

But this disappointment was not our last. Another unpleasant surprise was in store for poor Craig. We could not find a natural material for the making of the screens. We tried everything, — iron, copper, and other metals. But it was only necessary to think of the weight of such screens to forget metal forever. To use such screens we would have been forced to rebuild the entire theatre and to install electric scenery shifts. We tried wooden screens and showed them to Craig, but neither he nor our stage hands desired to move the terrible and dangerous walls. These threatened to fall at any moment and to crush all who stood on the stage. We tried cork screens, but even these were too heavy. In the end of things we had to make peace with simple theatrical unpainted canvas on light wooden frames. Their light tone was out of harmony with the gloomy mood of the palace. But nevertheless, Craig decided to use them, for they took on the variegated colors and half tones of electric lighting which were entirely lost when darker screens were used. The play of light was very necessary for the interpretation of the mood of the play during the realization of the scenic ideas of Craig.

But here we met another trouble. The great screens could not stand up well and would fall. If a single screen fell, all the others followed it. We invented countless methods for preventing the fall of the screens, but all of them demanded special scenic construction and architectural changes for which we had neither the technical means nor the money.

The shifting of the screens demanded many long rehearsals with the stage hands. For a long time we were unsuccessful; now a workman would unexpectedly jump to the forestage and show himself to the spectators; now a crack would form between two moving screens and the audience would see the life backstage; now the back of the scenery would show; now a screen would become stuck in one place. And one hour before the first night performance there was a real catastrophe. I was sitting in the auditorium and rehearsing the maneuvers of shifting the screens for the last time. The rehearsal ended. The scenery was put up for the first scene of the play and the stage hands were allowed to rest and drink tea before the beginning of the performance. The stage grew empty, the auditorium was as quiet as a grave. But suddenly one of the screens began to lean sideways more and more, then fell on the screen next to it, and the entire scenery fell to the floor like a house of cards. There was the crack of breaking wooden frames, the sound of ripping canvas, and then the formless mass of broken and torn screens all over the stage. The audience was already entering the theatre, when nervous work to rebuild the scene began behind the lowered curtain. In order to avoid a catastrophe during the performance itself, we were forced to deny ourselves the joy of shifting the screens in full view of the audience and to accept the help of the traditional theatrical curtain, which coarsely but loyally hid the hard work of the stage hands. And what oneness and unison the Craigian manner of shifting the screens would have given to the entire performance!

Another disappointment, no smaller than the one I have just described, awaited Craig in the matter of the actors' interpretation. When Craig came back to Moscow he had looked over our work with the actors and it had not satisfied him. He did not acknowledge the usual theatrical playing of actors, nor did we, but he did not even accept simplified though truthful interpretation of high feelings. We also did not accept such simplification. There was no noble simplicity, no grand assurance, no masterly restraint. There were no sonorous voices and beautiful speech, harmonic movement and plastics. But there was that which we feared most of all, — either usual theatrical pathos or the other pole, a very tiresome, heavy and prosaic living over of 'the parts. Why could we not find the golden mean? We had found it in contemporary plays, where we spoke, though badly, still humanly, but as soon as we attempted verse we fell back upon declamation, a dead seesaw rhythm, and a methodical flow of monotonous voices and monotonous conventionalization of speech. And the worst of it is that this appealed and appeals to all actors who have no taste, and whose name is legion.

I broke my head in struggling with this obstacle and inventing methods to conquer it. One evening, after a long working day, we began to speak over our tea for the hundredth time about actors, their art and the demands made on it. This conversation took on an especially lively character due to the presence of my wife, Lilina, who not only knew English well, but who, being an actress to Craig's liking, understood the theme of the discussion and was therefore an ideal interpreter. In order to better understand each other, I began to read and act before Craig in various methods and manners individual places and scenes from my repertoire of rôles. In the beginning I read in the old and conventional French manner, then in the

German, the Italian, the Russian declamatory, the Russian realistic. I showed the new impressionistic method also.

Nothing of all this was to Craig's liking. With all his strength he protested on the one hand against the old conventionality of the theatre, and on the other hand he would not accept the humdrum naturalness and simplicity which robbed my interpretations of all poetry. Craig wanted perfection, the ideal, that is, simple, strong, deep, uplifting, artistic and beautiful expression of living human emotion.

I had failed before Craig, and I was very much confused. On the next day, in order to quiet myself, I retired with Sulerjitsky to one of the rehearsal rooms of our theatre and began playing for him many of my parts, asking him to stop me every time he doubted the sincerity of my feelings or was dissatisfied with the artistic form of their realization. Alas, Sulerjitsky had a great deal of work to do with me and was forced to stop me at every step. This seance turned out to be very important, even historical in my life. That day I understood that much which seemed natural to me was in reality born of old theatrical frumpery. The most terrible thing of all is when self-conceit deceives the actor and when a disjointedness is formed between his body and his soul, between living over a part and its incarnification, when a muscular rebirth goes on in the body of the actor. Then his nature, his voice, his gestures, his mimetics, become crippled, like a spoiled and badly tuned piano. I was shaken in my convictions and passed many anxious months and years after that day.

Was it possible that all my work over the so-called " system " was without any result?

The production of " Hamlet " met with great success. Some people were enthusiastic, others criticized, but everybody was excited, and debated, read reports, wrote articles, while the other theatres in the country quietly appropriated the ideas of Craig, publishing them as their own.

Apparently we could not expect a greater success. But I was not happy within myself. Firstly, because I had not been able to show Craig as I wanted to show him, secondly because this important production had brought new doubts into my work and my researches. We had wanted to make the production as simple and as modest as possible. Of course this modesty was to be a result of rich imagination. There was very much imagination and simplicity, but the production seemed unusually luxurious, grandiose, affected to such an extent that its beauty attacked the eye and hid the actors in its pomp. This new quality of the stage was a surprise to me. The more we tried to make the production simple the stronger it reminded us of itself, the more it seemed pretentious and displayed its showy naïveté.

I suffered even greater confusion from the viewpoint of the acting in the production. The actors of the Art Theatre who had learned to a certain extent the methods of the new inner technique used them with some degree of success in the plays of our modern repertoire which were near to their own lives. Apparently it still lay before us to go through the same work and to find analogical methods and means for plays in the heroic and the grand style. When "Hamlet" was first produced by us, our Theatre had not yet begun its quest in that direction.

CHAPTER LV

THE FIRST STUDIO

SULERJITSKY began to feel my loneliness in art, my pains of research; he became interested in what I was doing and encouraged me with his interest in my work. Together, we tried to preach the new discoveries to the actors, but we did not succeed. Then we turned to the young people and began to give lessons to young actors and actresses picked from among the supernumeraries in the Theatre and the pupils of the school. But this was also unsuccessful. At last Sulerjitsky went to a private dramatic school run by one of the actors of our Theatre and established a class according to my plans. After several years this class yielded results and many of its pupils were accepted in the Theatre. Among them was Yevgeniy Vakhtangov, who was also fated to play a large part in the history of our Theatre. The initial impetus had been given, and some of the actors and the young people, seeing results in reality, asked us to give them an opportunity to learn and to show themselves to advantage, as it was very hard for them to do so because of the daily performances and the great amount of theatrical work in the Theatre itself. Among those who asked were many who later became famous in Russia and even abroad.

In the very middle of the fermentation which was caused in the Theatre when Sulerjitsky and I began the teaching of my system to the supernumeraries, the young people and the pupils, and all this not in the Theatre itself, there arrived the production of Tolstoy's "The Living Corpse". In it there is an endless number of *dramatis personæ*. All the supernumeraries and some of the pupils were asked to take part in the production. Very unexpectedly, at the first pre-rehearsal meeting, Nemirovich-Danchenko delivered a speech to the entire company, in which he insisted that all my new methods of work should be studied in detail by the actors of the main group and accepted by the Theatre. With this goal in mind, Nemirovich-Danchenko considered it necessary that before any work was done on the production itself I should explain what they called my " system " in detail and that the new work would begin with my system in mind.

I was overcome by the help that Nemirovich-Danchenko had given me, I am grateful to him for it to this day. But I confess that at that time I was not yet prepared to solve the difficult problem that Nemirovich-Danchenko laid before me. I had not yet found simple words for the expression of my thoughts and I fulfilled my mission far from perfectly. There was nothing surprising in the fact that the actors did not become as enthused as I wanted them to be.

When I began to put the results of my new experiments into practice, in order to give my comrades the benefit of what I had found, I met with great resistance. At the beginning I credited this to their laziness, to their lack of interest, to ill will and intrigue, and sought for secret enemies among them, but in the end of things I began to understand the real reason of my lack of success.

All actors, and especially Russian actors, like to work and are energetic in the sphere of purely physical work. Make them rehearse a hundred times, shout at the top of their voices, strain themselves, create the causeless outer physical emotion in the periphery of their bodies, and they will patiently and unmurmuringly do all in order to learn how such and such a rôle is *acted*. But if you touch their wills ever so lightly, and put before them inner spiritual problems, so as to call forth their conscious or superconscious emotions, you will be met with a rebuff, for the will of the actor is not well exercised; it is lazy, capricious. In order to awaken it one needs praise, success, applause, curtain calls, material presents, or simply narcotics and alcohol. The actor will be obstinate until you force him to action by your own personal interest in the work. The poor stage director must play for ten, sweat for ten, in order that the lazy will of the actor may react to his desires for at least one moment. That inner technique of which I preached and which is necessary for the creation of the proper creative mood is based in its most important parts on the process of will. This is why the troupe was deaf to my desires. For years, at all rehearsals, in all rooms and corridors of the theatre, on the street, I preached my new artistic credo with enthusiasm, but without any success whatever. They listened to me with respect, they practiced a meaningful silence, walked away, and whispered to each other:

" Why has he begun to play worse himself? He was much better off without his theories, when he played simply, played without any monkey business about it."

And they were right. As an actor who had changed for the time being his habitual work for the researches of an experimenter, I naturally receded. And this was noticed by all, not only by my comrades, — but by the spectators. It made me very anxious. It was hard for me not to change my steadfast new course, but I still managed to retain a small part of my actor's and stage director's authority. Nevertheless I continued to make my experiments, notwithstanding the fact that the majority of these experiments were incorrect.

My teaching was in its primary stages and was not accepted by the actors, for I had not yet found the right words that build a road not to the mind but to the heart of the actor, to his superconscious intuition. Carefully and energetically I tried to break a vent through the wall of my listeners' indifference. At times I had to lasso them.

" Let him play himself in his new way so that I may be persuaded. Then I will believe him and listen to him. Meanwhile I see that

Stanislavsky played better before he became so learned," my comrades reiterated obstinately.

But in the heat of my enthusiasm I could not, I did not want to work otherwise than my new discoveries demanded. My obstinacy made me more and more unpopular. The actors worked with me against their wills. A wall rose between me and the company. For years our relations were cold. I locked myself in my dressing room, accused them of ungratefulness, of disloyalty, of treason, and continued my researches with greater and greater devotion. That little self-love which so often controls actors had sent its subtle poison into my soul, and I painted the smallest facts in the falsest light imaginable. This made my mutual relations with the actors even sharper. The actors found it hard to work with me. I found it hard to work with them. At that time I attributed this to their ill will, but now it is clear to me that the reason was altogether different, and that the only one to blame was I.

The still unploughed spiritual soil of the young people, the supernumeraries, and the pupils, had accepted all that was sowed in their souls. They were easily enthused by all that was given them of the new. Inexperience made it seem to them that they had understood all that had been told them.

But finished actors, who had developed in themselves certain definite methods, could not accept the new without personal examination and criticism. They did not accept the system in its entirety, but they filtered it through the prisms of their experienced and well-trained artistic natures. Therefore all that had received finished form in my work and researches up to that time was accepted by them without youthful enthusiasm, but seriously, thoughtfully and deeply. They understood that it was only a theory which the actor himself was to turn into practice by long labor and wrestling with oneself. Each one of them accepted as best he could what little of real aid I could give them and began to develop it in his own way on the quiet.

But all that remained unfinished and unclear in my system at that time was severely criticized by the real actors.

I should have been overjoyed by this criticism and made use of it, but the impatience that was part of me, the enthusiasm for the new, perhaps a small self-conceit, interfered with true judgment of the facts. The words that were still unrealized by myself the actors understood with their minds, but not with their feelings, and this satisfied neither them nor me. Besides, my system cannot be explained in an hour or in a day even. It must be systematically and practically studied for years. It does good only when it becomes the second nature of the actor, when he stops thinking of it consciously, when it begins to appear naturally, as of itself. Time and patience were necessary for this, and I had neither.

Nevertheless, after Nemirovich-Danchenko's speech, my system was accepted in part by the Theatre. The actors carefully questioned me about the special terminology which was used by us during the study of the system. This was accompanied by one error on my part and on the part of the actors for which I am still paying, and heavily. To say the truth, not only the actors, but even the pupils of the Studio had accepted the system more or less on trust. They learned the terms, and then they used the terminology to cover their own perceptions which were at times creative, but mostly merely theatrical. The majority of them were the old well-known artificial habits, filled with theatricality and theatrical stencils. They were accepted to be that New of which the system talked. But the continuous exercises, like those of the singer who works day in, day out, over the placing and development of sound, like those of the violinist or 'cellist who develops in himself a true artistic tone, like those of the pianist who works over the technique of the fingers and the position of the hand, like those of every dancer who prepares his body for plastics and dancing, were conspicuous by their absence, and have never been performed even up to the present day, either by the actors or the pupils of the Studio. This is why I claim that my system has not yet shown any of its real results. Many learned to concentrate, but this only made them make all their old mistakes and made those mistakes display themselves more and more, perfected those mistakes, so to say. But the actor feels himself in comfort on the stage in that way, and he accepts this customary incorrectness of theatrical mood for the natural living over of his part. Such actors are convinced that they are living over their parts, that they have understood all, that my system has brought them unusual help, and they touchingly thank me and praise me for the discovery of a new America. But —

" I will find but ill health in that praise."

CHAPTER LVI

FOR the young people who came to seek my help I founded a Studio with my own means, and Sulerjitsky assumed its leadership. Accident furnished a remarkable coincidence. The hired home of the new Studio was located in the same place where the Society of Art and Literature was first founded, in the same place that once housed the Hunting Club. In one of the large halls on the top floor one room was furnished with a little stage on the level of the floor, for the height of the room did not allow a raised stage. The large hall housed everything that had to do with the Studio, — the classes, the rehearsals, the scenic workroom, the sewing room and the office. Here we gathered all who wanted to study the so-called Stanislavsky System, for this study was the main purpose of the founding of the Studio. Not only the supernumeraries came here, but also some of the actors from our Theatre. Not all of them were equally gifted, but almost all were enthusiastic about the work, for it was clear to them that here complete attention would be paid to them individually, while in the Theatre, with its daily rehearsals, it would have been hard to find enough free time for systematic study with them. I began to give a full course of study in the shape in which I had at that time formed it. Its aim was to give practical and conscious methods for the awakening of superconscious creativeness. It was a great pity that I could not give a great deal of time to this work in the new Studio, but to make up for this Sulerjitsky worked all the harder, and taught all sorts of exercises according to my directions for the creation of the creative feeling, for the analysis of the rôle, and for the construction of the willed orchestration of the rôle on the bases of consistency and the logic of emotion. Parallel with the studies a production of " The Wreck of Hope " was being prepared. It was rehearsed by Boleslavsky and produced before the public by Sulerjitsky. The rehearsals were continually held up by the work of the actors in the Theatre itself, where a new play was also in the throes of production. There were moments when it seemed that there was no possibility of having the studies of the young actors take place in two places at once, and that it was necessary to give up the Studio production and the other Studio work. But to this I answered decisively:

" The performance must take place at any cost, even if we have to do the impossible. Remember that this production is the thing on which your future depends."

After this, the rehearsals of the Studio production took place at night and lasted till dawn. The production was rehearsed, then corrected by Sulerjitsky, shown to me, and at last there was announced a public dress rehearsal, and the actors of the Theatre, Nemirovich-Danchenko, the artist Benois and others were invited to see it. The rehearsal was exceptionally successful and clearly displayed in all those who took part in it a certain special and until that time unknown simplicity and depth in the interpretation of the life of the human spirit.

After this there began public performances with the sale of tickets, and the money so earned was used for the material needs of the Studio. There could yet be no talk of paying the actors for their work, and they worked gratis. A great deal was written and said in the newspapers, in society and in the theatres about the new Studio. At times it was cited as an example to us, the older actors, who began to feel that side by side with us there was growing competition, and competition as is well known is the best mover of progress, especially in all that is related to the theatre. The old actors began to think. They began to pay a great deal of attention to what I said about the new methods of acting. My popularity began to awaken again, especially among the young people. And the young people are always the best propagandists of new ideas.

Meanwhile, Vladimir Ivanovich Nemirovich-Danchenko, ripened into a perfect stage director, conducted his own lines of research. In this manner, both of us, while still remaining true to our mutual and fundamental principles, each took his own natural path in everything else. This was not at all a quarrel, nor was it a separation, — it was an unescapable and natural phenomenon. Every definitely perfected actor, artist and stage director must follow the line prompted by his talent and his nature. The same thing happened in our Theatre. Two stage directors, two individualities, wanted to make their own, separate, independent paths. It became hard for us to work together, and each one of us wanted complete independence. In the old days two stage directors sat at the stage director's table, Nemirovich-Danchenko and I. Now each one of us had his own table, his own play, his own production. The company, spoiled by its former work, was dissatisfied with our natural parting of the ways. It was still less satisfied with the Studio, which drew me to itself from the Theatre. All this caused a very cold relationship on the part of the actors toward the Studio. The Studio was but badly related to the Theatre.

There were still other and more important reasons. The former quiet and balanced life of Russia was over. Our generation, which grew up on the full cup, had its own education. After 1905, when the system of education was changed in the schools, youth had won a great deal more of rights and freedom than we had had in our day. The pillars of government were beginning to tremble. The generation of the First Revolution seemed to be altogether different people than we were. If we advance a little in point of time, we see that the following generation was just as sharply differentiated from the generation of the First Studio as they were differentiated from us. This new generation went even further in the sense of freedom, in the weakening of discipline, in the strengthening of independence, — they knew the years of the war. After them came still another generation brought up amidst the thunder of cannon, the insidiousness of poison gases, bombs, catastrophes, world perturbations, Biblical hunger, all sorts of cares and national poverty, which history will remember with horror. All these generations that grew up before our eyes do not understand each other well. This was one of the reasons why one Studio after another came to life around our Theatre. These Studios were born because one generation could not fuse with another. Time will show what the result of this will be, whether the art whose principles were always the same will perish, or whether it will grow richer by the discoveries of new technical methods and the researches in the sphere of outward form.

Due to one of these reasons, or to all of them, no rapprochement could take place between the Theatre and the Studio, which still continued to help in the productions of the Theatre proper. This unexpected result worried me very much, for from the very beginning it changed my purposes. I had dreamed that the actor who grew up in the Studio would make his first timid artistic steps in a small room which was built so as not to violate the inner creative life of the beginning artist. With this aim in mind the auditorium of the Studio was built in a private apartment and seated between one hundred and one hundred and fifty spectators, who were arranged in an amphitheatre that rose upward from the stage. The stage itself was not even separated from the first row of seats. There were no traditional footlights, for the light came from above. The actors were separated from the public by a simple cloth curtain. This created an altogether exceptional intimacy, and it seemed to the spectators that they were sitting in the very place where the action of the play was going on, that they were not spectators, but accidental witnesses of a strange life. The intimacy of the impression created by this was one of the chief reasons for the exceptional success of the Studio. This intimacy gave the actors the possibility to appear without any dangerous strain which would have been necessary for them in a large theatre, and to begin to live their rôles, naturally developing and strengthening at the daily performances their voices, gestures, the definiteness of the interpretation of the inner orchestration of the rôle and its image. Only after all the artistic qualities of the Studio pupil were strengthened and it would be easy for him to carry his rôle to a large stage, would he be taken by us into the family of the older actors of the Theatre proper, into the midst of the true preservers of the traditions of Russian art.

But what happened was something altogether different. Perhaps because the desired rapprochement between the Theatre and the Studio could not take place, the actors who grew up in the Studio preferred to remain the first in a village rather than to become the second in Rome. In the Studio they soon became famous. But when they came to us in the Theatre they were only ordinary actors in our group. God knows what such a phenomenon threatened! Perhaps the Studios, demanding so little of themselves, would become good little theatres with small desires which they would be able to fulfil beautifully. Could such little theatres serve the Eternal in art, which must always make tremendous demands on the artist, demands that are always higher than his abilities? Or perhaps these little theatres would be satisfied with fashionable, speedy and cheap success, which this sphere of our art always yields. These were the thoughts that worried me at the time.

Meanwhile the work in the First Studio, under the talented control of Sulerjitsky, was going on rather well. He was a man of ideals, a humanist, a Tolstoyan. In the theatre he demanded from his pupils a life of service to art. In this he met with the warmest support from me. All vulgarity, bad manners and impudence on the part of his pupils hurt him to the quick. He quarreled with them, he persuaded them, he taught them by his own example, he educated this new generation, which, because of social and political circumstances, had not received a proper education. Happily they had received a certain discipline of theatrical character when they served as supernumeraries in the Theatre proper. Almost all of them had appeared hundreds of times in " The Blue Bird ", unseen by the public and making various objects fly across the stage during the performance. Such labor, hard and of a simple supernumerary nature, developed a certain outer discipline in them, which was necessary in the theatre.

But in all the rest they needed a re-education, which Sulerjitsky gave them, and not easily, but so to say with blood in his heart, for his love and passion cost him a great deal of health of which he had but little left. At that time the doctors had already diagnosed in him the nephritis which he had caught in Canada. It is not easy to educate adults who are old enough to want to be independent and teach others. But Sulerjitsky had a happy and lively nature. His scoldings and orders were interspersed with jokes and jests, which no one knew how to use better than he. It is impossible to remember all of the jests and practical jokes he let loose, not only in his free time, but also when it was necessary for the freshening of the atmosphere at rehearsals. Here is one of them. One young and talented pupil easily fell into despair from the least failure at rehearsals. He had to be patted on the back, praised, persuaded that he had great gifts, and he would take on life and hope again. In order not to repeat the same encouragement all the time Sulerjitsky printed a poster with the following: " X is a very talented man ". This poster was nailed to a stick and as soon as X grew the least bit doubtful of himself, the poster would be carried in procession through the rehearsal room. The process of the opening of the door, the comically serious appearance of the one who carried the poster, caused general laughter. Fully aware of the importance of his mission, the bearer of the poster would pass out through another door. The atmosphere of the rehearsal was refreshed, X became happy, and the rehearsal would go on with a new lease on life.

Sulerjitsky and I dreamed of creating a spiritual order of actors. Its members were to be men and women of broad and uplifted views, of wide horizons and ideas, who knew the soul of man and aimed at noble artistic ideals, who could worship in the theatre as in a temple. In our dreams we thought of all sorts of projects. For instance, one should not pay money in the theatre, for like a temple, it must be free to all. But these dreams, because they were unrealizable, had to wait for a better time. It was wrong to conceive that people came to the theatre accidentally, just to find release from their occupations. Such tired spectators were but poor apparatus for the reception of anything that was uplifting. We dreamed of other things, we wanted to hire an estate that was connected with the city by a car line or the railroad, and to construct a stage in the main building of the estate, where the performances of the Studio were to take place. The actors were to live continually in this house, and its wings were to be remodelled into a hotel for the guests, who, with their tickets, would receive the right to occupy a room for the night. They were to come long before the beginning of the performance. Having taken a walk in the park around the house, having rested, having dined together with the actors, having shaken the dust of the city from their shoulders, the spectators with cleansed and purified souls were to enter the theatre. In this way they would be able to receive what art was to give them. And art was also to be able to give much that was chosen, that was purified through a severe æsthetic filter.

The finances of such a Studio were to come not only from the performances, but from household economy and from the cultivation of the soil. In the spring the sowing, and in the autumn the harvesting, were to be done by the actors of the Studio themselves. This would bear greatly on the general mood and the atmosphere of the whole Studio. People who meet daily in the nervous atmosphere of the stage cannot establish those close and friendly relations which are necessary for true co-operation in art. But, if besides meeting on the stage, they met in nature, in common work on the soil, in fresh air, in the light of the sun, their souls would open, their physical labor would aid in the creation of unison among them. During the spring and the fall their stage work would stop only to be resumed again after the months of outdoor labor were over. In the winter, when they were free from their creative work on the soil, they were to work on the production of plays, they were to paint scenery, to sew costumes, to make models. The idea of household economy and the cultivation of the soil was one of the oldest dreams of Sulerjitsky. He was its initiator, for he could not live, especially in the spring, summer, and autumn, without being in close touch with nature. He longed for country life. And so the farming life of the Studio was to go on under his personal control. But all that we dreamed of at that time was nothing but a dream. And yet we were able to carry some part of it out in life.

I bought a large plot of land on the shore of the Black Sea in the Crimea, some few miles from the city of Eupatoria, and presented it to the Studio. On this plot there were built the communal buildings, a small hotel, a stable, a cow shed, barns for farming implements, and an icehouse. Each of the actors of the Studio was to build his own house with the labor of his own hands, and the house was to become his own property.

During two or three years a group of the Studio actors under the leadership of Sulerjitsky went to Eupatoria for the summers and lived the life of primeval men. They brought stones and cut them for the building of houses and put these up in temporary form. All the men passed the entire summer exposed to the sun and became as brown as berries. Sulerjitsky repeated the methods he had used with the Dukhobors in Canada, and established a severe régime. Each of the actors had his communal duty, — one was a cook, the other a coachman, the third a housekeeper, the fourth a boatman, and so on. The fame of the primeval group spread through all of the Crimea, and attracted excursions of the curious, who came to see the wild actors of the Studio of the Moscow Art Theatre. The entire enterprise aimed at the bringing together of the actors in good and interesting conditions of life, amidst healthy physical work, after the close and nervous atmosphere of the stage that always spoils peaceful relations. This summer life in the lap of nature was not in vain. It really brought the actors of the Studio very close to each other.

The First Studio was in the very bloom of its life, warmed by the fiery heart of Sulerjitsky, the ex-revolutionist, the Tolstoyan, the leader of the Dukhobors, the ideal stage director. His tenderly human heart sought for a repertoire that would be its true complement. He, and after him the entire Studio, came to love Charles Dickens, finding in that writer the echoes of all that Sulerjitsky lived by. They wanted to see the works of the great Englishman on the stage, but as he had not dedicated them to the theatre and yet the images in his novels and stories seemed to be created for the stage, it was decided to dramatize one of his creations. We chose " The Cricket on the Hearth ". Sulerjitsky put all his heart into this work. He spent many high feelings, spiritual strength, warm beliefs, and beautiful dreams on the actors of the Studio, until they were literally infected with his ardor, which made the production unusually spiritual and touching. The play did not demand simple theatrical acting; it begged for an acting that was intimate, near to the spectator, flowing into his very heart. The very construction of the Studio, where the spectator felt himself to be sitting in the same room where the action took place, helped this.

It was in this production, perhaps, that there sounded for the first time those deep and heartfelt notes of superconscious feeling in the measure and the form in which I dreamed of them at that time, and which did not find place in the large and uncomfortable auditorium of a regular theatre where the actors were forced to raise and strain their voices and to stress their acting theatrically. The spectator did not know the true reasons, nor our ingenuity which gave him a feeling of intimacy and nearness with the actors, and credited the whole result to the actors themselves. The scenery and properties were of the simplest, without any unnecessary details. The properties, like shelves with various objects on them, or a dish closet, were painted on flats and then cut out. Almost the entire scenery was made by the hands of the actors of the Studio, among whom there was an artist. It resulted in a very unusual mood. It was impossible to call the scenery artistic in the sense of painting and color, but it was peculiarly scenic. Here I may tell of a happening that had to do with this simple and seemingly very usual scenery, a happening which amazed me to no small extent.

During one of my summer vacations, I often met a well-known artist who was a connoisseur of painting. During our morning promenades, the talk naturally ran to painting on the stage. We examined and criticized the qualities and faults of the scenic work of many Russian and foreign artists in their relation to the problems of the theatre and especially to the problems of the actor.

" Tell me, what set of scenery do you consider the most successful, not as an example of painting, but as a fitting artistic background for the actor and the play? " I asked the artist.

" Let me think," he answered.

Quite a few days passed. He still did not answer my question, notwithstanding our many meetings.

" I am still thinking," he excused himself.

At one of our meetings he waved to me when he was still at a

[540]

distance from me, to come to him. I approached him and saw that he was excited.

"I know," he proclaimed triumphantly to me. "The scenery I saw that best fitted the problems of the actor was the scenery in 'The Cricket on the Hearth'."

I had not at all expected such an answer, but when he began to explain his reasons, and I put them side by side with what I knew of the production of plays and the making of scenery, I understood that my companion considered that the most successful which the actors had done moved by their inner wants, prompted by the spiritual problems of their rôles in order to help their acting and the fundamental thought that they were interpreting in the play.

CHAPTER LVII

"A MONTH IN THE COUNTRY"

WHAT directed us toward Turgenev, who has long ago been denied as a dramatist? We needed a play of complex psychology for laboratory work. And Turgenev's "A Month in the Country" is built on the most delicate curves of love experience.

The heroine of the play, Natalia Petrovna, has passed her life in a luxurious sitting room, amidst all the conventionalities of a tightly corseted epoch that was as far as it could be from nature. Due to the arrival of the eternal triangle, her relations with those near to her and the psychology of her soul are in a state of chaos. The proximity of her husband, whom she does not love, and of Rakitin, to whom she does not dare to give herself, the friendship of her husband with Rakitin, the delicacy of their feelings, so far as she is concerned, make her life unbearable.

In direct contradistinction to this trio of hothouse plants Turgenev shows the lovers Verochka and Beliaev. If in the house of the gentry love is of the hothouse variety, then here it is natural, naïve, and simple. Seeing the lovers, and attracted by the simplicity of their relations to each other, Natalia Petrovna hears the call of nature. The hothouse rose wants to become a wild flower, the society dame dreams of field and forest. She falls in love with Beliaev. This leads to a general catastrophe. Natalia Petrovna frightens away the simple and natural love of poor Verochka, confuses the student, but does not go away with him, loses her eternal admirer Rakitin, and remains forever with her husband, whom she knows how to respect but not how to love. And again she immures herself in her stiff little sitting room.

The lacework of the psychology of love which Turgenev weaves in such masterly fashion demands a special sort of playing on the part of the actors, a playing that might allow the spectator to see closely into the peculiar design of the emotions of loving, suffering, jealous, male and female hearts.

How was the actor to display his heart to such an extent that the spectator might be able to look into it and read all that was written there? That was a hard scenic problem. It could not be solved by the use of feet or hands or any of the accepted methods of stage representation. One needed some sort of unseen rayings out of creative will, emotion, longing; one needed eyes, mimetics, hardly palpable intonations of the voice, psychological pauses. Besides, it was necessary to do away with all that might interfere with the spectator's process of entering into the souls of the actors through the eyes or from receiving through the voice and its intonations the inner essence of the feelings and thoughts of the characters in the play.

For this it was necessary again to take advantage of immovability and the absence of gesture, to do away with all crossings on the stage, and to annul all the *mises en scène* of the stage director. Let the actors sit without moving, let them feel, speak, and infect the spectator with the manner in which they live their rôles. Let there be only a bench or a divan on the stage, and let all the persons in the play sit on it so as to display the inner essence and the word picture of the spiritual lacework of Turgenev.

Notwithstanding the failure of an analogous experiment in " The Drama of Life ", I decided to repeat it again, hoping that in the time that had passed since the production of the Hamsun play our stage technique had moved forward. Stanislavski the actor, who played the part of Rakitin, knew only too well the nature of the problem that Stanislavski the stage director had placed before him. And again I put myself entirely into the hands of the actor, refusing the help of the stage director. At least, I thought, I would find out if there were true artists in our company who were able to create the life of the human spirit. At least we would try out in practice whether it was true that the actor was the prime figure and the prime creator in the theatre. To weave delicate lacework without tearing its tender threads one must have the perfect technique of a virtuoso and not the technique of a day laborer with the coarse strain of muscles which tears the threads of emotion. It was first of all necessary to destroy this strain of muscle so abundantly present in most actors. It is not easy to accomplish this. It is even harder to make the physical freedom and immovability of the actor unforced and natural.

In comparison with "The Drama of Life" there was still another hardship, less in one way, greater in another. Less because it was not necessary to display such great and powerful feelings while immovable, and greater because Turgenev's picture of the souls of men is delicate in comparison with the primitive human passions in "The Drama of Life", — delicate, complex, and chaotic. In order to understand the delicate picture the entire attention of the spectator is required, he is forced to enter into the soul of the actor. And the actor needs greater strength in his spiritual rayings out and greater carefulness in the sense of their outer display.

As I became more and more disappointed in the means of theatrical production and entered more and more into the inner creative work of the actor — as actors of talent and technique grew and expanded in our troupe — the outward side of our productions retreated more and more to the background. Meanwhile in the other theatres of Moscow and Petrograd more and more interest was displayed in the outward appearances in contradistinction to the inner contents of plays. The result was that we, who were among the first in the eighties of the last century to bring great painters like Korovin and Levitan on the boards of the stage, surrendered our palm in this sphere to other theatres. In the imperial theatres of Moscow and Petrograd, the scenic work was in the hands of painters with great names — Benois, Korovin, Golovin, Dobujinsky. Painters had become not only desirable, but necessary members of the family of the theatre, and the tastes and demands of the spectators naturally assumed larger and more complex form. But where were we to find a painter who could answer all our needs? It was far from possible to talk with most of them about the essence of our art. Many of them did not have the necessary literary preparation to be able to make head or tail of the ideas in a play and the problems of the author, of psychology, of questions of scenic art in general. Many painters still demonstratively ignored all these problems which are fundamental to dramatic art. They entered the theatre either because of material reasons or for their own painting purposes. They looked on the proscenium arch in the light of a large frame for their pictures, and on the theatre in the light of an art gallery where they could daily show their work to thousands of people. Until that time the theatre had made no great demands of a special character on the painters, for they had painted scenery only for the opera and the ballet, where the purely scenic demands of inner character were not very great at the time. But could they be given the same complete independence in the spoken drama? Far from many of them could take true advantage of that independence. It often happened that the painter's model was accepted, the *mise en scène* written to fit it, and the play rehearsed for several months in accordance with it, — and then the scenery would be altogether different than in the model, changed by the artist for his own purposes, without any attention being paid to the fact that the changes destroyed all the plans and the labors of the stage director and the actors. At one time it was altogether impossible to work in the theatre with these field marshals of painting, and our Theatre was forced to turn to the younger artists, who were more adaptable and less spoiled.

But during one of our journeys to Petrograd I became acquainted with Benois and his circle, " The World of Art ", which at that time was considered very advanced. The broad and many-sided culture of Benois in all spheres of art and knowledge forced me to wonder how it was possible for one human mind and memory to retain such a store of information in itself. He was the leader of the group, and he enriched all his friends with his tremendous knowledge, answering all their questions as if he were a walking encyclopædia. Himself a great artist, he knew how to surround himself with talented men. His circle of artists had already shown the calibre of its work in the theatre in the productions of the Diagilev Ballet abroad. The Petrograd theatres also employed them and this gave them a great deal of practice and experience. They really knew the whole business of scenery, costume, and properties in the theatre. This group was the one that suited the demands of our Theatre best. But there was one great BUT. First-class workers must receive first-class pay. What the imperial theatres, which were subsidized by the government could allow themselves was impossible for us, a comparatively poor private theatre. This is why we could but rarely afford the luxury of working with those great painters who were not alien to the problems of our own art.

CHAPTER LVIII

THE WAR

JUST before we were overtaken by the terrible years of the world catastrophe, my wife went straight from Moscow to Marienbad, while I and my children went to see what the First Studio was doing in its colony near Eupatoria. In saying my farewells to the actors of the Studio I waved my hat until my carriage turned a corner and they were shut out from my view. Here something happened to me. Premonition and unrest took hold of me and I came near fainting. At one moment I even wanted to return and not to go abroad. But I remembered that my wife was waiting for me and continued on my way. In Lvov the night was unquiet. Soldiers passed continually by the window of my room, as if they were searching for something or somebody. The anxiety that had entered my heart in the Crimea did not leave me in Marienbad. I did not sleep in the nights and had premonitions of a great disaster. I wrote my children that if anything happened, then Kiev, where they were spending the summer with Sulerjitsky, would be in a very dangerous position and very near the possible battle front, and I gave them instructions what to do and where to go. My premonitions did not deceive me. War was declared. We wanted to go back to Russia, but there were no more railroad connections, for Austria had already begun fighting with Serbia. We managed to get out of Austria and found ourselves in Germany. When we left our train in Munich we saw before us the great yellow placards of mobilization. All human relations were changed. I will not describe all that the alien had to bear in an enemy country. My wife, Kachalov, the woman writer Gurevich, and I were arrested and led along the streets under armed guard to the fortress where we were detained for some time. After many tortures and adventures we were sent to Switzerland, suspected of being Russian spies. It is but natural that the Swiss should receive us unwillingly. Until it became clear that we were not spies, several weeks passed. In Switzerland we met a group of our actors who were trying to get back to Russia. For some time we were fed and boarded gratis by the owner of one of the best hotels in Beatenberg. Then we made our way to Geneva. Thanks to the kindness of one of the bank directors and several other people in that city, we secured money which we returned as soon as we got back to Russia. We made our way home by way of Marseilles, Athens, Smyrna, Constantinople and Odessa.

On the way we lived through many unexpected adventures and met the German cruiser *Goeben* in the open sea, but were able to escape it.

In Moscow life was at a boiling point. The theatres worked as never before. They tried to fit their repertoire to the moment and produced a series of quickly baked patriotic plays. And art showed that it had nothing in common with tendencies, politics, and the topics of the day.

When during the Russo-Japanese War somebody advised Chekhov to write a play about the war, the great writer was insulted.

" Listen," he said, " it is necessary that twenty years should pass. It is impossible to speak of it now. It is necessary that the soul should be in repose. Only then can an author be unprejudiced."

The newly baked patriotic plays failed, one after the other, and there was nothing remarkable in that. Can theatrical, pasteboard war vie with what was felt on the streets, in the souls of men, in their homes, with what thundered and destroyed them on the front? Was it necessary to tear apart the souls of men at a time when those souls were bleeding as it was? Theatrical war at such time is only a caricature, insulting and harmful. The patriotic spirit should be expressed only in the creation of the greatest masterpieces of the national genius. A performance of Pushkin in the scenery of Benois — that is how we expressed our patriotism.

But alas! Good will was not enough. The ability to do the thing was also necessary, and we did not have enough of it to be able to produce plays in the grand poetic style of a genius like Pushkin.

Beautiful in the plans of the artist and stage director Benois, and striking in his scenery and his costumes, the production of Pushkin's plays showed the actors and me especially the full imperfection of our art and technique.

In prose plays, even when they have large spiritual contents, we are able to create something. But in poetical works of a grand nature which speak not of individual men or individual classes, but of all human passions, our technique and our experience were not strong enough. I think that in the part of Salieri which I played in " Mozart and Salieri ", all that came from the heart to the tongue, from the heart to the face and its mimetics, from the heart to the arms and the periphery of the body, I lived over deeply and correctly. I felt and lived the part.

But when it became necessary to incarnify all that was lived over inwardly by the sound of the voice, by the poetic phrase, by resonant and rhythmic words, by controlled motions, I saw myself that I had neither voice nor diction, plastics, nor rhythm, nor tempo. I was a mere dilettante. What torture it is to feel truthfully but to incarnify your true feelings falsely and in unworthy form. I bore these pains for two seasons in the rôle of Salieri, a rôle beyond my strength, in which every phrase is so deep and broad that it might well be the sub-ject for a five-act play. What is important is that after this production I could say to myself: " I know that I know nothing."

My quest began once more. It seemed that all my life in art had been lived in vain, that I had accomplished nothing, that I had followed the wrong road.

CHAPTER LIX

BUT now there thundered about us the Second Revolution and after it the Third, all in 1917. The Theatre added a new mission to its work; it was to open its doors to the widest masses of spectators, to those millions of people who until that time had had no opportunity to enjoy cultural delights. As in Andreiev's "Anathema" in which crowds demanded bread from the good Leizer, forcing the latter to despair, notwithstanding his riches, of being able to feed millions of people, so we too were helpless in the face of the multitude that came to our Theatre. But our hearts beat anxiously and joyfully at the consciousness of the tremendous importance of the mission that had fallen to our part. In the beginning we tried to find out how the simple spectator would react toward our intellectual repertoire which was not written for a simple and naïve audience. There exists an opinion that one must play for the peasant plays of his own life, plays that are fitted to his idea of what the world is; that for the burgess one must play plays of the burgess' own life. This is not only a misunderstanding — it is completely untrue. The peasant, seeing a play of his own life, criticizes it, finds it unlike life as he knows it, does not recognize the language that is his own, for he speaks altogether differently than the people on the stage. He declares that he has grown tired of this life at home, that he has seen enough of it as it is, that he is infinitely more interested in seeing how other people live. The simple spectator longs for the life beautiful.

For some time after the revolution the public in the theatre was mixed; it was poor and rich, intelligent and nonintelligent, — teachers, students, coachmen, janitors, clerks, street cleaners, chauffeurs, conductors, workmen, domestics, soldiers. We gave our usual repertoire once or twice during the week in the tremendous building of the Solodovnikovsky Theatre, dragging our scenery and properties from the Art Theatre across the way. It is but natural that the scenery of the performance and the play which were intended for an intimate theatre should lose a great deal in the tremendous and uncomfortable house. Nevertheless, our performances took place accompanied by the strained attention of the spectator and a gravelike silence in the overfilled auditorium.

The Russian, more than any one else, is infected with the passion for spectacles. The more the spectacle excites and captivates the soul, the more it attracts him. The simple Russian spectator loves a drama at which one can weep a little, philosophize about life, listen to words of wisdom, more than any noisy vaudeville act after which nothing is left to feed the soul. The spirit of the plays in our repertoire was unconsciously absorbed by the new spectator. True, some of the fine points did not reach him, did not call forth the customary reaction and laughter in the auditorium, but other places suddenly found unexpected reactions and the new laughter would open to the actor the hidden comism underneath the text which had somehow escaped him before. It is a pity that the law of mass reaction to scenic impressions is not yet learned. Its importance to the actor cannot be exaggerated. It remains unknown why certain places in a play are laughed at by everybody at all performances in one city, while altogether different places in the same play produce the same results in other cities. We did not know why the new spectator did not accept the famous laughing places in a play as such, nor did we know how to change our individual and collective performances in order to reach the seat of his emotions.

They were interesting performances, and they taught us a great deal; they forced us to feel an altogether new atmosphere in the auditorium. We began to understand that these people came to the theatre not in order to be amused, but in order to learn. I remember one peasant, who was a good friend of mine, who came once a year to Moscow with the express purpose of seeing the entire repertoire of our Theatre.

Usually he stopped at my sister's, took out of a bundle a yellow silk shirt which became too short and narrow for him with the passing years, put on a pair of new boots, velvet trousers, oiled his hair, and then came to have dinner with me. Here he could not hide a smile of joy when he walked across the parquet floor, when he sat down to a clean, well-covered dinner table with an air of something akin to piety, when he put a clean napkin under his collar, took a silver spoon in his hand, and seemed to make a religious ceremony of our everyday meal. He did not eat the soup, he seemed to make a ceremony of transsubstantiation of eating the soup.

And after the dinner he would ask us for news of our Theatre with even greater joy, and then go to the theatre in his wonderful costume. Watching the performance, he would redden and pale from excitement and enthusiasm, and when the play ended he could not return home to sleep; he walked alone for hours in the streets, in order to clarify his impressions and to place his thoughts and emotions on the mental shelves where they belonged. When he returned, my sister would help him in this work, so difficult for him.

Having seen our entire repertoire, he folded his silk shirt, his trousers and his boots, tied them in a bundle, and returned to his home for the ensuing year. From there he would write numerous philosophical letters which helped him to digest and continue to live over the store of impressions which he had brought home with himself from Moscow. I think that not a few such spectators appeared at our Theatre. We felt their presence and our artistic duty towards them.

" Yes," I thought at that time, " our art is not eternal, but it is the most inescapable of all arts so far as our contemporaries are concerned. What strength there is in it! Its action is created not by one man, but simultaneously by a group of actors, artists, stage directors, and musicians; not by one art, but simultaneously by many most diverse arts, music, drama, painting, declamation, dancing. This theatrical action is received not by one man, but simultaneously by a crowd of human beings which develops a mass emotion that sharpens the moments of receptivity. This collectivity, that is, the simultaneous creation of many different artists, this comprehensivity, that is, the action not of one, but of many arts at one time, this herd feeling of receptivity, show their full strength in the impression they make on this new, unspoiled, trusting, and unsophisticated spectator."

This force of the scenic power over the spectator was shown in strongest relief at one performance which I will always remember. This performance was given almost on the eve of the Third Revolution. On that night the soldiery was gathering around the Kremlin, mysterious preparations were being made, gray-clad mobs were walking somewhere, some of the streets were completely empty, the lanterns were out, the police patrols removed, and in the Solodovnikovsky Theatre there gathered a thousand-headed crowd of the common people to see Chekhov's " Cherry Orchard ", in which the life of that class against whom the common people were preparing for final revolt was painted in deep and sympathetic tones.

The auditorium, filled almost exclusively by the common people, buzzed with excitement. The mood on both sides of the footlights was one of worry. We actors, in our make-ups, waiting for the performance to begin, stood near the curtain and listened to the buzzing of the audience in the thickened atmosphere of the auditorium.

" We won't be able to finish the performance," we said to each other. " There will be a scandal. Either they will drive us from the stage or they will attack us."

When the curtains parted, our hearts beat in the expectation of a possible excess. But — the lyricism of Chekhov, the eternal beauty of Russian poetry, the life-mood of country gentility in old Russia, caused a reaction even under the existing conditions. It was one of our most successful performances from the viewpoint of the attention of the spectators. It seemed to us that all of them wanted to wrap themselves in the atmosphere of poetry and to rest there and bid peaceful farewell forever to the old and beautiful life that now demanded its purifying sacrifices. The performance was ended by a tremendous ovation, and the spectators left the theatre in silence, and who knows — perhaps many of them went straight to the barricades. Soon shooting began in the city. Hardly able to find cover, we made our way to our homes in the night. In the darkness I ran into a priest, and thought:

"They are shooting there, and we are in duty bound to go, he to the church, I to the theatre. He to pray, I to create for those who seek respite."

There came the Third Revolution. The doors of our Theatre opened exclusively for the poor people and closed for a time to the intelligentsia. Our performances were free to all who received their tickets from factories and institutions where we sent them, and we met face to face right after the issuance of the decree with spectators altogether new to us, many of whom, perhaps the majority, knew nothing not only of our Theatre but of any theatre. But yesterday our Theatre had been filled by the old public which we had educated through many decades, and to-day we were faced by an altogether new audience which we did not know how to approach. Neither did the audience know how to approach us and how to live with us in the theatre. We were forced to begin at the very beginning, to teach this new spectator how to sit quietly, how not to talk, how to come into the theatre at the proper time, not to smoke, not to eat nuts in public, not to bring food into the theatre and eat it there, to dress in his best so as to fit more into the atmosphere of beauty that was worshipped in the theatre. At first this was very hard to do, and two or three times after the end of an act the atmosphere of which was spoiled by the crowd of still uneducated spectators, I was forced to come before the curtain with a plea in the name of the actors who were placed in an impasse.

On one occasion I could not restrain myself, and spoke more sharply than I should have spoken. The crowd was silent and listened to me very attentively. Until the present day I cannot imagine how these two or three audiences managed to tell of what had happened to all the other visitors in our Theatre. Nothing was written about it in the papers, no new decrees were issued on the score of what had happened. Why did a complete change in the behavior of the audience take place after what had happened? They came to the theatre fifteen minutes before the curtain, they stopped smoking and cracking nuts, they brought no food with them, and when I, unoccupied in the performance, passed through the corridors of the Theatre which were filled with our new spectators, boys would rush to all the corners of the foyers, warning those present:

" He is coming."

During the war and the revolution a tremendous quantity of people passed through the doors of our Theatre, — people of all descriptions, from all the provinces and of all the nationalities that compose Russia. If the Western Front gave before the enemy Moscow would be filled with newcomers who sought to find respite in the theatre. The new audience brought its own habits, its good and bad qualities; we were forced to educate them up to the discipline of our Theatre, and we had hardly done so, when the tragic fate of Russia dealt it a new and cruel blow, and a new stream of exiles would pour into Moscow from the north, or from the east, or from the south. They all came in through the doors of our Theatre and passed out through them perhaps forever. With the coming of the Revolution many classes of society passed through our Theatre — there was the period of soldiers, of deputies from all the ends of Russia, of children and young people, and last, of workingmen and peasants. They were spectators in the best sense of the word; they came into our Theatre not through accident but with trembling and the expectation of something important, something they had never experienced before. They treated the actors with peculiarly touching admiration, but the pity was that the unrest of the Revolution threw up a large quantity of giftless men who claimed to call themselves artists of the theatre. There appeared crowds of men who bore no relation whatsoever to art except the ability of exploiting it coarsely and the talent of sticking like moss to a good and profitable business. They compromised us who always served beauty and nobleness. And this harmed to a great extent the warm relationships between the actors and the simple Russian spectator. Besides, after about a year and a half of the Revolution, material circumstances brought about a change in the theatrical policy of the government, and our doors opened again to the richer portion of the public, which alone was able to bear the weight of theatrical expenditures.

The best test of the spectator from among the working and peasant class was the production of Byron's philosophical tragedy, " Cain ", with that remarkable tragedian, Leonid Leonidov, in the leading rôle. This is an inspired thesis in dramatic form, and in producing it in the theatre one can reckon on the attention only of the most intelligent audience. But at the dress rehearsal the auditorium was filled by a crowd of simple workingmen and peasants. They listened to what was going on on the stage in the deepest of silences. The serious, thoughtful mood of the dramatic poem prevented them from staging an ordinary theatrical ovation. After the end of the performance the spectators sat for a long time without any movement and departed without any noise, as if they were leaving a temple of worship after prayer.

Because of the illness of some of the actors, the play was soon removed from the repertoire of the Theatre. But for a long time we had inquiries from the simple new spectators as to when "Cain" was to be produced again.

Soon there was another catastrophe. A group of our actors, including Kachalov, Knipper, Germanova, Massalitinov and Baksheiev went on a guest journey to Kharkov, and was divided from us by the unexpected advance of the armies of Denikin. They could not cross the front and for several years our main theatrical troupe was divided in half.

The small numbers of those who remained took away all chance of producing any new plays and also of continuing our old repertoire. The same obstacle lay in the path of those of our comrades who had been cut away from us. We had to fill our ranks with actors from the Studios, they with actors who had nothing to do with the Art Theatre.

CHAPTER LX

MY manner of reading verse, unaccepted in "Mozart and Salieri," gave me no rest. I was criticized for my slow rhythm, I was accused of the absence of rhythm altogether. The manner of other actors in other theatres was quoted, that is, that method of reading from which I ran as from the plague. I would have done anything but read as they did. It is better not to read verse at all, than read it in the way which is considered lawful, requisite and patented in the sense of poetry and musicalness. Rhythm does not consist in stressing iambs and anapæsts. I cannot bear the marchlike beating out of rhythm. I want to sleep when I hear the reading of verse in a solemnly monotonous voice with chromatic tones crawling up. I cannot bear vocal leaps to the terza or quinta with a fall at the end of each line to a secunda. There is nothing more vulgar than a made, sweetish, quasi-poetical voice in lyric poems, which rises and falls like waves during a dead calm. What can be more terrible than the female readers at concerts, those tender, posing, soulful young ladies in light gowns who read from a pink velvet-bound book dear verses like: "Little star, little star, why are you still?"

Kind fate came to my aid again. The Great Moscow Opera wanted to put the dramatic side of its performances on a higher footing. It asked the Moscow Art Theatre to help it. Nemirovich-Danchenko and Luzhsky agreed to direct one of the operas. I offered to organize a Studio in which the artists of the Opera might consult me on questions of operatic acting, and younger artists might study, systematically passing a requisite course established by myself. The

[558]

rapprochement of the Great Opera and the Moscow Art Theatre was accepted enthusiastically, and in December, 1918, or January, 1919, there was a triumphant rout. The artists of the Opera were hosts to the actors of the Moscow Art Theatre. The whole evening was joyful, touching, and memorable. Tables and a stage were placed in the halls and foyer of the Great Theatre. The divas and the male artists of the Opera waited on us and gave us food that was luxurious in those hungry days. All were in evening dress, partly because the ball gowns and the evening coats in which the artists appeared at concerts were preserved better than the everyday clothes that had reached a state of extreme unreliability.

When the company of the Moscow Art Theatre arrived, all the soloists stood up on the stage and sang a triumphant cantata composed for the occasion. Then there was a comradely supper with speeches and mutual greetings. The soloists of the Opera, Nezhdanova, the tenor Smirnov, the basso Petrov, and others sang songs on the stage; Kachalov, Moskvin and I read. After supper came the actors from the Studios of the Moscow Art Theatre with a series of entertaining numbers very much like those which we used in creating the Cabbage Parties of our younger years. Later there was dancing, *petits jeux,* legerdemain.

After a few days I met the singers of the Opera for a heart-to-heart talk about art in the foyer of the Great Theatre. They asked me questions. I answered them, I demonstrated what I meant, I sang as best I could. Gradually in my soul there awoke again those old and half-forgotten feelings and enthusiasms which remained in me since my operatic studies with the elder Kommissarjevsky. Again there began to play in me love for dramatic, rhythmic action while singing, which had always remained unsatisfied.

I cannot complain about the reception the singers gave me. They were very attentive to me. Many of them were interested in the experiments and exercises which I showed them. They worked willingly and without any false theatrical shame. Others did not consider it convenient to appear in the rôle of pupils and were present merely as spectators, mistakenly thinking that with the aid of simple observation they would learn all the nuances of dramatic art. But they were hardly right. One cannot become stronger from simply watching others perform exercises. And our art demands a great deal of systematic exercise. Those who studied and continued to study made much progress, and after some time drew general attention to their acting. Others, who for various reasons could not study, began to console themselves with the denial of the necessity for acting in the opera and a general negation of all that was taking place in the Studio. This is usual human psychology in such cases.

A small group of singers who appreciated the new Studio brought great sacrifices to its altar and conducted themselves heroically. They worked without reward and at a time when order was still not established in the city after all the peripatetics of the Revolution; when it was still dangerous to walk on the streets at night, for shooting, pillage, and murder stalked abroad. Many singers with beautiful voices were forced to tramp the snow and the wetness without rubbers on their torn shoes. Nevertheless they did everything in their power to attend the classes in the Studio.

But there were conditions with which they could not struggle. For instance, their appearances in the operatic performances of the Great Theatre were unconquerable obstacles to their work in the Studio, as well as their concerts for the winning of enough bread to last through the day. But what was to be done? The salaries they received were not enough to feed them and their families, and a side occupation was necessary.

At that time there was a rage for concerts, for the entire mass of the new public fell hungrily on art. There was never enough place in theatres and concert halls, people arranged private concerts in various institutions and state buildings. In the rooms where economic business was transacted of mornings, art reigned at night. All Moscow sang and declaimed. The demand for singers and actors was tremendous, for the new public was sincerely and purely interested in art. Their interest helped the artists and gave them the necessary means for making ends meet, but it belittled and spoiled the art of the singers and interfered with their studies, for it took away those with whom excerpts of operas were being prepared in the Studio. During the winter I was unable to gather a complete quartette for the rehearsal of a given excerpt. To-day the soprano could not come, to-morrow the tenor, the day after the mezzo. Or it would happen that the basso, because of a concert, was free only from eight to nine, and the tenor, because of an appearance in the first act of the current opera in the Great Theatre, was free only after nine. In the beginning of the rehearsal of the quartette we would do without the tenor, and when he came, without the basso, who hurried to his concert. Conquering the unusual obstacles with great hardship, we were able, at the end of the season — that is, in spring — to prepare several excerpts from operas with the singers of the Great Theatre, which we showed in the hall of the Studio to several specialists, without any decoration or costumes, for it was not in scenery and costumes that the gist of the matter lay, and besides, we had no means to buy them. The special rehearsal was very successful and created much discussion. But what is most important was that it convinced me of the fact that I could be of help to the art of the opera.

In the next season I agreed to continue the work of the Opera Studio, but on other conditions. The members of the Studio were to be chosen from among young singers, who, under my guidance, were to study a number of subjects thoroughly before they were to be allowed to appear on the boards of the Studio as artists. I established a system of classes in subjects that had never been taught in other schools before, the theory and practice of what is called the System of Stanislavsky, various exercises in the development of the feeling of rhythm not only in movement, but in the inner sensations and in sight, and so on. The process of sight is the raying out of spiritual juices that come from us and enter into us. These rayings out have movement, and once there is movement, there is also its tempo and its rhythm. The same thing is true of the sense of touch. In order to differentiate silk and velvet one needs another tempo and rhythm than in differentiating the bristles of a clothesbrush. To smell ammonia one needs another tempo and rhythm than in smelling lilies of the valley. If one smells ammonia as one smells lilies of the valley, with rapid breathings-in of various duration and rhythm, one runs the risk of burning the whole mucous membrane of the nose. In a series of variegated exercises I tried to develop in my pupils not the outward rhythm of movement and action, but the inner rhythm of that unseen energy which calls out movement and action. In this manner I was able to develop in my pupils the sensation of movement and gesture, walking, and the entire inner pulse of life. These are purely practical methods and theses, which are useful in our work, and it would be a mistake to look in them for any scientific bases, from which I feel myself to be very far. To the accompaniment of a pianist's improvisations, the pupils lived for hours in rhythm, explaining in their actions how they felt the music. Relying on the same bases of the sensation of inner rhythm and action, they learned to walk, to do gymnastics, plastic and other exercises in my system for the development of correct consciousness of self in which rhythm plays a great and important part. There was a whole series of exercises and classes for the development of the feeling for the word and speech, for an altogether exceptional amount of attention was paid to diction in the opera.

CHAPTER LXI

I AM not young, and my artistic career approaches its last act. The present evolution of dramatic art begins again its new circle in eternity. In this or in that form, in a larger or lesser degree, I see a repetition of what I saw in my artistic youth. Again, as in our time, there have appeared new people with new ideals, dreams, demands, criticisms, impatience, self-conceit. New geniuses are born and write their new laws in interdependence with the new conditions of life. My old comrades and I also assume rôles that are new to us. We have become the representatives of experience; we have been placed as conservatives with whom it is the holy duty of the innovator to struggle. One must have enemies to attack. Our new rôle is not so attractive as our old one was. But — each generation has its own limitations. I do not complain, I am only constituting a fact. It would be a sin for us to complain. We have lived. More, we must thank the Lord for letting us see with one eye into the mists of the future, into what will come after us. We must try to understand those perspectives, that final goal, which attract the young generation. It is interesting to be able to live and watch what is going on in the minds and hearts of youth. But in my new position I would like to avoid playing two rôles. I am afraid to become a young old man, " a mousy colt of art " who flatters youth and tries to look as young as youth, and share its tastes, its convictions, — who tries to be abreast with the foremost and notwithstanding his lack of wind, limping and stumbling, trots behind youth, afraid that it might disown him. In a word, I do not want to become a young old man with gray hair and a bald spot, who courts every nice-looking high school girl and tries to rival his grandchildren.

I do not want to play the other rôle either, a rôle that is the exact opposite of the first. I am afraid to become too experienced an ancient, who thinks he has seen everything, who is impatient, irascible, opposed to everything that is new, forgetful of the researches and mistakes of his own youth.

In my last years of life I would like to be what I am in reality, what I must be by the strength of the laws of nature under whose guidance I have lived and worked and still live and work in art.

What am I and what do I represent in the new and nascent life of the theatre? Can I still, as of old, understand all that goes on and all that enthuses youth in all its details? I think that I can no longer understand organically much in the longings of present-day youth. One must be courageous to acknowledge this. You know from what I have told you how we were educated in our childhood and youth. Compare our life with the life of the present generation of youth brought up on a régime of poverty and danger. We spent our youth in a Russia that was peaceful; we drank from the full cup of life. The present generation has grown up amidst war, hunger, world catastrophe, mutual misunderstanding and hate. We knew much joy and did not share it with those near to us to any great degree, and now we are paying for our egotism. The new generation does not know the joy that we knew, it seeks and creates joy in agreement with the circumstances of life, and tries each moment to regain and make its own again those years of youth that it has lost. It is not for us to condemn them for this. It is for us to sympathize with them, to follow with interest and good wishes the unrolling evolution of the new art and the new life created by the laws of nature.

But there is a sphere in which we have not grown too old. Here we can still do a great deal and help youth with our knowledge and experience. What is more, youth cannot get along without us in this sphere unless it simply wishes to rediscover an already discovered America. Much in creativeness is incumbent upon all, the young and the old, men and women, the gifted and the giftless. All men are forced to put food in their mouths, to hear with their ears, to see with their eyes, to breathe with their lungs, and all actors without exception must receive creative food according to the laws of nature, must treasure what they receive in their intellectual and emotional memory, must rework the material in their artistic imagination, according to well-known laws that are incumbent upon all, must give birth to the image and the life of the human spirit, and having lived them over, incarnify them naturally.

In the sphere of rhythm, plastics, the laws of speech, the placing of the voice, breathing, the logic of the continuity of human feelings, there is much that is incumbent upon all. And it is in that sphere which is incumbent upon all that beginning actors strain and cripple their natures most often. We can help them, we can save them from disaster, and they may well listen to what we have to tell them from the store of our experience. How many gifted men and women this would save! From how many mistakes, unnecessary experiments and researches it would protect young actors! We know from our personal experience many mistakes and obstacles which every one is bound to meet on the stage, and it is our duty, in so far as we are able, to warn the inexperienced and prevent them from taking the wrong road. Of course we understand the general outline of what youth wants.

The life that Chekhov painted is gone, but his art is still with us. Many young people know nothing of that life, for they appeared on the scene long after it passed. Revolutions and wars created cruel but interesting moments in the life of man, who in one day, sometimes in one hour, passed through what it took a man of the generation before him tens of years to live over. For the reflection of this bright, colorful, sharp life on the stage there is needed talent, great inner strength, bright technique, an ideal, the consciousness of one's social and cultural mission, religion. How can all these elements be united in one man? Nature is unkind to man and rarely gives him what he needs in life. The perfect actor is as yet unborn. Longing for such an actor, youth makes compromises so as to be able to satisfy in part its need for sharpness and strength of artistic creativeness. It does not reach the desired result, but nevertheless it makes certain conquests which are necessary but which may not be properly evaluated or used in practice. The most important thing is not to leave the fundamental roadway along which art moves forward from times immemorial. And he who does not know this eternal road is fated to endless wanderings in impasses, along bypaths that lead to the jungle and not to light and freedom.

What is this path of the progress of art? It is the path of natural evolution. One must travel over it without hurrying. But the Revolution and its generation are impatient. New life does not want to wait, it demands quick results, another and a quickened tempo of life. Without waiting for natural creative evolution, it violates art, stuffing it with sharpness of form and content. Such condiment in piquant food is on the one hand the crying luxury and richness, the colorful scenery and costumes, the futuristic bravado and the unexpectedness of production effects, overacting and full tone. On the other hand there is created an exaggerated scenic simplicity, the complete absence of scenery, the putting in its place of all sorts of so-called simple constructive platforms, turning wheels and machines and other inventions of the stage director made, so to say, in the name of simplification. But this simplicity is worse than outright thievery; it cries aloud on the stage and disturbs the eye even more than the colorful luxury and richness of production.

Nature cannot be outwitted. Its true organic creativeness cannot be supplanted either by poverty-stricken or luxurious theatricality. A time will come when the evolution of art shall have completed its predestined circle and nature itself will teach us methods and technique for the interpretation of the sharpness of the new life.

In this evolutionary process of art we can help the new generation, for much that we have experienced is being repeated at present, and only differs in name from what we knew. The grotesque, synthesis, generalization, are not new phenomena in art; in one or another form they have lived always, at all times, among all innovators and revolutionists. Is not Othello-Salvini a tragic grotesque? Are not Jivokini and Varlamov bright comic grotesques which we have never yet seen repeated? Did not the radical movement of the past which was called impressionism move art along the very same path which has brought it to futurism and the absolute? The forms and the names are new, but the nature of evolution and its chief laws are the same.

There exists an old legend that the actor on the stage needs only talent and inspiration. Talent is given by God and inspiration is sent by Apollo. Therefore one is to rely on them alone. In support of such an opinion they bring the examples of geniuses like our Mochalov who seemingly proves this opinion at first glance in his artistic life. They do not forget Kean as he is pictured in the famous melodrama. He is the final example quoted and he strengthens the myth in the eyes of those actors who are poorly acquainted with their art and know nothing of its technique. Try to tell these men that you acknowledge technique, and they will shriek:

" Then you deny talent ! "

There is still another legend, very widespread among the practitioners of our art, that the first thing needed is technique, and so far as talent is concerned, of course it is never in the way. Actors of this ilk, when they hear your acknowledgment of technique, will at first applaud you. But if you try to tell them that technique is all right so far as it goes, but that before it come talent, inspiration, superconsciousness, and the living over of a part, and that it is for these that technique is created, that it consciously serves to awaken the creative mood, they will be horrified by your words.

" The creative mood! Living a part over!" they will cry. " That's only an old story!"

Is it not because these people are afraid of living emotion and living a part over on the stage that they cannot feel or live a part over on the stage themselves?

Both prejudices have become strongly fixed in the minds and hearts of actors. The best actors of the inspirational school, when they are not at once successful in a rôle, justify their failure and build a wall between themselves and artistic technique by means of the same myth about talent.

" It is a failure because I don't feel it yet. As soon as I begin to feel the rôle it will be a success."

Is this not the same as saying, " I don't play well because I don't play well. But when I begin to play well then I will play well?"

Nine tenths of the labor of an actor, nine tenths of everything lies in beginning to live and feel the rôle spiritually. When this is done, the rôle is almost ready, and it is meaningless to place nine tenths of the labor on simple accident, leaving but one tenth to one's art. Let us agree that exceptional talents feel and create their rôles at once. Laws are not written for them. They write their own laws. But what is most astounding is that I have never heard from them that technique is unnecessary and talent necessary or that technique is first and talent secondary. Just the opposite, — the greater the actor, the more he is interested in the technique of his art.

" The bigger the talent, the more development and technique it needs," said a great actor to me. " When men with small voices yell and falsify sound one is uncomfortable, but if Tamagno would begin to falsify with his tremendous voice it would be terrible."

That was the answer of a genius.

All great actors wrote about their technique. All of them until the

very last years of their life daily developed and strengthened their technique with singing, fencing, gymnastics, and sport. For years they studied the psychology of a rôle and worked over it innerly. Only homemade geniuses boast of their nearness to Apollo, of their all-embracing inner fire, and they inspire themselves with alcohol and narcotics and prematurely wear out their temperament, ability and gifts. Let some one explain to me why the violinist who plays in an orchestra on the tenth violin must daily perform hour-long exercises or lose his power to play? Why does the dancer work daily over every muscle in his body? Why do the painter, the sculptor, the writer practice their art each day and count that day lost when they do not work? And why may the dramatic artist do nothing, spend his day in coffee houses and hope for the gift of Apollo in the evening? Enough. Is this an art when its priests speak like amateurs? There is no art that does not demand virtuosity.

Having tried in the theatre all the means and methods of creative work; having paid homage to the enthusiasm for all sorts of productions along all the lines of creativeness, those of history and manners, those of the symbol, those of fantasy, and so on; having learned the forms of production of all artistic tendencies, realistic, naturalistic, impressionistic, futuristic, statuary, schematized, exaggeratedly simple, with drapes, screens, tulle, and all sorts of effects of light and direction, — I have come to the conclusion that all these things mean nothing and do not create an inner, active dramatic art. The only king and ruler of the stage is the talented actor. But alas, I cannot find for him a true scenic background which would not interfere with, but would help his complex spiritual work. What is needed is a simple background, but simplicity is the result either of a poor imagination or of a very rich one. I don't know how to keep the simplicity that is the result of rich imagination from forcing itself to the front of the stage even more than exaggerated and rich theatricality. The simplicity of screens, drapes, velvet, rope scenery was a simplicity that was worse than theft. It attracted more attention than the customary scenery of the theatre to which our eye is used and which it is beginning to stop noticing. If there is not born a very great painter who will give the most difficult of all scenic sets a simple but artistic background for the actor, the true actor can only dream·of a simple board stage on which he could come out like a singer or a musician and interpret with his unaided inner and outer qualities, his art and his technique, the beautiful and artistic life of the human spirit in the rôles which he portrays.

There is no art that does not demand virtuosity. There is no final measure for the fullness of this virtuosity. The French painter Dégas said, "If you own a hundred thousand francs' worth of craftsmanship, spend five sous to buy more." This necessity for the acquirement of experience and craftsmanship is especially apparent in the art of the theatre. The tradition of painting is preserved in museums and collections; the tradition of the arts of speech in books; the traditions of music in notes. The young painter may stand for hours before a picture, gradually perceiving the coloration of Titian, the harmony of Velasquez, the drawing of Ingres. The inspired lines of Dante and the finished pages of Flaubert can be read and re-read. It is possible to examine every curve of the creations of Bach and Beethoven. But a work of art born on the stage lives only for a moment, and no matter how beautiful it may be it cannot be commanded to stay with us.

The tradition of scenic art lives only in the talent and the ability of the actor. The impossibility of repeating the impression received by the spectator limits the rôle of the theatre as a place for the study of the art of the stage. In this sense the theatre cannot give the beginner such results as the library and the museum give to the writer and the artist. It would be possible, what with the present age of perfected invention, to try to enter the voices of dramatic artists on phonograph records, and their gestures and mimics on the films of the cinema and this would give a great deal of help to young actors. But nothing can fix and pass on to our descendants those inner paths of feeling, that conscious road to the gates of the unconscious, which, and which alone, are the true foundation of the art of the theatre. This is the sphere of living tradition. This is a torch which can only be passed from hand to hand, and not from the stage, but through personal teaching, by the way of the discovery of mysteries on one side, and exercises, obstinate and inspired labor for the acceptance of these mysteries on the other side.

The main difference between the art of the actor and all other arts is that every other artist may create whenever he is in the mood of inspiration. But the artist of the stage must be the master of his own inspiration and must know how to call it forth when it is announced on the posters of the theatre. This is the chief secret of our art. Without this the most perfect technique, the greatest gifts, are fruitless. And this secret, more is the pity, is very jealously guarded. The great masters of the stage, with but few execptions, not only did not try to disclose this secret to their younger comrades, but they kept it behind an insurmountable barrier. The absence of this tradition sentenced our art to become dilettantism. From the inability to find a conscious path to unconscious creativeness, actors reached destructive prejudices which denied spiritual technique; they grew cold in the surface layers of scenic craft and accepted empty theatrical self-consciousness for true inspiration. I know only one method of combating this so dangerous circumstance for the actor. This is to describe in a well-balanced system all that I have reached after long researches and in this manner give actors and those who long to walk the boards a guide, a series of exercises which may show them practically, by way of work over oneself and over the material of the rôle, how the actor may create the conditions that are favorable to true scenic inspiration, and in the same manner call it forth at the moments necessary for his art.

When I look back over the roads that I have traveled during my long life in art, I want to compare myself to a gold-seeker who must first make his way through almost impassable jungles in order to find a place where he may discover a streak of gold, and later wash hundreds of tons of sand and stones in order to find at last several grains of the noble metal. And, like the gold-seeker, I cannot will to my heirs my labors, my quests, my losses, my joys and my disappointments, but only the few grains of gold that it has taken me all my life to find.

May the Lord aid me in this task!

APPENDICES

LIST OF THE PRODUCTIONS OF THE ALEXEIEV CIRCLE

1877
 September 5 "The Old Mathematician"
        "A Cup of Tea"
        "Which of the Two?"

1879
 March 18   "A Dainty Bit"
        "The Capricious Woman"

1880
 July 8   "A Room with Two Beds"
        "The Hurly-Burly in the Shtcherbakovsky Alley"
 August 3   "A and Z"
        "The Barbershop"

1881
 July 11   "The Secret of Woman" ("A Woman's Secret")
        "The Weak String"
        "Karl the Brave"
 November 25 "A Wife for Hire"
        "A Dainty Bit"
        "The Weak String"

1882
 July 24   "The Love Philtre"

1883
 April 28   "Hercules"
        "Javotta"
        "A Peculiar Disaster"
        "Aida" (from Act III)
 August 20 "The Practical Man"
        "Let Every Cricket Know His Own Hearth"

1884
 January 28 "Mischief"
        "Comtesse de la Frontmer"
 August 18 "Mademoiselle Nitouche"
        "The Little Red Sun" (Act I)

1886
 February 7 "Don't Fly Near the Fire"
        "The Hearth-Fairy Jests"
 February 18 "The Money Kings"
        "Lili" (an operetta)

1887
 February 6 "One Word to the Minister"
        "The Gamblers" (Gogol)
        "Les Plaideurs" (Racine
 February 11 "The Case of Pleianov"
        "A Cup of Tea"
 April 18   "The Mikado"
        "Lili"
 September 15 "The Major's Lady" (Shpajinsky)
 December 6 "The Forest"
 December 15 "Conquerors Are Not Judged"
        "We Must Be Divorced"

1888
    January 31   "Poverty is not a Sin"
                      "The Secret of Woman"
    February 29   "The Favorite" (Krilov)
                      "The Secret of Woman"

LIST OF THE PRODUCTIONS OF THE SOCIETY OF ART AND LITERATURE

1888
    December 8   "The Miser Knight" (Pushkin)
                     "Godunov"
                     "Georges Dandin"
    December 11   "Bitter Fate"
                     "The Bear Matched Them"
1889
    January 10   "The Favorite"
    January 15   "The Stone Guest"
    February 9   "The Rouble"
    March 11   "Burning Letters"
    November 23 "Villainy and Love"
    November 26 "Usurpers of the Law"
1890
    ———   "Don't Live to Please Yourself but to Please the Lord"
                     "If He Only Knew"
    April 5   "The Dowerless Bride"
1891
    February 8   "The Fruits of Knowledge"
    September 14 "Foma"
                     "In the Judge's Chambers"
    December 1   "Sin and Disaster Visit All"
1892
    January 4   "We Must Be Divorced"
    January 23   "Anna de Coeurvilliers"
                     "A Scandal in a Noble Family"
                     "The Love Philtre"
    February 11   "The Sinecure"
    February 29   "There Was Not Even a Penny"
1893
    January 28   "The Bread of Labor"
    March 4   "The Blind Alley"
    October 22   "Mischief"
    November 26 "The Forest"
1894
    February 7   "The Tutor"
                     "Each One Speaks of His Own Grievance"
    February 21   "The Last Sacrifice"
    April 20   "The Wild Woman"
    October 2   "The Topics of the Day"
    December 9   "The Bravo"

APPENDICES

1895
    January 9   "Uriel Acosta"
    November 2   "We'll Settle It Among Ourselves"
1896
    January 25   "Othello"
    April 3   "The Assumption of Hannele"
    April 7   "The Marriage of Krechinsky"
    October 29   "Marriage"
                  "The Betrothal in Galernaya"
    October 31   "Don't Sit in a Stranger's Sleigh"
    November 19 "The Polish Jew"
                  "Two Hounds on One Trail"
    December 12 "On the Farm"
    December 19 "The Dowerless Bride"
1897
    January 19   "We'll Settle It Among Ourselves"
                  "The Proposal"
    January 23   "Lazybones"
    February 6   "Much Ado About Nothing"
    February 7   "The Duck and the Glass of Water"
    March 3   "A Peculiar Disaster"
    October 30   "The Hot Heart"
    November 6   "A Strange Feast Brings Drunkenness"
                  "Breakfast at the Chairman's"
    November 13 "Fofan"
    December 17 "The Twelfth Night"
1898
    January 10   "The Mistress of the Inn"
    January 19   "The Slavery of Husbands"
    January 29   "The Sunken Bell"
    November 26 "The Tutor"

LIST OF THE PRODUCTIONS OF THE MOSCOW ART THEATRE

In the Hermitage Theatre
1898
    October 14   "Tsar Fyodor"
    October 21   "The Merchant of Venice"
    December 2   "The Mistress of the Inn," "Greta's Joy"
    December 17 "The Seagull"
1899
    January 12   "Antigone"
    February 19   "Hedda Gabler"
    September 29 "The Death of Ivan the Terrible"
    October 5   "Fuhrmann Henschel"
    October 26   "Uncle Vanya"
    December 16 "Lonely Lives"
1900
    September 24 "The Snow Maiden"
    October 24   "The Enemy of the People"
    November 28 "When We Dead Awaken"
1901
    January 31   "Three Sisters"
    September 19 "The Wild Duck"
    October 27   "Michael Kramer"
    December 21 "Dreams"

In the Kamergersky Theatre
1902
    October 25   "Small People"
    November 5   "The Power of Darkness"
    December 18 "The Lower Depths"
1903
    February 24   "The Pillars of Society"
    October 2   "Julius Cæsar"
1904
    January 17   "The Cherry Orchard"
    October 2   "The Blind," "Interior," "The Unbidden Guest"
    October 19   "Ivanov"
    December 21 "Near the Monastery," "Surgery," "The Evil
                One," "Non-Com Prishibeiev"

1905
    January 28   "The Prodigal Son," "Ivan Mironich"
    March 31   "Ghosts"
    October 24   "The Children of the Sun"
1905
    September 26 "Trouble From Reason"
    December 20 "Brand"

1907
    February 8   "The Drama of Life"
    April 2   "Walls"
    October 10   "Boris Godunov" (A. Tolstoy)
    December 12   "The Life of Man"
1908
    March 5   "Rosmersholm"
    September 30   "The Blue Bird"
    December 18   "The Inspector General"
1909
    March 9   "At the Gates of the Kingdom"
    October 2   "Anathema"
    December 9   "A Month in the Country"
1910
    February 9   The First Cabbage Party
    March 11   "Enough Stupidity in Every Wise Man"
    October 12   "The Brothers Karamazov"
    December 17   "Miserere"
1911
    March 1   "In the Claws of Life"
    ———   The Second Cabbage Party
    September 23   "The Living Corpse"
    December 23   "Hamlet"
1912
    March 5   "The Lady from the Provinces" and two other plays
    March 14   The Third Cabbage Party
    October 9   "Peer Gynt"
    December 17   "Ekaterina Ivanovna"
1913
    March 27   "The Forced Marriage," "The Man Who Thought He
                          Was Sick" (Molière)
    October 23   "Nikolai Stavrogin"
1914
    February 3   "The Mistress of the Inn"
    March 17   "Thought"
    December 31   "The Death of Pazukhin"
1915
    March 26   "The Pushkin Plays"
    April 14   "Autumn Violins"
1916
    February 3   "There Will Be Joy"
1917
    September 26   "The Village of Stepanchikovo"
1920
    April 4   "Cain"
1921
    May 25   "The Inspector General" (dress rehearsal)
    October 8   "The Inspector General" (first performance)

INDEX

INDEX

INDEX

INDEX

458, 481, 488
Sudbinin, Serafim, 304
Sudeikin, 430
Sulerjitsky, Leopold, 224, 452, 454, 455,
    468-471, 481-483, 489, 508, 510, 519, 523,
    525, 531, 532, 535, 536, 537, 538, 539,
    547
Sunken Bell, the, 237, 256-264, 449
Sunset Glow, 472
Suvorin, Alexey, 221

Taglioni, 428
Talents and Admirers, 74
Tamagno, 33, 35-37, 568
Tamberlik, 11
Taneiev, 77
Tarassov, Nikolai, 457
Tchaikovsky, Petr, 77, 105, 132, 362
Teller, 197
Theatre of the Literary Art Society, 221
Three Sisters, the, 366, 370-375, 454
Titian, 570
Tolstoy, Alexey, 337, 447
Tolstoy, Lev Nikolaevich, 110, 169, 207,
    208, 215, 217-225, 400-403, 469, 470,
    525
Tolstoy, Sergey, 401
Tolstoy, Sofia, 222
Tretyakov, Pavel, 12
Tretyakov, Sergey, 77
Tretyakovskaya Gallery, 12, 77
Trouble from Reason, 346, 472, 508
Tsar's Bride, the, 14
Tsar Candale, 83
Tsar Fyodor Ivanovich, 301, 309, 312,
    315, 316, 317, 327, 331, 335-337, 385,
    443, 444, 445, 446, 447
Turgenev, Ivan, 92, 93, 104, 215, 346, 347,
    383, 542, 543, 544
Tutor, the, 215-216

Uncle Vanya, 360-363, 366, 448
Uriel Acosta, 226-237, 245

Usurpers of the Law, the, 180-184, 202

Vakhtangov, Yevgeniy, 525
Varlamov, 93, 567
Varley, 21
Vasnetsov, Victor, 14, 141
Vassiliev, an actor, 93
Vassiliev, a critic, 365
Velasquez, 570
Verdi, 37
Viardot, 11
Village of Stepanchikovo, the, 211-215,
    407
Villainy and Love, 177
Vincent, 55
Vishnevsky, A., 424, 441
Volkenstein, Count, 10
Volkonsky, Prince, 10
Volkov, Fyodor, 10, 93, 349
Volnini, 11
Volpini, 34
Vonsiatsky, 147
Vrubel, 141, 426-427, 435

Weak String, the, 67, 117, 184
Weimar Theatre, 92
Wild Duck, the, 345
Wilhelm, Kaiser of Germany, 445-446
Witte, Count, 392
Woman's Secret, the, 67, 117, 184, 196
World of Art, 546
World War, 547-549
Worms, 235
Wreck of Hope, the, 532

Yakovlev, V. A., 21
Yegorov, 489
Yelpatyevsky, 367
Yermolova, Maria, 92, 93, 233, 458, 463,
    510
Yuzhin, 138

Zucchi, 130-131

[582]